Alfred F. Young

MASQUERADE

Alfred F. Young is Emeritus Professor of History at Northern Illinois University and Senior Research Fellow at the Newberry Library in Chicago. In 2000, the Organization of American Historians honored him with its Distinguished Service Award. He is the author of *The Shoemaker and the Tea Party*, *We the People* (with others), and *The Democratic Republicans of New York*, and has edited numerous other volumes.

ALSO BY ALFRED F. YOUNG

The Democratic Republicans of New York:
The Origins, 1763–1797

We the People: Voices and Images of the New Nation
(with Terry J. Fife and Mary E. Janzen)

The Shoemaker and the Tea Party:
Memory and the American Revolution

EDITED WORKS

The American Heritage Series
(55 vols.; with Leonard W. Levy)

The American Revolution:
Explorations in the History of American Radicalism

Beyond the American Revolution:
Explorations in the History of American Radicalism

Past Imperfect:
The Essays of Lawrence W. Towner on History, Libraries, and the Humanities
(with Robert W. Karrow)

Masquerade

Deborah Sampson, *portrait by Joseph Stone, 1797. Courtesy Rhode Island Historical Society, RHi x5 25.*

Masquerade

The Life and Times of
Deborah Sampson, Continental Soldier

ALFRED F. YOUNG

VINTAGE BOOKS
A DIVISION OF RANDOM HOUSE, INC.
NEW YORK

FIRST VINTAGE BOOKS EDITION, MARCH 2005

Copyright © 2004 by Alfred F. Young

All rights reserved under International and Pan-American Copyright Conventions.
Published in the United States by Vintage Books, a division of Random House, Inc.,
New York, and simultaneously in Canada by Random House of Canada Limited,
Toronto. Originally published in hardcover in the United States by Alfred A. Knopf,
a division of Random House, Inc., New York, in 2004.

Vintage and colophon are registered trademarks of Random House, Inc.

The Library of Congress has cataloged the Knopf edition as follows:
Young, Alfred Fabian, [date]
Masquerade : the life and times of Deborah Sampson, Continental soldier / Alfred F. Young.
—1st ed.
p. cm.
Includes bibliographical references and index.
1. Gannett, Deborah Sampson, 1760–1827. 2. United States—History—Revolution,
1775–1783—Participation, Female. 3. Women soldiers—United States—Biography. 4. Soldiers—
United States—Biography. I. Title.
E276.G36Y68 2004
973.3'092—dc21
[B] 2003047549

Vintage ISBN: 978-0-679-76185-3

Book design by Iris Weinstein
Maps by David Lindroth

www.vintagebooks.com

FOR MY DAUGHTERS,
Sarah, Emily, and Elizabeth

Contents

Contents

Illustrations and Maps

Illustrations and Maps

MAPS

MASQUERADE

Prologue

"A lively comely young nymph . . . dressed in man's apparal has been discovered"

O N J A N U A R Y 1 0 , 1 7 8 4 , three months after the news of a peace treaty with Britain had arrived in the United States, two months after a British army had sailed away from New York City, and a few weeks after the last of the Continental Army at West Point had been disbanded, the *New York Gazette* published the first report of the successful masquerade in the American army of a woman who had taken the name "Robert Shurtliff." The printer, Elizabeth Holt, who had recently taken over the management of the paper after the death of her husband, ran the story as a long, unsigned paragraph in a prominent place under the sideline "New York," without a headline, the journalistic style of the day. A month or so later, the item was reprinted in Boston and elsewhere.

Composed on the heels of the woman's discharge at West Point in late October 1783, the article was probably written by one of her senior officers, but the information in it could only have come from her. The short account embodied the tangle of fact, invention, and mystery that would characterize the telling of her story for the rest of her life, and ever since:

An extraordinary instance of virtue in a *female soldier,* has occurred lately in the American army, in the Massachusetts line viz, a lively comely young nymph, 19 years old, dressed in man's apparal has been discovered; and what redounds to her honor, she has served in the character of a soldier for near three years undiscovered; during which time she displayed herself with activity, alertness, chastity and valour, having been in several skirmishes with the enemy, and receiving two wounds; a small shot remaining in her to this day; she was a remarkably vigilant soldier on her post, and always gained the admiration and applause of her officers; was never found in liquor, and always kept company with the most upright and temperate soldiers.

For several months this galantress served with credit as a waiter in a General officer's family; a violent illness (when the troops were at Philadelphia) led to the discovery of her sex; she has since been honorably discharged from the army with a reward, and sent to her connexions who it appears live to the Eastward of Boston, at a place called Munduncook.

The cause of her personating a man, it is said, proceeded from the rigour of her parents, who exercised their prerogative, to induce her marriage with a young man she had conceived a great antipathy for, together with her being a remarkable heroine, and being warmly attached to her country, in the service of which, it must be acknowledged, she gained reputation; and no doubt will be noticed by the compilers of the history of our grand revolution. She passed by the name of Robert Shurtlieff, while in the army, and was borne on the rolls of the regiment as such: For particular reasons, her real name is withheld, but the facts aforementioned are unquestionable and unembellished.

By the time the article appeared, Deborah Sampson, who had taken the name "Robert Shurtliff," had returned to Massachusetts, to Sharon, a town about twenty miles southeast of Boston, where she made her way to the farm of her aunt and uncle. One of the few accounts of her service given in her name—Deborah Gannett, after she married in 1785—puts a few more bare bones on the story. In 1792, in a petition to the Massachusetts legislature for the pay she never received while serving in the Massachusetts line of the Continental Army, she offered a succinct summary of her military service. This was probably accurate because it was reviewed by a committee that included former officers who recommended granting her request:

She "from Zeal for the good of her Country was induc'd, and by the name of Robert Shirtliff did on May 20, 1782, inlist as a Soldier in the Continental Service for three years. . . . She was constant & faithful in doing Duty with other Soldiers & was engag'd with the Enemy at Tarry Town New York & was wounded there by the Enemy & continued in service until discharg'd, by General Knox at West Point, October 25, 1783."[1]

The newspaper article of 1784 could only have been written by someone who had gotten the story from her own lips. The narrator was straining to set down the facts as he heard them—a good clue is his misspelling of the difficult Indian name of the town in Maine to which she said she was going, actually not Munduncook, but Medundock (later renamed to the more felicitous Friendship). The most likely author was General John Paterson, the "General officer" in whose military "family" she served as a "waiter," the army's term for orderly. Twenty years later, in the diary recording her lecture tour of New England and New York in 1802–03, in the course of which she spent a month with Paterson in western New York, she called him "my old friend."[2]

But the article, for all its earnest facticity, accepted the persona Sampson had adopted to carry out her masquerade. The basic facts of her military service were more or less "unquestionable." She enlisted, saw active service, was in skirmishes, was wounded, and the article itself was rich testimony that she had won the "applause" of her officers.

Some claims, however, were questionable. First, she was older than she said. She may have been a "comely young nymph" of nineteen in the eyes of her middle-aged male beholders. But, born in December 1760 (or possibly 1759), she was at least twenty-one in the spring of 1782 when she enlisted, and close to her twenty-third birthday when she was discharged. She had presented herself as younger—seventeen or eighteen—to account for being a "smock faced boy," the term soldiers used to taunt beardless young men; and when discovered, she stuck to this feigned age. Second, it was stretching it to say she had served "near three years." The documents she submitted in 1792 show she had enlisted May 20, 1782, for a three-year *term* and was discharged October 25, 1783, which came to seventeen months. It was easy for her admirers in a celebratory mood to say she had served "near three years," and it was not a time when an officer could check out a soldier's service record.

The facts in the article, moreover, were hardly "unembellished." "The cause of her personating a man" emphasized the motives she had found out were acceptable to justify a woman joining the army: romantic love and patriotism. The claim that she was escaping to the army to avoid an unwanted suitor foisted on her by the "rigour" of her parents was a variant of the romantic image in the ballads about women warriors so popular in England and the colonies. They often went into the army or navy *in pursuit of* a lover their parents had forbidden them to marry. Deborah Sampson's parents, however, were not a presence in her life; her father had disappeared when she was a child, her mother was in the next town, and Deborah was completely on her own.

She had become "warmly attached to her country"—her army service alone shows this—but to what extent patriotism moved her to enlist awaits the telling. She was among the last of the "three year men" recruited in a Massachusetts draft call for fifteen hundred soldiers in the spring of 1782, when American patriotism was at its lowest ebb. The decisive Battle of Yorktown occurred in October 1781, and with the news that peace negotiators were meeting in London, the odds were against renewed combat. Like several thousand American soldiers, she was recruited by a bounty agent as a substitute for a class of men facing the draft and she received a hefty reward for enlisting.

The picture of her in the newspaper account as an exemplary soldier, a model in the eyes of her officers, was, we shall see, very much a reality, but the persona was a creation by Sampson and her officers. That she had served with "chastity" added the virtue indispensable for granting a woman recognition of any sort. Other claims raised intriguing mysteries: where she fought and what skirmishes she engaged in; when and where she was wounded; whether a "small shot" remained in her body; and if "a violent illness" in Philadelphia led to her "discovery." And, of course, the account totally avoided the biggest mystery of all—how a woman got away with passing as a man for seventeen months in the most male of American institutions.

The newspaper report, in short, presented the persona she had used to carry out her deception. She had engaged in one masquerade; she would take up another. Unraveling this double masquerade may enable us to reconstruct a kind of life in the era of the American Revolution that has never been recovered.

Women Warriors and Passing Women

Deborah Sampson was not the only woman to serve in the Continental Army disguised as a man, and, entering a war that in the spring of 1782 was in its seventh year, she was hardly the first—but she very likely was the most successful. In the army for seventeen months, she probably served longer than any other woman passing as a man in the Revolutionary War.

From what little we know, for example, about two other women who enlisted in Massachusetts, they were "discovered" early on, tried, and punished. Ann (or Nancy) Bailey of Boston, identified only as a "spinster," who enlisted in February 1777 as "Sam Gay" and received a bounty of £15 10s., was rapidly promoted to corporal, and three weeks later was found out, "discharged, being a woman dressed in man's apparel." She fled, was arrested, and found guilty by a civilian court of "fraudulently intending to cheat & injure the inhabitants of the state" in that she "pretended that she was a young man" (a double crime). She was fined and sentenced to two months in prison. In the spring of 1782 in Springfield in western Massachusetts, Anne Smith, who had enlisted as "Samuel Smith," "after many enquiries and very minute examination" by the mustering officer "was discovered to be of the female sex" and imprisoned, just missing a bounty of $80. In jail, she claimed that "she had been a soldier and in actual service for three months, undiscovered." The newspaper account breathed admiration: "She acted the man so perfectly well through the whole that she might probably have passed had not the want of a beard and the redundance of some other matters led to a detection."[3]

A young woman who in 1778 enlisted as a man near Elizabethtown, New Jersey, suggests the fate of other would-be soldiers less skilled in "acting the man." She was detected almost at once and humiliated. As Lieutenant William Barton, her commanding officer, told the story, while waiting at Barton's table in uniform and asked "to hand the Tankard to the Table he did so and Made a Courtesy [curtsy]," which gave her away. An officer pretending to be a doctor examined her and "soon made the discovery by pulling out the Teats of a Plump young girl." The woman pleaded with Barton: she had gone into the army because "she wanted to marry a young man and her Father would not permit her." To no avail. Barton "ordered the drums to beat her Threw the town with the whores march."[4]

"It was not an unusual circumstance to find women on the ranks disguised as men," a writer in a New York City newspaper reflected in 1822, on the occasion of Pennsylvania awarding a woman soldier a pension, adding, "It would be interesting to collect anecdotes of the services rendered by women during the revolutionary war." No wonder that Linda Grant De

Hannah Snell, as depicted in an excerpt from "The Life and Adventures of a Female Soldier," the narrative of the most famous cross-dressing British soldier of the century. It appeared in Isaiah Thomas's New England Almanack *(Boston, 1774). Printers recycled the image on other imprints. Courtesy American Antiquarian Society.*

Pauw, a historian who has long collected such anecdotal histories for the Revolutionary War, is convinced that "we should allow for women serving undetected and even serving detected with no one giving a damn."[5]

In the larger Atlantic world of the eighteenth century, Sampson would not have raised many eyebrows. "To march off to war as men did, to rebel by passing as men: cross-dressing was one of the traditional forms of popular protest," Arlette Farge, a scholar of European women in the era from 1500 to 1800, concludes. "Virtually all the examples of 'passing women' that have survived"—including women soldiers—writes Martha Vicinus, who has studied them in England and Western Europe, "are of working-class and peasant women who sought more job opportunities, better pay, and greater freedom."[6]

For the American colonies in the eighteenth century, the tantalizingly brief reports of passing women that have come to light suggest similar patterns. They might be runaway indentured servants (like Catherine Davidson, advertised in Pennsylvania as "a convict servant woman" whose accomplice had "attired her in men's clothes" and who "speaks man like"); or runaway slaves (like "a mulattoe woman slave, named Maria," or a quadroon in Virginia who joined the Continental Army as a drummer boy). Or they were free women who had taken jobs gendered male (like "Charles," a sailor in Marblehead who resisted being stripped for a whipping by the ship's master, confessing that she was a woman who had been to sea for four years). They might be pregnant single women fleeing the site of their shame (like Mary Gorman, who in North Carolina dressed as a sailor on a coastal vessel). How many ended up in court (like Martha Kingsley of Attleborough, Massachusetts, who as "Philip Ammadour" was charged with paying suit to a woman "uncivilly"), we do not know. Sometimes a newspaper reported a spectacular masquerade: Charlotte Hamilton, a woman of twenty-eight who was transported from England as an indentured servant, passed herself off as "Charles Hamilton," a doctor, boasting "that she had used the disguise for several years," traveling through Virginia, Maryland, and Pennsylvania. There was a hidden world of plebeian deception and disguise.[7]

The disguised women warriors of England were widely known in the eighteenth century to an Anglo-American audience through newspapers, magazines, and memoirs, as well as ballads, more than a hundred of which have been identified. "Ballad-makers regularized the heroine as they did few others," Dianne Dugaw writes; "far from being isolated and idiosyncratic, the Female Warrior and her story assumed the status of an imaginary archetype in popular ballads, a standard motif." One of the most popular as-told-to memoirs, *The Female Soldier: The Adventures of Hannah Snell* (1750), circulated in several forms in New England.[8]

In Western European culture, high and low, Amazons were "part of the literary landscape," the historian Natalie Davis tells us, "while accounts of Jeanne d'Arc with her banner reminded the French of what a woman could achieve in leading men to battle." Such traditions were familiar enough for American patriots to invoke them. In the military crisis of 1776, when Washington's armies were in desperate retreat across New York and New Jersey, Thomas Paine, in *The American Crisis* papers that began "These are the times that try men's souls," called for "some Jersey maid to spirit up her countryman" as did "a woman, Joan of Arc," who helped drive back "the whole English army." Abigail Adams boasted to her husband, John, that "If our Men are all drawn of [f] and we should be attacked, you would find a Race of Amazons in America." The unlearned often got the spelling wrong— "amozones," "amazoons," "amisons"—but they got the idea.[9]

Sampson should not be confused with the large number of women in army camps who accompanied husbands or loved ones or were simply women set adrift in the maelstrom of war in search of a living. Over seven years of war, several thousand women were attached to the American army. In 1782, when Sampson entered an army of about 11,000 at West Point, a "Return of the number of women and children in the several regiments" accounted for 405 women. "Camp followers" was their derogatory name, but as their importance grew on him, George Washington called them "Women of the army." The historian Holly A. Mayer sums up their roles: "They cooked the food, did the wash, mended clothing, took care of the sick and wounded, helped their fellow women, lay with men, and then bore and raised their children." Indeed, eighteenth-century armies could not function without such women. Occasionally, a camp follower fought alongside her partner. Decades later, "Molly Pitcher" was a generic name for several women attached to artillery units who replaced their fallen husbands at their cannons. Other women took over more prosaic military chores, like Sarah Osborn, who on one occasion put on her husband's overcoat, shouldered his gun, and took his place on sentinel duty. Such women, unlike most women warriors, were visibly female.[10]

Still other American women wielded guns, hatchets, or pitchforks in defense of their homes. Some performed as spies, scouts, or couriers, galloping through the night on horseback. In New England, when danger threatened in the absence of the local militia, some women formed home guard militia units like the women of Pepperill, Massachusetts. In the backcountry, in areas riven by bitter civil war, women warded off attacks on their homes by Tory civilians or by Indians, as they had for generations.[11] In New England, the tradition of frontier women who had disguised themselves as men and fought with "Amazonian" courage against the Indians and French was alive in the era of the Revolution, as was the memory of women who resisted their Indian captors.

Deborah Sampson thus was by no means the only American woman to bear arms or see service in the Revolutionary War. Yet we know more about her than any other American woman warrior or a woman of the army. Unlike the composite "Molly Pitcher," she was a real person. And she alone became, in her own lifetime, a celebrated figure, the subject of a book-length memoir, and a public lecturer. To jump ahead of our story—and over some personal history that we shall see is not quite as simple as it seems—in November 1783, Deborah returned to civilian life to work on her uncle and aunt's farm in Sharon, Massachusetts, in her "regimentals." She returned, not as Deborah Sampson but for a while as her brother, "Ephraim Sampson"—or so her biographer claimed. In 1784, she became engaged; in 1785, she married Benjamin Gannett, Jr., a farmer; and between 1785 and 1790, she bore three children. In 1792, in response to her petition, the Massachusetts legislature awarded Mrs. Gannett back pay for her "extraordinary instance of female heroism." She then cooperated with Herman Mann (1770–1833), a schoolteacher with literary aspirations, on a book about her exploits, which appeared in 1797—part memoir, part novel, part factual, in good part fantasy—in which she was presented as "The American Heroine."[12]

Like a good many other veterans, but alone among women who saw combat, Sampson waged a persistent public campaign over nearly three decades for the benefits to which she considered herself entitled. In 1802–03, as part of this campaign, unlike any other veteran who has come to light, she went on a tour, delivering an "address" about her exploits, occasionally donning a uniform to perform the soldier's manual exercise of arms. She was America's first itinerant woman lecturer, advertising herself as "the Celebrated Mrs Gannett." She won her pension in 1805.

She lived the rest of her life on a hardscrabble farm in Sharon. Never prosperous, she spent some of her pension payments on tokens of refinement in a quest for gentility. She was recognized by some as "a woman of handsome talents"; to others she was a subject of malicious gossip. Known locally in her last years as "the old soldier," she died in 1827 at sixty-seven after intermittent illness, the fame from her memoir faded, the applause of her lecture audiences long since died away, her pension payments swallowed up by doctors' bills. On her death, there was no more public notice than a paragraph in the county paper picked up here and there by other publications.

Yet, in her day, there was no American story quite like hers. Of all the "founding fathers," Benjamin Franklin might have appreciated her most. He was, after all, America's most famous master of masquerade: the sophisticated urbanite who in his almanacs played "Poor Richard," dispensing wise aphorisms to country yokels; the libertine who in his autobiography palmed himself off as a man keeping daily track of his youthful lust; the cosmopolitan minister to France who, in Paris, posed as a homespun Yankee in a coonskin cap. The two shared a world in common that is as important to recover as is their distance from one another in power, social esteem, and visibility. Franklin, the epitome of the self-made man in America, might have found Sampson a kindred spirit: a self-taught person of many skills, someone who was also a master of the art of self-fashioning, a would-be self-made woman.[13] But despite this shared aptitude for masquerade, Deborah Sampson Gannett faced challenges that Franklin as a man would never know.

How Do We Know?

Recovering the life of a relatively little known woman who engaged in a masquerade more than two hundred years ago is a challenge. She was, after all, very skilled at deception. Spectacularly successful in one disguise, Deborah Sampson then spent a good part of her life guarding a persona that obscured herself.

The task is daunting because she herself left such a meager written record and because she has come down to us by way of such a frustrating source, Herman Mann's memoir of 1797. The surviving written record *by* her is heartbreaking for its sparseness: a short diary/account book kept for one year during her lecture tour of 1802–03, and for no other period; two one-page letters, one in 1804, the other in 1806, both to creditors; a half-dozen short petitions in which she gave little more than an outline of her military service. She probably wrote more. These few documents are tantalizing because they hint at what she could have done. The diary is unusually rich, and the two letters are artful, together revealing the writing skills and vocabulary of a person who unmistakably was also a reader. These sources also exhibit an array of emotions: the petitions, her anger; the diary, her love for her children and her sheer delight in social acceptance; one letter, her longing for friendship. The diary also shows her as a curious, careful observer and as a meticulous keeper of records. It is a wonderful source, brimming with implications for her life as a whole.

Over several years of searching, I recovered not a single letter *to* her. There are no "Deborah Sampson Papers." I suspect she either destroyed such letters in a somewhat embittered old age, or after her death an indifferent family lost them. I found only three letters *about* her from contemporaries: one from an illustrious political supporter who visited her in 1804 (Paul Revere); one from a sergeant in her regiment irked to offer a paragraph of skeptical comment on her memoir to a newspaper (Calvin Munn); the third from a veterans' advocate in Dedham (William Ellis), who observed her in later life. There is one captivating commentary about her lecture appearance. I found not one letter or reminiscence from a contemporary member of her immediate family or a senior army officer.

Thus, her voice comes down to us for the most part mediated by Herman Mann, who wrote and published not only the memoir, entitled *The Female Review,* in 1797 but her public "address" in 1802, and who after her death in 1827 revised the memoir, leaving on his own death a rambling, unpublished manuscript. It is easy to discredit Mann and dismiss him altogether, but we cannot afford this luxury. She chose him to write about her, and she talked to him only a decade after the war, when her memory was clear and her speech "deliberate and articulate." While she recounted her exploits to others, he was the only person who set them down. I blow hot and cold on him, as will be apparent.

As historians weigh sources, a memoir written years after an event is flawed, and an "as-told-to" memoir strained through a second voice is doubly inauthentic. This axiom has led scholars to dismiss a large number of potentially valuable sources that they should try to decode, peeling off the layers imposed by the subject's memory and the memoir writer's bias. In Mann's case, the flaws are so serious they make us skeptical of the entire work. He was an inept, inexperienced writer who was in a project over his head. A schoolteacher in his early twenties, in 1797 he began a long career as a country printer and editor in Dedham, Massachusetts. Thirty years later, he confessed that for the memoir he "wanted [lacked] the facts I have since obtained," was rushed into print by his friends, and "thus exposed my inability" as a writer. Actually, it took him three or four years to pull the book together because he strained to make it so literary. He wrote in a stilted, prolix style filled with elegant euphemisms and opaque passages.[14]

Mann fabricated events, most notably describing Sampson in vivid detail at the Battle of Yorktown—which took place in September–October 1781, seven months before her enlistment—moving back its date a full year, to May 1781. Her enlistment can be documented for May 1782 and for no other time. At the end of the book he fantasized a series of improbable adventures for her among western Indians, and could not resist embellishing her likely prosaic military episodes in the Hudson Valley. Shamelessly, Mann lifted from a variety of other works. In fact, there are enough parallels between his *The Female Review: or, Memoirs of an American Young Lady* and *The Female Soldier; or, The Surprising Life and Adventures of Hannah Snell* (London,

1750) to suggest that he and/or Sampson were familiar with the English narrative. He thought of his work as "a novel based on fact," a genre that gave him license to let his imagination run wild. This is why Calvin Munn, Robert Shurtliff's drill sergeant, could dismiss the book as "a novel not one fourth of which is fact."[15]

Mann was ideological, a "republican educator," who, as the literary historian Judith Hiltner writes, "had no qualms about altering biography in the service of ideology" and whose "agenda . . . shaped his appropriation of her experience."[16] He was also prurient, describing lurid sexually titillating scenes: Sampson bathing nude in the Hudson; Sampson rescuing a woman captured by Indians by "marrying" her but refusing to sleep with her on a bear-skin rug. His accounts of a romantic encounter by his heroine in Philadelphia with an enraptured young heiress and of flirtations with women on her return to civilian life seem cut from this same cloth. In his 1797 book, he reassured readers the romance between the "two lovers" was chaste; in his revised manuscript in the 1830s, he turned it into a passionate erotic encounter. Either of course is possible, but both are better taken as evidence of Mann's literary imagination.

For all these maddening flaws, in describing Deborah's youth and army experiences there is simply no substitute for Mann's narrative. Although there was much in the book that embarrassed her, she collaborated with him a second time on her address. He wrote it, she memorized and delivered it, and he published it, writing an introduction. Afterward, she remained on close terms with Mann, his wife, and his son. Then, sometime in the last decade of her life, she cooperated with him a third time, giving her blessing for another edition of the memoir, on the proviso that he not publish it until after her death.

When I started doing research on Deborah Sampson, I thought of Mann as a young, inept "con" man, spinning outlandish tales about Sampson so he could rise to fame and fortune. I still do, but as I picked up the episodes she hid from him, I could see where she was leading him around by the nose. When I found no corroboration for his outlandish tales, they seemed to be the fruits of his inventiveness. Most of the particulars about her early life and prosaic military actions, I believe, came from her (and some could have come only from her), while the fantasies were his. Which is which, where to draw the line, is sometimes vexing, and I am not sure I always get it right. Perhaps we should call them both "confidence" artists.

Sergeant Munn got the genre half-right when he called the memoir a novel, but not the proportion of fact to fiction. More than one fourth was factual, and, because we have few alternative sources, the problem is to figure out what in it was likely, unlikely, or improbable. Mann packaged her; to get to her, we have to unpackage him.

Slender Clues and Historic Contexts

What does a biographer do when his subject speaks so rarely in her own voice and her voice is strained through an author who blurs fact and fiction? My research strategy was to test the Mann/Gannett account (which covers the first third of her life, 1760 to 1784) by building up a body of independent evidence, which might also help map the last two thirds of her life, from 1784 to 1827. Frustrated by the meager documentary record, I have gone down a number of unconventional paths.

First, I have played detective, hunting especially for small clues that might fit into the different jigsaw puzzles of her life, paying special attention to sources dug up by the many people who have pursued Sampson before me. Two centuries later, the trail is very cold, but by trying to walk in the tracks of those who came before me, I thought I might be able to piece some of the shards they discovered into patterns that might have eluded them. Carlo Ginzburg, a historian skillful in recovering the worldview of common people, calls such evidence "slender clues," "discarded information," or "details usually considered of little importance"—the sort of unconscious evidence Sherlock Holmes or Sigmund Freud might have delighted in.[17]

I looked for such inadvertent clues, for example, in the different versions of Mann's book. There are no less than four texts for *The Female Review:* the book he published in Dedham in 1797 as "A Citizen of Massachusetts"; his unpublished revision composed between 1827 and 1833; his son Herman Junior's condensed version of his father's manuscript, entitled "The American Heroine," rejected by a publisher in 1850; and an 1866 reprint of Mann's 1797 text with a scholarly introduction by John Adams Vinton and excerpts from the elder Mann's manuscript in footnotes. Here and there a variation in the texts was helpful. Mann's revised manuscript, however, was disappointing; while it occasionally makes clear what was murky, he plagiarizes more and is less restrained in his fantasies. Vinton, the editor, a Dartmouth graduate and a minister, often corrects Mann's facts, heckling him from his footnotes, but he has misled many readers by reprinting fanciful excerpts from the unpublished manuscript as if they were reliable. Mann himself left a few other clues in his newspaper, other publications, and private papers, while his son left a useful journal.[18]

I also looked for small clues in the mounds of sources left by Sampson's twentieth-century devotees: reminiscences about the Gannetts and the town collected from townsfolk by the founder of the Sharon Historical Society around 1900; the family scrapbook of memorabilia, kept by Muriel Nelson (born in 1910), Deborah's great-great-granddaughter, who as a child lived in the Gannett house; the notes of Pauline Moody, author of an anecdotal biography in 1975. The small band of enthusiasts who succeeded in having Sampson declared state heroine of Massachusetts in 1982 scoured local depositories for documents that now bulge out of scrapbooks in the Plympton Historical Society assembled by Charles Bricknell, or are in the personal collection of Patrick Leonard. Their research was incorporated in a book self-published by Emil Guba.

Second, I have looked hard at the surviving evidence of the material world Deborah inhabited. I scrambled over sites in the three Massachusetts towns where she lived (Plympton, Middleborough, and Sharon), and at the encampment at New Windsor above West Point, where she was stationed in the winter of 1782–83. I explored the three houses she lived in, remodeled but very much intact. I stared at objects passed down to descendants, such as an elegant imported porcelain cup plate used with a teacup. Sites and artifacts are mute—they do not "speak for themselves" any more than do written documents, yet they thrust questions forward with an uncommon force.

You go to sites with questions: What kind of a farm did the Gannetts live on? What level of life would it have supported? Daniel and Peggy Arguimbau, who own and work the same Sharon farm and live in the same farmhouse in which Deborah Gannett lived from 1813 to 1827, walked me over the meadows and woodlands she trod, and around the same weatherbeaten barn in which the Gannett family sheltered their few cows. Sites also set off alarm bells. Early in my research, when I walked out of the reconstructed log hut of the sort Robert Shurtliff could have lived in at the New Windsor encampment, I had a feeling in the pit of my stomach that I had made a terrible mistake: How could a woman have lived with six to eight men in these cramped quarters over a snowy winter and escaped detection? Had I fallen for a hoax? This set me off on a train of inquiry: Where *was* her light infantry company stationed in 1782–83? Where did she live when she became General Paterson's "waiter"?

Holding clothing in my hands prompted similar reactions. After I tried on a reproduction of a light infantry uniform at New Windsor, I made my way to a modern tailor of uniforms of the Revolutionary War to puzzle out the little mysteries of a woman wearing a man's uniform. You also find the unexpected: in search of a diary, I visited Beatrice Bostock, a great-great-granddaughter on Cape Cod, a woman in her eighties. Her daughter, Ann Gilbert, brought out a dress handed down in the family as Deborah's, a pretty ankle-length gown with large blue designs. After a skilled costume historian authenticated it as an eighteenth-century dress, dated it to about 1785, and said it could easily have been a wedding dress for a country woman, it struck me that more than likely this was the dress our returning soldier was married in. What role did clothing play in her enacting gender?

Third, because there was often no alternative, I have put effort into reconstructing one historical context after another. I have tried to understand the towns she lived in, the churches she belonged to (and the Baptist Church she was thrown out of), and the families she was part of. It is remarkable how much one can intuit about one person from the groups she was part of, groups now emerging into the light of history thanks to a generation of social historians: indentured servants, weavers, Baptist converts, ordinary soldiers, the "women of the army," war veterans, yeomen farmers, country women in search of refinement, common readers—the list could go on. Where the documentary record was the most treacherous—for the war—I constructed a template on which I might lay the flimsy pieces of evidence about her and weigh what was likely, possible, or improbable.

Finally, I have been attentive to intangible evidence that scholars blessed with a plethora of printed sources often disdain: "the old folks traditions" about Deborah Sampson, collected by a Middleborough antiquarian; the "thousands of anecdotes and stories" soldiers were said to have passed on about her; and the "taunts and jeers" whispered by Mrs. Gannett's Sharon neighbors. I have thought about the names parents gave children, and what children might have made of their names. I have listened carefully to the dream Mann reported as Deborah's with a message from the book of Judges.

Going down these many paths, I learned far more about Sampson than I believed it was possible to learn about a woman Mann rightly said was of "low birth and station" when I set out. Time and again, I was amazed at what you could find—if you only looked. Repeatedly, I reopened research on a topic in my excitement over an unexpected discovery. If others share my sense of amazement, I hope it encourages them to try to piece together the lives of people that scholars too often say are beyond recovery. Yet, when all is said and done, there are a great many things about Deborah Sampson Gannett—including the most important things—we do not know and perhaps never will.

I HAVE TRIED to tell Sampson's story as it seemed to unfold, in four periods of her life, using the name or designation by which she was commonly known in each. Part 1, "Deborah Samson" (without a "p"), is about the girl and young woman from 1760 to 1782. Here is the child, the servant, the spinner and weaver, the schoolteacher, the dreamer, the religious rebel, the woman coming of age in Middleborough, Massachusetts, in the era of the American Revolution.

Part 2, "Robert Shurtliff," follows her through the army, 1782–83, tracking her in her light infantry regiment in the Hudson Valley in the all but forgotten final years of the Revolutionary War after Yorktown. I recount her likely adventures in Westchester County, her service as General John Paterson's "waiter," and her near-death experience in Philadelphia, as well as Mann's stories of her improbable adventures among the Indians and her less than likely romance.

Part 3, "The Celebrated Mrs. Gannett," picks up her civilian life in late 1783, when she returned to Massachusetts and became a Gannett in Sharon, a wife and mother, and began her long quest for recognition as a petitioner, the subject of a memoir, and a public performer, taking her through the lecture tour of 1802–03.

Part 4 is about the "Old Soldier," as she was known in the last decades of her life until her death in 1827: the Gannett family's desperate search for security, her success as a petitioner, her poignant quest for tokens of gentility, and her reputation as a conversationalist. It follows her in her last illness and then reprises her husband's career.

In Part 5, chapters 10 and 11 are an effort to bring together the public memory of Deborah Sampson over two centuries: what history has made of her, as opposed to what she did in history, the ways she has been recurrently lost, found, and appropriated. An epilogue attempts to piece together the "what-ifs" of her life.

I have tried to tell Sampson's story in a way that invites readers into weighing the often elusive evidence. At no point have I invented dialogue or interior thoughts for her, although I have occasionally reported thoughts or dialogue Herman Mann attributed to her. I have frequently tried to imagine, however, what she and the other actors in her life might have thought or very likely did, always in light of the available evidence and the historic context. Where alternative interpretations are possible, I have tried to suggest them. I hope this kindles the reader's imagination. In recovering the subjectivity of an ordinary person when the record is so tantalizing, biography, perhaps more than any other branch of history, invites the collaboration of reader with author.

PART ONE

DEBORAH SAMSON

Chapter One

Deborah

W HEN EITHER of the sexes reverses its common sphere of action," her memoirist Herman Mann wrote in 1797, "our curiosity is excited to know the cause and event." Mann was not of an analytical mind, but, in five rambling chapters about Deborah Samson as a child, youth, and young adult, using the clues she provided, Mann offered answers to the question he posed. Judging by the number of times he attributes her as his source ("she informs," "she has often said," "she has assured me," "she has said"), for her youth she was his major source of information. She even revealed something of her inner life in a riveting dream. A child in effect without parents after she was five, Deborah was placed as an indentured servant in a farm household, and after she was a free person became a weaver and for a time a teacher. Setting the scraps of her biography in what we can piece together about the different worlds she entered gives us a story of a remarkable transformation. To use Mann's words, she was a "young female of low birth and station" who rebelled against "a contracted female sphere."

1. *The Child*

"As I was born to be unfortunate, my sun soon clouded"

At an early age, Deborah Samson was a near orphan. She was born into a family of unusually prominent ancestry that had already slid to a point near the bottom of colonial society, a slope of downward mobility Americans have pushed out of their national myths. She was a Bradford. Her mother, Deborah Bradford, was the great-granddaughter of William Bradford (1590–1657), the first governor of the Plymouth colony. Living in Plymouth County, in what had once been a separate Pilgrim colony until it was absorbed by Massachusetts in the 1690s, she grew up with a heritage that was being celebrated anew in the Revolutionary era.

On the side of her father, Jonathan Samson, Jr., she was also descended from a settler who had come over on the *Mayflower,* Henry Samson. The Samsons knew their ancestry—in 1785, she (or someone else with the same name) bought and inscribed a copy of a sermon by Reverend Robert Cushman, the first preached in the Pilgrim colony, reprinted in 1785. How much the Bradford name meant to her is left to our imagination; in her dark days as a child and servant, it could have been a source of shame that she had sunk so far below the expectations the community had for someone with so illustrious an ancestry, but it might also have been a source of pride and inspiration. In 1785, she would name her firstborn child Earl Bradford Gannett.[1]

She was born in Plympton, a small inland farming village adjoining the seaport, Plymouth, according to family tradition, in the house of her grandfather, Jonathan Samson, Sr., a prosperous respected farmer. The house still stands, enveloped by subsequent additions and layers of renovation. The core of the original house, as far as one can tell, was a one-story cottage organized around a multipurpose room with a huge hearth, and small bedrooms at either end. Jan Lewis Nelson, who was caretaker of the house in 1974, thought it was not much changed from the original: wide pine planks in the floor, pine on the walls, a fireplace with wrought-iron fixtures for cooking over an open hearth, built-in beehive ovens. As farmhouses went in colonial New England, it was a comfortable dwelling, but it is not where Deborah lived for long.[2]

Deborah was born December 17, 1760—at least that is the date she gave Mann; no birth record has been found. It is possible she was born a year or so before. Exactly where Jonathan and Deborah Bradford Samson lived after

Deborah Samson's birthplace—the house of her grandparents, in Plympton, Massachusetts, as it appeared around 1900. Still standing and outwardly similar to the original, this is the house where she may have lived in her early years. Photograph from a postcard, c. 1900. Courtesy David Browne.

they were married in 1751 is cloudy. In 1758, Jonathan was identified as a "labourer" in a legal document, which meant he very likely moved around for work, as agricultural laborers often had to do. Many decades later, the Plympton town clerk explained to the descendants of Ephraim, Deborah's brother, that he thought the Samsons led "a rather transient and unsettled life," which accounts for the birth dates of their children not always being registered. Deborah seems to have been the fifth of seven children: Jonathan (1753), Elisha (1755), Hannah (1756), Ephraim (1759[?]), Nehemiah (1764), and Sylvia (1766).[3]

One suspects her mother was responsible for the children's biblical names, all save Sylvia taken from the Old Testament. Such names were still in vogue in conservative areas of New England like Plymouth County, even as they were passing out of fashion elsewhere. In naming a daughter Deborah,

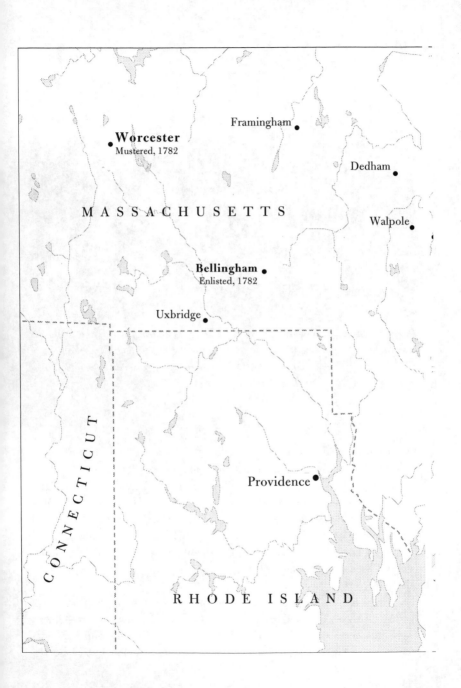

Framingham

Worcester
Mustered, 1782

Dedham

M A S S A C H U S E T T S

Walpole

Bellingham
Enlisted, 1782

Uxbridge

C O N N E C T I C U T

Providence

R H O D E   I S L A N D

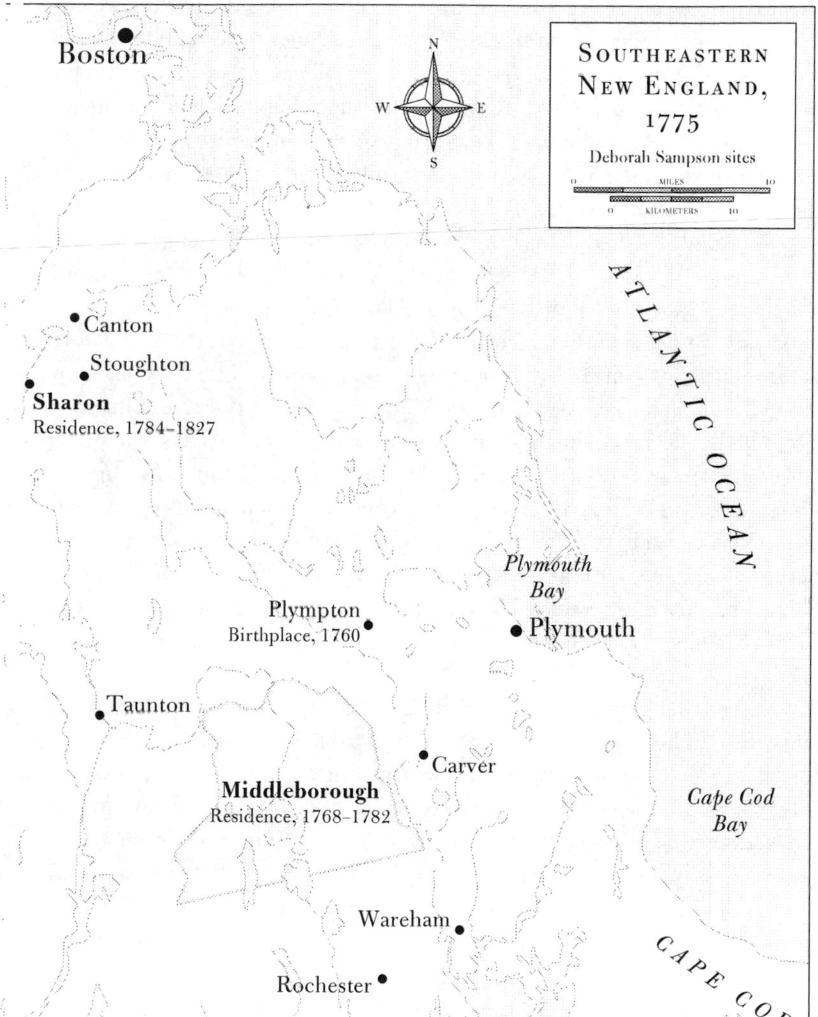

Boston

SOUTHEASTERN
NEW ENGLAND,
1775

Deborah Sampson sites

0   MILES   10
0   KILOMETERS   10

ATLANTIC OCEAN

Canton

Stoughton

Sharon
Residence, 1784–1827

Plymouth
Bay

Plympton
Birthplace, 1760

Plymouth

Taunton

Carver

Middleborough
Residence, 1768–1782

Cape Cod
Bay

Wareham

Rochester

CAPE COD

New
Bedford

Buzzards
Bay

she was passing on a name common in her family—no less than a dozen Deborahs came before her in the Bradford line. Our Deborah could hardly have escaped the story of her namesake in Judges, the prophet in Israel who inspired men to battle, or of Jael, who in the same chapter killed the enemy general Sisera. "A good name," as an English Puritan minister put it, "is a thread tyed about the finger, to make us mindful of the errand we came into the world to do for our Master."[4]

The family spelled their name "Samson" without a "p." Her grandfather and father and mother are Samson in legal documents. John Adams Vinton, who in the 1850s worked on a genealogy of the family, wrote that "the name is Samson in nearly all the records, down to a late period. . . . But as the name now almost universally appears with a *p* he would follow the modern usage."[5] Deborah never signed her maiden name on any document that has survived, but at two landmark events where her name was taken down orally, she was Samson: at her admission to the Third Baptist Church in Middleborough; and at her marriage. After she became a Gannett, it did not seem to matter very much to her. On her lecture tour in 1802–03, when she arranged her own publicity, she was "the celebrated Mrs. Gannett, the late Deborah Sampson." Her family name is Samson, and I have spelled it so in this part of the book about her youth, but I have left it Sampson thereafter, the common spelling.[6]

In 1758, her grandfather on her father's side died, and according to the story the children were told which Deborah passed on, a brother-in-law by his "ill designs, conniving and insinuations" cheated her father out of his inheritance, after which her father went off to sea to seek his fortune, "from whence he was not heard for some years." Eventually, "her mother was informed he had perished in a shipwreck." This is the kind of story a proud mother might tell her children because she was unable to face the fact that her husband had deserted her.[7]

Deborah's father never reappeared in her life. "She informs she had little knowledge of her father during her juvenile years," Mann wrote. Or if he did, she was too ashamed of his scandalous life to talk about him. Her parents seem to have had a tempestuous marriage. In the mid-nineteenth century the Plympton town clerk wrote, "I am told by older people who well recollected [Jonathan Samson, Jr.] that he and his wife quarreled, which led to their separation."[8]

The story that her father was cheated by a wicked brother-in-law smacks of a fairy tale. His father died intestate and the estate was divided by administrators among Jonathan Junior's mother, his five sisters, and himself. As the only son, he may possibly have received a double share, but he may have expected more had his father made a will. In February 1758, within three weeks of his father's death, Jonathan Samson, Jr., sold his share of the estate to a brother-in-law, a "cordwainer," according to the deed.[9] The fact that her brother Ephraim did not know either the place or date of his birth, and that Nehemiah was born in Stoughton in 1764 and Deborah in Plympton in 1760, suggests that the family moved about. Deborah was born in her grandfather's house probably because her parents' house at best was small and cramped; an old-timer who knew the town in the nineteenth century thought the house might have been not "much more than a shanty. There were plenty around Plympton when I was a child."[10]

Sometime in the mid-1760s, Jonathan Samson abandoned his family and, by 1770, appears to have started a new life, not by going to sea but by migrating to Lincoln County, Maine (then a frontier region of Massachusetts). In 1773, Reverend Jacob Bailey of Pownalboro, reporting that "five or six murders have been committed on the Kennebec River in Maine" since 1760, wrote that "indictments for capital crimes were found in that county against . . . Jonathan Sampson (1770)." Whether or not this was our Jonathan Samson is not certain. The case, it seems, never went to trial. We know that he lived in the area with a woman, Martha (nicknamed Patty), who became his common-law wife and by whom he had two or more children, and that both he and she ended up on poor relief, charges of the town of Fayette. So did his legal wife back in Plympton. We know this because years later the penny-pinching selectmen of Plympton, who were paying for poor relief for Deborah Bradford Samson, sent one of their own up to Maine to get Fayette to assume financial responsibility for her as the legal spouse of one of their residents. We also know from military records that in the 1770s Jonathan served a short stint or two in the army. In 1794, he came back to Plympton briefly to attend to a property transaction. He and his common-law wife died in poverty in Maine, he sometime after 1807. Thus, he did not perish at sea in a shipwreck (the family mythology that Deborah was passing on in the 1790s), but he seems to have lived a storm-tossed life.[11]

Around 1765, in the space of about a year, when Deborah was barely five, she faced a calamity: her grandmother on her mother's side died; her father took off; and, to use Mann's words, her mother in "indigent circum-

stance was obliged, at length, to disband her family and to scatter her children abroad." Deborah was put out to live in the homes of strangers—the
eighteenth-century way in New England of providing for dependent children. She was placed first with "a distant relation of her mother, an elderly
maiden by the name of Fuller," where is not clear. After less than three years,
Miss Fuller "was seized of a violent malady" and died. Then, when the
young girl was about eight, she was placed in Middleborough with the
widow of Reverend Peter Thacher, a woman in her eighties. She stayed with
Widow Thacher for "about two years" before she, too, passed away. Middleborough was the next town over from Plympton, but as a huge town, one of
the largest in Massachusetts, its center, where the minister's house stood,
was a good trip from Plympton. Her mother was not exactly next door.
Finally, when Deborah was about ten, "her mother removed her" to the family of Jeremiah Thomas in Middleborough. Deborah remarked of these
years, "As I was born to be unfortunate, my sun soon clouded," a poetic
comment—either hers or Mann's—that suggests how grim these years of
being shunted about may have been for her. She had every reason to feel
abandoned. The adults in her life recurrently disappeared.[12]

2. The Servant
"You are always hammering upon some book"

Deborah was a servant in the family of Jeremiah and Susannah Thomas
from about the age of ten, if custom was followed, probably until she was
eighteen, roughly 1770 to 1778. Her life as a servant is a story of incessant
work, of the mastery of an unusual combination of skills, and of the successful pursuit of an education in books in defiance of her master—in short, of
the emergence of a young woman with a sense of herself.

Thomas family descendants later referred to Deborah as an "indentured
servant" or a "bound girl." Mann did not use these terms, possibly because
there was no such formal indenture, but just as likely, because in presenting
her to the public, it was a source of embarrassment. He also elevated the status of his heroine in the army from "waiter" to "aide" to make her more
respectable.

In colonial Massachusetts, there was a variety of arrangements for "putting out" children in what today might be called foster homes. For orphans or children whose parents were too poor to provide for them, a law of 1692 allowed local justices of the peace to bind out boys to the age of twenty-one and girls to the age of eighteen "or time of marriage." Often such children were apprenticed very young, between five and nine. In the average country town, the selectmen placed such children but invariably were wary of assuming jurisdiction over poor children from another town. In 1766, for example, Middleborough tried to return Josiah and Sarah Marshall and their three daughters, Sarah, Mary, and Deborah, to Plympton, "being poor persons and unable to support themselves." It was also fairly common for parents who were not necessarily poor to "put out" their children to service with another family. Thus, in Middleborough, Deborah might have been among a goodly number of young boys and girls who had been placed as servants.[13]

No evidence survives of either a private contract indenturing Deborah or the town fathers putting her to service. Most likely, after Widow Thacher died, there was an informal arrangement. Either Deborah's mother "removed her" to Jeremiah Thomas, or Reverend Sylvanus Conant, who had followed Thacher as Congregational minister, had a hand in it. The successor minister would have felt a special responsibility for a child who was a ward of the former minister's widow. If custom was followed, Deborah was not paid and was not free until she was eighteen.[14]

Deborah would have been referred to as a "servant," "servant girl," or perhaps "servant maid." In the colonial era, the term "servant" was widely used—apprentices were servants—and no odium was attached to it. It became invidious among young white native-born men and women in the North when "servant" became identified primarily with indentured servants imported from the British Isles and with African-American slaves in the South. Exactly when this happened is hard to pin down, but clearly at some time in the Revolutionary era a leveling spirit led free people who worked for wages to bristle at the word "servant." After the war, they wanted to be referred to as "help," "helper," "helps," or "hired girl," more fitting for a voluntary relationship in a more egalitarian society.[15]

Jeremiah Thomas probably would have met the town's expectations for a master, that he be "a man of sober life and conversation." The Thomases were legion in town—their section of town was called Thomastown. The patriarch of the clan was Benjamin Thomas, chosen in 1776 as deacon of the Congregational Church. Susannah Thomas was Benjamin's daughter, Jeremiah, his son-in-law. Benjamin, as the church historian put it, "though not of a cultivated mind in other respects, was well versed in the Scriptures, of inflexible virtue, [and] of sound and clear orthodoxy." Mann first identified Deborah's master as Jeremiah Thomas and then called him "Deacon Thomas," a mistake which could have stemmed either from his confusion or possibly from Deborah conflating the two in her memory. Benjamin, who lived a scant two miles from his daughter, very likely became a presence in young Deborah's life. Perhaps Jeremiah, a very strict master, sounded so much like the "inflexible" Benjamin that she remembered him as a church deacon.[16]

The Thomases probably followed the common practices for children placed with them as servants. Such a child was not without legal rights and was not usually treated as a Cinderella, but neither was she on a par with the other children in the family. According to late-nineteenth-century family mythology, Deborah grew up with the five Thomas boys as brothers and went into the army to join them, a recollection which does not square with either the ages of the boys or the record of their military service, and softens the reality that she was a nursemaid to three of them. Susannah Thomas would have been delighted to have a servant girl whose duties involved taking care of her brood. The older boys could have been Deborah's playmates (assuming she had time to play), but there was an age difference that would have widened as she matured. When Deborah was fifteen, the three older boys were thirteen, eleven, and ten, and prepubescent. As it happened, she went into the army four years after she left the Thomases.[17]

She spoke to Mann about the Thomases "with respect and gratitude." After all, she once again had become part of a family. Her actions later in life provide several small clues to how important this was to her. In Sharon, in 1796, she adopted a baby, Susanna Shephard, whose mother had died in childbirth, and raised her as her own daughter. In effect an adopted child herself, Deborah embraced someone else's motherless child. The second clue is the loving way she later treated her own servant, Patience Payson, self-identified as "helper," who stayed with the family for more than forty years. A former servant, Deborah knew how important it was to be treated as a member of the family.[18]

Middleborough was an agricultural town of small farms. The farm Jeremiah Thomas had inherited from his father was about 50 acres, with another 25 acres in woodland lots scattered about, a total somewhat above the average. Most farmers produced enough to feed their families and their livestock, exchanged produce with neighbors, and grew flax for linen or raised sheep for wool. As their "cash crop," farmers sold timber or dug iron from the many bogs in town. Women in charge of the dairy sold or exchanged butter or cheese with neighbors. Today, only a few acres of the original farm are attached to the Thomas house; in Deborah's day, it would have had pastures to support livestock and sheep, a vegetable garden, a barnyard for fowl, a fruit orchard, a barn, and a flock of outbuildings.[19]

The farmhouse was small. The present owner, Kenneth Crest, measuring the original foundations, came up with 25 by 22 feet, making a first floor of 550 square feet, only slightly larger than the average New England colonial farmhouse. It probably consisted of two rooms on the first floor, one a large multipurpose workroom, kitchen, and dining area, the other a bedroom for the parents. The loft above would have been for the children. Today, the solid rough-hewn beams in the low ceiling of the cellar are all that suggest the aura of the original house. Deborah probably slept in the loft with the children, a common arrangement.[20]

"Men's and women's tasks on American farms were intertwined and almost totally interdependent," the historian Jack Larkin tells us. "But in space, time, tools and authority they were distinct. Farmyard, garden, house, kitchen and hearth, in diminishing concentric circles, enclosed and bounded women's daily realm," save that female servants might be called upon to work in the men's spaces as well. In Susannah Thomas's circle, Deborah would have worked, first, to help care for her young children; second, to share her unceasing rounds of household labor in kitchen and hearth; and third, to do the woman's chores in the farmyard: milking cows, feeding fowl, tending vegetables.[21]

She also seems to have crossed over into the men's circle. Mann's narrative did not depict Deborah at work. He mentioned only that the Thomases allowed her "the use of a number of fowls, sheep &c. on the condition that she would appropriate the profit" to some useful end. But Reverend Stillman Pratt, writing a life of Deborah in the Middleborough paper in the 1850s, when he could still talk to a few people who had been alive in her day,

The farmhouse in Middleborough on Sachem Street where Deborah was a servant in the family of Jeremiah and Susannah Thomas, as pictured on a postcard c. 1895 before it was remodeled to its present appearance. Courtesy Middleborough Historical Association.

enumerated an unusual combination of activities gendered male as well as female, even if he bathed his account in nostalgia for a golden era of rural life that never existed:

> She became acquainted with almost all kinds of manual labor. It was pastime for her to work amidst fragrant hay in summer time, or husk the yellow corn in the mellow light of autumn. . . . If occasion required, she could harness the horse and ride him to plough, or to town on errands. She could rake hay, or stow it away in the barn: was familiar with the milkmaid's task.[22]

Some of these tasks were gendered female. Plowing was not. Haying was usually done by men, unless there was a frantic battle to bring in the ripe hay when a storm threatened. Pratt also portrayed Deborah as "a tolerable mechanic. If she wanted a basket, a milking stool or sled she could make them. With the use of a jack knife she was familiar, and could work out a weather cock, with that instrument as well as a man." This meant she would have been adept with a variety of men's tools. To "work out a weather cock" (a weathervane shaped like a rooster) means that she could whittle, which is corroborated by another clue. By family lore Deborah whittled pie-crimpers and sold them door-to-door. There were other small objects that kept farm families whittling away through the winter, such as spools and quills used in spinning and weaving. She also used a knife in the army. The evidence for woodworking, however, is problematic.[23]

Physically, Deborah may have been the equal of the boys in the Thomas family, but she was not treated as their equal, and she expressed her resentment. She was denied the limited education the boys got at the town school. Towns were required to keep schools, but attendance was not compulsory for boys or girls, much less servants. The Thomas boys went to a neighborhood one-room schoolhouse in "the warm season of the year," but Deborah went not at all, "because she could not be spared," as she told Mann later. She could already read. She would have learned her ABC's from her mother or grandmother, the common custom. Then Miss Fuller "[took] charge of her education." Miss Fuller and Widow Thacher, both elderly, their eyes failing, may have had Deborah read to them from the Bible.[24]

At the Thomases, she told Mann, "she used to obtain what school books and copies she could from the children of the family," though this did not satisfy her. "She has often said with emotion," wrote Mann (and this was the only point he reported her making "often" and "with emotion"), "that the most mortifying punishment she ever received from her master was, —'You are always hammering upon some book—I wish you wouldn't spend so much time in scrabbling over paper.' " "Hammering upon" implies she went back to her reading again and again; "scrabbling" (a corruption of scrawling and scribbling) means she was also writing. Hostility to book learning for girls was common among conservative farmers. For a rock-ribbed fundamentalist like Deacon Benjamin Thomas, it was enough that a girl learned Scripture.[25]

Mann could not say enough about Deborah's hunger for learning. While this may have reflected his interest in promoting female education, which came into fashion in the 1790s, his praise for her was exceptional. She had "*unusual* propensities for learning," an "*inherent* propensity for learning," and a "*thirst* for knowledge" (emphasis added). He singled out the quality of her intellect: "a mind quick of perception and of strong penetration" and an "inquisitive and curious mind." She also had an excellent memory; she could recite the Catechism verbatim, no mean feat. (The Westminster Catechism consisted of 107 questions and answers defining the mysteries of justification, sanctification, and glorification.) She kept a journal and at twelve began a correspondence with "a young lady of polite accomplishments" (possibly a girl from Boston who, according to family lore, visited Middleborough). To top this off, he claimed that "she was able to read, with propriety, in almost any book in her language"—suggesting that she was a precocious child reading above her age level in whatever she could find.[26]

What would a New England girl from ten to eighteen have been reading in the 1770s?[27] Mann was explicit about two sources for her books and about her intellectual interests. The remarkable findings of scholars in the history of popular reading help us fill in possible titles. One source, already mentioned, was schoolbooks brought home by the Thomas boys: a speller, a psalter, and of course *The New England Primer*. A second source was the Reverend Sylvanus Conant. She won "the esteem and approbation of her village curate," who made "a donation of a few books," wrote Mann. Conant's predecessor, Peter Thacher, was known to have had one of the largest collections of Puritan authors in New England and we know some of his books were passed on to Conant. He may have given her "Godly" books, such as those steady sellers, John Bunyan's *Pilgrim's Progress* and *The Prodigal Daughter*.[28]

Deborah very likely also had access to the world of "chapbooks," paper-covered books which sold for only a few pennies and were especially popular with young readers. Imported or reprinted by Boston printers, they would have been available in a crossroads town like Middleborough, hawked by peddlers from their saddlebags or sold in Andrew Leach's grocery store.[29]

Mann was precise as to her interests. Her "taste for nature and Natural Philosophy," which he said ran to astronomy and the solar system, might have been whetted by country almanacs like Nathaniel Ames's *Astronomical Diary: or Almanack,* with its reports on eclipses, "lunations," and the "sun & moon Rising & Setting." "Her taste for geography," Mann observed, "must have been chiefly spontaneous; as the study of it in books was unfashionable among the female yeomanry"; it might have been stirred by novels like *Gulliver's Travels* and *Robinson Crusoe,* whose heroes voyaged to distant exotic lands.

The staple themes of chapbooks were adventure, heroism, and war, whether in "histories" of kings, soldiers, or pirates. She would have encountered women protagonists, in the much-read novels *Pamela* or *Clarissa* or in a chapbook, *The Maid of Orleans,* about Joan of Arc, or a captivity narrative by New England's Mary Rowlandson. There is no limit to what a girl who Mann tells us "was able to read, with propriety, in almost any book in her language" could have chosen. She may also have read any number of books devoid of propriety, like the narrative of Hannah Snell, the woman warrior. The limits were set by what she could borrow, read in a public house, or afford to buy. Whatever she read, perhaps the most important point is that she became a reader and remained one through her life. Her reading contributed to her sense of empowerment as well as to her aspirations.

3. A "Masterless Woman"
Spinner, Weaver, Teacher

At the end of 1778, when Deborah turned eighteen, the customary age at which an indentured servant or a child put out to service would have completed her obligations, she was free. For more than three years, from 1779 until the spring of 1782, when she left Middleborough, she supported herself as a spinner and weaver, and for two "seasons" was a teacher as well. These were remarkable choices, contributing, like her reading, to a changing sense of herself. She became a "masterless woman," a status fraught with meaning in her world.

The teens, a Boston minister told a youthful audience in a sermon that would have been a stock theme elsewhere, is "your *chusing time.*" "Now you commonly chuse your Trade . . . and how you tend to be employ'd all your days. Now you chuse your *Master* and your Education or Occupation." After addressing himself obviously to boys, he turned to the girls. "And now you dispose of yourself in *Marriage* ordinarily, place your *Affections,* give away your hearts, look out for some companion of life, whose to be as long as you live."[30]

For a servant like Deborah in an inland rural town, as for most young women whatever their class, there were not many choices at "*chusing time.*" Access to further education was almost nonexistent. Even Boston did not open its famous public schools to girls until the 1780s. Private academies at the secondary level did not flourish until after the war. No male trades apprenticed women; the occasional woman blacksmith, printer, or silversmith we hear about almost always had inherited the business from her husband. In the cities, there were some "she-merchants," but women were at best petty shopkeepers or in the needle trades; many were servants, washerwomen, and wet nurses; at worst they were common laborers or prostitutes.[31]

How Deborah acquired her skills as a weaver is guesswork. Almost every colonial farm girl learned how to spin from her mother or grandmother (or mistress if she was a servant); almost every farmhouse had a spinning wheel, but a minority had a loom for weaving. A large loom took up space—about 64 square feet, the size of a four-poster double bed. It was just too big for the average two-room Cape Cod–style house, unless an ell was added or the ceiling in the loft was unusually high. The Thomas farmhouse was small. There was room for a spinning wheel or two, but hardly for a loom. Deborah might have learned to work a small hand-held loom for weaving tape or narrow fabrics, but she probably did not weave. She would have had to learn the intricacies of the large loom from a skilled weaver, perhaps a widow, perhaps another young woman. The families where Deborah was said to have worked—the Bournes, the Mortons, the Leonards—all lived in large two-story houses, big enough for a room to be set aside for both a loom and a large walking wheel for spinning. The Sproat tavern, another place where she worked, was also a very large building.[32]

Traditionally, in old England, weaving was a male trade and weavers were often itinerant. William Bradford, Deborah's ancestor, was a fustian weaver before the great Pilgrim migration from Holland, which he led. In seventeenth-century New England, women spun but did not weave; yet "long before the Revolution . . . New England women began to weave," as the historian Laurel Thatcher Ulrich points out. Men continued in the craft, but the proportion of male artisans declined as weaving became a household trade. The newer weavers, the historian Gloria Main explains, were women "who took up weaving as a nearly full-time activity in the years before marriage or during widowhood."[33]

Indeed, Plymouth, Deborah's home county, was unusual as a major center of female weavers. In the mid-eighteenth century, about two out of every five households had a loom. The ratio of looms to spinning wheels in the county was one of the highest in all New England. Middleborough also supported a fulling mill, where coarse woven fabrics were softened. All this was well under way before the patriot movement of the mid-1760s and before the needs of the army in the 1770s intensified the demand for home manufacturing. Deborah had the added advantage of entering this labor market in the midst of the war.[34]

Women weavers produced cloth for the local market as well as their own households. There was no putting-out system with merchant intermediaries delivering wool and collecting cloth, as in England, but rather a system of "bespoke," that is, made-to-order work. The diary of Abigail Foote of East Haddam, Connecticut, a woman about the same age as Deborah, suggests the range of activities for a young woman living at home doing weaving jobs for neighbors. Here is a sampling of her entries from June and July 1775: "I wove . . . I carded 4 pound of tow . . . I wove in the afternoon . . . I spooled and quilled for Mrs Wiles . . . I spooled and warped a piece for Mr. Amos Wells . . . I finished spooling Noah Foot's piece and warped it . . . I wove and ironed and raked hay and quilled and went a gooseberrying with David Wile's wife . . . I wove three yards." On July 28, seventeen days after she began, Abigail finished 24 ½ yards of Noah Foot's piece. This may resemble Deborah's life, save that, unlike Abigail Foote, who stayed put, she moved about from house to house.[35]

The boycott of British imports gave a patriotic glow to the activity of spinners and weavers. In response to the movement for domestic manufactures encouraged by patriots, women might gather on a village green, or, more commonly, in the house of the local minister, where they conducted spinning bees for the cause. In October 1775, after warfare began, Elizabeth Foote, Abigail's sister, made an entry in her diary, after she carded "two pound of whole wool" and "spun to take off 10 knots," that she "felt nationly into the bargain." When towns had to equip their own militia, weavers could see the patriotic fruits of their labor in uniforms, blankets, and shirts. As the war ground on for seven years, cutting off all imports from England, there was also a demand for a variety of finer fabrics from local consumers.[36]

Weaving had "its own repertoire of liberating opportunities" for women, and it is not hard to imagine the effect success as a weaver might have had on Deborah. Weaving required skills of a high order, learned in a kind of intermittent apprentice-master relationship. It also led to a constant "neighborhood exchange of labor and tools," bringing an individual into contact with other women. As a servant, Deborah had had to stay put; now she moved about town. And spinning and weaving produced a cash income. As a servant, she had gone unpaid, save for some money she earned from the few chickens she tended. Textile production was one of the few household trades for which a woman received payment. A spinster was paid either by the day with "keep"—boarding—or by the number of skeins of thread; a weaver, by the yard. In 1777, in response to state law, the town fixed prices by the yard for a range of "quality Good yard wide cloth," ranging from tow (a coarse linen) and flannel cloth at the bottom of the scale to cotton and linen, both finer fabrics, at the top. An experienced weaver could spin several yards a day, which meant that Deborah could make in one day more than the price the town fixed for a man mowing and reaping or doing common labor.[37]

Her aspirations were raised. Most weavers wove a range of fabrics, according to their skills and the demands of their customers. Granville Temple Sproat, a Middleborough antiquarian, said Deborah was remembered by the "old folks" as "a famous spinner of linen and worsted, and was engaged by many of the old residents to do their nicest and finest spinning." In the mid-1790s, Mann wrote that "she has just shown me pieces of *lawn* and *muslin* which were manufactured with her own hands, soon after the commencement of the war." These, too, were quality fabrics; lawn was linen, made from flax; muslin was made from cotton. Deborah obviously had enough pride in her weaving to hold on to her handiwork for years. It was in these years of working with fine fabrics and moving about the more genteel houses in town that she also acquired a taste for elegant clothes which, as we shall see, she carried throughout her life.[38]

There was more to weaving than making money. Weaving was one of the very few androgynous trades in New England. Male weavers often traveled from village to village. Deborah was itinerant within the village. When she was paid by the piece, she was getting equal pay for equal work, the only colonial trade of which this could be said. At the Thomases, she had learned she could do a woman's work (and much more); as a weaver, she learned she could do a man's work.

Weaving had its downside: it was "tedious and boring," Jane Nylander, a historian of everyday life, reminds us. Elizabeth Fuller, after spending six days weaving 31½ yards of linen, wrote a couplet in her diary: "Welcome sweet Liberty once more to me / How have I longed to meet again with thee." Spinning was even more monotonous. Both occupations thus could be mind-deadening—unless they freed a woman whose mind was being nourished by her reading to wander to distant places and wonder about another life. So, if Deborah acquired from her trade a sense of independence, she may also have acquired a desire to escape from it.[39]

For two seasons Deborah was also a teacher, which may have enhanced her sense of herself in still other ways. Teaching for a "season" meant during the summer, after planting and before harvesting, when children could be spared from farm chores. Towns often had a two-tiered system: "women usually taught the younger children and girls during the summer, often for only half the wages of the young male college graduates who took the older children the rest of the year." The women taught the children to read, the men to write and do sums. In the war years, when there was a shortage of men, the county pressured towns that failed to appoint teachers. In 1779, the local selectmen appointed Deborah to teach "six months in the warm season," Mann's phrase. The following winter, she herself attended "a good man school," his term for a more advanced school on the second tier, and was renewed for a second season in 1780.[40]

She boarded out in different homes, the New England way of paying public school teachers. In 1773, for example, the selectmen paid Benjamin Thomas £1 16s. to board a schoolmaster for six weeks. The minutes have no entry for townsfolk boarding Deborah, but given Deacon Thomas's status, he probably had something to do with her appointment. Middleborough was a big township with several one-room schoolhouses or rooms in private houses set aside as schoolrooms, scattered in the several precincts. To accommodate far-flung pupils, the teacher moved about, which explains why residents in two different parts of town later claimed Deborah had taught there. She taught in a building then near the center of town and subsequently moved to what is now called the Jenks house (a small, plain room with a low ceiling enveloped by a house built around it). In the 1850s, however, Miss Hannah Perkins "remembers well attending on her [Samson's] instructions when she taught in a private house on Mad Mare's Neck," in the extreme southern end of town, at least ten miles away from the center. It was a sprawling town, and Deborah would have boarded in the area she taught, which explains why, when she became a convert to the Baptists, it was at the Third Baptist Church, close to her school in the southern part of town.[41]

She mastered teaching, and she took up teaching again in Sharon in the 1790s, but no one spoke of it as her principal occupation. Teaching was not considered a career. It meant taking charge of an assortment of unruly boys and girls of all ages and sizes in a one-room ungraded classroom, keeping order as much as teaching. For books she probably used the same elementary texts the Thomas boys had brought home. Teaching was not lucrative and brought no elevated status. It may, however, have given her a feeling of vindication: the girl whose master could not spare her to go to school became a teacher.[42]

Between weaving and teaching, she became in these years a "masterless woman," a free single woman. The law prescribed a female as always subject to someone else as her master. A father was master to his children, an employer master to his servants, and when a woman married, she was legally subordinate to her husband. When a woman of this era used the phrase "lord and master" to describe her husband, it might be a gibe to take him down a peg, but it referred to a legal status in the common law: lord and woman, baron and femme. A woman on her own, in other words, a non-dependent woman with her own income, was uncommon in early America; most likely she was a widow who took over her husband's business. Deborah Samson, at ages nineteen through twenty-two between 1779 and 1782, was a woman without a master. As a weaver, she would have been beholden to her customers, and as a teacher, to the selectmen, but this was not quite the same as a legal dependence. In fact, as a weaver with a reputation for fine work, she would have been sought out.

Authority feared "masterless" men and women. In East Anglia in England, the courts had long taken action to place "single men," "Bachelors," and "masterless men" under "family governance." Massachusetts did the same. The Puritans and Pilgrims knew what they were doing. In writing the history of the mid-seventeenth-century English Revolution, the historian Christopher Hill has identified "masterless men" as a major source of radicalism. It was during these years as a "masterless woman," living without the watchful eye of mistress and master, that Deborah made the decisions that transgressed the norms of her society.[43]

4. Masculine/Feminine
"I have probably imbibed something of the masculine . . ."

What was young Deborah Samson like? What did she look like? And what traits did people observe in her? It is hard not to begin with the body and face her contemporaries saw and her physical attributes. Unfortunately, our testimony about her as a young woman in Middleborough and Sharon is almost all retrospective and all from men: from Herman Mann, attempting to describe the woman he saw in the 1790s as she was fifteen years before, at twenty-one (or the woman he imagined when he revised his book in the 1830s); from Joseph Stone, who painted her portrait in 1797 at Mann's bequest; and from Granville Temple Sproat, a Middleborough resident later known as "the Shaker poet," who in the second quarter of the nineteenth century collected what he called "The Old Folks Traditions of Deborah Sampson," based on the reminiscences of people who had known her before the war.[44]

Among the young women of the town, Deborah was different. Sproat wrote that she was "tall, muscular and very erect and considered one of the very best specimens of womanhood among the hardy and vigorous population of Middleboro of that day." Mann wrote that "her stature is perhaps more than middle size," five feet seven inches (which he changed later to five seven and a half). This meant she was not only taller than most women (who then averaged about five feet), but as tall as most men (who were around five foot five). In height, Deborah may have resembled both her father, who in a military muster roll was recorded as six feet tall, and her brother Ephraim, described as "a tall, spare man."[45]

"Her waist," Mann wrote, "might displease a coquette," implying she was not thin, but "her limbs [legs] are regularly proportioned. Ladies of taste considered them handsome when in the masculine garb." (In the eighteenth century, a gentleman's stockinged leg was a source of sex appeal.) Her breasts were small. In 1797, Mann only mentioned in a footnote that in the army she bound them with a linen cloth. But in his revised manuscript in the 1830s, when he warmed to pretending to be her (writing in the first person), he wrote: "My breasts were much smaller than I have seen in some young women even before marriage, and were not flabby." This rings true; from what we know about women disguising themselves in the army who were detected, large breasts were a giveaway.

The gentlemanly officer who described Samson as a "comely young nymph" in his admiring report in 1784 may be pardoned for his hyperbole. So may the romantic gentleman who was so carried away by her performance in Northampton on her later lecturing tour in 1802 that he thought she was "beautiful in an eminent degree." Mann, even though he had a stake in presenting her as a feminine heroine, was more frank: "The features of her face are regular; but not what a physiognomist would term the most beauti-ful."[46] Then, compensating for what a reader might construe as a slight, he added: "Her eye is lively and penetrating. She has a skin naturally clear and flushed with a blooming carnation." Thirty years later, he filled in the details:

> My eyes are inclining to hazel; tinctured, however, with a little blue. . . . My nose is rather of the Roman cast; not perfectly straight, nor aquiline. My mouth is of middling size; lips not nigh so thick as a negro's. . . . My teeth had considerable regularity. . . . My ears are of a medium size. . . . My hair which I almost forgot, is neither black, brown, nor perfectly auburn; it is pretty fine—some of it is now a little grey. . . . My complexion was not olive, nor lilly-white. It is now somewhat sun-burnt, powder-burnt, and weather-beaten.

Daniel Johnson, a Sharon resident who knew her as an elderly woman when he was a boy, looked back on her "as a person of plain features."[47]

Joseph Stone's unflattering likeness of 1797 (frontispiece), drawn from life, supports Mann's description. Stone, a folk artist from Framingham, Massachusetts, of limited skills as a portrait painter, is not entirely reliable. Neither is he to be dismissed. Mann thought enough of the portrait to send it on to an engraver to make the frontispiece for his book. In a small oil paint-ing on paper (which remarkably still survives), Stone portrayed a woman with a long face, a large, prominent Roman nose, and a jutting lantern jaw. Her long, wavy hair comes down to her neck, and a high-waisted dress is draped over her small bosom. Yet for all the feminine diversions of the cloth-ing, the face has a masculine cast. Zilpah Tolman, born 1830, who married into the family, thought the engraving of Deborah which was based on the painting "must be a correct likeness as her relatives that I knew had the same rather long face."[48] A long "lantern" jaw was characteristic of English migrants to New England from East Anglia. In the twentieth century, a descendant said to resemble Deborah (for whom the claim is likely) also had a "long face" in her youth.[49]

By the standards of their day, where did contemporary observers place Deborah on some continuum of masculinity and femininity? Sproat, relying on the visual memories of "the old folks" *after* they knew she had become a soldier, was emphatic: "People often thought as they looked on her stalwart form Deborah Sampson should have been a man and they often said so." Mann was equivocal: he saw a woman in her mid-thirties, softened by motherhood, and, of course, he was trying to convey a feminine heroine. His emphasis was on her bearing and behavior as opposed to her appearance. "But her aspect is rather masculine and serene," he wrote, "than effeminate and sillily jocose. Her movement is erect, quick and strong: gestures naturally mild, animating and graceful; speech deliberate with firm articulation. Her voice is not disagreeable for a female." After her death, when he returned to striking this balance, he again emphasized that her acquired traits were masculine, having her say: "I have probably imbibed something of the masculine both in speech and gestures."[50]

We have moved closer to how people perceived Deborah's personality. Mann, speaking of her as a youth, was confident that she had "a natural sweetness and pliability of temper," a "uniform and tranquil" temper, and "a native

What did Deborah Sampson look like? A number of her twentieth-century descendants who know her only through the image in the painting or engraving of 1797 believe that a member of their family resembled her. The best claim is for Pauline Hildreth Monk Wise (1914–1994), whose father, Rodney Monk (1883–1975), believed Pauline looked like Deborah. She was twenty-three in this snapshot. Photograph courtesy Carolyn Myrick.

modesty and softness of expression." In sum, she was sweet, calm, and soft. He also portrayed a woman who was "a lover of order" and "punctuality," who "showed an aversion to all irregular and untimely diversions," disdaining "revelry, gossiping, detraction and orgies." In other words, she had a strong Protestant work ethic, was serious, systematic, and dedicated. And these, one supposes, were the virtues he wanted her to exemplify.[51]

The perception of people who talked to Sproat, who had seen her working in people's houses or walking down country lanes, is more like the second part of Mann's description: severe and intense, as well as explosive. "She is described," Sproat wrote, as a woman "who didn't talk much, was very industrious—would spin from sunrise to sunset almost without stopping to rest and always carried with her an earnest and rather severe look." "Very industrious"—here was the spinner and weaver being paid by the piece, anxious to accumulate money; "an earnest and rather severe look" hints at a person who did not invite conversation or small talk. (The weaver, Laurel Thatcher Ulrich reminds us, was "her own most demanding mistress.")[52]

Two fragments of lore that survive from the Middleborough years support a picture of a quick-tempered Deborah rather than a sweet, tranquil Deborah. They suggest a young woman with emotions that might be released in a burst. "One day while engaged in spinning for a family living in the vicinity of Barden Hills," as Sproat tells the story, "having no wood prepared for cooking her dinner, Deborah Sampson seized an axe and wielded it with such dexterity, that the lookers-on said she cut wood like an old experienced chopper." The episode suggests letting go of pent-up anger. Men were supposed to chop the wood; women were supposed to cook. There was no man around: she would show them she could do what any man could.

The second anecdote, about Deborah as a teacher, suggests a tough disciplinarian quick to rein in unruly children with physical force. The school in the Mad Mare's Neck part of town where she taught was in a private house with exposed rafters. As Hannah Chapin, her former pupil, recalled the incident, "Miss Sampson took one refractory scholar, tied his hands together by a line, and throwing one end over the timber, raised him aloft, to the great consternation of the little urchins who thought the fellow's arms would be dislocated if his life was not taken. She had no idea of spoiling the child by sparing correction." Obviously, it was the kind of terrifying event that stuck in a child's memory. At the end of her life, she was remembered by her grandson as a disciplinarian who pointed to a whip on the wall to curb the unruly grandchildren living with her.[53]

A young woman with "an earnest and rather severe look" who was not beautiful may have been disadvantaged in the marriage market, although not necessarily because of her looks. A pretty woman might be able to land a man of a higher "station." A woman's marriageability, however, was usually determined more by her class, family status, and wealth than by her beauty or personality. From the point of view of a young farmer taking a wife, Deborah had few tangible assets. The Samsons were poor; her father had disappeared; her mother would become a public charge. She brought to a marriage neither property, family connections, nor a dowry. To a young man who did not have to worry about such things, she was a very good catch. She was strong, tough, and skilled, not only in housewifery but also in spinning and weaving, which could bring in extra income, and she was book-smart. The problem in Middleborough was that the size of the farms young men were inheriting was shrinking. Most farm boys in the town would think twice about courting a woman who would bring them no property, especially if she enjoyed "hammering" at books and "scrabbling" in journals. Consequently, the pool of men who might be interested in Deborah was small to begin with, much less the men she might be interested in. From her point of view, not many young men in town were her match.[54]

The war would have dried up the pool even further. Over the seven years of a war that began in 1775, the Continental Army recruited 106 men in Middleborough out of a total of 1,066 men in town aged over sixteen, or one in ten. In the years when Deborah came of age—she was eighteen in 1778, twenty-one in 1781—New England enlistees were drawn more and more from the ranks of the landless young men who were the most likely suitors for the hand of a woman like Deborah. The pattern was similar in Middleborough.[55]

Given the limited prospects for marriage for someone of her class, Deborah's "severe" look hints at a woman who may have withdrawn from the marriage market. She knew firsthand the lot of a farm wife and mother. Over eight years she had observed Susannah Thomas, who had had four children by the time Deborah arrived and gave birth to two more. Eight children was still common at a time when there was little will or capacity for family limitation. She knew what the female sphere on a farm was like. Besides, as a spinner and weaver and teacher she had found, if not quite a living, a kind of independence she was in no hurry to give up.

The story that Deborah told her officers in 1783, that she went into the army to escape a marriage her "parents" had arranged with "a young man she had conceived a great antipathy for," is possible, but under the circumstances, unlikely. There were, of course, no parents playing an active role in her life. And Mann's embroidered revision of this story in his later manuscript in which the suitor became "a young gentleman of fortune and agreeable deportment" was "mere moonshine," as his 1866 editor, John Adams Vinton, cracked in a footnote. Why would a wealthy gentleman woo so plain a girl as Deborah? Years later, Mann told this as a comic story. In words he gave Deborah, the suitor was "a lump of a man," who "on a certain parade day he came to me, with all the sang-froid of a Frenchman and the silliness of a baboon, intoxicated, not with love but with rum. From that moment I set him down a fool." But neither a young gentleman of fortune nor a drunken baboon was likely.[56]

By the age of twenty-one, Deborah was already a woman who had broken gender norms: an avid reader, a servant who mastered male as well as female skills; a weaver and a teacher. In becoming a "masterless woman," she gained new vistas. One suspects she was not ready to become a wife and mother; her reading had given her too much sense of a wider world and her experiences too much of a sense of herself and of other possibilities.

5. *Deborah*
"Arise, stand on your feet, gird yourself . . ."

Deborah's suit of stern armor may also have been a way of warding off unwanted sexual attention. Plain or pretty, young female servants had good reason to be fearful of sexually aggressive males. Ordinarily, without explicit evidence, one can only speculate about the sexual experience of a single individual, or extrapolate from the pattern of a group. In Deborah's case, arguably, she revealed something about her sexual fears in a dream, and, in so doing, revealed even more about the kind of person she was becoming.

Rape in the colonial era often was forced on a woman by a man she already knew. Female servants were particularly at risk from the lust of masters, their sons, or other men in the homes in which they worked, all aware of their vulnerability. The line between consensual and coerced sex, moreover, could be thin. With no property to lure men into marriage, servants may have been willing to attract them through sex. But sex was risky business. If a single woman was accused of having intercourse, as Mary Beth Norton points out, she was subject to the criminal charge of fornication, "defined by colonial law as sexual intercourse by any man with a single woman." In the Revolutionary War years, it was a rare session of the Plymouth County Court of General Sessions that did not fine a few young women for this crime. Men, on the other hand, rarely appeared before the court on this charge, evidence for what Cornelia Hughes Dayton calls "an entrenched double standard."[57]

The presence of British soldiers heightened sexual fears. Several British army regiments, it will be remembered, were stationed in Boston after 1768 to enforce the Navigation Acts, and thousands more arrived in the aftermath of the Tea Party, turning Boston into a garrison town. British soldiers were portrayed as the aggressors, as in Paul Revere's engraving of the Boston Massacre, in which the blood of innocent victims shot down by soldiers ran through the street. The events of 1775—the military occupation of Boston, the British army expedition to Lexington and Concord, the bombardment of Bunker Hill—were further proof to New Englanders of this aggression.[58]

Rape was a major theme of the patriot political campaign to oust the army in 1768–70. Then, after the first military encounters in 1775, rape escalated in public consciousness. A Revere engraving on the cover of a New London almanac depicted America as an Indian maiden lying on the ground, the victim of lascivious attention by British ministers. Mercy Otis Warren, who experienced the war from her home in Plymouth, incorporated in her history of the Revolution a folk memory of the "shrieks of infant innocence" from young girls "subjected to the brutal lust" of British or Hessian soldiers. It was not far-fetched that Mann should write that "Miss Sampson learned that many of her own sex were either ravished, or deluded to the sacrifice of their chastity, which she had been taught to revere, even as dear as life itself." After war broke out, "the country inhabitants" were frequently alarmed by "idle and ignorant reports" that British troops were "penetrating with the greatest rapidity into the country, ravaging, plundering and butchering all before them." In response, "more than once was Miss Sampson persuaded to join her female circle . . . to seek security in the dreary desert or deserted cottage."[59]

Against this background, Mann recounted a vivid dream that Deborah, by then Mrs. Gannett, reported to him in the 1790s, which I interpret as growing out of this pervasive fear of aggression, sexual and military. In early America, people in all classes searched dreams for signs of omens that predicted the future. They believed in portents, visions, and prophecies, patronizing fortune-tellers and "cunning" men and women. They also interpreted comets and eclipses as signs of God's providence. Dreams remained for many, especially in the countryside, part of "a world of wonders."[60]

Deborah's truly extraordinary dream is meaningful in this context.

When I first read Mann's account of it, I was skeptical, putting it aside as one of his more lurid flights of imagination. Mechal Sobel, a scholar who has analyzed the dreams of some two hundred early Americans, convinced me that it was indeed Deborah's dream. It was a dream, Mann reported her saying, that had recurred three times—"the traditional magic number," says Sobel, "that was widely believed to provide assurance that it was from God and would come true." This talisman aside, the more I returned to it, it seemed to be a dream that was beyond even Mann's considerable powers of invention and was most likely to have been experienced by a young woman, especially an adolescent. Further, the dream reported a scriptural revelation not at all in keeping with Mann's outlook—he was something of a deist—yet consistent with Samson becoming an evangelical Baptist convert a few years later.[61]

The dream, as Mann reported it, first occurred on April 15, 1775, four days before the Battle of Lexington. If so, she would have been about fifteen. She dated a personal event by associating it with an electrifying public event, something we all do, which psychologists call "flashbulb" memories. Since she reported having the dream three times, it might have recurred when impending military actions would have heightened fears of British soldiers sallying forth into the countryside. British troops did not evacuate Boston until mid-March 1776, and after that, a justifiable fear remained that they would reappear in southern New England. The Middleborough militia marched off on several "alarms" to cope with British threats to other points on the seacoast.[62]

The dream reveals not only Deborah's fear of aggression—whether or not it was sexual—but her extraordinary capacity to respond to it. It was a kaleidoscopic nightmare. Mann told it in the first person, speaking as Deborah, a mode in which he was usually fluent; and while he undoubtedly embellished it to heighten the drama, he probably captured her emotions. Her mood was one of terror. The dream begins in a scene of bucolic serenity, the sun going down on a hillside overlooking "the pleasant and fertile meadow," herds grazing, farmers in the fields, breezes from gentle "zephyrs" wafting "ravishing odours"—in all, an idyllic pastoral countryside. She is filled with "sublime ideas of Creation and that being who has caused it all to exist." Then, a sudden change occurs, which invokes "astonishment and horror." The sky darkens, there is "incessant lightning and tremendous peals of thunder," with "stenches of sulphur" (the smell of Hell). The waters below are "convulsed" with mountainous waves and ships are "at once dismasted, dashing against rocks and one another, or foundering amidst the surges."[63]

The dreamer now confronted horrifying dangers. Farmers dispersed, fleeing for safety. After hearing "a volcano which shook with the perpetual roar of thunder," she sees "the most hideous serpent roll itself from the ocean." It approaches at great speed and she flees to her home. As she looks back, "the streets through which he passed [were] drenched in blood, I fell into a swoon. . . . At length I found myself (as I really was) in my own apartment"—her bedroom. But instead of safety, she saw "the door of the apartment open of itself" and the serpent reappeared "in a more frightful form." "He was of immense bigness, his mouth opened wide and teeth of great length. His tongue appeared to have a sharp sting in the end." He entered the room "and advanced toward my bedside, his head raised as nearly as I conjectured about five or six feet, his eyes resembled balls of fire. I was frightened beyond description. I thought I covered my head and tried to call for assistance but could make no noise."

Thus far, she was a truly helpless victim (as most people are in nightmares), but now her mood changes abruptly. She is in bed, unclothed or scantily clothed. "At length I heard a voice saying, 'Arise, stand on your feet, gird yourself, and prepare to encounter your enemy.' I rose up, stood upon the bed; but before I had time to dress the serpent approached and seemed to swallow me whole." She calls on God for assistance. "And at that instant I beheld at my feet a bludgeon which I readily took into my hands and immediately had a severe combat with the enemy." The serpent retreats, lashing at her with a tail that "resembled that of a fish, more than that of a serpent. It was divided in several parts and on each branch were capital letters of yellow gilt"—saying what, is not clear. She pursues him, striking him, "till at length I dislocated every joint, which fell into pieces to the ground."

She then underwent a second trial. The monster took new form, the fractured pieces reuniting "in the form of an ox. He came at me a second time, roaring and trying to gore me with his horns." She beat him, too, with her bludgeon, so that "he fell into pieces to the ground. When I ran to gather them, but on survey found them nothing but a *gelly*—and I immediately awoke."

This dream may be analyzed on several levels: for its emotional content; for its symbolism; and for clues to Deborah's personality. The overall emotion conveyed by Mann's account is of sheer terror in the face of overwhelming danger. The image of ships "dashing against rocks" and "foundering amidst the surges" of the ocean has the emotional resonance of the story she was told as a child of her father going off to sea and being shipwrecked. The serpent could be no more than a common garden variety of snake and the horned ox could have been a bull in some farmer's meadow. But familiar dangers to a farm girl in the agricultural countryside could also be easily transformed into grotesque images of horror.[64]

It is difficult, however, for present-day readers not to see symbols of sexual aggression at the core of the dream. Deborah clearly refers to both animals as male. Moreover, she is in her own bed, unclothed ("before I had time to dress"), and the serpent "of immense bigness" is about to swallow her. Both animals project phallic symbols: the ox (more properly a bull) is "roaring and trying to gore me with his horns"; the serpent has a lashing tongue with "a sharp sting in the end." The serpent's tongue and thrashing fishlike tail and the ox's horns evoke (to us) an erect, active penis and the "*gelly*" on the ground evokes semen, an ejaculate from the spent animals. She did not make these sexual associations, but could they not have arisen from an emotional matrix of sexual fears intensified by military threats? The serpent and ox could have stood for British soldiers or for other men who threatened women.[65]

Serpents had taken on a political meaning at the time of Deborah's dream. In the Christian tradition, the serpent, of course, was preeminent as a source of evil—in particular, sexual temptation. The devil was often referred to as "the old serpent." More immediately, as the colonists moved toward war, serpents were in the air as a symbol of patriot resistance. In 1774 and 1775, the masthead of Isaiah Thomas's *Massachusetts Spy* (which had a large country circulation) featured Revere's engraving of a snake divided in pieces confronting a menacing dragon, each segment marked with the abbreviation of a colony/state, with the slogan beneath: "Join or Die." The "capital letters of yellow gilt" that Deborah could not make out in her dream hint at the capital letters on the pieces of this scotched snake. In the ensuing war, any number of military units adopted as their flag the symbol of a coiled rattlesnake about to strike, with the slogan: "Don't Tread on Me."[66]

Deborah gave no hint to Mann of any experiences expressing sexual fears. We are left to speculate. She was a farm girl, aware of animal sexuality in the barnyard. She could hardly have been unaware of male anatomy; privacy in a small colonial farmhouse was unknown. While people undressed

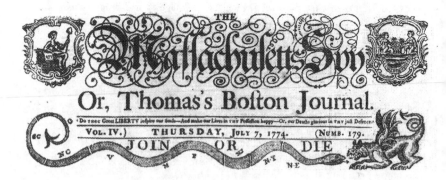

"Join or Die," *the divided snake, each part lettered with the abbreviation of an American colony, may be the visual source for a similar image in young Deborah's dream. According to Mann's memoir, the dream first occurred soon after the battles of Lexington and Concord, in mid-April 1775. This engraving by Paul Revere appeared in* The Massachusetts Spy, *published in Boston by Isaiah Thomas, in issues between July 7, 1774, and April 6, 1775. Courtesy American Antiquarian Society.*

infrequently, she could have seen naked males: her father (a man given to drink), her master, certainly the Thomas boys who slept in the attic with her. Court depositions by servant women who brought charges against rapists occasionally testified to men seeking them out in their beds—the site of Deborah's dream. She also could have seen or heard the Thomases engaged in sexual intercourse in the chamber below, and she might have seen one of the older Thomas boys masturbating, the biblical sin attributed to Onan that ministers never tired of preaching against. In the town, she might have been the object of propositions or horseplay by men of all sorts. At such harvest frolics as cornhusking, ribald rituals in the barn gave license to bawdy play. Hence, the dream might have either relived a sexual encounter (or warding one off), or it could have reflected a young woman's fear of and/or desire for such an experience.[67]

The blood—"the streets through which he [the serpent] passed [were] drenched in blood"—could have represented blood from menstruation or the breaking of her hymen. In the eighteenth century, the average age of menarche was usually around fifteen, Deborah's age in 1775. (Only in the twentieth century with improved health and nutrition has the age of first menstruation dropped to about twelve.) The image in the dream was resonant of the "streets stain'd with blood" both in Revere's engraving of the Massacre (literally red in hand-colored copies) and in sermons commemorating the event.[68]

In the memoir, neither Deborah nor Mann drew any sexual implications. Whether or not the dream was sexual, to my mind, the most remarkable thing about it is her active resistance to the threats confronting her, distinguishing it from common nightmares in which the dreamer is transfixed as a terrified victim. Her emotions of fear and helplessness changed rapidly to defiance; she summoned up the courage and physical strength to bludgeon both monsters to death.

Deborah would also have known the story of Samson in the Bible, for which her family name was a constant reminder. Samson took up the jawbone of an animal to club his enemies to death. The kaleidoscope of the dream thus amalgamated the biblical Deborah and the biblical Samson with contemporary political symbols. She takes action, moreover, in response to a voice ("Arise, stand on your feet, gird yourself, and prepare to encounter your enemy"), which unmistakably paraphrases the passage in the Song of Deborah that follows the narrative in Judges 5:12: "Awake, awake, Deborah: awake, awake, utter a song: arise, Barak, and lead thy captivity captive, thou son of Abinoam." A person who revered the Bible might have rendered this passage more exactly. But that was not Mann.[69]

Deborah must have known the story of her famous namesake. In many homes it was a common practice for children to read aloud to the family from the Bible. Joseph Buckingham, a printer, later recalled that, when he was an apprentice, he regularly read aloud in the presence of his master and mistress "at least one chapter, and often two or three chapters in the Bible." He had no doubt that he "read the Bible through in course at least a dozen times before I was sixteen years old." One grown-up after another Deborah encountered as a child could have instructed her in the virtues of the woman she was named after. Every scripture-reading, churchgoing Protestant in New England would also have known the story of Jael, with whom Deborah was linked in Judges. Indeed, Deborah's great-grandmother was named Jael Hobart Bradford. There was a reminder for a child![70]

Deborah, as the story is told in Judges, was a prophetess consulted by Barak, a general in Israel, when he was threatened by a formidable army of Canaanites with "nine hundred iron chariots" led by Sisera. Deborah counseled Barak to take ten thousand men and attack, but Barak refused unless she agreed to go with the army. Deborah agreed, prophesying that Sisera would fall into the power of a woman. Barak's army defeated the enemies of Israel, and Sisera fled, ending up at the tent of Jael, wife of the King of Hasor, who was at peace with Canaan and presumably neutral. Jael, as Laurel Thatcher Ulrich sums up the story, "led Sisera into her tent, fed him, lulled him into sleep, and then murdered him by driving a tent peg through his head," one of the grimmest stories in the Old Testament.[71]

The story acquired special resonance in New England in the valorization of frontier women who took up arms against Indians. Cotton Mather hailed Hannah Duston, who killed ten of her captors and escaped to tell the tale and bring back their scalps, for emulating "the action of Jael upon Sisera" and, by indirection, Deborah. What is striking in our Deborah's dream is that she carried the story a step beyond her biblical namesake. In the book of Judges, Deborah arouses others to do battle. In her dream, our Deborah takes up arms herself and bludgeons her two enemies to death, which makes her more akin to Jael. Deborah and Jael, as Ulrich comments, "were equal to any biblical male in courage and fierceness."[72]

The scriptural Deborah was also interpreted in other less bloody ways by Americans. In 1702, when a Quaker missionary wanted to epitomize the place held by Mary Coffin Starbuck, a highly successful "she-merchant," as a leader on Nantucket Island, he said, "she who was looked upon as a Deborah by these people." A century later, in 1801, in the pamphlet *The Female Advocate,* a Connecticut woman held up the biblical Deborah as a model for the woman as citizen: "Behold her wielding the sword with one hand, and the pen with the other; her sitting at the council board, and there, by her superior talents conducting the arduous affairs of military enterprise!"[73]

In time of war, the biblical Deborah was invoked by ministers to inspire military ardor in men. During the Revolutionary War, women invoked her to inspire female patriotism. When the women of Philadelphia publicized their door-to-door campaign to raise money for the troops, they spoke of "our ambition . . . kindled by the fame of those heroines of antiquity who have rendered their sex illustrious," listing first "the zeal and the resolution of Deborah, of Judith, of Esther."[74]

WHAT DID the dream mean to Deborah Samson of Middleborough? After he summed it up, Mann wrote: "This very singular dream had an uncommon effect on her mind and seemed to presage some great event. The novelty and momentous ideas it inspired induced her to record it, but she kept it secreted from others. At that time she attempted no particular interpretation of it." As Mann presented it, it presaged her serving as a soldier seven years later.[75]

There are a few rubs to his account. For one, it is doubtful that, at the time, Deborah kept the dream secret. It was terrifying, hardly the kind of dream one would keep to oneself. She had to interpret it and would have sought help to do so. A few years later, when she was undecided about enlisting in the army, Mann said she consulted a "prognosticator." She may have done so earlier. Fortune-tellers also interpreted dreams, drawing on both oral tradition and handbooks. When we turn to these popular handbooks, it is astonishing how congruent some of their symbolism is with the message of resistance from Judges in the Old Testament. In *The Universal Dream Book: or Interpreter of all Manner of Dreams,* a compendium of the wisdom of Aristotle, the Greek soothsayer Artemidorus, and ten other classical and Renaissance scholars, the entry for "serpent" was unequivocal: "to dream that you have killed a serpent is a sign you will overcome your enemies: to dream of beating a serpent is very good. . . ." To Hannah Heaton (1721–1794), an evangelical Connecticut farm wife, who dreamed of Satan embodied in the "shape of a great snake all on flame with his sting out," the snake was an omen of a "great trial" ahead. Thus, whether from Judges, Artemidorus, or folk wisdom, the message of the snake in Deborah's dream was similar: You face a trial, but you have the power to overcome your enemies.[76]

It is unlikely that at fifteen—if the dream occurred in 1775 as Mann said—she took it as a portent of her military exploit seven years later, in 1782. This may be all that Mann wanted to see in it. It is significant that she remembered the dream twenty years later and told it to him; it may have meant a good deal more to her than to him. "Dream reports and dream analysis," Mechal Sobel concludes, "were extremely important at turning points in the lives" of people she calls "dramatic narrators." Dreams "of utmost significance supported deviant behavior that they would not have undertaken without the legitimation of what they regarded as spiritual direction." Deborah might have prized the dream for encouraging her to continue to defy the norms for her gender and class.[77]

Quotations from the scriptures dropping from on high were especially common among evangelical converts—which, to anticipate the next chapter in this book, is what Deborah Samson became. Indeed, "Biblical impulses"—"verbatim quotations from scripture that suddenly sprang to mind without thought or warning"—were often cited by radical evangelicals to justify their actions, the historian Douglas Winiarski concludes.[78]

Whether or not we read the dream as sexual, the trajectory of the dream as a whole seems crucial. It ends in a call to take action and in the conquest of her enemies. The words from Judges express the overriding sense of the dream and the spirit of a life that was emerging. The child who thought, "As I was born to be unfortunate, my sun soon clouded," received a message from on high, "Arise, stand on your feet, gird yourself, and prepare to encounter your enemy." In short, the girl becoming a woman was no longer a passive victim wafted by events she could not control; she had a sense of herself as a person with the capacity to shape her own life, the kind of person she was becoming.

Chapter Two

The Rebel

Τhe stream of revolution," the much-esteemed historian J. Franklin Jameson wrote many years ago, "once started, could not be confined within narrow banks, but spread abroad upon the land. . . . Many economic desires, many social aspirations were set free by the political struggle." In Middleborough, this stream overflowed two banks. It swept away the town's most wealthy and powerful family, headed by Judge Peter Oliver, an arch Loyalist, the town's most famous political figure. And in religion the waves of the crusade by the Baptist Church led by Elder Isaac Backus, the town's most famous religious figure, lapped against Massachusetts's Congregationalist Church establishment, the Standing Order. Oliver and his family were forced into exile in England, where the upheavals in Middleborough were very much on his mind when, in an embittered history of the "late horrid rebellion," he wrote that "this material world is turned topsy turvey every Day."[1]

Arguably, Deborah Samson was an unusual woman who would have found a way to break out of what Herman Mann called the "narrow" and "contracted sphere" that set the boundaries for her sex at any time. But she crossed that boundary in the midst of a war by enlisting in the Continental Army, an opportunity not available in peacetime. And she crossed it only after she first passed a boundary in religion—leaving the Congregational

Church to join the Baptist Church in the midst of a major evangelical revival. Deborah Samson was a close witness to the "stream of revolution" in Middleborough that created a new political order, and a full-fledged participant in the religious awakening, each contributing in different ways to her transgressions of gender.

1. *A "Topsy Turvey" World*
"Rebells or Devills" Confront Judge Oliver

Middleborough was "aptly named," as two recent town historians have remarked. "It was the center for all inland routes of travel in Plymouth County." Roads connected the town to Plymouth, a small seaport on the Atlantic fourteen miles to the east, to New Bedford, a port nineteen miles to the south, and to Taunton ten miles to the west, which led to Providence, forty miles away. Boston was about thirty miles to the north. Thus, although an inland town, Middleborough was not terribly far from the sea and was within a circle in which information was diffused from two provincial capitals, Boston and Providence. Its two best-known citizens were itinerant: Peter Oliver, who went back and forth to his court in Boston; and Isaac Backus, who was forever on the road in New England, organizing his host. The official town Committee of Correspondence, appointed in 1774, was in touch with its counterpart in Boston. News of major events traveled rapidly by "a contagious diffusion." Reports of the battles of Lexington and Concord reached the town within a day. When Boston got the news that Congress had adopted a Declaration of Independence and rang all its church bells, before long Ichabod Tupper was racing across fields in Middleborough to tell his father, William, a patriot leader, "Father, all the bells are ringing between here and Boston. And we are free!"[2]

The center of town was the green, which consisted of little more than the Congregational meetinghouse (also the place of the town meeting), an open field where the militia trained, the "new" cemetery, and Ebenezer Sproat's imposing two-story tavern and barn. "Public houses," or "ordinaries," as they were also called, were centers of public life. The original church building erected in 1745 lasted until 1827, when it was replaced by the church that still stands astride the green—a tall, white-spired building in a picture postcard New England setting. Sproat's public house survived only until

The Sproat public house on the green in Middleborough, a center of town life where, in 1775, the tavern sign read: "Entertainment for All Sons of Liberty." Here Deborah did weaving and may have gotten drunk, testing her first failed enlistment as "Timothy Thayer." Courtesy Middleborough Historical Association.

1898, but its huge barn still stands, tottering and precarious, clearly large enough for carriages as well as horses, a reminder of the travelers who stayed overnight when they passed through town.[3]

All this landscape would have been familiar to Deborah Samson. The green was about two miles from where she lived with the Thomases (on today's Sachem Street), not much of a walk for a strong country girl, and not far from the other houses in which she later did weaving. She dutifully attended the meetinghouse with the Thomas family and did spinning and weaving for the Sproats in their public house. On the green, swarms of girls and young women watched the militia go through its exercises. She lived close to the center of town activity.

As towns in colonial Massachusetts are sorted out by historians, Middleborough ranks as a "secondary country town with a very low level of commercial development," which means it was—with the notable exception of the Olivers—a town of farmers who did not produce very much for a market or rise to affluence. In 1775, a population of about 4,500 sprawled over 70,000 acres, making it one of the largest, yet most sparsely settled townships in the entire colony. It stretched twelve and a half by thirteen and a half miles. Settlement was clustered in a host of neighborhoods: the green, Eddyville, Warrentown, Muttock, Titticut, Lakeville, Thomastown, Beachwoods, and The Rock. Today, the thick forests in the southernmost part of town suggest the wooded character the area as a whole had in the eighteenth century.[4]

Middleborough was a town of struggling farmers who raised corn or rye and pastured cattle and some sheep for wool for the growing number of weavers. Their cash crops were timber or iron ore, dug from the bogs in the town's numerous lakes and ponds. A handful of mechanics scattered in the countryside catered to farmers, while a cluster around Muttock worked for the Olivers. In this widely spread town there was but one lawyer, one doctor, and only four men licensed to run general stores and a dozen to keep public houses.[5]

For all of America's nostalgia about an age of thriving self-sufficient farmers, most farmers in the town cultivated "shriveling parcels" of land, "whose sandy soil already displayed symptoms of exhaustion." The historian Leigh Johnsen found that the size of the parcels changing ownership went from 72 acres in the first decade of the century to only 28 in the 1770s. A consequence was "a skewed distribution of wealth," in which "the most affluent twenty percent of the residents owned more than half of the community's wealth" while the poorest 20 percent owned only 2 percent of the property. Not surprisingly, migration was well under way to western and northern New England. By the mid-1790s, Elder Backus thought that "as many people . . . could be found in other places that have sprung from Middleborough . . . as all who are now in the town." This explains why the town's population hovered around 4,500 for every decade from 1775 to 1810.[6]

On this landscape of declining opportunity, the resources and wealth of the Olivers stood out starkly. Peter Oliver, Sr., Chief Justice of the highest court in Massachusetts, owned one of the largest and the most profitable iron furnaces and forges in the province in Muttock, where he dwelled in what his modern biographer calls "the most elegant mansion in the province." Later, "old folks" remembered the colonial era as "a time when George was King and Oliver was Judge."[7]

Today, the stone ruins one can climb over on the Nemasket River are haunting reminders of Oliver's once-bustling industrial complex: a dam stopping the waters, sluiceways feeding into what once were waterwheels, huge stone foundations for a bevy of buildings. It is not hard to imagine the sounds of the throbbing, noisy manufactories that once flourished here: a blast furnace, an iron forge, a foundry, a slitting mill, as well as a sawmill, a gristmill, and a host of storehouses. All this went into the manufacture of military hardware, finished ironware, and nailrods. Oliver employed several score artisans directly: ironworkers, smiths, carpenters, as well as cartmen and laborers.[8]

The Oliver family was a living symbol in their midst of the "corruption" that made patriot leaders like John and Samuel Adams livid: a concentration of family power, plural officeholding, and private profit. When Reverend Conant excoriated the British for "exhorbitant pride and avarice," his flock might have taken him to be speaking of the Olivers. The family owed its business success to the military contracts brought by the Olivers' connections with Thomas Hutchinson, lieutenant governor and then governor until 1775. Peter Oliver, Sr., who had settled in the town in the mid-1740s, had been, since 1762, Associate Justice and, since 1771, Chief Justice of the Supreme Court of the Province. His older brother, Andrew, was province secretary, Stamp Act commissioner designate in 1765, and lieutenant governor until his death in 1774. The Olivers intermarried with the Hutchinsons: Andrew married Hutchinson's sister-in-law; in 1770, Peter Oliver, Jr., married Hutchinson's daughter, Sara. Decades later, the Oliver housekeeper, Mary Norcutt, could regale people with tales of the sumptuous four-day wedding celebration for the couple in the "great hall."[9]

The judge, American-born and a Harvard graduate, displayed all the trappings of his wealth and office. He traveled "in a coach emblazoned with his arms accompanied by postilions and outriders in scarlet livery." He lived in baronial splendor, his estate stretching along a bluff above the Nemasket River overlooking the ironworks below. Oliver Hall was called the "great Oliver" to distinguish it from the "little Oliver" built by "Judge Oliver" as a wedding gift to his son, Dr. Peter Oliver, Jr.[10]

Within the "great Oliver" the "great hall" was decorated with imported

English woodwork, hangings, and wallpaper, tapestried chairs, and Turkish carpets. White servants and black slaves maintained this finery. Here the Olivers entertained everybody who was anybody in the colony. It was Thomas Hutchinson's favorite vacation spot. Today, not a trace of the mansion remains; the "little Oliver" alone stands, a handsome two-story house, its symmetrical Georgian style a reminder of the balance of a world the Olivers lost with the Revolution.[11] Deborah Samson would have heard stories about the goings-on at the "great Oliver" from Jennie, daughter of one of Oliver's two black slaves, later a servant at a house where she did weaving. Young Deborah might have gone along with her master Jeremiah Thomas when he hauled a cartload of wood to Oliver's furnace. On her own she probably patronized Mr. Leach's general store in Muttock.[12]

In Middleborough, the Revolution rung down the curtain on deference to the Olivers. For two decades after Peter Senior settled in the town in the mid-1740s, townsfolk kowtowed to him. In the meetinghouse, the Olivers owned pews close to the pulpit on the main floor. The town meeting chose Peter Senior as delegate to the General Court and in 1765 elected him selectman; sending Daniel, his younger son, as delegate with instructions to make amends to the Boston residents whose homes were damaged by the Stamp Act demonstrators—namely, his uncle Andrew Oliver and Thomas Hutchinson. But after 1765 it elected no Oliver to any office.[13]

The town at first responded conservatively to the imperial crisis. But in 1774, when Boston was starved by the British blockade, the town sent 51 bushels of rye and 30 bushels of corn to its "industrious poor." When it was clear that Britain's "Coercive Acts" canceled the colony's "old Charter," the "Middleborough people and indeed the Province in general," Dr. Oliver reported, "declare solemnly never to submit to this new plan of government."[14] By mid-1774, the Olivers and Hutchinson became the principal objects of patriot wrath. In Boston, the mood was so ugly that when Andrew Oliver died, Judge Oliver was afraid to appear at his brother's funeral. In Middleborough, the popular upsurge focused on the Olivers with an intensity that suggested the release of long-pent-up antagonisms of poor farmers to the great family's ostentatious presence and power.[15]

Patriots attempted to force local officeholders who received their commissions from the royal government to resign. In his running letters to the family in Boston, Dr. Oliver registered his mounting sense of terror and aristocratic contempt. In August 1774, "Men deputed from 40 Middlebg.

brutes" waited on the judge's house, shouting "threats and insults. I never knew what mobbing was before." In September, Dr. Oliver "was visited by about 30 Middleborough puppies," who forced him to renounce his commission as justice of the peace. They then carried off Silas Wood, "and threatened his life if he would not sign their paper to stand by the old Charter. . . ."[16]

In October, Deborah Samson very likely was present at the next dramatic event that unfolded on the green, when the militia officers collectively resigned their royal commissions. In a ceremony reported sarcastically by Dr. Oliver, "Our Sons of Lyberty put up a lyberty Pole on the Green, Our Minister grac'd the solemnity with his presence, and made a prayer under the Pole, and an harangue upon Lyberty. Mr. Conant took the pikes and gave them to the New Officers." In Oliver's eyes, Conant "rendered himself very ridiculous"; but not at all so to his predominantly Whig parishioners or to the young woman to whom he had loaned books.[17]

The Sproats hung a sign outside their tavern—"Sons of Liberty Entertained Here"—and when hostilities broke out at Lexington, local Minute Men marched off to the camp near Boston and the selectmen established a Committee of Inspection to suppress local Tories. No sooner had the fighting begun than Judge Oliver made a mad dash on horseback from Boston to Oliver Hall, removed his valuables from a secret drawer, and returned to the safety of the British army. In June, Dr. Oliver fled. He later heard that "a number set out to destroy and burn our interest but that the Selectmen interposed and saved them." Confiscation of their property and sale of the ironworks followed.[18]

As Dr. Oliver watched one person after another he thought of as allies go over to the patriots, he was bewildered: "but a very few in Middleborough but what are Rebells or Devills. The parson stands foremost in the list." To the Olivers, unable to comprehend that ordinary people could make political decisions on their own, the Congregational clergy were "the black regiment" of sedition. In 1776, the Olivers sailed into exile to Great Britain, their arrogance intact, Peter Senior raging at "that infernal Hydra Rebellion, with its hundred Heads," which "spread desolation . . . and ravaged the peaceful mansions of its inhabitants."[19]

In 1778, the family's worst nightmare came true: Oliver Hall went up in flames, the target of political arson. As Mrs. Norcutt, the housekeeper, told the story: "A good many people" gathered at the fire but made no effort to put it out. With flames lapping from the windows, "they had broken in the doors and were running through the building with the hopes of finding something to lay their hands on," but almost everything had already been removed. In the guest parlor nothing was left but the elegant wallpaper, all gilt and velvet. Women, Mrs. Norcutt pointedly recalled, "tore off the paper and took it home with them. They used to wear the sprigs of gold in their hair, when they went to a dance in town for years afterward." How appropriate. Among rebels in England an evergreen sprig worn by a woman in her hair, or by a man on his hat, was a time-honored badge of defiance. The same year, 1778, Washington ordered his soldiers "to adorn their Hats with *Green Boughs.*"[20]

All in all, there was something audacious about the Revolution in Middleborough. No one had to propagandize the town into independence. Reverend Conant, in a sermon in 1776, spoke of the crown demanding "unconditional jurisdiction . . . [over] our properties, liberties and lives." Once the threat was perceived this way, the sentiment for independence welled up from below. On May 20, 1776, the town meeting boldly voted that if the Continental Congress chose independence, "they the said inhabitants will solemnly engage with their lives and fortunes to support the measure." Followers were ahead of leaders.[21]

Locally, it was not a revolution in which the have-nots overthrew the haves. Members of the same solid yeoman families continued in office as selectmen. Judging by Dr. Oliver's comments, however, the activists in the mobs were youthful ("puppies") and strong ("brutes"), suggesting they were young farmers or mechanics. Clearly, new men were taking part in politics "out of doors," while new solid citizens were coming forward to assume office. Emblematic of the latter, in 1776, the town sent as its delegate to the Provincial Congress Benjamin Thomas, the patriarch of Thomastown, chosen for the first time to public office (the same year he was elected a deacon in the Congregational Church).[22]

Conservative to the innovations of Great Britain, Middleborough resisted the efforts of Massachusetts' would-be rulers to draw up a state government that would balance the "democratic" with the "aristocratic." In June 1780, a town meeting of 220 men took up the Massachusetts constitution drafted with the guidance of John Adams, clause by clause. "We have Run through it all," they said of the Declaration of Rights with thirty articles, and a "Frame of Government" with six chapters, and they did not like it.

They submitted page after page of "observations" that began with: "We object," "We object against," and "We still object." The religious provisions "encroached upon the consciences" of individuals; the property requirements for election to the Senate meant that "money makes Senators and not men." With a requirement of property worth £1,000 to be governor, they asked sarcastically, what would happen if the people's choice for governor had only £999? One provision after another was "Contrary to the Rights of Nature." In the end, the voters rejected the document 220 to 0, and then voted 173 to 3 to accept it only with amendments.[23]

Where was Deborah amidst all this defiance? She was fifteen in 1775, when New England soldiers, after their encounters at Lexington, Concord, and Bunker Hill, began singing "Yankee Doodle," an anthem celebrating the rustics who stood up to Britain; she was sixteen in 1776, when John Adams expressed alarm at reports of "a leveling spirit" and a "spirit of innovation" in Massachusetts; and twenty in 1780, when the state's new Declaration of Rights proclaimed that "all men are created equal." Mann reported Deborah becoming a patriot in these years, but he had no sense of the larger explosions and portrayed none of the events in Middleborough we have described. In the 1790s, conservatives were erasing all such internal radicalisms from the public memory of the Revolution: the mob actions, the debates over democracy, the way "the stream of revolution" set free social aspirations.[24]

Her memory of these years was of a political awakening. She was not off in some distant cranny of the far-flung town but close to the center of action on the green. Until 1778, she was a servant in a family that would have been tutored in Whiggery by her mistress's father, Benjamin Thomas. She heard the Whig sermons of Reverend Conant and likely grieved for him when he died in the smallpox epidemic of 1777. And 1778, when patriots burned down Oliver Hall, was the year she turned eighteen and became a free woman. With no master to tell her she was not to go out at night, she could easily have been among the women who tore pieces of gold-leaf wallpaper from the "great Oliver" and wore them in their hair.

In each home in which she worked or dwelled, she would have gotten firsthand accounts of stirring military events: from Abner Bourne, a captain in the militia (in whose house she boarded while a teacher), about the militia companies who responded to an alarm in Rhode Island; from the Sproats (in whose tavern she worked as a spinner and weaver) about their son Ebenezer, six feet four inches tall, an army major appointed Inspector General by General von Steuben; from the Mortons about their son, who enlisted in the Continental Army. And in the patriot Benjamin Leonard family (where she did weaving) she could have heard all about the Tory black sheep of the family, Zebulon Leonard, pronounced "enimical" by the town.[25]

Working at Sproat's tavern, she would have seen the crossroads come alive. "She had frequent opportunity," Mann writes, "of viewing the American soldiers, as they marched from one part to another." Four militia companies responded to alarms for the defense of the coast. A hundred or so Middleborough men enlisted in the Continental Army. She saw young men whom she knew, no smarter and no stronger than she, marching off to war. Standing near the notch marked off in front of the tavern which measured the minimum height for Continental soldiers, she could see that, at five feet seven inches, she was above the qualification.[26] After Massachusetts instituted a draft, she would have seen would-be recruits going from place to place in search of the best bounty offered by a town to fill its draft quota. She certainly would have caught wind of runaway apprentices and farm boys with a wanderlust heading for the seaports and a berth on a privateering vessel.

The travelers and peddlers who stopped at Sproat's public house would have brought in the print culture that bloomed in the Revolution. Here she may have seen a copy of Isaiah Thomas's *Massachusetts Spy*, which for a year ran the divided snake and the slogan "Join or Die." Here, too, is where the avid reader may have encountered Thomas Paine's pamphlet *The American Crisis*, calling for some "Jersey maid" to become the American Joan of Arc.[27] The almanacs hanging on hooks on the tavern wall (or in the necessary house) printed mileage charts for travelers, ticking off distances from one town to another. If she saw Isaiah Thomas's almanac for 1776 (a copy of which passed down in the Gannett family to this day), she also could have read "Directions for Preserving the Health of the Soldiers in the Camps."[28]

Thus, the inhabitants of sleepy, sprawling Middleborough, whose plow joggers normally reckoned themselves dwellers of Muttock or Thomastown or Eddyville, became citizens of a state and of a nation. It was a little world not only in motion, but "turned topsy turvey." They were years when a young woman like Deborah Samson, living with a growing sense of her own capacities, might entertain thoughts about possibilities not otherwise open to a person of her gender in her class.

2. A "Come-outer"
Baptists Confront the "Standing Order"

On the crest of a wave of evangelical fervor sweeping New England, in November 1780, a few weeks short of her twentieth birthday (or perhaps her twenty-first), Deborah Samson was "received" into the Third Baptist Church of Middleborough. The Revolution in Middleborough was very likely a source of political awakening, but for her the possibilities for rebellion appeared first in religion. A woman caught up in the spirit of defiance might express it "out of doors" in crowd actions or as a spectator cheering male activism, but had no way to voice it within the institutions of government, a male sphere. In Massachusetts, women were not members of the town meeting where all the voting took place, did not hold office or sit on juries. It is therefore not surprising that they should express themselves in the meetinghouse, where they were usually the numerical majority, and where the "sisters" were addressed attentively by ministers.[29]

Someone who left one church for another was sometimes called a "come-outer." This was familiar vocabulary. In the 1740s, in the first Great Awakening which in Middleborough split the Congregational Church, the deacon of the "new lights" made "a solemn speech" to the "old lights" to "come out from among them, and be ye separate." A Baptist elder might say of someone who had seen the light that he or she was "brought out." It involved a distinct sense of transition, and after crossing one threshold, there was no telling what others a person might cross.[30]

The minutes of the clerk leave no doubt that Deborah Samson was admitted to the Third Baptist Church of Middleborough in 1780 and suspended in 1782. But fifteen years later, she and Herman Mann fogged up what had happened. As he wrote his narrative in the late 1790s, he said of the revival only that she was "in the midst of it and was excited to observe its operations," but he denied she had ever joined the Baptists. She hid the affair because it was a source of multiple embarrassments: a commitment to a religious enthusiasm looked upon with disfavor by conservatives, the shame of being in effect excommunicated, and the fiasco of a botched enlistment in the army. For his part, Mann, a deist of sorts, was so prejudiced against evangelical religion that he gave a completely hostile account of the revival—it was a "penetrating disorder" and a "contagion" spread by the clergy for their own aggrandizement—and accepted her disavowal. He did not want even an ex-Baptist as his heroine.[31]

That a rebellious woman of religious disposition in Middleborough should gravitate to the Baptists is not at all surprising. She was raised on the Old Testament. Recall her dream with the message associated with her namesake in the book of Judges. The Bible seems to have stayed with her. (In 1802, she could invoke a parable from Scripture.) As a child she would have gone to Sabbath exercises as the ward of the widow of the former minister, then as a servant to the daughter of Deacon-to-be Benjamin Thomas. Recall, too, that Reverend Conant was her benefactor, a lender of "Godly" books.

Middleborough, by the 1780s, was home to "the largest concentration of Separatist Baptists of any town in New England." It had no less than three Baptist churches. Elder Isaac Backus, a towering figure in the Baptist struggle for religious liberty in New England, was pastor of the town's First Baptist Church from 1756 to the end of his life in 1806. Middleborough was "the mother of churches," and the First Baptist Church "the mother of ministers."[32]

The Baptists in New England, as their most prolific historian William McLoughlin observed, were invariably "regarded as outsiders and eccentrics"; they were "decidedly an out group, lacking any significant ties of kinship, wealth, social status or political influence with the ruling elite." For Middleborough, a town spread all over the map, the very physical location of the churches embodied this social geography. The sole Congregational meetinghouse commanded the upper green at the center of town, but Backus's First Baptist Church was in Titicut far to the north: the Second Baptist was in Lakeville to the southwest, and the Third Baptist was in the southernmost part of town in an area known as The Rock. Until the awakenings of 1779–80, the Baptists were few in numbers: around 1760, the First had fifty-nine members and the Third ten. After the 1740s, for thirty years, writes Leigh Johnsen, Backus and his associates "presided over a handful of small, withdrawn, and harassed sectarian congregations on the outskirts of town."[33]

The social gulf between the two denominations was visible in the physical differences in their meetinghouses and in the "seating of the meeting." For an observant young woman like Deborah, attending Sabbath exercises in the Congregational church was an exquisite weekly instruction in the social ordering of the community by class, gender, age, and race. The meeting-house was big enough to accommodate a congregation that had grown to 456 members in the Great Awakening of the 1740s. Raised in 1745, it was an imposing building: 55 feet long, 45 feet wide, and 25 feet at its walls, with a higher ceiling. Within, there were galleries on three sides. On the two sides of the main floor were the sheltered pews bought by the more well-to-do proprietors, "square, about five feet high, the upper part lattice work, through which the occupants would see the adjoining pews." The dozen most expensive pews, which sold for £20 and more, were for genteel families like the Olivers, while the less expensive ones in the first gallery ranging from £10 up went to solid citizens like Benjamin Thomas. On the main floor, "the space in the center was filled with benches without backs for people who could not afford to own pews." There was also "a woman's side" on the main floor.[34]

In the second gallery, a section was set aside for the town's small number of blacks (some slave, some free, almost all servants of well-to-do parishioners) and Indians, while another section was for boys and still another for girls. On the west side stood a lofty pulpit the minister reached by climbing a set of stairs. In front was an enclosure for the "deef" seats, as well as an elevated seat for the deacons who sat before the communion table. As a child, Deborah might have accompanied Widow Thacher to an honored place on the main floor; later, she might have sat either in the Thomas family pew in the first gallery or in the section of the second gallery set aside for servants.

The Baptists, by contrast, at first met in private houses or out of doors; one afternoon Backus preached "under the shadey trees." The first meeting-houses they put up were usually small, plain, unadorned frame structures that looked like one-room schoolhouses; indeed, some later doubled as such, like the Bell School in the Lakeville section. In seating arrangements, in the early years there was little differentiation by class. "Young and old, men and women, rich and poor, educated and unlettered stood side by side in undifferentiated space," the historian Susan Juster remarks. Later, when the Baptists prospered, they, too, auctioned off their pews.[35]

The equalitarian traditions of the first Great Awakening lingered on among the Baptists. "The common people," Backus declared, "claim as good right to judge and act for themselves in matters of religion as civil rulers or the learned clergy." The town's succession of Congregational ministers

A Baptist meetinghouse which doubled as a schoolhouse, the Bell School or the Neck School of Lakeville, typical of the plain architecture of early Baptist churches. It was erected in 1796 on Assawampsett Neck. Postcard courtesy Walter O. Thompson.

were learned Harvard or Yale graduates. Baptist ministers, called "Elder" rather than "Reverend," were not usually college graduates and, until congregations were large enough to support them, were itinerant. Even when "settled," they were likely to pursue an occupation of farmer or artisan.[36]

Baptists had long attracted large numbers of women, especially young, single women. Members were addressed as "brothers" and "sisters," and there was a tradition of lay exhorters, who occasionally were women and might even be children. (Decades earlier, the county court had fined a boy preacher in Middleborough.) In governance, men ruled, but some congregations followed the dictum, "admit the sisters to equal votes," and feisty Baptist women were known to challenge ministers. The church offered enough of "a widening of women's sphere of authority" to attract strong-willed women.[37]

The wartime awakenings boomed Baptist membership in New England. With about 6,000 members in 1777 in 119 churches, by 1784 the denomination had 8,000 members in 151 churches, an increase of one third. In Middleborough, the First Baptist went from 59 members in the early 1760s to 138 by 1779, and the Third, Deborah's church, from 10 to 194 by 1782. Historians disagree as to the weight attached to secular influences in the awakenings, but Backus himself was quite aware that natural calamities awakened people to a sense of their mortality. In 1778, in Middleborough, the mortality rate had "at least doubled" from "dysentery and slow fever," and in 1779, he wrote, the town experienced "the greatest scarcity of food last spring as has been known for a hundred years." Then came the "dark day," May 19, 1780, in which "the clouds and vapors were so thick over us that at noon day it was darker than ordinary moon light. Many in town and countrey thought the day of judgment . . . had come." During the late summer and fall of 1780, the Baptist revival peaked.[38]

In 1780, Elder Asa Hunt sent triumphant battle reports to his co-workers on the spiritual awakening in southern Middleborough where Deborah was living. May 31: "God is doing wonders among us . . . not far from thirty more hopefully brought into liberty." July 12: "In the number are four boys about twelve years old." September: "about one hundred souls [in all] have been turned from darkness to light." October 14: "half a dozen young converts brought out clear," making for a total of 113 converts. And there would be more in the fall.[39]

It is possible to sketch a rough social profile of the new converts. Hunt's language makes their youth clear: "young Christians," "young converts," even "boys about twelve years old." The minutes of the Third Baptist show that among these converts women were numerous. In September, for example, seven of the nine brought over were women, and on November 12, when Deborah was received, she was one of eight women and eight men. This pattern continued. In 1781, six of the seven converts in July and five of the seven in September were women. The congregation was flooded with women. They would have included daughters of farmers, servants, former servants, spinsters, and weavers—in other words, women like Deborah. A scholar tracing the men who joined both the First and Third finds that the converts who owned land "owned relatively little acreage," and that a large number were not on the tax lists at all; a good scattering were artisans, ironworkers, and laborers. In short, the new converts, men and women, were for the most part poor.[40]

For Deborah, it was not a spur-of-the-moment action. She probably weighed her decision over the summer of 1780, a time when she most likely was teaching school in south Middleborough, home to the Third Baptist. She did not take this momentous step, however, until November, at a moment when another event may have played on her emotions. That month, the Congregationalists gave an extraordinary sign of rejecting equality for the "sisters." In 1778, after Conant died, the congregation called to their pulpit Abraham Camp, a twenty-six-year-old graduate of Yale College, class of 1773, for a period of probation, the customary practice. In the eyes of Backus, Camp appeared "to be a man both of gifts and gracious experience." In February 1779, after the voting members of the congregation (all men) decided almost unanimously to ask him to accept a permanent appointment, he "hesitated to accept and asked that the vote of the sisters in the church might also be taken." This was an unusual request that would have been the talk of the town. In November 1780, when a second poll was taken (among the men alone), even though the vote was 20 to 5 in his favor, Camp declined, possibly because he did not want to minister to a congregation in which his request had proven so divisive. He left town for another pulpit in Berkshire County in western Massachusetts, where he died two years later.[41]

The clerk of the Third Baptist recorded "Deborah Samson" as "received" on November 12, 1780, the month the Congregationalists voted on Camp. Was there an unseen personal drama behind her religious decision? Had she waited to see if the "brethren" would allow the "sisters" to vote and/or whether they might appoint Camp? As the story passed down in town and was picked up by Reverend Pratt in the 1850s, Camp was "said to have been an advocate of woman's rights and had a high appreciation of the talents and character of the subject of this memoir and regarded her departure as a serious loss." "Woman's rights," of course, was a later term made popular after the Seneca Falls Convention in 1848; "high appreciation" hints at some kind of personal recognition by Camp. Was the twenty-one-year-old Deborah smitten with the "gracious" twenty-six-year-old advocate of a vote for the "sisters" who took an interest in her? Had she then rejected the church that rejected him? The timing of her decision allows us to gossip, the way townsfolk seem to have done, but there is no way of knowing.[42]

To be "received" by the Baptists, an individual would have to undergo a conversion, a deeply emotional event. Her awakening would have led her to come forward in the meeting space, and to make a likely "confession of faith" before the congregation, followed by a warm ceremony of acceptance. Sometime thereafter, the ritual of immersion or adult baptism followed, which in south Middleborough would have taken place in one of the area's numerous lakes or ponds.[43] So momentous a decision was usually taken after much inner turmoil, and sometimes after comforting biblical texts "dropped into one's head as if from heaven." Others heard "voices that called from the heavens," which were often "the 'trigger mechanism' for the conversion." Deborah's earlier dream, in which she heard a voice booming her instructions with a passage from Judges, was typical of such an impulse.[44]

Deborah was a Baptist for a year and a half, from November 12, 1780, into the spring of 1782. Becoming a Baptist meant many things for her. First, it resolved for the time being an inner turmoil as she feared for her soul. It permitted her to believe that she was of special significance in the eyes of God. It was also a way station on an intellectual journey that continued and led her by the 1790s (if Mann is right) to "setting aside doctrines of total depravity, election and a few others" and to reject "being bound by any set religion." In short, she did not stay a Baptist.[45]

Second, becoming a Baptist meant being embraced by a new family, meaningful for a child abandoned by her own family, shunted from one household to another, and no longer living with her surrogate family, the Thomases. She entered a close-knit fellowship of men and women, a sub-community. It also meant joining a large assembly of other strong-willed women.

Third, if the Revolution began her political education, the Baptists took it a step further, teaching her civil disobedience, the principle of individual resistance to unjust laws in defense of a higher law. Deborah joined the Baptists at a high point in their struggle for "soul liberty." Backus embraced the patriot war as "our cause," but as Massachusetts went through a long process of adopting a constitution (1778–80), he poured his energies into an unrelenting campaign to free dissenters from compulsory taxes for the support of Congregational ministers—from the "Standing Order," as the established church was known.[46]

Middleborough's town meeting accommodated its large Baptist minority, electing Backus to the committee that drew up its objections to the new constitution, including the establishment clause. Despite statewide opposition, however, Article III was adopted, requiring members of dissenting churches to submit certificates if they wanted to be exempt from taxes. It granted toleration but not religious liberty. Baptists then began a campaign of noncompliance. Deborah could have read one of Backus's fervent tracts or heard his circular letter read: "brethren face them down boldly upon this point and they cannot stand." She would have heard all about Elijah Balkcom of nearby North Attleborough, who refused to pay his religious tax, was carted off to jail, and brought suit to test the law. The Baptist mood in 1780–82 was one of defiant individual resistance to injustice.[47]

If becoming a Baptist meant all these liberating things to Deborah, it also meant being subject to a discipline more severe than any she had known. As the Baptists grew, their leaders were bent on winning respectability, which meant they were zealous in shaping up their new flock, especially the young women. The elders had what Susan Juster calls "an obsessive, almost paranoid concern with discipline" and, as a result, created "a climate of constant suspicion."[48] The "generally sexualized climate" of the revivals, Juster observes, often led to "a blatant disregard for conventional sexual boundaries." For a convert, the experience of coming out of one state and adopting another one was liminal; it put a person on a threshold. "Individuals undergoing liminal rites of passage," Juster remarks, "experience a profound sense of freedom from social conventions and indeed from society itself." Something like this seems to have happened to Deborah Samson.[49]

If Samson had thoughts of trying to escape her "contracted" female sphere, she had joined a community that narrowed that sphere still further. If she felt empowered by becoming a Baptist, she would have to draw on the powerful examples of Baptist disobedience to injustice to make good her escape. Indeed, in the spring of 1782, the effort of Baptist "brethren" to discipline her was the straw that broke the camel's back, leading her to a flight from town.

3. Enlistee
"She determined to burst the bands, which . . . held her sex in awe"

Deborah Samson enlisted in the Continental Army twice, the first time in Middleborough as "Timothy Thayer," probably between mid-March and late April 1782. It was a disaster: she was discovered, was threatened with legal prosecution, and brought down the wrath of the Baptist Church. The second time, she was successful. She fled Middleborough, not at all clear as to what she would do, and ended up in the middle of the state, where on May 20, 1782, she enlisted as "Robert Shurtliff."

The sequence of events is crucial to grasp her state of mind. She hid the story of the first enlistment from Mann, who picked it up as a rumor but dismissed it in the only skeptical footnote in his book. "It has been reported," he wrote, "that she enlisted, as a Continental soldier for a class in Middle-borough—that she received a part of the stipulated bounty—that she was immediately discovered, and refunded the bounty. I have no account of this from her, nor is the report in the least authenticated." It was true, however. She did not tell him the story for the same reason she did not tell him about becoming a Baptist, because it would have damaged the persona she was helping him shape. And he had no incentive to run it down. But the report can be "authenticated."[50]

We know of the event because it was recorded in the minutes of the Third Baptist Church the following September and because it was transmitted in local lore. It was picked up by Reverend Pratt from "a person who remembered Deborah Sampson," and it was passed down in the family of Captain Benjamin Leonard, at whose house Deborah put on her disguise. It was also discovered by John Adams Vinton, Mann's 1866 editor, who got it not only from his fellow biographer Pratt, but from "that distinguished antiquary, Mr. Samuel Adams Drake of Boston whose wife was a near relative of Captain Leonard," who got it from a family descendant. Drake was the author of a number of reliable antiquarian books about Boston history. This chain of transmission, like the story, has its comic side, but it comes down with the kind of specific detail about people and places that makes it credible, especially when combined with the church minutes.[51]

As Pratt told the story, Samson was staying at the home of Captain Benjamin Leonard, who "lived East of the upper Nemasket works, and with him a negro woman by the name of Jennie, daughter of Judge Oliver's slave, Phillip." Deborah, "by the aid of this negro . . . dressed herself up in a suit of clothes belonging to a young man named Samuel Leonard. Thus clad, she started for the recruiting office at the house of Mr. Israel Wood. There she signed the papers of enlistment as a soldier under the feigned name of Timothy Thayer. Having now become a soldier she went, thus attired, to the tavern kept near the place where Dr. Putnam resides." She "called for a dram of liquor, talked and staggered like any other military character. During the night, however, she returned home; crept into bed with the negro; and when morning dawned, the young man of the previous evening donned as usual her ladies dress and engaged in her business as though nothing had occurred." The detail in this seventy-year-old account is astonishing.

Pratt did not flinch at attributing mundane motives to his heroine (whom he otherwise likened to Joan of Arc): "It is supposed that being short of funds she contrived this mode of replenishing her purse, not then intending to go into the army. Some of the bounty money she received was actually spent for wearing apparel." A few nights after the episode, he wrote, "she appeared at a singing school held at the house near the [current] residence of Mr. Earl Sproat somewhat dashed [dashing] in a new costume. On that occasion she made a present of a pair of long gloves to a young lady of her acquaintance to whom she felt indebted for special kindness during a season of sickness."

When the time came for the new recruits to muster, "no Timothy Thayer could be found." Pratt was explicit as to how she was discovered: "Now Deborah being a school dame was a notorious character and having lost by means of a felon the use of a forefinger[,] an old lady who sat in the corner carding wool when the young soldier signed the articles of agreement said he held the pen just like Deb. Sampson did." "Notorious character" meant no more than that as a schoolteacher she was well known; a "felon" was an inflammation of the tissue of the finger, which for her could have been the result of an accident while weaving, whittling, or chopping wood. "When therefore no such person appeared she suggested that it must have been said Deborah acting a borrowed part." Authority now moved into action. "Inquiry being made, Black Jennie let the whole secret out and the part she acted in dressing her up in men's clothes. She [Deborah] however gave up what bounty money had not been spent and henceforth kept close, fearing she might be taken up and suffer legal punishment. . . ." "Kept close" means she did not talk about it for good reason: she could be prosecuted either for wearing a man's apparel—a crime—or for defrauding the government, or both.

Vinton added a juicy bit of misogynist lore: "Tradition affirms that Samuel Leonard was so shocked at the idea of his clothes having been used by a woman, that he never wore them afterward." It is not hard to see why villagers passed on the story—it had taken on the dimensions of a folk legend embellished with a young man's sexual panic. It was a very good tale about a fascinating subject, how a woman passed as a man, with an element of mystery as to how she was detected.

The cast of characters was present in the town in the 1780s. The Leonards were a family where Deborah "hired out" to do spinning and weaving. Benjamin Leonard was a militia officer; Samuel Leonard a private; and the recruiter, more likely, was Isaac Wood, who was licensed to maintain a public house, the usual site for an army recruiter. "Black Jennie," who belonged to Dr. Peter Oliver, in 1782 would have been a free person and, if so, very likely a servant. Contemporaries would not have attached any sexual connotation to "crept into bed with the negro," or to racial mingling among women of the laboring classes. The places in the story can also be identified. All were within walking distance of one another, close to the upper green. Deborah risked so perilous an adventure not in some distant corner of the town, but where she was known. No wonder she was caught. The episode is a puzzle: part trial run, part moneymaking, perhaps in good part a lark.[52]

The name "Timothy Thayer" is interesting. Later lore had it she identified herself as "Timothy Thayer of Carver." For a would-be woman soldier, a disguise name and place of origin was important, both at the point of recruitment if it was in a town where everyone knew everyone else, and in the army whose regiments were often organized by area and where a soldier might meet someone from his own county, if not his own neck of the woods. An assumed name did not have to be the name of an actual person—in fact, there was a risk in impersonating a real person who might be known. But it had to be the name of a real family from a real place about which the masquerader could be knowledgeable if questioned in everyday banter. Within a town, the first hurdle was the civilian recruiting agent. Thus, she had to pass herself off as someone from out of town.

Deborah's first disguise name and place of origin qualified. Carver was the town immediately adjacent to the Thomastown area of Middleborough, with which she would have been familiar. Thayer was a very common name: on the compiled list of Massachusetts soldiers, there are several score Thayers and many Timothy Thayers, none explicitly from Carver, but any number from the eastern part of the state. It is likely that she knew a particular family named Thayer that she could pretend to be part of: the family of Captain Nathan Thayer of Medway about thirty miles from Middleborough. The source is an oral tradition picked up by Elizabeth Ellet in the late 1840s for her biographical sketch of Deborah. Although unreliable for details of Deborah's life, Ellet had it on the authority of a niece of Captain James Tisdale of Medfield that Deborah spent seven weeks with the Thayers in Medway in 1778 masquerading as a male soldier, during which time she had a "love passage" with a young woman, which upset Mrs. Thayer no end. On her lecture tour in 1802, Deborah Gannett did indeed stay in Medfield with Captain Tisdale, where his niece could have heard such a story. There is no proof at all for such an enlistment in 1778 or any other time, or for the romance. But in the garbled way in which stories are transmitted over time, it offers a clue as to why she may have chosen the name "Timothy Thayer."[53]

Deborah's two enlistments in the spring of '82 are understandable only in the context of the army's recruiting practices and the origins of recruits in the last years of the war. John Shy, a dean of military historians of the Revolution, warns against creating a "mythology" that "popular support never flagged, and that the army of the Revolution was a great egalitarian phalanx. Because popular support did flag, and the army did have to scrape the social barrel for soldiers." After the initial enthusiasm for the war faded, Massachusetts resorted to a draft to meet its quota of Continental troops. By 1777, and especially in '81 and '82, most men went into the army either because they were drafted or to gain a bounty as a substitute for a draftee. On March 8, 1782, to raise fifteen hundred three-year men, the state legislature voted the last of these drafts, once again assigning quotas to each town. As explained by George Robert Twelves Hewes, formerly a Boston shoemaker who had been drafted in Wrentham, the state required all men of military age to serve, "or to form themselves into classes of nine men, and each class to hire an able bodied man, on such terms as they could, and pay him for his services, while they were to receive their pay of the state."[54]

The bait for an impoverished recruit was a bounty, collected from an agent acting on behalf of a class of drafted men. The Middleborough selectmen debated how much they would offer as their bounty, and after going as high as 100 silver dollars, settled on 50, a princely sum because silver was a hedge against inflation at a time when paper money was "not worth a continental." Would-be recruits often shopped around from town to town for the best bounty and also jumped bounties. Deborah, between her first and second enlistments, in effect did both.[55]

Getting into the army was a snap. There was no physical examination and no request for proof of age, residence, or citizenship. A recruit just showed up. Moreover, the civilian agent who got a commission on the bounty had a stake in keeping one eye closed, and the army officer assigned to rounding up raw recruits usually gave them only an eyeball once-over. There seems to have been a requirement as to height, possibly five feet five inches, but officers seem to have had latitude in interpreting eligibility. A man had to be tall enough to ram a rod down a muzzle-loading musket, which was almost five feet long. And he had to be able to keep up a stride marching with fellow infantrymen. A woman dressed in man's clothing who was tall enough could get away with it as long as her physique did not give her away.[56]

In desperation to meet quotas, the hurdles were dropped to a new low for this last draft of the war. In the spring of 1782, Washington court-martialed one Massachusetts officer at West Point for having accepted among his recruits four deserters (two from the British army, two from the French), as well as four "boys undersized," two immigrants who decamped, "a Negro lame in the ankle," and George West, "an idiot"—a parade of the unqualified that gives new meaning to "scraping the bottom of the barrel."[57]

Deborah's first enlistment took place sometime between late March 1782 (by which time the towns were required to respond to the state draft) and early May, when she left town, most likely in April. The account in the church minutes for September 3, 1782, locating the event as "last Spring," confirms the contours of the episode and suggests her frame of mind. The clerk wrote:

> Considered the case of Deborah Sampson, a member of the church who last Spring was accused of dressing in men's cloths and inlisting as a soldier in the army and although she was not convicted, yet was strongly suspected of being guilty, and for sometime before behaved very loose and unChristian like, and at last left our parts in a secret manner, and it is not known among us where she is gone; and after considerable discourse, it appeared that as several brethren had labored with her before she went away without obtaining satisfaction concluded it is the church's Duty to withdraw fellowship until she returns and makes Christian Satisfaction.[58]

It is not hard to re-create what happened from what we know about Baptist disciplinary practices. "Dressing in men's cloths," of course, violated the biblical injunction in Deuteronomy 22:5: "The woman shall not wear that which pertaineth unto a man, neither shall a man put on a woman's garment: for all that do so are abomination unto the Lord thy God." It also violated a Massachusetts statute of the 1690s which was not at all a dead letter. "Accused . . . and although . . . not convicted, yet was strongly suspected of being guilty" suggests she might have been accused by a local justice of the peace, but that the court either took no action or dismissed the case, or that it was still pending. For the Baptist inquisitors, however, suspicion alone was

Minutes of the Third Baptist Church, Middleborough, September 3, 1782. Courtesy Franklin Trask Library, Andover–Newton Theological School.

cause enough to act; and by the time they reported to the congregation in September, she had left town, which in their eyes, of course, confirmed her guilt.

"For sometime before behaved very loose and unChristian like" is a puzzle. It could have referred to her post-enlistment display of drunkenness in a tavern: "loose" does not necessarily have a sexual implication; had her sin been in any way sexual, the elders had a richer biblical vocabulary to draw on. No one accused her of being a "harlot" or a "whore" or spoke of any "wanton" or "unnatural" act. Baptists attached a very broad meaning to "loose and unChristianlike." But "for sometime before" clearly implies this was not the first time Deborah had run afoul of church standards. We are in the dark. It may have referred to something as simple as failure to attend Sabbath exercises regularly at the Third Baptist meetinghouse, which was close by when she joined and was living in the southern part of town, but very far from the upper green where she was living in 1782. In any case, the change referred to a general attitude Deborah conveyed.

"Several brethren had labored with her" means that a small committee (explicitly "brethren" and no "sisters") traveled up from The Rock in the southern part of the township to confront her and ask her to admit to and explain her transgressions. Saving a soul was important to them. "Without obtaining satisfaction" suggests that Deborah either denied the incident (remember, Pratt's storyteller said she "kept close," to protect herself), or worse, she questioned the right of "the brethren" to conduct an inquiry into her private life. If so, she would have compounded her original sins by defying church authority. She was not repentant or remorseful.

To make "Christian satisfaction" means she would have to confess her sins before the congregation and plead for forgiveness. An entry in the church minutes for another errant sister suggests what it would entail to "withdraw fellowship": not until a sinner confessed to misconduct before the congregation were the members "free to commune with her." In other words, Deborah faced the prospect of being shunned by the people who had taken her into their fellowship—a terrible fate in a town made up of neighborhood communities further divided on a denominational basis, especially for a single woman. Remember, she had left the Congregational Church, whose members could hardly offer solace to a lapsed Congregationalist, now a lapsed Baptist guilty of a secular crime as well. Is it any wonder, then, that by late April or early May she was in full flight from Middleborough?

Susan Juster, the historian who has made the fullest study of women in Massachusetts Baptist churches in the eighteenth century, was struck by several things in this record of Deborah Samson's encounter with the church. First, "her stormy career at the Third Baptist conforms to the pattern of other revival converts in the 1780s, many of whom joined in a burst of enthusiasm only to fall away (or be disowned) within a year or two." Second, to Juster, "it is the swiftness of the church's judgment that stands out." The contrast between her rapid dismissal and what the minutes reveal of the church's treatment the same year of a male offender, Moses Thomas, "is striking." Thomas contested the church's action against him repeatedly over more than a year. "It is entirely fitting," Juster writes, "that she chooses to respond to the church's labor by going away secretly rather than staying and fighting it out." Finally, Juster sees the charge of Samson behaving "very loose and unChristianlike" as "a general condemnation of her furtive and unreliable character." This is typical of female offenders in this period, who were more likely to be disciplined "for vague 'unChristian character' rather than discrete sins." Her sin was dissimulation, which to Baptists in quest of respectability was a major lapse. Samson, in short, was one of the "disorderly women" Baptists wanted either to tame or to disown.[59]

SO DEBORAH SAMSON left town. Whatever the underlying impulses, her departure was in immediate response to her confrontation with the Baptist elders in the wake of her failed enlistment. What's more, she left in a panic, in a warranted fear that civil authority might still bring charges. She was probably planning such a move for some time, but clearly she was escaping. All of this she hid from Mann.[60]

Mann, knowing nothing about her urgent need to escape (or not wanting to know), gave as her central motives for leaving town a desire to see the world and serve her country. He broke down her thought processes with some clarity. To accomplish these goals, there were "but two methods . . . the first is that of traveling in the character of a gentleman.—The second, that of taking an effective part in the CAUSE of her COUNTRY by joining the army in the character of a voluntary soldier." She chose "the latter after many severe struggles between prudence, delicacy and virtue." He was frank: "the thought of traveling without a companion or protector" was "imprudent" and her "greatest obstacle was the want of that current specie." In sum, she was afraid to take to the road alone as a woman and she was broke.

This part of his account rings true. "The many dangers we are subject to from your Sex," Abigail Adams wrote her cousin, "Renders it almost impossible for a Single Lady to travel without injury to her character."[61] A woman of Samson's status on the road alone had added reason to be apprehensive. She had to go on foot. There were stagecoach lines between major cities but not between the smaller ones and rides were costly. She knew how to ride a horse but was not prepared to steal one. But a young white woman walking on the open road was suspect either as a runaway indentured servant, a runaway wife, as one of the "strolling poor" warned out of one town on the way to another, or as a fugitive from justice—which she had good reason to consider herself. If she stopped at a public house for the night (assuming she could afford one), she would have been subject to scrutiny at the common table and asked to share a bed. Traveling disguised as a man got around most of these obstacles.[62]

Uncertain of what course to take, Mann reported, "she dressed herself in a handsome suit of man's apparel and repaired to a prognosticator." A believer in dreams, Deborah might also have believed in fortune-tellers. She was making a momentous decision and she needed reassurance; she also had to test her ability to pass. Like any good fortune-teller, the one she chose told the person of ambiguous gender before her what she calculated she wanted to hear: "that she had propensities for uncommon enterprises," predicting that her success "would more than compensate a few difficulties"— or so Mann worded it. Deborah returned, "her resolution strengthened," with thoughts of going to Philadelphia, "the metropolis of America."[63]

She made her own suit from "a handsome piece of cloth" she herself had woven. She made herself a "genteel coat, waistcoat and breeches" and bought what she could not make, a hat and a pair of shoes, "under invented pretexts." By family lore she did her sewing out of doors at the Leonards and made her purchases at Andrew Leach's store in Muttock. What excuse could she give Mr. Leach for buying men's clothing? Perhaps that she was buying an outfit for her brother Ephraim.

At this point, Mann introduced the romantic motive mentioned in chapter 1, the story of her rejecting a suitor pressed on her by her mother. Mann was explicit, however: this was not "the cause" of her volunteering for the army; it was "a love of liberty." To support this patriotic motive, he told an unlikely story of an incident on the eve of her departure in a "rural festivity" with her friends. She was in tears at the news that the brother of one of their friends had been "killed in the battle of Long Island" (unlikely, because it occurred some six years before). At midnight the next night, she put on her new clothes and left town.[64]

In this way, Mann gave Deborah a bundle of motives—patriotic, romantic, educational—but he also made her an unmistakable rebel against gender restrictions. "Very justly did she consider the female sphere of action, in many respects, too contracted," he wrote. She debated whether she should "swerve from my sex's sphere . . . or shall I submit without reluctance I cannot to a prison where I must drag out the remainder of my days in ignorance." And at length, "she determined to burst the bands, which, it must be confessed, have too often held her sex in awe."[65]

The pattern of flight confirms Mann's claim that Deborah was undecided as to her course of action. She skittered hither and yon, suggesting she was anxious about her ability to pass and trying alternatives. She headed for Taunton, nine miles due west, "in hopes of meeting with some stranger who was going directly to the Headquarters, then at the southward." At dawn, however, she was seen in Taunton by her "near neighbor," William Bennett (a person who did indeed live down the road from the Jeremiah Thomases). She thought "he had discovered her masquerade," panicked, left the road, lost her way in "a thicket of wood," fell asleep exhausted, and then found the road and made her way back to Middleborough to find out whether she had been recognized. She had not.[66]

She took off again, this time heading south, through Rochester to New Bedford, a seaport. There the "commander of a cruiser," dangling the prospect of money, "gained her consent to go as his waiter to sea." "Waiter" was the term for an officer's orderly, and on board ship for a cabin boy. She abandoned the plan after she learned about the captain's reputation for "austerity." Later, Mann put it that she "partially contracted with the captain of a privateer at New Bedford." "Austerity" is a mild word for the harsh regime of a captain who was a tyrant at sea; "partially contracted" means she may have been recruited in a tavern by a crimp, signed up, got wind about the captain from other seamen, came to her senses just in time, and fled.

This adventure is credible. The sea was never far out of mind in New England as a safety valve for escape, even in inland towns. Taking off on an oceangoing vessel was a time-honored way for boys to satisfy their wanderlust, for young men without the prospect of land to make good, or for older men to shed their burdens. The sea, moreover, may have long been in the back of her mind. After all, her father had disappeared at sea and her cousin, Simeon Samson of Plymouth, was a sea captain who had made good his escape as a prisoner of war in 1762 by dressing as a woman, a tale passed down in family lore. During the war, there was what Abigail Adams called a "rage for privateering" in Massachusetts, as literally tens of thousands of men responded to the blandishments of recruiters. The ballads about women who disguised themselves as sailors, cabin boys, or pirates might also have echoed in her head.[67]

Having been tempted once, however, she did not go to sea. After New Bedford, her trail was zigzag. Mann reports she went to Boston, fifty-six miles away. Perhaps she was looking for a more benevolent privateering captain. Just to walk amidst the hustle and bustle on the teeming Long Wharf or among the noisy shipyards and workshops of Boston's North End would have been an adventure. Even in wartime she could have found work in Boston at common labor. From Boston, according to Mann, she headed in a southerly direction, passing through Roxbury, Dedham, Medfield, and Wrentham, ending up in Bellingham, in the southern part of Worcester County, a trip of more than forty miles. In all, she covered easily 150 to 200 miles.

Bellingham was the site of the home church of Noah Alden, a Baptist elder who exchanged pulpits with Middleborough's Third Baptist Church. She would hardly have turned to him for pastoral help; she may have been testing her disguise. By this point she may have decided she had no choice but the army and may have been hunting for the best bounty offer.[68] At the public house across the road from Alden's she met "a speculator"—an agent hunting for draft substitutes—from Uxbridge, the next town over, who signed her up on May 20. On May 23, when she passed muster at Worcester, the county seat, about fifteen miles away, she received £60 from Noah Taft, "Chairman of Class No. 2 for the Town of Uxbridge as a bounty to serve in the Continental Army for the term of three years," for which she signed a receipt in a bold hand: "Robert Shurtliff." If the bounty was in hard money, this was a healthy sum.[69]

"Robert Shurtliff" fits the bill for a disguise name. It was common; there are a score of Shurtliffs from Plymouth County alone on the master list of Massachusetts soldiers, spelled every which way, among them a few other Robert Shurtliffs. There were Shurtliffs in Middleborough, including a family down the road from the Thomases, and two Shurtliffs, Levi and Mary, who joined the Third Baptist the same year she did. There was a Shurtliff family in Plympton and a Robert Shurtliff in Carver. If asked about where she came from, she could say she was from a place she knew, describe every glen and glade, and rattle off the names of others in her family. Robert was a common name, and Bob, the common nickname for Robert, by subsequent lore is what she was called.[70]

Captain Eliphalet Thorp, the "muster master" who enrolled her and testified to May 23, 1782, as the date of her mustering at Worcester, said she was "sent on to camp soon after." Calvin Munn, a drill sergeant elected by his fellow sergeants in the Fourth Massachusetts Regiment, testified to coming up from West Point to shape up this last batch of three-year men of the war,

Receipt for a bounty for "the sum of Sixty pounds" to serve in the Continental Army for a three-year term, signed by Samson as "Robert Shurtliff" (possibly "Shurtlieff"), May 23, 1782, the date of the muster. The bounty is from Noah Taft, on behalf of "Class No. 2" in Uxbridge, a group responsible for coming up with a draftee. They are paying for a substitute, a common practice. Massachusetts Archives.

Certificate by Eliphalet Thorp, in 1791, attesting that Mrs. Deborah Gannett, as "Robert Shirtlief," enlisted May 20, 1782, and was mustered May 23, 1782. Thorp identified himself as "Capt. 7th. M[assachusetts] Reg[iment] M. Master," which in his other military records was "muster master." Mrs. Gannett submitted this document in January 1792 in support of her successful petition to the Massachusetts General Court for back pay. Massachusetts Archives.

Deborah Samson among them. Under his command, she and about fifty other recruits assembled at Worcester, marched to the Hudson, and crossed the river to West Point to join the Massachusetts Fourth Regiment. She was in the army.[71]

WHAT GOT her there? As Mann presented the story, Deborah was a self-educated woman, hungry for knowledge of the wider world, whose aspirations could not be met within a "contracted" gender system. True enough. And yet, Mann's interpretation of a patriotic-romantic-rebellious heroine does not convey the matrix of personal influences shaping her decisions.

She was a tall, strong, robust woman, with a range of farm, household, and craft skills, as well as book learning—an unusual combination. From eighteen to twenty-two, as spinner, weaver, and schoolteacher, she was a "masterless woman," a free, single woman not under family governance. In a town with many poor young farmers with grim prospects for inheriting land, she was a plain-looking woman who could offer a potential husband neither land nor dowry nor family connections. For the time being, she seems to have withdrawn from the marriage market.

She became politically aware during a time of revolution when her town seethed with defiance of authority and turned "topsy turvey" a world in which "George was King and Oliver was Judge." She rebelled first in religion, as did many other young women, converting to the evangelical Baptist faith, and then was empowered by the example of Baptist civil disobedience for "soul liberty" to defy their disciplinary action. She left Middleborough to escape Baptist wrath and the threat of legal prosecution. She was possibly inspired by the plebeian traditions of warrior women of the Old World and New England. She was certainly conscious of the biblical tradition of her namesake, Deborah, whose words in Judges spoke to her. She was a person with enough of a sense of herself to become someone else.

And yet this does not quite do justice to the larger intangible influences that might have shaped her decision. She might have known about other young women who tried to pass. She moved in circles of young single women who might have talked about such things: fellow weavers, the many women converts to the Baptist faith. As a reader who gobbled up print, she could have encountered women warriors. The narrative of Hannah Snell was available in New England not only as a cheap imprint but in a three-page excerpt in Isaiah Thomas's almanac for 1775. A Connecticut newspaper

CORNWALLIS *turned* NURSE, *and his* MISTRESS *a* SOLDIER.

A Prifoner from Virginia's coaſt,
   Cornwallis has return'd, ſir;
Toolong, toolong he rul'd the roaſt
   And for our ruin burn'd, ſir.
Before he was, in wretched plight,
   By armed men ſurrounded,
He ſhow'd himſelf a man of might
   And every thing confounded.
But when they thunder'd at his door
   He prov'd by this diſaſter,
His race was run, his battles done
   And Waſhington his maſter.
His miſtreſs in a paſſion cry'd,
   She could have aſted bolder;
So put his ſword upon her ſide,
   His muſquet on her ſhoulder.

Like Hercules, renown'd of old,
   The diſtaff is his calling;
And while he hears his miſtreſs
   ſcold,   [ing.
   He keeps her brat from bawl-
Behold him here and ſhed a tear,
   Sir Henry and Knyphauſen;
And Arnold too may quake with
   fear,
   Whom Satan has his claws on.
Each valiant chief ſhall ſee with
   grief,
   Their horrid revolution;
Cornwallis forc'd to ſpin for
   bread,
   Burgoyne to thump a cuſhion.

"Cornwallis Turned Nurse, and His Mistress a Soldier," appeared in
The Continental Almanac for 1782 *(Philadelphia: Francis Bailey, 1781).*
Library of Congress.

spoke of "the famous Hannah Snell" as "among the Amazons" in London who rescued a poor countryman from a navy press gang by beating up the recruiting officer. Moreover, Snell's image, a crude cut of a woman (in a dress) carrying a gun and powderhorn, was run by colonial printers as an attention-grabbing device on a variety of unrelated imprints. She obviously was the stuff of legends.[72]

Disguise was in the air in the Revolutionary era. Members of mobs often blackened their faces to avoid detection or hung effigies in the dark of the night. The destruction of the tea in Boston's harbor, in which some of the boarding parties put soot on their faces and others put on Indian regalia, was an electrifying event known up and down the colonies, which legitimized disguise in ways that cannot be measured. Farmers in rural rebellions would resort to Indian disguise decades later. The spirit of disguise was exhilaration; it freed a person of constraints.[73]

She entered the war at a moment of national exhilaration—not when the New England countryside was aflame with the patriotic "Spirit of '76" or in response to the desperation of the winters at Valley Forge. She enlisted seven months after Washington's triumph over Cornwallis at Yorktown in October 1781 presaged an American victory in the war. Her bold personal act of reversal followed the most gigantic military reversal of the war. According to legend, British fifers at the surrender ceremony played "The World Turned Upside Down," a song well known in the colonies as a nursery rhyme. In chapbook versions, the rhymes were accompanied by pictures of a dozen reversals that tickled the hearts of children: the ox turned butcher, the horse turned groom, the son spanking his father.[74]

A few months after Yorktown, a cartoon appeared in a Philadelphia almanac parodying an image from the chapbook, depicting Lord Cornwallis "Turned Nurse, and His Mistress a Soldier," with a woman shouldering a gun, the general holding the baby and wielding a spinning distaff. Such an image resonated with young women, almost all of whom served in their households both as nursemaids and spinsters. In 1782, it expressed a mood of elation. Peter Oliver bitterly deplored a world turned "topsy turvey" from the vantage point of those who had lost their world. "The World Turned Upside Down"—the song, the rhyme, the cartoon—celebrated it from the point of view of those who had a world to gain.[75]

PART TWO

"ROBERT SHURTLIFF"

Chapter Three

The Continental Army

"THE CURTAIN is now up—a scene opens to your view," Mrs. Gannett said at a dramatic moment in her public address in 1802 when she began to recount her military experiences. "What shall I say further? Shall I not stop short, and leave to your imaginations to pourtray the tragic deeds of war?" And she did just that; she stopped short, depriving her audience of the answers to a host of questions that coursed through their minds as they saw before them the woman who had served as a Continental soldier. She teased her audience to make a comparison between herself and camp followers, "between the perils and sexual inconveniences of a girl in her teens" who saw duty in the field, and "those who go to the camp without a masquerade and consequently [were] subject only to what toils and sacrifices they please." But she revealed no secrets.[1]

Disguised as Robert Shurtliff, Deborah Sampson (as we will now call her) served in the Continental Army a total of seventeen months—from May 23, 1782, until her formal discharge on October 23, 1783. She was not "discovered," it seems, until the summer of 1783, after more than a year of military service. What did she do as a soldier? How did she succeed in her "masquerade"—a word that her memoirist used? When I began exploring her life in the army, I thought these were two separate questions. The more her experiences sank in, the more it seemed that the answer to the second question—How did she get away with it?—lay in the answers to the first. This led to a series of inquiries: In what unit did she serve? What did this service do? Where did she see action? What did it mean to be in the American army in the Hudson Valley in the period between the victory at Yorktown and the disbandment of the army in November 1783? She accomplished her deception by becoming an outstanding soldier in the light infantry, a branch of service engaged in a very active kind of warfare in Westchester County that sputtered on in the last two years of the war. She hid herself as a woman, paradoxical as it may seem, by standing out as a man.

1. *Between War and Peace*
"In a state of suspense"

The war in the Hudson Valley that Deborah Sampson joined in 1782–83 has been erased from the popular historical memory of the Revolutionary War, which assumes there was no military action after the decisive victory at Yorktown in October 1781, the last full-scale battle of the war. It is almost as unknown to later generations as it was to her countrymen at the time, which is why she could get away with the stories told about her. To General George Washington, an American victory was far from secure. Some 26,000 British regulars remained on North American shores, 13,000 of them occupying New York City, 3,300 in Charleston, 5,000 in Canada. Washington feared British duplicity. "Notwithstanding all the pacific declarations of the British . . . ," he wrote in the fall of '82, a full year after Yorktown, their "principal Design was to gain time by lulling us into security." News that American and British commissioners were negotiating a peace treaty did not reach American shores until August 1782, and news of the preliminary treaty signed in Paris at the end of November, not until March 1783. We are "in a state of suspense," Washington wrote in January 1783. Thomas Paine was still writing his *American Crisis* articles to buoy up public support for the military effort.[2]

In 1782, Washington's strategy was to maintain a large army of at least 10,000 men in the Hudson Highlands prepared for a number of eventualities. His headquarters at Newburgh, twelve miles above West Point, were a token of the importance he attached to this theatre of war. The Hudson River was the "Key to America," he had said in 1777, and the magnificently engineered system of forts at West Point was still America's Gibraltar. The forts, together with the amazing 1,700-foot-long chain of 1,200 iron links, weighing 60 tons, which stretched across the river, had achieved the goal of preventing a British naval attack up the Hudson.[3] In August '82, the army conducted a rehearsal for an amphibious invasion of New York City, moving five infantry brigades from the west bank of the Hudson across the river in military formation, ready to be deployed in battle when they landed. Had French naval support been available, Washington might have launched an attack on the British army occupying Manhattan, and Deborah Sampson might have made her appearance in arms in an invasion of New York City.

Washington attempted no such large-scale military ventures, however. In the freezing winter of '83, he authorized an expedition of 500 troops to western New York to capture Fort Oswego to counter the threat of British-inspired Indian attacks. It turned out to be a disaster. In February '83, he asked his commanders to calculate what it would take to oust the British from New York City, but there was no such action. In reality, at this stage of the war, the "neutral ground" in Westchester County, lying between the British army in Manhattan and the American army in the northern sector of the county, was one of the few scenes of ongoing small-scale military action outside the South.[4]

Deborah Sampson entered a huge, well-organized army that in August 1782 counted 11,132 officers and men in the infantry, plus another 1,000 in the artillery defense of the fortress. It was the best-equipped, best-clothed, best-fed American army of the war. And the village of huts for 7,000 built late in 1782 at New Windsor, a few miles north of West Point—the largest military installation on the North American continent—made it the best-housed American army at any point in the war. In June 1782, the officer making an inventory of the regiment Sampson had just entered pronounced it "in very good order." The men's "clothing is uniform and their arms clean and handsome," and "no exertion seems to be wanting" by the officers "to advance the reputation of the regiment." All in all, the army was the mirror opposite of Valley Forge.[5]

This Hudson Valley army sustained a military community in which women were relatively more numerous and more accepted than at any other time in the war: "washing, mending and cooking for the soldiers," as the camp follower Sarah Osborn summed up her activities. Washington, who earlier had dealt with such women as a cumbersome drag on army marches, came to recognize the "women of the army" as indispensable. By the end of the war, the army set a ratio of 1 woman for every 15 men in a regiment, which the commander in chief allowed to go to 1 to 11 in his key artillery units or risk losing "some of the oldest and best soldiers in the Service." In the winter of 1783, the Fourth Massachusetts Regiment, which Sampson joined, counted 15 women to 553 enlisted men, a ratio of 1 to 37. The army obviously counted women; it gave them and their children rations; it inoculated them against smallpox and housed them in tents or huts. Women were a visible presence, with implications for a woman disguised as an infantryman to which we will return.[6]

From the vantage point of most officers, life in the Hudson Valley encampments in 1782 was hardly arduous. In fact, thanks to the French alliance, it was an uncommon time for official celebrations, climaxed in the fall by the review of the massed American and French armies as the French encamped in Westchester on their way to embarking from Boston. Officers recorded a year of pleasant "entertainments," dinners, teas, and dance assemblies.[7] For most enlisted men, while there was a respite from military campaigns, it was a time of boredom and restlessness. They marked time in garrison duty, foraging, and building the huts and a huge assembly hall at New Windsor. To the acerbic memoirist Sergeant Joseph Plumb Martin, soldiers at West Point "fared better" during the last years of the war than in the first three or four, but he still "lived half the winter [1782–83] on tripe and cowheels, and the other half on what I could get. . . . We always had very short carnivals but lengthy fasts."[8]

The fall of '82 through the spring of '83 was a time of "dissatisfactions" in the army. Officers were in the thick of an organized campaign for pensions that led to the so-called Newburgh Conspiracy. Enlisted men, impatient to return home, were bitter at the government's failure to meet their demands for back pay and a settlement. Courts-martial ground on, trying men for desertions, petty thievery, and other forms of insubordination.[9] Mutiny, the term authority gave to collective protest, was recurrent. The memory of the large-scale mutiny of the Pennsylvania line in January 1781 had not faded. In late January 1782, there was a mutiny of the New Jersey line put down by New England troops. In May 1782, when Connecticut troops conspired to march on the state legislature in Hartford, the leader was shot. Then, in late June 1783, after most enlisted men had been discharged under the guise of a furlough, another mutiny flared in Pennsylvania, prompting Washington to rush 1,500 troops from West Point to Philadelphia to suppress it.[10]

While Deborah Sampson served in the army when the war was winding down, it was a time when a soldier could still be tested both in military action against the enemy and in his loyalties—whether he was an insubordinate rebel or a "good and faithful soldier." Robert Shurtliff would be put to both tests.

2. *The Light Infantry*
"All chosen men, men of sprightly genius . . ."

Within a few days after she arrived at West Point, Deborah Sampson was chosen for the light infantry company of the Fourth Massachusetts Regiment. Captain George Webb commanded the company; Colonel William Shepard the regiment (until he was replaced, in November 1782, by Colonel Henry Jackson); and General John Paterson the brigade. A company usually had from 50 to 60 men, a regiment from 8 to 10 companies or from 400 to 500 men. In 1782 and 1783 in the Hudson Valley, while most soldiers were marking time, the light infantry was the single most active branch of service. Indeed, as the military activity of the rest of the army decreased, for the light infantry it increased.

The "light corps," as the service was dubbed, was an innovation of European and English armies in the eighteenth century adopted by the American army in 1777. It was composed of "younger, more athletic and intelligent soldiers, suited for missions requiring endurance, agility and initiative," the military historian John Shy explains. They were so called, according to an encyclopedist, "because they were light in equipment and armament to give them maximum mobility for their primary role as skirmishers." One light company was chosen by each regiment, which might be combined with others into a corps, and sometimes a larger unit. In the Virginia campaign in the fall of 1781, the Marquis de Lafayette commanded a light infantry division of about 2,000 men. Baron von Steuben gave personal instruction to this unit and vowed to make it "the terror of our enemies."[11]

Late in the war in the Hudson Valley, the role of the light infantry shifted. They had the major burden of carrying out the army's mission

A drummer, a private, and a company officer in the Light Infantry Company of the Fourth Massachusetts Regiment of 1782, as depicted by H. Charles McBarron, Jr., a military illustrator who follows the tradition that this service was reserved for tall men. From The Company of Military Historians, Military Uniforms in America: The Era of the American Revolution, 1755–1795 *(1974). Courtesy The Company of Military Historians.*

in Westchester. The American army, writes Shy, made "a continuous effort to put pressure on the British, gather information, and contest those unstable areas with Loyalist irregulars— the quasi-guerrillas, quasi-bandits who made life dangerous in the lower Hudson Valley." Washington, nervous lest he be caught off guard, gave priority to collecting "the most authentic intelligence" of enemy movements, especially any sign in New York City that the British might be disembarking.[12] Given the role anticipated for them, it is not surprising that in mid-May 1782, as recruits from the spring draft trickled into West Point, his priority was to bring the light infantry companies up to full strength "out of the first recruits of a proper description."[13]

The light corps nursed its elite reputation. In 1780, General Chastellux of the French army observed that "this troop made a good appearance; they were better clothed than the rest of the army; their uniforms both of the officers and men were smart and military." Officers in search of glory, like Alexander Hamilton, begged for assignment to the light infantry. Dr. James Thacher of Plymouth, an army physician since 1775, considered himself honored to be tapped for "this select corps, consisting of the most active and soldierly young men and officers . . . constantly prepared for active and hazardous service."[14] Sergeant Joseph Plumb Martin, a seven-year veteran, was less rosy. The duty of the light infantry was "the hardest, while in the field, of any troops in the army, if there is any *hardest*. During the time the army keeps the field they are always on the lines near the enemy, and consequently always on the alert, constantly on the watch." The service, he thought, was among the most dangerous. "There is never any great danger of Light Infantry men dying of the scurvy."[15]

Hyperbole infused soldiers in the light infantry with an esprit de corps. In the spring of '82, as Lieutenant Benjamin Gilbert eyed the fifty rank-and-file members of his light infantry company of the Fifth Massachusetts, he thought they were "all chosen men, men of sprightly genius, Noble dispositions and undoubted courage." He would have told them so. In past campaigns, men in the light corps were told that "the eyes of every individual" or "the eyes of the world" were upon them, or that "the eyes of Citizens and Country would be more fully upon the American Light Infantry than any other part of the army." Ironically, with everyone's eyes on the light infantry, it would be the last place in the army anyone would expect to see a woman disguised as a man.[16]

Deborah Sampson was probably tapped for this service in the first days after she appeared on the drill parade late in May 1782. Private Roger Barrett, who arrived at the same time, remembers being chosen for the same company on his second day. She was very likely on the company roster for June, although the first and only roster bearing the name "Robert Shurtliff" that has survived is for November 1782. One can watch the count of recruits assigned to the company grow, week by week, as the "return" goes from thirty-seven in May to fifty-nine by July. And one can follow the flow of equipment into the company, day by day, as Captain George Webb signs receipts written in the large, clear hand of the commissary, Africa Hamlin, for uniforms, tents, canteens, and cooking kettles, as well as for muskets, bayonets, flints, and cartridges. This army of the last year of the war was nothing if not well equipped, and well accounted for in the bookkeeping.[17]

Webb's muster roll of March '82 showed his company down to thirty-five privates, while the next surviving muster for November '82 shows a total of fifty-nine enlisted men. Sampson was one of sixteen raw recruits who joined fifteen men who had enlisted the year before and a score of veterans who had been in the war longer. She would have drilled with this company, perhaps under the supervision of Baron von Steuben, although not for very long. Within a month her unit crossed the Hudson and was stationed at a field camp; a few weeks later she saw action.[18]

The fact that Sampson was chosen for the crack light infantry is a prime clue to the mystery of how she avoided detection. Deborah, as we know, was relatively tall and robust. In Britain, it was said of Maria Knowles, who made good her disguise as a man in His Majesty's 66th Regiment of Foot, that "her height covered her deception"; in her hometown she was known as "the tall girl." Something of the same could be said about Deborah. At five foot seven or seven and a half, she was taller than the average male soldier. In a sample of enlisted men from Massachusetts late in the war, the average height was five feet five and three-quarter inches, which meant there were a good many men shorter than that. In her class of three-year recruits of 1782, she literally stood out. By contrast, the gaggle of men drummed up by recruiting officers in the draft of the last two years of the war included a large number of boys as well as men physically unfit for military service. In 1782, von Steuben "created a special guard or company of boys who were too young and small to serve in the line but were to continue with the army for the campaign." Most ended up as waiters to officers, or as fifers or drummers. The army was awash with undersized beardless boys.[19]

The tension among officers over meeting recruiting standards reveals in a flash why Sampson was snapped up so easily in Massachusetts and then tapped for the light infantry. Washington was in the midst of court-martialing the officer who had recruited the parade of misfits mentioned in the previous chapter. Recruiting officers were being chewed out for their laxness.[20] In May 1782, after the army adopted a new regulation of a minimum height of five feet five inches for recruits, Colonel Ebenezer Huntington of the Connecticut line fumed at the new order. He was "as proper a judge of a man for a Soldier" as any other mustering officer. The new rule, he wrote, would exclude "nearly ⅖ths of the men obliged by law to do military duty" who were "under that size." Jokingly, Huntington proposed that the army recruit women. "As the Women appear to be more zealous for recruiting & keeping up the Army than the men I have proposed to some of [my?] friends that the Classes [of civilians subject to the draft] should have the liberty to hire Women." He ended on a more misanthropic note: "tho at same time I would recommend that tall Girls be procured that the offspring may be five feet six inches high," that is, over the new minimum.[21] The height requirement for the light infantry traditionally was set higher than for enlisted men. According to a calculation of one sample, the rank and file in the light infantry averaged from five seven to five ten. Here, too, Sampson more than met army standards. She was a find.[22]

Height aside, Sampson would have blended in with the average Massachusetts soldiers at the end of the war. We know a good deal about them because for some units the army compiled descriptive rolls, setting down in column form alongside a soldier's name his age, town of origin, occupation, height, and complexion. One scholar has counted noses for soldiers from four Massachusetts regiments late in the war, including Sampson's for the year before she entered. The average age at enlistment was 23.2, the median 20.5, with two out of five men under 21. (Sampson was 22 in 1782 but presented herself as 18.) The majority were Massachusetts-born but no longer lived in the town of their birth (which was also true of her). Most men were the sons of farm owners or farm laborers (very few were yeoman landholders), or else they were laborers and artisans in the lower trades. They were "landless and footloose," as historian John Sellers sums them up. Thus, Sampson was as skilled as most soldiers, if not more so. They were men used to outdoor work, and if their skin was more sunburnt and their hands more callused than hers, it was not by much. On the other hand, as a schoolmarm, she was more literate than most soldiers and capable of writing a clear hand. Otherwise, she shared with her comrades a common small-town Protestant New England culture. She fit in.[23]

At a stage of the war when large-scale pitched battles were not in the offing, a soldier would have been picked for the light infantry for more than his physical attributes. He, of course, had to be strong enough to march double-time, maybe ten miles a day carrying 30 pounds of arms and ammunition—a musket, a linen or canvas knapsack for spare clothing, a cartridge box for ammunition, a wooden canteen, a haversack for rations and personal possessions, and often a "fusil" (a large sidearm). He had to master wielding a musket with a bayonet at the end of it. Above all, he had to be alert to danger and quick to size up a situation. He also had to be enthusiastic, ready to volunteer for risky missions or take the initiative in unanticipated crises; in short, he had to be what a modern army would call a "gung-ho" soldier. And he had to fit into a unit that needed to act together in moments of sudden, unpredictable danger.[24]

As officers walked down the regimental line of new recruits looking for light infantry candidates, there must have been something in Sampson's bearing that caught their eye: the alert way she held herself, as if on guard against danger, an eagerness to please, or perhaps the speed with which she manipulated her new musket to the commands of Sergeant Calvin Munn. Twenty years later, she could still perform the manual exercise of arms in a Boston theatre with an éclat that brought down the house. As a weaver, she had deft hands accustomed to detail. As a sometime teacher, she may even have exuded an air of command acquired in disciplining unruly children; and, as the ruler of her classroom, she knew what it meant to respond quickly to authority.[25]

Ironically, the attributes Sampson needed to maintain her deception—to be alert, quick, and street smart—were the very ones that made her an ideal choice for the light infantry. Everyone who testified to her as a soldier inadvertently confirmed this. The officer who wrote about her service in 1784, without saying as much, singled out what officers prized most in a light infantryman: "she displayed much *alertness,* chastity and valour" and was "a remarkable, *vigilant* soldier on her post." Sergeant Munn, who "taught her the first rudiments of military exercise," said that "she was *prompt* and *expert,* and did her duty faithfully as a soldier." (He remembered this in 1827!) Herman Mann reported similar skills. "She says she learned the manual exercise with *facility* and *dispatch.*" In his description of what she was like in 1782, Mann wrote: "Her eye is *lively* and penetrating. . . . Her movement is erect, *quick* and strong." These adjectives all point to a woman with exactly the right stuff to be a successful light infantryman. "Vigilant" rolled up all these qualities in one word. Vigilance, of course, was the sine qua non for keeping up her disguise.[26]

A military uniform was an especially good costume for a woman pretending to be a man; the uniform was gendered male and no one expected to find a woman dressed in one. It was a costume in which awkward country bumpkins, furtive runaway indentured servants, and undersized shoemakers could all masquerade as soldiers. Its purpose, after all, was to create the illusion of uniformity and suppress the individuality of the wearer. On the parade ground, lined-up soldiers looked more or less the same. Had Sampson served early in the war, however, when soldiers were dressed in a wild diversity of clothing, "rag tag and bobtail," whatever she wore would have called attention to her individuality. If she had been in the army in the winter of American despair in 1777, she might have been "bare footed, bare-legged [and] bare-breeched," as one officer put it, or "not only shirtless and barefoot, but destitute of all other clothing," as Sergeant Martin recalled. In 1782, recruits wore spanking new uniforms, all alike. After their uniforms became worn, moreover, the light infantry units were among the first to be issued fresh ones.[27]

The light infantry uniform was meant to be diverting, a marker that it clothed an elite soldier. Amazing as it may seem, the description of this service's uniform, which military historians and illustrators have used ever since, is taken verbatim from a paragraph about Sampson's clothing in Mann's 1797 book. As such, the description came either from her or from Mann's observation of the uniform she had saved and took out of a chest in Sharon in the

The uniform of a member of the light infantry in a Massachusetts regiment depicted by a present-day military illustrator, George C. Woodbridge. Courtesy George C. Woodbridge.

1790s to show him. (She would wear it later on the stage in Boston, in 1802, perhaps let out.) The uniform, Mann wrote, "consisted of a blue coat lined with white, with white wings on the shoulder and cords on the arms and pockets; a white waistcoat, breeches or overhauls and stockings, with black straps about the knees; half boots, a black velvet stock [for display around the neck] and a cap with a variegated cockade, on one side, a plume tipped with red on the other, and a white sash about the crown."[28]

The "wings" (an epaulet on each shoulder) and decorative cord (braiding), and especially the brightly colored feathers on the hat, were intended for dress parade. The "overhauls" (overalls), on the other hand, were meant for the field: "long trousers cut snug to the leg and shaped to fit over the top of the shoe like a gater." They provided "freedom of action and more protection than the knee breeches and stockings worn earlier in the war." Either "on the parade" or in the field, the uniform of a member of the light corps set him off as a soldier who was special.[29]

Clothes did make the soldier. In donning the uniform, performing the duties, and learning the drills, Deborah Sampson was on the way to becoming Private Robert Shurtliff, light infantryman.

3. *"Smock faced boy"*
Coping with the "trials of her sex"

While she was being broken into this elite corps, Deborah Sampson had to confront the dangers facing a woman trying to avoid being found out. The "trials of her sex," as Mann called them, were never-ending, straining our imagination to recover the day-by-day world of a soldier in the Revolutionary War.[30]

One of the first tasks for a recruit, fitting the uniform, was probably less a trial for her than it may seem to those of us today familiar with the ways of a tailor altering a suit. Early in 1782, Massachusetts sent some two thousand uniforms to the army, most likely loosely sized, which had to be taken in or let out. There would have been tailors in a large garrison like West Point, but it was not uncommon for a man in the regiment with such skills to do sewing for his comrades. Deborah, with skills as a seamstress—she had made her own male garment in Middleborough—could have done her own alterations without attracting attention. This was the obvious way to avoid the close scrutiny or wandering hands of a tailor.[31]

In any case, the uniform was not tailored in a way that could reveal her as a woman. "She wore a bandage about her breasts, during her disguise," Mann wrote in a footnote, her only revelation to him of a "delicate" matter in her masquerade. In his later revised manuscript, he explained that her breasts were smaller than he had seen in other young women. This could be the difference between success and failure in disguise. Christian Davies, for example, described in her memoir as "the British Amazon," made a point of saying that her breasts "were not large enough to betray my sex."[32]

A soldier's breeches were generally loosely cut rather than form-fitting, like some officers' dress pants, which meant there was no need for a woman to stuff them to feign male genitalia. Answering "a call of nature" wearing breeches, however, presented a problem. A soldier did not wear undergarments (nor did males of the laboring classes), but he wore a long shirt, the tails hanging down in front to his crotch and in back to cover his "arse."

Breeches had a "front fall," a flap buttoned across at the top (unlike the fly of later years, which buttoned up and down). To ease himself, a man had to unbutton the flap and let it fall. In order to squat to urinate, a woman wearing breeches would have had to lower them; she obviously required more privacy than a man, who could go over to the nearest tree.

It was possible, of course, that Sampson taught herself to urinate standing up, thrusting her pelvis forward to direct the stream. Other women have. There is also a chance that she used some sort of tube. Christian Davies used a "urinary instrument," which her memoirist described as "a Silver Tube painted over, and fastened about her with Leather straps," claiming that "without such an implement she could never hope to pass long concealed." As for defecation, both women and men had to lower their breeches to sit or squat. Consequently, if Robert Shurtliff was seen squatting, soldiers might assume he was defecating. A woman did not talk about such things to a man, and an author as attuned to his female readers as was Mann hardly wanted to take up such delicate matters.[33]

In her first weeks in the army, Sampson, like other green recruits, had to put up with hazing. Her company included a good number of seasoned veterans. Benjamin Hobbs, for example, in his application for a pension, listed thirteen battles from Long Island to Yorktown. A number were at Yorktown. Old-timers razzed neophytes as "Bounty Boys," "Quotamen," or "The Long Faced People." Until she proved herself, she had to endure the taunts aimed at beardless boys. Mann occasionally referred to her as the "smock faced boy" or the "blooming boy," phrases for teenage boys without facial hair. But the fact that there were so many such boys in the army in 1782–83 diminished the significance of beardlessness. Puberty for boys came later in the eighteenth century than in the twenty-first (just as menarche came later for girls), which meant there could have been any number of sixteen-, seventeen-, and even eighteen-year-olds (the age she claimed) without facial hair or other secondary sexual characteristics. Nor would her voice have given her away. Mann's comment, that "her voice was not disagreeable for a female," suggests it was not high-pitched to begin with. But even if it was, she would have been among many adolescent boys whose voices had not yet dropped.[34]

She may possibly have been teased as a "molly." On board ship, English sailors taunted the cross-dressing Hannah Snell, who had taken the name "James Gray," as "Miss Molly Gray," until she issued a challenge "to prove herself as good a man as any of these on board." Molly, of course, was a diminutive for Mary and Margaret, but in England it had long been slang for an effeminate man (whence: "Don't mollycoddle the boy"). Beginning early in eighteenth-century London, it was slang for a man who had sex with other men in one of the city's numerous "molly houses," or public places. Margaret Corbin, who was wounded filling in for her husband in the artillery, and who became a member of the Invalid Corps at West Point, was dubbed "Captain Molly." Several different women were known as "Molly Pitcher." In Deborah's case, teasing nicknames may also have registered some gender confusion on the part of soldiers attracted to a youthful, relatively handsome effeminate person of their own sex.[35]

Physically, aside from her lack of a beard, there was little about Deborah to give her away. If she kept her long hair, it would not have been a problem. The army fought an unending battle with rebellious young men who wanted to wear their hair long. A general order at West Point in 1782 required soldiers "to wear the hair cut or tied in the same manner" as their company, which could well have precipitated debates: cut or tied. Today's ponytail was then called a "queue," or "clubbed," "plaited," or "braided" hair. In garrisons like West Point where there were barbers, soldiers were required to have their hair dressed at intervals and to be shaved. My guess is that if she had a choice, Deborah, anxious both to conform and to avoid the implication of effeminacy in long hair, cut her hair short.[36]

Living quarters in a garrison at West Point could have been a serious "trial of her sex." To house several thousand enlisted men, West Point had an array of buildings on a plateau and in the hills amidst woods: a few large barracks each crowding in hundreds of soldiers, and many smaller crudely built huts and tents. In the spring of '82, the recruits who poured in probably were put up in tents, six or more to a tent. Barracks and tents posed different dangers.

Wherever she ended up, there was relative safety in the lax standards of the day for hygiene. There was no daily occasion when soldiers were expected to undress; they slept in their clothes. Nor was it a custom in the army to bathe one's entire body regularly. In summer weather, troops might be sent into a river or pond to bathe in the nude. At daily inspection, a soldier only had to give the outward appearance of cleanliness. "No soldier is to come on the parade . . . with his face or hands dirty," ran one of Washington's orders of the day, and that required no more than splashing on some water from a basin or trough.[37]

Army standards on sanitation also worked in her favor. At every stage of the war, the army conducted a battle to get soldiers to "ease themselves" in what were variously called the "necessary" house, the "little house," "vaults," or "sinks," as opposed to using the woods or any convenient area in camp. In one order of the day at West Point issued after an outbreak of small-pox, Washington threatened soldiers who did not use a necessary house with thirty lashes on the spot, an embarrassing as well as painful punishment. Such orders may have been honored more in the breach than in the observance. For Deborah, a necessary built for one occupant would have provided privacy, but if it was a long house with many seats, none at all; the woods out of sight of other soldiers was her best bet. Once she was in a field camp or on the road in thickly forested Westchester, there was more chance for privacy by going off to the woods to answer "a call of nature."[38]

How she managed her "monthly courses" may also be less of a mystery than it seems at first. It is very possible that months passed without her menstruating, as a result of her state of high tension from the combined fears of discovery and combat. We have only present-day evidence to go on. Of 119 women in the first group of women admitted to officer training at West Point on July 4, 1976, by the end of intensive "beast" training, "most of the women had stopped menstruating" and "many woman missed their periods until November—some, like women in concentration camps, missed them for a year." Amenorrhea of this severity is familiar to other women in intensive training, such as professional athletes or ballet dancers, where biologists report that "as many as forty or fifty percent may be amenorrheic." Mann tells us that once at West Point, Sampson "lost her appetite" (a sure sign of extreme anxiety), from which "she afterwards recovered" (a sign that she was able to come to grips with it). When she menstruated—she was in the army seventeen months—she could have dealt with the flow of blood, as did other women at the time, by wearing a clean cloth or kerchief, which she herself could wash in a stream or pond. That would not be unusual because soldiers were expected to wash their own clothes, unless they could afford to pay a "washwoman" attached to the regiment.[39]

Inspection at daily roll call and at drill with a corporal or a sergeant glowering in her face would have been a trial until it settled into routine. Von Steuben's manual enjoined officers that "they must inspect into the dress of their men; see that their clothes are whole and put on properly; their hands and faces washed clean; their hair combed; their accoutrements properly fixed, and every article about them in the greatest order." The army inspected appearances. The way to avoid calling attention to oneself was to be all spit and polish.[40]

Clearly, there were things she had to avoid. She had to steer clear of close contact with her comrades: on marches, on fatigue duty requiring heavy shared labor, in sleeping. In camp she had to avoid horsing around or a sport like wrestling. Physical contact might lead to anatomical discoveries or bewildering sexual attractions. Avoiding body contact would have been especially hard in the small field tents in which six soldiers usually had to crowd together on the ground. On cold nights she could hardly risk "spooning" with her buddies, a common practice to stay warm. She had to guard against anything that might lead to a loss of control, like excessive drink.[41]

She also had to minimize risks that increased the chance of being found out. The chance of detection was greater in a large encampment like West Point or New Windsor, with masses of men in close quarters, more prying eyes, and more frequent inspections. The more she was on a tour of duty on the road in a small detachment, and the more her unit was focused on danger from the enemy, the less the threat to her. She must have sensed this early on, realizing she had lucked out by landing in the one service that in 1782 would lessen the danger of detection—by placing her in danger of losing life and limb.

4. *The War in Westchester*
"Great numbers wore masks"

"Great numbers wore masks," wrote James Fenimore Cooper of the war in Westchester County several decades later, "which even to this day have not been thrown aside." Deception was the central theme of Cooper's *The Spy: A Tale of the Neutral Ground* (1821), set in Westchester, actually the first American historical novel. The hero is Harvey Birch, an American spy serving George Washington who poses as a Loyalist to deceive aristocratic Westchester Loyalists. Henry Wharton, another character, engages in two masquerades. Caught wearing a wig and an eyepatch, he is jailed under suspicion of spying, and then escapes, disguised as his black servant, Caesar. The novel, in which uncertainty about appearances provides a constant tension, was an epitome of the war in Westchester. For anyone engaged in deception, the strange warfare being waged in the county where Sampson saw almost all of her military action provided an almost ideal forest of protective coloring.[42]

Westchester was a large county of about a half million acres due north of the island of Manhattan, lying between the North River to the west (the Hudson, as it was later called) and the East River that broadened into Long Island Sound to the east. Dutchess County bordered it on the north, Connecticut on the east. Its wartime population was about 28,000, of whom 4,000 were African-American slaves, a large presence. During the war, most of the county lay in the "neutral ground"—a vast area in between a zone in the south secured by British troops and another in the north held by American troops. The British, whose main army was stationed in Manhattan, commanded Harlem (today, the Bronx) and the lower part of Westchester. The American army held only a small zone in the northwestern part of the county above the Croton River. It maintained field camps at Fishkill, the Continental Village, Peekskill, and Verplancks Point, the latter two just north of the Croton. It also held fortified posts—blockhouses—to the south on the banks of the Hudson guarding the major river crossings at King's Ferry, Dobbs Ferry, and Philipse Manor. This "neutral ground" was about thirty miles from north to south and twenty miles wide.[43] Light infantry troops rotated from the west bank of the river at West Point to the large field camps on the east bank in the north and thence to the fortified posts to the south along the Hudson.[44]

For almost seven years Westchester was racked by internal civil war. The large-scale battle at White Plains in 1776, when Washington's retreating army was defeated in a hopeless rearguard action, was never repeated, but another kind of warfare ground on endlessly. One might be tempted to call it "guerrilla" warfare or "low-intensity" warfare, except that these modern terms attribute too much system to what had become a chaotic, multilayered civil war, lost to the public memory of the Revolutionary War that can only visualize two clearly defined sides. With two voracious armies poised at either end of a rich agricultural area, "a fierce scramble developed between them for livestock, hay, vegetables, diary products and grains." Foraging expeditions reached into obscure parts of the county.[45]

This contest between the two armies was accompanied by a bitter civilian conflict between Loyalists and patriots. A large proportion of the population was Loyalist, as was true in Manhattan and the other counties surrounding the city. In Westchester, Loyalists were recruited into both the regular British army and as "irregulars." Colonel James DeLancey, former sheriff of the county, commanded a corps of about sixty horsemen who conducted hit-and-run cavalry raids using sabers as a weapon of terror. He claimed to have had 480 men in all under his command. His troops, known as the "Westchester Refugees," together with other irregulars, were dubbed "cowboys"—they rounded up cattle on the hoof and drove them south to the British army. Their opposite numbers on the American side were "skinners," who "skinned their victims first and asked about their political affiliation later," robbing them of all they could.[46]

This civil war was layered over a long-smoldering tension between landlords and tenants. Two thirds of the county was in tenanted estates owned by large landlords: the DeLanceys, the Philipses, the Morrises, all Loyalist. The DeLanceys within the British zone to the south were leaders of Loyalist resistance. The Van Cortlandts were almost the only Whig landlords, holding an estate north of the Croton River in the protected American military zone. Tenants in Dutchess and Albany counties were either in outright rebellion against their landlords (Whig or Tory) or indifferent to a patriot cause in which they had no stake. In Westchester, where tenants were generally more prosperous and their leases more secure, they were diverse in their political allegiances. Loyalism, neutralism, and sheer self-preservation seemed to guide most residents of the county.[47]

Through most of the time Sampson was in the army there was warfare in Westchester. In the spring and summer of 1782, international "politics notwithstanding," a recent scholar writes, "the brutal war between the two armies continued unabated" in the county. In the fall and winter of 1782–83, "the partisan warfare slackened considerably," writes Mark V. Kwasny, yet "Continental detachments and New York militia units continued to patrol." Even after peace was declared in 1783, "the situation in Westchester remained volatile after eight years of civil war and raids between neighbors." In July 1783, the war over, eight companies of American light infantry had to be dispatched to the county to maintain order.[48]

Within Westchester, long before 1782, it was a war of every man for himself and every widow left husbandless by the slaughter fending for herself. Neither "cowboys" nor "skinners," Washington Irving wryly observed, "stopped to ask the politics of horse or cow they drove into captivity; nor when they wrung the neck of a rooster did they trouble their heads to ascertain whether he was crowing for congress or King George." "The unhappy inhabitants," wrote Timothy Dwight, at the time an army chaplain, "often were actually plundered, and always were liable to this calamity. They feared everybody who they saw and loved nobody."[49]

This was the very dangerous theatre of war into which light infantry companies were thrust. It was the epitome of what students of warfare called the "petit guerre," in which "the same deceptions, Manoeuvres, and Strategems are frequently used by the Commander of a party and by the general of an army." For infantrymen, it was a war of skirmishes by small detachments, in which troops mingled with civilians whose political loyalties they could never be sure of. For civilians, it had become, out of self-preservation, a war of deception, with Tories posing as patriots and patriots as Tories, depending upon which side menaced them. To survive, men and women took on whatever identity they had to.[50]

The most famous event associated with the war in Westchester, the capture of Major John André, General Benedict Arnold's key accomplice in his treasonous plot to turn over West Point to the British, encapsulated this pervasive uncertainty about identities. In 1780, André, a high-ranking British officer traveling on horseback incognito in civilian clothes as a gentleman, was stopped near Tarrytown by three young farmers who had previously fought on the American side and were now either irregulars or skinners. André was confused as to whether they were bandits or friends. One of the men, released from a British prison, wore the green jacket of a Hessian soldier—what was he? Knowing the territory, André offered to buy the men off. They took his watch, horse, and saddle, but when they removed his boots and found papers that uncovered the plot, they turned him in. The captors were rewarded as patriot heroes, but at the time, an American officer identified them as belonging to "that class of people who passed between both armies as often in one camp as the other."[51]

Deception was a way of life in this war, and that was the way it was remembered by residents whose seared memories were taken down decades later. One such resident, Jeremiah Anderson, recalled that his father "was whipped tortured and hanged for his money both by Skinners and cowboys." He also remembered smuggling a wounded American soldier out of the family house in a woman's nightcap "so as to pass him off as a woman." It was a war of assumed identities; had local residents learned that an American regular soldier in their midst was a woman passing as a man, her masquerade would have seemed no more bizarre to them than any others they had seen or heard about.[52]

For members of the light infantry who often patrolled in vulnerable small parties, deception added to the tension. On the road, no one knew where the enemy might be lurking in ambush or, in truth, who the enemy might be. Soldiers had their eyes peeled to distinguish American irregulars from British irregulars, "skinners" from "cowboys," civilian friend from civilian foe. A civilian who wore a friendly patriot face might turn out to be a treacherous Tory. Soldiers were alert to such distinctions, on which their own survival depended. The possibility of a person of ambiguous gender within their own ranks was the last thing on their minds.

Chapter Four

The Light Infantryman

WHAT DID Deborah Sampson do in this army from the time she arrived at West Point, in late May 1782, until she was discharged at the end of October 1783? Unfortunately, she herself provided only sparse accounts in her own words (or words to which she gave her assent). She filed six petitions based on her military service. Of these, we know what she testified to in only three, and in each of these she offered only the most perfunctory statement as to what she did, little more than a sentence or two. Copies of the others are lost, including those for a pension as an invalid veteran, unfortunate because the law required a full set of medical documents and testimonials. The 1784 article in the New York newspaper (reprinted in the Prologue) is important because it could only have been based on what Sampson told her principal officers prior to her discharge and what they otherwise knew about her.[1]

If we put together these documents originating with her, and add what we learn from the few shards of testimony from individual officers (a deposition by her mustering officer, a certificate from her regimental commander, a brief letter by her drill sergeant), this is as much as we can say about her military service with reasonable certainty:

1. She enlisted May 20, 1782; was mustered into the army May 23, 1782, at Worcester, Massachusetts; and was stationed at West Point.

2. She served in the Light Infantry Company of the Fourth Massachusetts Regiment.

3. She "was in several skirmishes and received two wounds, a shot remaining in her to this day," the testimony of her officer's account of 1784.

4. She "was engag'd with the enemy at Tarry Town, New York & was wounded there by the enemy & continued in service until discharged," her testimony in her petition of 1792, accepted by a knowledgeable committee of the Massachusetts legislature, which included two officers who had served at West Point.

5. She served "as a waiter in a general officer's family," at New Windsor and West Point, namely, General John Paterson, her officer's testimony confirmed by her own later action.

6. She was discharged October 23, 1783, at West Point by General Henry Knox.

These, indeed, are bare bones. The only writer who put flesh on them was Herman Mann, who in a 250-page book devoted chapters 7 through 12 to the adventures of Robert Shurtliff in the army. Mann, as we have already seen in reconstructing her youth, while sometimes reliable, at other times was maddeningly untrustworthy. Yet, for her year and a half in the army, there is no alternative. He fabricated events, most glaringly putting his heroine at the Battle of Yorktown in September–October 1781. For well-known events of the Revolution, like Bunker Hill and Yorktown, he plagiarized from other authors, a common practice. For a key personal event, her wounding, he may have borrowed from the memoir of England's Hannah Snell.

At the Battle of Yorktown, Mann inserted his heroine in a famous large-scale event close to well-known heroes, Washington and Lafayette, like Woody Allen's Zelig or Tom Hanks's Forrest Gump. At the end of her military action, in a series of wildly improbable episodes among Indians, he depicted her among unknown people and places. In between these two fantasies, however, he described a string of petty encounters in Westchester— the kind of events, known only to the participants, that did not make their way into history books—with a combination of believable prosaic detail and unbelievable embellishments.

For these events, the heart of her military experiences, Deborah, once she had become Mrs. Gannett, seems his most likely source.[2] She appears to have identified for Mann the actions she was in, giving him the names of fellow soldiers, officers, and Westchester civilians. We can identify (after a fashion) most of these soldiers and officers. And thanks to detective work by Jane Keiter, a historian of Westchester County, we can identify the civilians and locate the sites of action. Mann misspelled unfamiliar place names, but in its own way, his phonetic spelling confirms an oral transmission from Mrs. Gannett, who would have known place names only as she heard them. If she remembered the wrong first name of a member of her company or telescoped two names into one, this is a common quirk of memory.[3]

Chronologically and geographically, however, Mann's episodes are a jumble. By placing her enlistment in May 1781, he took on the burden of accounting for an entire year when she was not in the army. He had to invent activity for her for the spring and summer of 1781, take her to Yorktown for a battle in September and October, bring her back to West Point for the winter, after which he had to fill in, until June 1782. Sometimes he took episodes that occurred later and placed them earlier, sometimes the other way around. How much help he had from Mrs. Gannett in all of this is hard to say.

The stories in *The Female Review,* as a whole, as I have already suggested, fall into one of three categories of credibility: likely, unlikely, and improbable. For the war, the likely events can be confirmed by other evidence and appear credible given the known context; the unlikely events are unsupported by evidence or are supported by only the thinnest proof; the improbable events are negated by contradictory testimony or are improbable because of what we know about the historical context.

How do we test and unjumble Mann, given the absence of the kind of military records that might enable one to trace a single soldier? My strategy was to track Sampson's company—the smallest formal military unit in the army. My goal was to create a template on which to test the five fullest episodes in the Mann/Gannett narrative, and to see if I could arrange them in a chronology and locate them on a geography that might fit on the template. I was amazed by what I found.

1. *Searching for a Light Infantry Company*
Private Roger Barrett's Memories

It is possible to track the Light Infantry Company of the Fourth Massachusetts Regiment. But the surviving official records for the company for these years are few. For 1781–82, there are five "muster rolls" for the company (the monthly listing of soldiers by name and rank), one of which bore Robert Shurtliff's name. I found no "orderly books" (the journals kept by company officers recording military orders, courts-martial, and other events). For her regiment, there are manuscript records that include "returns" (charting the total number of troops in each military unit, month by month), quartermaster's records of equipment dispensed to each company, lists of deserters, and other housekeeping documents. All these help locate her regiment but do not get us down to company *actions*. Alas, none of her commanding senior officers (Captain George Webb, Colonels William Shepard and Henry Jackson, and General John Paterson) left either a diary, a journal, or a set of letters; only the commander in chief, George Washington.[4]

It is possible, however, to get a good sense of the company in action through three bodies of sources, each originating at a different vantage point: first, through General Washington's general orders and letters to officers in the field; second, through the recollections of one member of the company, Roger Barrett, set down in 1832 in his application for a pension; and third, through the diary and letters of Benjamin Gilbert, a lieutenant in the Light Infantry Company of the Fifth Massachusetts Regiment in active service at the same time. Taken together, these three sources enable us to construct a clear, multidimensional template.[5]

General Washington's Orders: Washington's orders tell us where the light companies as a whole were posted and what he ordered them to do. The commander in chief was particularly attentive to the light infantry companies because at this stage of the war they usually were his only military units in the lower Hudson Valley on active duty.

As the war wound down for the main army, it ratcheted up for the light corps. In early June 1782, after he had ordered the companies brought up to full strength with new recruits, Washington assigned "entire companies of light infantry in rotation" to the lines in northern Westchester, where their camp was at Peekskill. Early in August, he ordered a regrouping of all the light infantry units.[6] At the end of August, to protect the massive amphibious

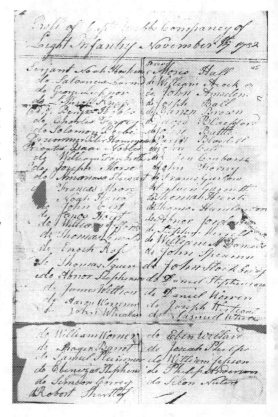

The roll of Captain George Webb's Light Infantry Company of the Fourth Massachusetts Regiment, November 17, 1782, is the only surviving roll for the company for 1781 and 1782 on which the name "Robert Shirtlef" appears (lower left). This was a list from which the mustering officer would enter the names in tabular form on the formal muster roll. Courtesy American Antiquarian Society.

operation simulating an invasion, the light infantry units were "ordered in front of the army . . . [to] keep out proper picquets and small scouts to patrol as far as the Croton [River]." From mid-September to mid-October 1782, with a French army of seven thousand troops encamped in northern Westchester, they were put on special alert. Typically, in late October, Washington ordered two light companies to the Croton River to be "continually moving from place to place & keeping up Patroles incessantly to cover the Country & prevent surprise." They were commanded to "send out scouts to enemy lines." Other light infantry units were sent out all over Westchester: to reconnoiter the British army; "to assist in covering a foraging party"; or to respond to British raids.[7] These were orders; they tell us very clearly what the companies en masse were told to do, but not what Sampson's company actually did.

Private Roger Barrett's Memories: One private's recollections tell us about where her company was when Sampson was a member. Barrett's memories come down to us in his petition for a pension in 1832 submitted to meet the requirement for applicants to give "a very full account" of their actions to prove their service.[8] Taking the only muster roll of Captain Webb's company on which Robert Shurtliff's name appeared (November 12, 1782), I ran down the service records of fifty-nine men and then looked for them in a master index of pension applicants. After locating about two dozen applicants, I turned to their petitions in the National Archives, looking especially for those who had filed under the 1832 law.[9]

Of these applicants, three reported on the action of the company in 1782–83, two sparingly because it was only a minor part of a long service record, and one, Barrett—for whom it was his only military service—at length, in a clear, sequential account. At age sixteen, Roger Barrett enlisted at Watertown, Massachusetts, "some time in the month of May" 1782, "about the middle of the month," and "in a few days thereafter he joined Captain Webb's company" at West Point, entering the company at the same time as Sampson. In 1832, at age sixty-six, he recalled the experiences he had absorbed at sixteen and seventeen, an age when new and exciting events are often well encoded in memory and, after an initial loss, well retained into old age.[10]

After establishing his credentials with a formulaic listing of his senior officers (who matched Sampson's and included some others) and his time of service, Barrett began the account of his activities with a disclaimer, the modesty of which supports his credibility. "He was in no battle during said service." Where was he? Most of the time his company was "on the lines" or on a tour of duty in Westchester. On occasion the company was split up into smaller units, a conclusion that can be drawn from the fact that he and Sampson each mention serving under a non-commissioned officer the other does not mention.

Warfare in the eighteenth century was geared to the seasons. Barrett remembered the activity of his company by the places to which it was posted, and the time by the seasons, not the months, conveying a good sense of both chronology and geography (see map, opposite). "After joining his company & regiment at West Point [in late May] . . . he remained there a

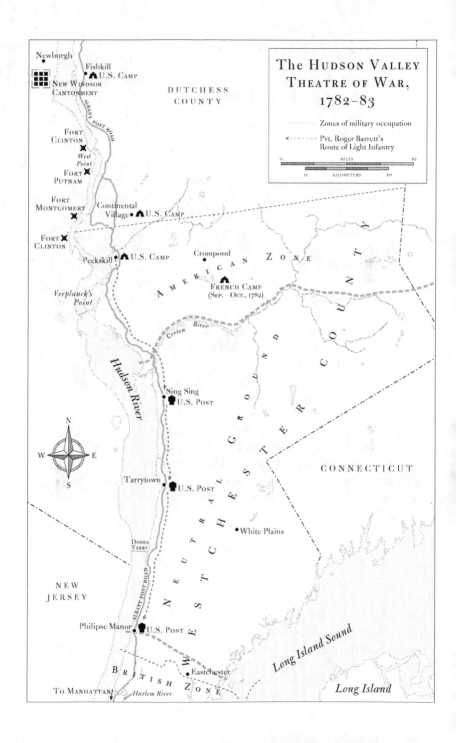

The HUDSON VALLEY
THEATRE OF WAR,
1782–83

············ Zones of military occupation

◄·—·—·— Pvt. Roger Barrett's
Route of Light Infantry

0 ▦▦▦▦▦ MILES ▦▦▦▦▦ 10
0 ▦▦▦▦▦ KILOMETERS ▦▦▦▦▦ 10

Newburgh
Fishkill
▲U.S. Camp
NEW WINDSOR
CANTONMENT

DUTCHESS
COUNTY

FORT
CLINTON
West
Point
FORT
PUTNAM

FORT
MONTGOMERY   Continental
Village ● ▲U.S. CAMP

FORT
CLINTON

Peekskill ● ▲U.S. CAMP   Crompond

AMERICAN ZONE

WESTCHESTER COUNTY

French Camp
(Sep.–Oct., 1782)

Verplanck's
Point

Croton River

Hudson River

Sing Sing
U.S. Post

N
W   E
S

CONNECTICUT

Tarrytown
U.S. Post

NEUTRAL GROUND

Dobbs
Ferry

White Plains

NEW
JERSEY

ALBANY POST ROAD

Philipse Manor ● U.S. Post

B R I T I S H   Z O N E

Eastchester

TO MANHATTAN   Harlem River

Long Island Sound

Long Island

month or six weeks [i.e., until late June or early July] when he marched with Captain Webb's company, detached from his Regiment southerly to Croton River which was then this line between American and British armies [near?] Peekskill where he was stationed all that season until late in the fall during which time he was frequently marched with detachments to Sing Sing, Tarry Town, Dobb's Ferry, Phillipse Manor and other places in that vicinity." Barrett's geography was accurate; he named military stations in the "neutral ground" along the Hudson, as he would have encountered them while marching from north to south.

"His winter quarter following that campaign was at New Burgh two miles back of the town or Village," a location commonly given for the encampment at New Windsor.

In the Spring of 1783 he was again marched [south] on the ice to West Point with said company & Regiment where he was stationed for a month or two when he was marched with said Company and Regiment to the same place where he was stationed the previous season on Croton River where he was again stationed for the most part until the close of the war.

After the Peace was proclaimed [spring 1783] he was transferred, being a three years' man, into an other company of Colonel [Henry] Jackson on south thru Sing Sing, Tarry Town and Phillips Manor to New York, where he arrived the same day the British left the City [November 25, 1783]. He remained there a few weeks after which he returned with his said regiment to West Point where he remained during the winter following [1783–84]. Soon after he went into Winter Quarters he served as a Waiter for Major Gibbs of his Regiment until he was discharged which was in the first part of June, 1784 at West Point.

Barrett's account conveys a sense of the company being on the go from place to place from the early summer of 1782 through the winter of 1783. The trajectory is from the permanent encampments on the west bank (West Point or New Windsor) to the field camps on the east bank in northern Westchester above the Croton River, then to posts to the south along the Hudson held by American troops within the neutral ground, then back to the field camps and home to garrisons on the west bank. The company did not stay put for very long. This, then, provides both the time frame and geographic frame within which Deborah Sampson's military episodes in Westchester most likely occurred, unless—and it is an important exception—she was detached from her company in a small party or she volunteered for an action in which troops were drawn from different units.[11]

Barrett, while lucid as to when the company was where, said little, unfortunately, about what it did, which in itself may be a clue. He "was stationed" and he "frequently marched." While he speaks of being "detached" from the company, he mentions no skirmishes. This suggests either that he was not in any, or, if he was, that the actions were so uneventful they did not stay in his memory. It is entirely possible that Sampson was in patrols which encountered the enemy while Barrett was not.

Is there any other evidence that Sampson's company engaged in skirmishes? Two other soldiers on the company roster mentioned skirmishes in Westchester in their pension petitions. Solomon Beebe, a soldier since 1777, spoke simply of being in "many other skirmishes which might be superfluous [*sic*] to mention." And William Jeffords (a five-foot-three-inch sixteen-year-old when he joined the army) mentioned being "in several slight engagements but no noted battle."[12]

More revealing, George Webb, captain of the company, confirms that on one occasion he detached small parties from the company in anticipation of meeting the enemy. In a letter to his commanding officer, he described in detail an operation in the first week of October 1782 near Tarrytown on the Hudson, for which Webb was hauled on the carpet for moving his troops forward before the order to advance was given. Webb gave a sense of a company on the alert for skirmishes: "a party of men" here, four men led by a corporal there, some men on shore marching, some men on horseback, still others in two small boats on the river. In other words, he painted a picture of the normal chaos of a military encounter in which a captain dispersed his men in anticipation of an enemy threat. Robert Shurtliff could have been in this action.[13]

Lieutenant Benjamin Gilbert's Diary and Letters: Gilbert, commander of the light infantry of the Fifth Massachusetts, put down observations in his letters and diaries at the time that conveyed a feeling for day-to-day life in such a company in Westchester.[14]

His company, like Barrett's, was especially active in June, July, and August 1782, again in the fall, and in the snowy winter of 1782–83. Unlike the company in Barrett's memory, which hugged the posts along the Hudson, Gilbert's was one of those dispatched on inland sorties. He went on two circuits of the entire county, one to its southernmost reaches near the British lines (which Mann claimed for Sampson). This company also was heavily involved in the area around the Croton River (where three of Sampson's episodes took place). Occasionally, Gilbert states that it was divided into "small parties."

The accounts by Barrett and Gilbert, combined with Washington's orders, besides making clear that the period from June through the fall of 1782 was the most likely time for Robert Shurtliff's military activity, establish the area around the Croton River where the American zone bordered on the neutral ground as a major scene of light infantry action. The Croton River clearly was to soldiers in the light infantry in Westchester what the 38th parallel was to GIs in the Korean War or what the 17th parallel was in Vietnam: a dangerous line of demarcation between opposing troops where sudden encounters with the enemy were possible. It was also like the war in Vietnam in another way: it was fought amidst civilians on a landscape of farms and woods, where it was often not at all clear who was friend or foe.

Gilbert's entries capture something of what Sampson may have encountered on the road. In Westchester, when his company goes on a tour, they stop each night at the house of a civilian ostensibly friendly to the American cause ("Mr. Van Tassel," "widow Brown," "widow Hunt"). The troops billet one day in a barn, the next day in the woods, the next in a farmer's orchard. Tension is intermittent. The military encounters are all small-scale and with "irregulars." But Gilbert is ever on the alert for a surprise attack and sure to move his men from place to place each day. On occasion, they march "in small parties ambushing the roads," which means they were on the lookout for the enemy lying in wait in thick woods.

For the light infantry, it was a war of dangerous patrols and inglorious small party encounters. A comment by General Rufus Putnam, a veteran of many campaigns, about his service around the Croton River in 1780 could have been made in 1782–83, even though there was much less activity. Duty at the river, he wrote, was "far mre feteauging [fatiguing], Slavish, hazardous, & requiring much Greter vigilence, then [than] common reotean [routine] duty performed with the army. . . ."[15]

Here, then, composed from the testimony of Washington, Barrett, Gilbert, and Webb, is the template on which to try to test Mann's episodes about Robert Shurtliff. If we knew no more about Sampson's military career than what we know about her company from these sources, we would have enough to say she was on active duty for long stretches of time in a hazardous service that demanded constant vigilance. But we do know more: a surprising number of episodes in Mann's narrative fit on this template.

2. *The Adventures of Combat*
"A number of small skirmishes"

In spite of the mishmash he made of chronology and geography, Herman Mann grasped the function of the light infantry. He called them "rangers" and spoke of "scouting" as "a great part of their business" or their "common business." He recognized that they saw combat: they were called upon to "retaliate on the enemy" and were engaged in "a number of small skirmishes." He knew that they were "mostly on the lines" or on patrol. In his own stilted way he also caught the ceaseless tedium of military duty: "many marches forward and retrograde" and "numberless incidental activities and hardships." His accounts of Sampson's prosaic "small skirmishes" and "incidental activities," for all his overblown style, deserve to be analyzed.[16]

If we take the military episodes of the Hudson Valley in the Mann/Gannett account one by one and lay them on our template, five are described with enough detail to make them testable: (1) her first engagement, a skirmish; (2) a second, also a skirmish, in which she was wounded; (3) an interlude in which she nursed a dying soldier in the attic of a Tory; (4) a patrol in which she escaped from Tory deception across the icy Croton River; and (5) an expedition to northern New York in which she encountered hostile Indians.

Chronologically, four of the five episodes fit on the template. Mann spread them out from June 1781 into the winter of 1782–83. Most likely they occurred between June 1782 and January 1783, the first three in the summer and fall of 1782, a time of peak activity for the light infantry. Geographically, they also fit: the first four occurred in Westchester, either in the neutral ground or in the American zone very close to the Croton, the area of almost continuous light infantry patrols. The expedition to the north in the fifth episode does not fit, but is possible. All five episodes are either likely, probable, or possible. Yet the evidence is often garbled, places don't fit, and each episode includes scenes that seem to be a product of Mann's imagination. For each episode, the event as Mann presented it is first summarized, and then analyzed, below.

Episode One: A Baptism by Fire

The initial episode, a skirmish in which Sampson came under enemy fire for the first time, occurred in her company's first encounter with enemy troops soon after it was sent across the Hudson. Mann placed it in June–July 1781, near Tarrytown. It could have occurred near Tarrytown in June–July 1782. Emotionally, the account rings true as a soldier's first engagement in combat, yet some evidence is problematic.

To tell the story the way Mann told it, on June 10, Captain Webb's company was sent "on a scout," divided in two squads, Shurtliff's "under the command of Ensign Towne." They went south along the Hudson as far as Harlem, only eight miles above the British lines, and on their return, went north to White Plains in the center of the county and then back to the Hudson. There, on July 3 (changed to June 26 in his later manuscript), close to the river in the Tappan Bay neighborhood near Tarrytown, they encountered "a party of Dutch cavalry from Gen. Delancie's core then in Morsena." Armed with carbines and broadswords, the Loyalist horsemen poured two volleys into the American infantrymen before they could respond. British infantry landing from boats reinforced James DeLancey. The Americans fired, retreating to the woods. "The ground was then warmly disputed for a considerable time. At length, the [American] infantry were obliged to give way: but they were quickly reinforced by a detachment led on by Col. Sproat, a valiant officer of the second Massachusetts Regiment." The enemy retreated; the Americans regained their ground and then "retired to their encampment."

This was the military encounter. Sampson's memory of her reactions was uncommonly vivid, natural for someone recalling her first life-threatening experience under fire. "She says she underwent more with the fatigue and heat of the day, than by fear of being killed, although her left-hand man was shot dead the second fire." She also recalled intense thirst: "Our fair soldier with some others came near losing her life by drinking cold water." And she reported the first casualties she had seen: "She recollects but three on her side, who were killed," naming them. "She escaped with two shots through her coat, and one through her cap." By this account, it was a searing baptism by fire.

It could have happened. The event might have occurred soon after Washington ordered the light infantry companies into action in June 1782, but a detachment scouting so far south and so close to the British lines was unusual, and not in Private Barrett's memory as a movement of the company as a whole. The scale of the British response—army reinforcements sent by boat up the Hudson—fits more a known event near Tarrytown in 1781.

The military figures named can be identified. "Gen. Delancie's core then in Morsena" was Colonel James DeLancey's corps, the dread unit of irregulars based on the Morisania estate in the British zone in the southeastern part of the county. They would have been quick to respond to an American intrusion near their zone and were a cavalry that swooped down on infantrymen, broadswords their weapon of choice. On the American side, Colonel Sproat was Ebenezer Sproat, indeed, of the Second Massachusetts Regiment, six feet four inches tall. Sampson had special reason to know him as the son of the owner of the familiar Sproat's tavern in Middleborough. Whether or not his unit was there we cannot say. Ensign Towne was Jacob Towne, a veteran soldier on the muster roll for Sampson's company.

The account muddles the names of the three men it reported as killed: John Beeby, James Battles, and Nooble Sperrin. There were three men on the company's several rosters in 1781–82 with these last names. There was no John Beeby, but there was a Solomon Beebe. There was a James Battles who was reported dead as of December 1, 1781, but there was also a John Battles, his brother. There was no Nooble Sperrin, but there was a John Sperrin and an Isaac Nobles. Thus, there were three men in her company with the same *last* names that Mann gave, but different first names, who could have seen action with Sampson. However, the problem does not end there: if the men with her in the skirmish were these three, they were not killed in battle, but lived on after the war. Solomon Beebe in fact, as already noted, filed a pension application in which he spoke of skirmishes "which might be superflious to mention," one of which might have been this one. What might account for this double discrepancy: getting names wrong and naming men as killed who lived on? Assuming that the names came from Mrs. Gannett, she might have been confused as to who was there, mixing up first names and conflating two names into one. Or, more likely, Mann mixed them up, either taking down names wrong or writing up his notes carelessly. But how did he or she end up listing men as killed who were not? They could have been wounded and she thought they died; more likely, Mann, to heighten the drama of her encounter, needed three men killed in battle, and he chose names she had mentioned and garbled them.[17]

Sampson's physical reactions—intense thirst and extreme fatigue—were typical of a neophyte soldier in a first engagement. Drinking cold water to quench thirst after battle was so dangerous and so common early in the war that Dr. Benjamin Rush, the surgeon general of the Continental Army in 1777–78, had issued a warning about the possibly fatal "cold water disease." This part of the baptism by fire rings true.[18]

Episode Two: A Near-Fatal Skirmish

This was the skirmish in which Sampson claimed she was wounded. Calvin Munn, Sampson's drill sergeant, who thought Mann's book was "mainly false," was probably right in charging that "She was not wounded as is therein related." He does not seem to have questioned, however, that she was wounded; he only leaves us guessing as to which part of the account was untrue. The problem is that nearly everything about the incident is subject to contradictory claims—where and when the skirmish occurred, in what part of her body she was wounded, in what hospital she was treated and by whom, and whether she treated her own wound, and if so, how. The story is worth probing because a wound became central to her later persona.[19]

As Mann dramatized this episode, it had two parts, the skirmish and the treatment of the wound. The event began with her volunteering for action against the enemy: "she, with two sergeants, requested leave of their Captain to retaliate on the enemy, chiefly refugees and tories in New-York for their outrageous insults to the inhabitants beyond their lines." He replied, "You three dogs have contrived a plan this night to be killed, and I have no men to lose." She persisted; he consented; "they beat for volunteers," and she was one of a party of twenty, perhaps thirty, drawn from several companies. They traveled far south in the county to Eastchester, fairly close to the British lines, where they laid in ambush observing the enemy. They came upon two boys who led them to a cave "stored with provisions such as bacon, butter, cheese, crouts [sauerkraut?], early scrohons [scones?], and jars of honey," on which they gorged themselves, and then they set up a camp nearby "in a place called in Dutch, Vonhoite."[20]

In the middle of the night, "a large party chiefly on horseback and well armed" descended upon them, and "a severe combat ensued." Americans shot enemy soldiers from their horses. "Our gallantress . . . immediately mounted an excellent horse" and gave pursuit, driving the enemy into a quagmire. "They rushed them on the right and left, till as many as could escaped; the rest begged quarters." At this point, she realized she had been wounded. She had a saber cut to her head and a musket ball in her thigh. She thought she was near death and, fearing discovery, wanted to kill herself. Two comrades took her in hand and brought her on horseback to "an old hospital" at the "French encampment near what was called Cron Pond," where she was treated by a "French surgeon." The account of the skirmish ended with details on the casualties. "The Americans took nine prisoners and seven horses and killed a number of others on the spot. Of their wounded ROSE, STOCKBRIDGE, PLUMMER, and the invincible Fair [Mann's term for Deborah]. DISTON was killed."

The skirmish is not subject to corroboration. Her company, judging by Barrett's account, was not sent on such forays; but judging by Gilbert's account of his company, which was, it could have occurred. In the telling, however, the action was not by a company but by volunteers drawn from several units, a possibility. The geography is confusing. The military action would make more sense near the northern part of the county. Jane Keiter, a historian versed in Westchester, identifies "Vonhoite" as the likely home of William or Willis Hait or Haight, which translates into Dutch as Hoite, and "Von Hoite" as "the place of Hoite." She places this in the American zone in the north not far from Crompond. Caves were also in that area. Mrs. Gannett, in her first public petition, however, named Tarrytown as the site where she was wounded. For a severely wounded soldier, a trip from Tarrytown, midway in the neutral zone, to a hospital above the Croton River is more credible than one from Eastchester very far to the south.[21]

At the skirmish, three of the four other soldiers mentioned can be identified. This time, Gannett and/or Mann used only last names. The wounded men could have been Enoch Rose, John Stockbridge, and Samuel Plummer, all listed on the November 1782 muster with Robert Shurtliff. Diston, who was not a member of her company, cannot be identified even under variant spellings. Mann's timing of the episode in June 1782, however, is awry. If she was attended by a "French surgeon" in "an old hospital" in "the French encampment," it would have been between September 18, 1782, when the last of the French army arrived from Virginia, and October 22, when the army departed for Boston. French troops were encamped near Crompond (about nine miles east of Peekskill), where they had a building Americans used earlier as an army hospital, which could be called "an old hospital."[22]

Sampson's overwhelming fear of detection rings true. This would have been a constant source of tension for her in the field. "She had always thought she would rather die, than disclose her sex to the army," Mann wrote. After she was wounded, "almost in despair she drew a pistol from a holster and was nearly ready to execute the fatal deed," but she banished "the shocking act and idea of suicide."

For the second part of this episode, about the treatment of the wound, there are several versions of where it was on her body. In the Mann narrative, she received two wounds: "Putting her hand to it [her head] she found the blood gushed from the left side of her head very freely." This turned out to be a flesh wound. She also "found her boot in her right leg [revised by Mann in his 1830s manuscript to the left leg] filled with blood; and in her thigh, just below her groin, she found the incision of a ball, whence it [the blood] issued."[23]

As the story was retold over the years, some versions shifted the serious wound from her thigh to the upper part of her body. Sproat, the collector of Middleborough's oral lore, said that "in her first battle she was wounded by a musket ball in her left breast," and this was the way descendants were telling the story around 1900. As Elizabeth Ellet picked it up earlier, at mid-century, from someone who said she heard it from Deborah, "she was shot through the shoulder." Either upper body location would fit the story Philip Freneau's daughter told about the interview the poet/editor had with Mrs. Gannett in 1797 (about which more in chapter 6), when she was said to have shown him her scars. In her public address in 1802 (written by Mann), Mrs. Gannett added to the mystery by saying, "a dislocated limb draws fresh anguish from my heart." "Limb" was a genteel euphemism for a woman's arm or leg, but "a dislocated limb" sounds more like an injury to the shoulder or leg than to the upper thigh.[24]

The dramatic climax of the wound's treatment also comes in several versions. In the Mann narrative, it occurred when a French surgeon gave her a bottle of wine and prepared to dress her wounds. A French doctor in a French hospital in the French encampment, as has been suggested, is not far-fetched, although virtually impossible to trace. The rest of the story, however, tests our faith in Mann and Gannett. After an orderly bathed her head wound in rum, the alcohol presumably an antiseptic, Sampson then disappeared and "taking an opportunity with a penknife and needle, she extracted the ball from her thigh." Thirty years later, Mann added refinements. Putting the story as if in her own words, he says she took from the hospital "a silver probe with a little curve at the end, a needle, some lint, and some of the same kind of salve that had been applied to the wound in my head. I found that the ball had penetrated my thigh about two inches, and the wound was still moderately bleeding. The wine revived me, and God by his kind care watched over me. At the third attempt, I extracted the ball, which I still preserve as a sacred relick." This is the first mention of saving the ball. In Sproat's Middleborough lore, the story passed down in more rustic form: "that night by the light of the campfire, she dug out the ball with her own hands, using a soldier's pointed eating knife."

In the version first presented to the public in 1784 (predating Mann's book), the officer who had talked to Sampson at the time of her discharge wrote: "she received two wounds, a small shot remaining in her to this day." We don't know what she claimed when she received her pension as an "invalid veteran" in 1805 because the papers were lost. In her 1809 petition for a back pension, she said she "received wounds by which she has been disabled from performing the common occupations of life as she otherwise might have done." After her death, Patience Payson, the family servant for over forty years, testified that Deborah was wounded by two balls, that she extracted one but was unable to remove the other, which remained within her, the cause of her recurring ill health.[25]

The place of the wound thus remains a mystery. Had the shot lodged in her upper thigh, it might have affected the way she walked, yet no one ever referred to a limp. Had the shot been to her shoulder, it might have affected the movement of one arm, yet, at her appearances on a Boston stage in 1802, she handled a musket with such élan in going through the soldier's "manual of arms" that she drew applause for four nights. And in the subsequent lore of the family, while there are other relics, there is no mention of a musket ball.

The whole story of removing a ball from a wound in the groin smacks so much of a similar incident in the adventures of Hannah Snell that it seems that narrative could have been the inspiration for Mann (or Deborah, or both). Even the excerpt reprinted in Isaiah Thomas's country almanac included the graphic story of Snell extracting a ball from her groin. As it went, at the siege of Pondicherry in India, Snell received "a Shot in the Groin," was sent to the hospital "under the care of two able Physicians . . . but not willing to be discovered, extracted the ball out of her Groin herself, and always dresst the Wound, and in about three months was perfectly cured." Both women, of course, could have suffered a similar wound and dealt with it in a similar way to avoid detection.[26]

Or, the story of a wound in the groin could have been a hoax. For Mann, the sensationalist, a wound near the groin was a titillating metaphor that hinted at sexual penetration in a narrative announcing on the title page that his heroine had protected her chastity. For Mrs. Gannett, claiming a wound in so private a part of her body could have been a way of making credible an injury for which she had no formal proof. In the 1790s, requirements for a soldier trying to establish proof of disability for a pension as an "invalid veteran" were unbelievably stringent, including affidavits from a surgeon or officers about the cause of his disability during the war, and reports from two physicians who had recently examined him. On the other hand, to claim that you were treated by a French doctor (whose name you did not know) in a French hospital (whose records had departed with a disembarking army), and further, that you treated yourself rather than reveal your sex—all this was a way to get around these hurdles. Moreover, since the location claimed was such a delicate matter, it was not something to which many others would have been privy. If there was a scar near her groin, perhaps only a midwife or the women who attended her birthing rituals knew.[27]

I don't think the story was a hoax, however. I believe she was wounded, but probably in the upper part of her body. All the public testimony points to a wound. I give weight to the 1784 article by an officer who knew Sampson which reported her as wounded, "a shot remaining in her to this day." Her 1792 petition to the Massachusetts legislature, in which she said she "received a wound," was reviewed by a committee that included Dr. William Eustis, a surgeon at the West Point hospital. In 1797, on the occasion of her first appeal to Congress, her congressman, Harrison Gray Otis, said that her petition stated, "she is able *to produce certificates* not only of having served but of having been wounded." In 1805, when she was granted a pension as an "invalid veteran," Secretary of War Henry Dearborn wrote that she was "severely wounded." Cumulatively, this is impressive evidence.[28]

Wherever the wound was, she could have treated it herself. Many wounded soldiers did, out of a sheer impulse for survival. Wounded men often had to be dragged to army hospitals, where surgeons had only one remedy for a wound to a limb: amputation without anesthesia. Moreover, before the advent of antiseptics, army hospitals in the Revolutionary War were places where numerous soldiers died from infections and fevers.[29]

Whether she was shot in the thigh or shoulder or breast, whether or not one round lead musket ball remained in her, conceivably, after almost two hundred years, we might find out if her grave in Sharon were opened. But this is a ghoulish, unnecessary prospect. It really does not matter. There is strong evidence that she was wounded in action, but it is also likely that Sergeant Munn was right, that Mann's account of how she was wounded and what she did about it is flawed. She was wounded, she suffered pain, she had a scrape with death, and she lived to tell the tale—and to have others spin it into another tale. This, then, was the second episode.[30]

Episode Three: Nursing a Wounded Soldier

In the adventure that followed on the heels of being wounded, Robert Shurtliff, while recuperating, nursed a sick soldier named Richard Snow in the garret of a house near Collebarack belonging to an "old Dutchman named Van Tassel." After ten days of care, Snow died; Van Tassel turned out to be an active Tory, and his daughter, who was kind to Shurtliff, a patriot. Robert Shurtliff went back to camp. He then returned to the house at the head of a squad of soldiers and captured a dangerous party of Tory irregulars assembled there. The first part of this episode— nursing a wounded soldier—seems possible; the second part unlikely.[31]

The event took place in an area of the American zone where a Tory masquerading as a patriot was a commonplace. "Colabarack" (more accurately Collebarack, sometimes Colabaugh) was close to Crompond, site of the French hospital, and just north of the Croton River line of demarcation. It was a dangerous area because it was rife with Tories; a census of the Van Cortlandt manor in September 1782 listed 680 out of the 3,052 inhabitants as refugees from heavily Loyalist New York City. Van Tassel, although a common Dutch name, was the name of the owner of a house where Lieutenant Gilbert's company also stopped, which means Americans could have taken him as a seeming friend. Jane Keiter believes he was Abraham Van Tassel, who earlier fought with the Loyalist Refugee Corps and later filed a Loyalist claim with the British for his losses. She also identifies the daughter in the story as Mary, at the time a teenager.[32]

The circumstances of Sampson's action are plausible: "in their march to the line" from Collebarack, that is, on the way back to the main field camp at Peekskill, "she requested to be left with a sick soldier . . . mostly because she was unable to do duty with the army." She had recently been wounded. There was indeed a Richard Snow. He was on her company roster early in 1782 but not in November 1782, and other records show he died in the army, which suggests a death in the late fall of 1782, a time that would fit in with this action, if it followed her wounding.[33]

Although this much of the episode is possible, Mann's romantic additions seem contrived. After Snow's death, from the attic window, Sampson saw a party of Tories in the yard below. "At length she heard footsteps on the stairs. Her heart fluttered," but it turned out to be not an enemy but Van Tassel's daughter, "who seemed possessed of humanity." "If you please, sir, walk into my chamber." There, "they regaled themselves with a glass of wine and a beautiful serene air." In his generally more sexualized 1830s revision, Mann wrote: "She grasped my hand, and modestly suffered me to leave a kiss upon her sweet, ruby lips."[34]

The coda to the romance is even less likely. Sampson/Shurtliff rejoined her company, reporting Van Tassel's duplicity to her captain, who authorized retaliatory action. "She took command of a party" (hard to believe for a private) and returned to capture the Tory soldiers, one of whom "vented many bitter oaths, that Robert Shurtliff had stolen his girlfriend" (precisely as Hannah Snell had done with a villain in her narrative). All this is unlikely.

Episode Four: An Escape Across an Icy River

The fourth testable adventure of 1782 is credible. It involves an escape from an enemy attack in the dead of the winter across the icy Croton River and another act of deception by a Tory, this time the "Widow Hunt." The incident occurred December 1 on a road near the Croton River in the neutral ground. Sampson "and a party," so the story goes, "were surprised by a party of Dutch cavalry from an ambuscade" and made their way swiftly to a place called Croton Ferry, "where their only alternative was that of fording" the river to the safety of the American zone. They forced a Dutchman to "pilot them to the [sand]bar," where they "entered the watery element" and made good a passage to the other side.

Thinking themselves safe, "they went to the house of the Widow Hunt, who under the pretext of friendship sent black George," her slave, ostensibly for refreshments but secretly to inform nearby enemy troops. But our heroine, who was "more accustomed with the cunning of her sex" than the men, warned her patrol about the woman's guile. The troops went back to the river crossing, and after "a cold winter night," decided to recross the frozen stream. Two thirds of the way across, "our young FEMALE . . . was so exhausted" that she thought the swift stream would carry her to her death. But "she got hold of a string which they buoyed to her" and made it to the other side. "She rendezvoused with her company at Pixhill Hollow."[35]

The context and place make this event credible. An encounter by a light infantry patrol with the enemy in the winter of 1782 was likely, especially in the area around the Croton, the hot spot. On December 2, Washington ordered light infantry into the area. There was a ferry that crossed the Croton. Indeed, the ferry house on the Van Cortlandt estate, restored in the twentieth century, may be at the same site. Peekskill ("Pixhill Hollow") was the site of a major American light infantry field camp. The area, to repeat, was one where Loyalists would have played at being patriots to appease American troops. The only identifiable member of the cast of characters, "Widow Hunt," also appears in Lieutenant Gilbert's diary as the owner of a house near the Croton River, where his company stayed twice late in 1782, meaning it was a stopping place for light infantry companies. It very likely was a tavern. Jane Keiter identifies her as Mary Hunt, a widow, who ran a tavern near the Croton. "Black George" escapes identification, but slave servants were numerous in Westchester. This escape by Sampson with her patrol across the frozen Croton thus is probable.[36]

Episode Five: An Encounter with Indians

The last of the military adventures adds a heavy dose of fantasy to a possible event: an expedition in the winter of 1782–83, "to assist Gen. Schuyler in subduing the Indians on the frontiers." Mann presents it so clumsily and so briefly in a single paragraph at the end of a chapter as to make it almost unintelligible. In his later revision, he blew it up to twenty manuscript pages, which made the story clearer but even less credible.[37]

The basic military action was the army sending a detachment to the north. According to the narrative, Robert Shurtliff, stationed with his company at the newly built winter encampment at New Windsor, volunteered for a party commanded by one Captain Mills. (The company was not sent.) The party made its way north along the Hudson, and at Bradport met up with a settler whose house was under attack by Indians. At the house they saw his slain wife and two children "hung by the heels, one scalped and yet alive." After they captured several Indians, Sampson "thrust her hand into the bosom of one" to discover "his being the complexion of an Englishman except where he was painted." They sent him to headquarters and "executed the rest on the spot." They then returned to the New Windsor encampment, "their feet once more crimsoned the snow," and "her name resounds with plaudits"—she became a hero.

The basic event, an expedition of a small body of troops up the Hudson Valley in the winter of 1782–83, was possible, although it does not appear in military records. Earlier that winter, Washington had sent an expedition to seize Fort Oswego in far western New York. American troops were stationed at forts in the Albany area as a precaution against a British attack from Canada, and Washington repeatedly reassured General Philip Schuyler, now retired from active duty, of his concern for the region's security. Indians within New York remained an obsession with the American army, even after they had decimated Iroquois villages in the western part of the state. Thus, an expedition out of New Windsor to the Albany area might easily have been taken by the soldiers as one to "assist" Schuyler, a famous general.

As to the cast of characters, Captain Mills could have been John Mills or William Mills, both captains at West Point in 1782. Drawing volunteers from several companies was common for a hazardous enterprise. We haven't a clue as to the identity of the white man seized by the soldiers, but we know there were Anglo-Americans living among Indians who adopted Indian ways, "white Indians." There was a place called Bradport on the New York map above Albany. More than this cannot be said.[38]

But if such an expedition was possible, the event seems improbable. This late in the war there probably were no Indians left in upstate New York to be subdued. The tribes that had once occupied northeastern New York had migrated far to the west to be out of harm's way of the vengeful Americans. Mann's tale of Indians beating out the brains of a settler's children was a stock trope; later he threw in the massacre of Jane McCrae at Saratoga, the most famous Indian atrocity story of the war. In this later version, the army party visited a Seneca village which was unlikely to have been there. It also stopped at the headquarters of General Schuyler, where Sampson and Captain Mills were greeted by the famous general and his daughter, newly married to Alexander Hamilton—all imagined associations with the famous. The story was fantasy.[39]

The denouement of the expedition in the 1797 book suggests that Mann the novelist is teasing his readers—a woman disguised as a man thrusting her hand into a man's bosom and discovering him to be a white man disguised as an Indian. This also reminds readers that Sampson is passing as a man; it prefigures a doctor in a military hospital in Philadelphia thrusting his hand into Sampson's uniform to discover her sex.

SO, FOR THE FIVE EPISODES we have tested, there is corroborating evidence of varying strengths for the core events in four. The first four take place in the geographic area and within the time span established for light infantry activity: in other words, they fit on the template. The fifth does not. Three events (the wounding, the nursing, the crossing) take place in the principal area of frequent light infantry action around the Croton River. In the two skirmishes, the soldiers mentioned are identifiable as members of her company (albeit in a bewildering way). The other episodes include the name of at least one other identifiable person (Private Richard Snow, Von Hoite, Van Tassel, Widow Hunt, Captain Mills). Yet, while each episode opens with a realistic credible first act, three of the five end with fantasy second acts (the wounding, the nursing, the expedition). All the episodes suffer from Mann's self-imposed need to magnify Sampson's heroism.

There are themes that run through the episodes. In all five, Sampson suffered severe hardships: she was under fire twice; she was wounded; twice she froze, crossing an icy river or tramping through snow. She clearly was in a hazardous service. Mann's narrative is suffused, however, with the prime stereotype of suffering American soldiers: blood in the snow. Bloody footprints in the snow were of course possible—shoes were often in short supply, even in this well-equipped army. But the narrative caters to the public image of the army at Valley Forge.[40]

Putting aside Mann's fantasies, stripping away his literary additions, and allowing for his jumbling of events, places, and names, in their core form, four episodes fit on the template. They allow us to say this about Sampson as Shurtliff: (1) she was in actions entirely consistent with light infantry service in Westchester County at this stage of the war; (2) she was an active member of her company, who spent a major part of her time either "on the lines" (in which she resembled Private Barrett) or "on the scout" (in which she resembled Lieutenant Gilbert); (3) she was in a number of incidents involving civilians in rural settings (a house, a barn, a ferry crossing) in which she confronted Tories pretending to be patriots, consistent with the civil war in Westchester where, as James Fenimore Cooper wrote, "all wore masks"; (4) she was in two engagements in which there was an exchange of fire and soldiers were killed or wounded, in one of which she was wounded; and (5) she stood out as a soldier who volunteered and took the initiative.

The senior officers whose knowledge lay behind the New York newspaper article of 1784 accepted her claims because they knew what service in the light infantry was like. They knew the kind of actions a member of Captain Webb's company would have taken part in, even if they did not know the specifics. As a soldier, she was credible to them. She should be credible to us.

Chapter Five

The General's Waiter

I F   D E B O R A H   S A M P S O N   spent 1782 passing as an infantryman in the rank-and-file world of enlisted men in the field, she spent most of 1783 pursuing her deception in the world of officers from the vantage point of a "waiter" to a leading general. She was so successful she was not discovered until she was at death's door in a Philadelphia military hospital. What happened after this is unclear. In Herman Mann's dubious telling of her adventures, after she was nursed back to health by a benevolent doctor, she had a romance with a beautiful young heiress and went on a journey of wild adventures among Indians in western Pennsylvania. The romance is possible but unlikely; the journey is not at all credible. Her adventures as a general's waiter offer more clues to her deception. At the end of October 1783, she was discharged at West Point to the applause of her officers as a double success: both as a "good & loyal" soldier and as a woman able to disguise herself as a soldier.

1. *A Waiter*
"My old friend," General Paterson

"For several months," the newspaper account of 1784 reported, "she served with credit as a waiter in a General officer's family." The claim was accurate:

the officer was General John Paterson, a prominent general in the Hudson Highlands; "waiter" was a military term for an officer's servant or orderly; the "several months" were in 1783, very likely from late winter or early spring into the fall. A general officer's "family" was a term embracing the staff officers, waiters, and civilian servants attached to the headquarters of a senior officer: a general or a colonel. The experience opened up a world closed to most enlisted men and had a lasting impact on Sampson. Twenty years later, on her lecture tour, she made an arduous 125-mile detour from the Hudson Valley to visit Paterson at his estate on the distant New York State frontier, where she was his guest for a month. In the diary kept on the tour, she referred to him as "my old friend."[1]

The Mann/Gannett narrative portrayed the appointment as a promotion, a step up in Deborah's quest for recognition. This clearly is a theme of her wartime experiences. What began, however, as a protective strategy—to give an outstanding performance as a soldier and win approval to ward off suspicion—took on a life of its own. She had a compelling need in the army to prove herself. Mann as narrator had a need to portray her as a heroine who rose above the average soldier.

One thread in the narrative of the military episodes of 1782 already encountered is that she volunteered. Another is that she was promoted, or considered for promotion. Mann's text is explicit: "she did her duty, sometimes as a common soldier, and sometimes as a sergeant." At another point, he speaks of her as promoted in the field: "by reason of the absence of a non-commissioned officer she was appointed to supply his place." Mann placed this at Yorktown, a fiction, but it could have taken place elsewhere. In his appendix he added, "she never would accept a promotion in the army; though it is said, she was urged to take a Lieutenant's commission." All this is possible, even allowing for the joint need of both storytellers to magnify her role.[2]

Mann also insists that she was awarded an honor. He asserts flat out that "the honorary badge of distinction, as established by Gen. Washington, had been conferred on her, but for what particular exploit, I cannot say," a modest confession of ignorance so rare in his narrative as to be winning. There is no record of any award to her, but, then again, there is no general listing of soldiers given awards during the Revolutionary War. In the summer of 1782, Washington instituted three forms of recognition for the rank and file: chevrons for men enlisted for the duration (one for each three years); a cloth badge with a purple heart for "any singularly meritorious action" (awarded, as far as we know, to only three sergeants in 1783); and an "honorary badge," which could be awarded for meritorious service in general and was supposed to be recorded in a Book of Merit. Of these three, the last, if anything, is what she could have been awarded, but the Book of Merit is lost.[3]

There is no doubt that General Paterson "selected her as his waiter," and possibly it was after "he had previously become acquainted with her heroism and fidelity," as Mann put it. It may also be that he was attracted by "her martial deportment blended with the milder graces and vivacity of her sex and youth," in other words, her blend of masculine and feminine qualities. An enlisted man hardly had to be either a hero or handsome, however, for an officer to choose him as a waiter. Undersized boys were often candidates for the job. The army did not record the names of the literally thousands of soldiers who became orderlies, and there is no entry for waiter in Robert Shurtliff's incomplete service record; but the fact that the 1784 newspaper report written by an officer refers to her service "in a General officer's family" speaks loudly. So does her reference to Paterson on her visit to him in 1803 as "my old friend."[4]

She served as Paterson's waiter a good part of 1783. Mann dated the appointment as April 1, 1783, but in his revised manuscript he placed it "directly after our return to headquarters" from the expedition to northern New York, which he dated as January 1, 1783. So she may have begun earlier in the year; judging by events, she was in Paterson's service for at least six months. She would have been with him at the New Windsor encampment, where he signed one order "Commander of the Left Wing of the Newburgh Cantonment." In June, when the encampment was broken up, she would have moved with him to West Point to his new headquarters in "the red house" on the plains, which General Henry Knox assigned to him at his request. "I prefer a house to myself," Paterson had written. He had clout.[5]

The Revolution forced the "better sort" to show more deference to their "inferiors." "Waiter" may well be an American euphemism, elevating the status of a military servant in the same way that the designations "help" and "hired man" were preferred to "servant" by civilian servants late in the eighteenth century. No one caught the implications of this vocabulary better than the New England lawyer and former officer Royall Tyler in his enormously popular play, *The Contrast,* first performed in New York City in 1787. A major character was Jonathan, a Yankee farm boy who serves as a waiter to

Colonel Manly, an American officer. When Jessamy, a French-born servant, says to him, "I understand that Colonel Manly has the honour of having you as a servant," Jonathan is furious: "Servant, Sir, do you take me for a neger,— I am Colonel Manley's waiter."[6]

Mann was also concerned about the humbling implications "waiter" may have had for his readers, so, in reprinting the 1784 newspaper article in his appendix in 1797, he excised the words "as a waiter" to make the sentence read, "she served with credit in a General Officer's family." In his narrative, Mann implied that a waiter was an "aide," which elevated the position further. In his 1830s manuscript, he moved her status up still another notch, calling her an "aide de camp." But a waiter was not in the least an aide-de-camp, who was always a commissioned officer. Colonel Alexander Hamilton had been an aide-de-camp to General Washington. Earlier, Captain Elinathan Haskell was Paterson's aide; Lieutenant Edward Phelan was his aide during part of the time that Sampson was his waiter.[7]

Her duties would have varied. She could have been the general's body servant, taking care of his clothes, helping him to dress, and cleaning his boots. She might literally have waited on his table, serving food and drink for him and his guests—senior officers commonly entertained junior officers. Wives might have been present. She might have prepared food; she could have brought his laundry to a "washerwoman" attached to the regiment. And she might very well have served as a courier delivering Paterson's orders in a far-flung encampment. It was a job with some status. A soldier acting as a waiter for a highly ranked officer, the military historian Charles Niemeyer observes, "did have some weight regardless of conferred rank. Acting in his name, a soldier could have requests obeyed even by officers." This certainly is Sampson's frame of mind conveyed by the narrative; she thrived on the prestige of association with a general.[8]

At the end of the war, the sheer number of military servants at West Point had become a scandal. A servant was one of the perks of senior officers bolstering their class status. By January 1782, however, a high-ranking officer at West Point reported there were "not less than . . . one thousand soldiers employed as waiters on officers," all "taken out" of military service. A mild reform about this time, possibly in response to this criticism, limited servants to officers of the line. Paterson, as a brigadier general, was entitled to four, which meant Deborah had other servants for company.[9]

John Paterson, in the army since 1777, was the kind of gentleman Deborah Sampson had never encountered in Middleborough: a Yale graduate, a lawyer, and in the judgment of as knowledgeable a political leader as John Adams, "a Good Officer of a liberal Education ingenious and sensible." Paterson was one of the gentry in Berkshire County who had tried to tame the Revolution in tumultuous western Massachusetts (and would return to play a similar role in suppressing the rebellion named after Captain Daniel Shays). In his mansion in Lenox, he was accustomed to servants, including a slave, Agrippa Hull, whom he took with him into the army as a private. "Grippy" served as his body servant until 1779.[10]

Paterson, who had served at the battles of Boston, Trenton, Saratoga, and Monmouth, and in

Brigadier General John Paterson. The drawing, a heroic pose taken from a tablet at the battle monument at Monmouth, New Jersey, is based on a miniature portrait and appears as the frontispiece to a biography by a descendant. Courtesy The Newberry Library, Chicago.

the last years of the war was intermittently in command of West Point, was obviously held in high trust by Washington. He was also respected by his fellow officers, who elected him Grand Master of their Masonic lodge and an officer in the Society of the Cincinnati. When he migrated to western New York in the 1790s and became a large land proprietor, he practiced a paternalism that bent to the democratic ways of Yankees on the frontier. A Federalist in Massachusetts, he was elected to Congress in 1802 as a Republican. Six feet one and a half inches tall, with an athletic build, he was, in the eyes of a modern biographer, "a man of commanding presence." Indeed, he could have been a prototype for the upright "Colonel Manly" in Royall Tyler's play: stern, republican, and a benevolent defender of veterans. He was one of

A reconstructed hut at the New Windsor encampment above West Point in which Sampson lived with six to eight men for part of the winter of 1782–83. Theresa Ramppen Gaydos reenacts Deborah Sampson. Photograph, 1995, by William E. Fulton.

those officers who took seriously the admonition in von Steuben's manual to "win the love of his men." He clearly won Deborah over. Thirty-eight years old in 1783 when she was twenty-three, he may have been something of a father figure for a girl who had grown up without a father.[11]

Deborah probably wangled an appointment from Paterson as waiter because it rescued her from the perils of the close quarters at New Windsor. The snug huts which served as living quarters for enlisted men from November 1782 until June 1783 were described by the French general, the marquis de Chastellux, as "spacious, healthy and well built and consist in a row of 'log houses' containing two rooms, each inhabited by eight soldiers when full, which commonly means five or six men in actual fact." Each was 35 by 18 feet, divided into two rooms by a wall in the middle with bunks built into the walls and a large stone fireplace at either end for cooking and heat. Paterson thought the huts were "the best erected this war."[12]

When I walked into a reconstructed hut at New Windsor—low, window-less, with little room to move around—the meaning of "close quarters" hit me. Imagine, in the long northern winter with two feet of snow on the ground after mid-December, six to eight people living here cheek-by-jowl, sleeping, cooking, taking mess together, huddling around the fire, gambling, telling stories. Was it possible for a woman to maintain her disguise in such quarters? My second thought, after I learned more about the common practices for hygiene and sanitation in the army, was that it was somewhat possible. My third thought was that while deception was possible in this setting, the risks were high, and she made every effort to get out. The experience, John Shy observes, was also "a threat to her modesty and femininity—five or six male companions talking, swearing, farting, drinking, puking (all suggested by Lieutenant Benjamin Gilbert's experience). In the winter a pot may have been used for pissing." All this also lends some credibility to episode five in the previous chapter, the story of her volunteering for an expedition to northern New York in the winter of '83, and on her return, seizing an opportunity to become Paterson's servant—or perhaps making one.[13]

Idle soldiers holed up in winter quarters whiling away their time playing cards or pitching buttons would have been bored, restless, and curious. The army put them to work foraging for food, cutting down trees, building roads, and erecting the "Temple of Virtue," a huge assembly hall. "The timber was cut and drawn together by the soldiers, and mostly sawn by hand," Mann wrote. "Our Heroine worked against any hardy soldier. . . . In its raising, a joist fell and carried her from a considerable height to the ground," injuring her nose and ankle—a possible event. She probably got away with living in a hut at New Windsor because she did not live there very long and because she got out of quarters as much as she could.[14]

Appointment as a waiter set her apart physically from her fellow infantrymen. If a contemporary drawing of the village of almost seven hundred huts has it right, the light infantry would have been assigned huts on the left flank of the regiment. Today, the site where she might have lived with enlisted men is marked, but not the building where she might have lived with Paterson, probably a short distance away. The general had a more spacious hut; officers' huts, Lieutenant Gilbert thought, were big enough for a country dance.[15]

Serving as a waiter at a general's headquarters also set her apart psychologically. She had more creature comforts than enlisted men. She doubtless slept on a bed, and, if so, more than likely shared it on occasion with men, perhaps other servants. She did not take mess with class-conscious officers, but she doubtless ate more and better food than in the huts. Mann spoke of her riding a horse belonging to "Captain Phelon," Paterson's aide, when hers was lame and his available, a possibility. If she was a courier, she would have needed a horse to get around a large camp.[16]

She would have seen an array of officers: genteel, conservative New England men of a republican bent like Paterson and Colonel Henry Jackson; aristocrats like General Robert Howe, a slaveholding rice planter from South Carolina; junior officers like Lieutenant Benjamin Gilbert, who had scrambled up from the ranks. Paterson's headquarters was a good vantage point to observe the comings and goings of an officer class of gentlemen and would-be gentlemen. She would have seen them on military business as well as their own political business, organizing petitions to Congress and forming a Masonic order and a chapter of the Cincinnati. She would have heard about officers who fought duels, nursing their exaggerated sense of honor. She also would have gotten a glimpse of their high living: dining, drinking heavily, and bragging about their exploits in a "seraglio" a few miles from New Windsor. In 1783, Lieutenant Gilbert recorded no less than fourteen overnight visits to this brothel in the company of fellow officers.[17]

In the spring of 1783, she would have experienced life in the army as a strange mixture of tension and relaxation. She saw agitated officers at the height of their political activity. From the fall of '82 through March '83, the leading officers were in the thick of an intensive campaign to increase their government pensions: committees, petitions, fiery manifestos, a delegation to Congress. Paterson was a leading signer on every petition. Audaciously, the officers threatened to keep the army in the field after the peace treaty was adopted if Congress did not meet their demands. Washington, at a dramatic confrontation with several hundred officers who jammed the "Temple of Virtue" on March 15, 1783, called their bluff and the officers backed off, basically because their threats were hollow without the support of enlisted men. The "Newburgh Conspiracy," as it was later called, was as much an officers' rebellion as any mutiny by enlisted men, which the same officers put down in blood. For a woman excluded from the public sphere, the officers' campaign for pensions was a dramatic civics lesson she would not forget; she would spend more than twenty years campaigning for her own pension.[18]

Then, early in the spring of 1783, it was all over—or so it seemed. On March 26, news arrived that the peace treaty had been signed. On March 27, the officers celebrated. On March 28, "the joy of the soldiers was so great that they caroused all night," Lieutenant Gilbert reported, and on the 29th they "continued marching, Huzzahing and drinking all day." In mid-April, after Congress's proclamation of a cessation of hostilities arrived, there were solemn ceremonies at the "Temple": a concert, prayer, an anthem, and a toast by Washington to a lasting peace. Deborah must have been present through these festivities, but Mann's silence suggests either she did not join in the drunken revelry in which she might lose control of her masquerade; or she did, in which case it was not something to write about in a book about a proper heroine.[19]

In June 1783, the war officially over, the duration-of-the-war soldiers were discharged under the guise of a furlough, without a settlement for their back pay. Disbanded, they had little power to sway Congress. "There was policy in government," a politically astute sergeant like Joseph Plumb Martin recognized; "to discharge us in our present, pitiful, forlorn condition, it was feared, might cause some difficulties which might be too hard for government to get easily over." Solders were furloughed, Lieutenant Gilbert wrote, with nothing "but poverty in their pockets"; not one man in twenty had "a single farthing." "Where is the justice?" he asked. (He had once been a private and sergeant.) Meanwhile, the "three year men" who had enlisted in '81 or '82 had to stay on. In the first two weeks of June, the New England regiments were regrouped according to their home areas, given rations, and marched home under the command of officers, a politically safe dispersal. The army at West Point shrank from a grand total of 11,797 in March to 2,760 in June. Sampson, the waiter, moved with General Paterson into his new quarters at West Point.[20]

Then came a shock. On June 24, Washington received a frantic plea from the president of Congress to suppress another mutiny of the Pennsylvania line in Philadelphia, so he dispatched fifteen hundred troops to the capital, half of them under the command of General Paterson. For Deborah, the war was not over; in fact, terror lay ahead.

2. A Rescue
"The death-like doors of the hospital in Philadelphia"

In the summer of 1783, for Deborah Sampson the near paradise of "a general officer's family" turned into the hell of a Philadelphia army hospital. The melodramatic account in Mann's memoir—Sampson hovering near death in the Philadelphia hospital, Sampson "discovered" and rescued by "Dr. Bana," Sampson nursed back to health in his home, after which she had a romance with "the nymph of Baltimore"—I first placed in the category of the unlikely, with a heavy touch of fantasy. Gradually, I moved the hospital part of the story from unlikely to likely, leaving the romance in limbo, to which I will return.

Here is the hospital part of the story in Mann's narrative. In the summer of 1783, he wrote, "a detachment of 1500 men was ordered to march to Philadelphia from West Point for the suppression of a mutiny in the Pennsylvania line." Sampson, still a waiter to Paterson, "did not go till four days after the General left West Point. She rode in company with four gentlemen [officers]" through the Jerseys. Arriving outside Philadelphia, "she then found the troops encamped on a hill. . . . Here she had frequent occasion to visit the city, sometimes on business," where "the gentility of her dress and agreeable mien gained her access to company of both sexes of rank and elegance."[21]

An "epidemic disorder raged in the city," however; Sampson quickly succumbed and was "carried once more to the hospital," where "death itself could scarcely have presented a more gloomy prospect." "Multitudes were daily carried to Potter's Field" (the burial grounds for the friendless poor). "She begged not to be left in the loathsome bunks of soldiers. Accordingly she was lodged in a third loft, where were two other officers of the same line, who soon died." She was "alone in her wretchedness" except for "Doctor BANA and the Matron Mrs. PARKER whose solicitude she remembers with gratitude."

She fell unconscious, and "the inhuman sextons" prepared to remove her body for burial. "One JONES, the only English nurse, at that instant coming in," Sampson "once more rallied . . . and gave signs of life." The ghoulish undertakers withdrew and Jones informed the matron. "Doctor BANA at that instant entered; and putting his hand in her bosom to feel her pulse, was surprised to find an inner waistcoat tightly compressing her breasts. Ripping it in haste, he was still more shocked, not only on finding life, but the breasts and other tokens of a *female*." He ordered her removed to the matron's apartment, where she was "treated with all the care that art and expense could bestow."

The doctor then made her a "welcome guest" in his family, where she recuperated, continuing to dress in uniform as Robert Shurtliff. The doctor informed neither Sampson nor anyone else that he knew her gender. There ensued a romance with "a young lady of the suburbs of Baltimore, beautiful in form, with a well cultivated mind and a fortune." In her 1802 address, Deborah Sampson Gannett summed up this Philadelphia hospital experience in one short, enigmatic sentence: "Nor need I point you to the death-like doors of the hospital in Philadelphia whose avenues were crowded with the sick, the dying and the dead, though I myself made one of the unhappy crowd."[22]

Mann wrote a little Gothic tale worthy of the American novelist Charles Brockden Brown, who in *Arthur Mervyn* (1799–1800) captured similar horrors of the plague that later gripped Philadelphia. It is easy to punch holes in Mann's Philadelphia story. Take the claim that Robert Shurtliff, while recovering at the doctor's home, escorted his "discreet and amiable daughters" around town. The doctor's children—one a boy, one a girl—were ages two and four at the time. Mann had a penchant for invention; he also did not know when to leave a good story alone.[23]

As my research into the event unfolded—into the military context, the medical history of the city, and the cast of characters at the hospital—the hospital part of the Philadelphia story took on life.[24]

First, the military context. There was, indeed, a mutiny of the Pennsylvania line in June 1783, and Washington sent most of his depleted army from West Point to suppress it, unnecessarily, as it turned out. The mutiny was the result of Congress's decision to discharge enlisted men without providing for their back pay. "We will not accept your furloughs and demand a settlement," read the manifesto of the politicized soldiers in Lancaster. In mid-June, some seventy of them marched on Philadelphia, where they were joined by several hundred more already in the city. As Dr. James Thacher heard the story at West Point, there were "about three hundred in the whole," and "with fixed bayonets and drums beating," they marched to the State House (today's Independence Hall), the building which then housed Pennsylvania's Executive Council as well as the Continental Congress. They posted "sentinels at every door . . . and threatened to let loose an enraged soldiery." Although their target was the state government, Elias Boudinot, the president of Congress, interpreted the action as menacing Congress. The state militia was unreliable. Congress ordered Washington to send troops and then adjourned to the safety of Princeton, New Jersey.[25]

It was a perilous moment. "Furloughing" had brought the army at West Point down to 2,760 men, of whom 1,753 were fit for service. On June 24,

Washington, receiving news of what he branded an "infamous and outrageous mutiny," ordered three regiments, "all Men of tried fidelity," to march at once through New Jersey to Philadelphia. He was furious, contrasting "the arrogance, the folly and the wickedness of the Mutineers" with "the fidelity, the bravery and patriotism" of other veteran soldiers who went home "without the settlement of their accounts or a farthing of money in their pockets." He placed in command General Robert Howe, who, two years before, had put down a mutiny in the New Jersey line in blood.[26]

As it turned out, in June 1783 there was no need for military force. The Pennsylvania soldiers were willing to accept half-pay and the rest in certificates, and by June 25, they dissolved. On July 1, Boudinot informed Washington that the mutiny had been "quelled," but insisted that the troops continue on to Philadelphia as a show of force. The loyal soldiers were being deployed in a politically inspired law-and-order demonstration.

General Paterson, commanding a brigade, accompanied his troops to Philadelphia. When they arrived at camp outside the city, the rebellion had evaporated. Paterson then spent July and August presiding over the courts-martial that sentenced two sergeants to death by hanging and four privates to the lash (Congress later pardoned the sergeants). Over the summer, he was in and out of the city, honored in July, for example, at what the *Pennsylvania Gazette* called "an elegant entertainment at the State House" for the generals, their saviours. In all, General Paterson spent almost three months in the Philadelphia area; he was ordered to return to West Point on September 25.[27]

Deborah could have been in the Philadelphia area all this time. She loyally followed Paterson from West Point to the army camp a few days after he left. It was a chaotic moment at West Point: the main army had been sent home and the regrouped light infantry units had been posted to Westchester to preserve order; on the heels of this came news of the mutiny. She could just as easily have decamped and no one would have stopped her. Why didn't she? She was under orders, she was attached to her general (in both senses), and she was not going to miss out on a chance to see the capital city of the United States. (Recall, Mann said it was one of her goals when she left Middleborough.) Once in Philadelphia, she may have accompanied Paterson, but could easily have moved about town on her own until she was stricken.[28]

Second, the medical context. A medical crisis in the city lends further credence to the episode. An epidemic of smallpox and measles raged in

Philadelphia early in the summer of 1783. General Howe quarantined soldiers to the camp outside town because "so great a number of the troops" had not had "these disorders." For all of Washington's efforts to inoculate soldiers at the end of the war, smallpox was still a disease dreaded in the army. No one claimed Sampson came down with its telltale signs, but measles, a debilitating disease in adults, was a possibility. Whatever the source of the infection, she seems to have been delirious with a fever.[29]

Third, the hospital scene and cast of characters. Two of the three people named in the account can be established as in the employ of a military hospital in Philadelphia in 1783. "Dr. Bana" is Dr. Barnabas Binney, army surgeon, and "Matron Parker" is Mary Parker, matron of the hospital and an army employee. The army hospital, in a way, was hidden. Early in the war, the army set up a number of hospitals in Philadelphia, taking over existing buildings. One was in "the eastern" or "the southeast wing" of the Philadelphia Alms House or Bettering House, as it was also called, which the army leased intermittently from its Quaker managers. If the army kept records of patients housed there, these have not survived, but few military hospitals did. The records of the government's payment of rent, on the other hand, are clear proof that in 1783 this building was used as an army hospital, the only one in the city so late in the war.[30]

Dr. Barnabas Binney and Matron Mary Parker served in this hospital. In September 1782, when Dr. Thacher, the army surgeon, traveled from West Point to Philadelphia, he dined with his friend, "Dr. Benney of the hospital"; other records listed him as "Benning." Obviously, people had trouble with the name. The fact that Mann mangled the spelling as "Bana" suggests he took it down phonetically from Sampson. The name was of French origin, pronounced "Be-ane." In Boston, Apollos Rivoire, Paul's father, said the "Bumpkins" also had trouble with his French name before he anglicized it to Revere.[31]

Binney was listed as "hospital physician and surgeon" in the military records. Doctors were not given military ranks; they were simply attached to the army and drew a salary and provisions. They might wear a uniform—a miniature portrait of Binney by Charles Willson Peale depicts him in a suit that resembles a uniform. Any number of official records establish him as a physician or surgeon in the army from mid-1776 to early 1784, and place him in Philadelphia and at the Philadelphia hospital in 1783 and 1784.[32]

"Matron" was the correct title for the director of nursing in a hospital;

earlier, the Pennsylvania hospital advertised in the papers specifically for a "matron." And "Mary Parker, Matron" appears in 1781 on the same page with Dr. Binney in the "Return of Officers &c in the Genl Hospital of the United States" under the heading: "Where stationed & c Philadelphia, attending ye sick in Jail &c." Moreover, the Philadelphia Directory for 1785 lists three different women under "Parker, widow." Nursing was a common occupation for widows, who had few other economic opportunities. The third person in Mann's account, "One JONES," identified by him as "the only English nurse," if a woman, could have been one of five women listed as "Jones, widow" in the 1785 city directory. Conceivably, she was Rosanna Jones, listed as "Widow, Nurse for the sick" in a later directory.[33]

Mann, of course, was quite capable of throwing in names to add verisimilitude, but he usually did not invent people out of thin air, and he had too much imagination to make up so common a name as Jones. He got these names from Mrs. Gannett. Binney and Parker (and possibly Jones) were identifiable people attached to the army's Philadelphia hospital, and it is hard to imagine how Mrs. Gannett would have known these names had she not been a patient there, or how else Mann could have gotten them.

Dr. Barnabas Binney is very credible as a medical saviour. Born in Boston in 1751, in 1774 he was an honors graduate of Rhode Island College (later Brown University) and a man of humane, liberal views. A Baptist, his commencement oration was on "the right of private judgment in religious matters." After war broke out, he went to Philadelphia, attended Dr. Benjamin Rush's medical lectures at the University of Pennsylvania, and became a physician. He served the army through 1784, almost all that time in Philadelphia, and in the last years of the war was a senior surgeon in the army medical service. Binney died in 1787, leaving a wife and two small children, one of whom, Horace Binney, would become a luminary in the Philadelphia bar.[34]

The Binney family accepted the story of their ancestor rescuing Deborah. They knew it as it came down, not via Mann, but via Elizabeth Ellet, in whose sketch of Sampson the rescue is followed by a romance of Robert Shurtliff with Binney's *niece*. According to the family genealogist, "a son of Dr. Binney [Horace?] wrote that the first part of the story [about the rescue] is probably true, there was a tradition to that effect in the family, but the story of the niece is not true," a reassuring skepticism. The only other anecdote the family passed down about Binney as an army doctor supports his reputation as a humane rescuer. He once encountered a soldier left for dead after

Dr. Barnabas Binney *(1751–1787), Deborah Sampson's medical saviour, in a watercolor on ivory by Charles Willson Peale, painted after the war by the since famous Philadelphia artist. Courtesy The Society of the Cincinnati Museum, Washington, DC.*

battle "near the abandoned pile of men laid aside for burial. He thought he perceived signs of life in one of the heaps, [and] upon examination he discovered that the subject had been cut with a sabre lengthwise down the abdomen and that the bowels had been let loose." Binney sewed him up; "the soldier lived for many years . . . became a farmer," and brought him a present of "a fine cheese, a barrel or two of cider or apples." The story obviously stuck in family lore because of the veteran's gifts, which the family shared.[35]

Thus, for this fantastic, macabre hospital episode, the pieces of the jigsaw puzzle come together—the Pennsylvania mutiny, the Philadelphia epidemic, the hospital in the alms house, Dr. Binney and Matron Parker as the medical personnel—to make the episode more than likely. They support the summary by the officers in the 1784 newspaper article: "a violent illness (when the troops were at Philadelphia) led to the discovery of her sex." They also support the recollection set down in 1827 by Calvin Munn, Sampson's sergeant, who was so skeptical about Mann's tale of her earlier wound. Munn admitted he left the army in June 1783, so he did not have firsthand knowledge of the Philadelphia episode, but he obviously had followed her army history. The matter-of-fact way in which he told what he knew about her lends credence to his account:

I taught her the first rudiments of military discipline, and was very well acquainted with her until I left the army in June 1783. After that she went to Philadelphia with the army, fell very sick, was deranged, and by her symptoms was discovered to be a female.[36]

What followed is another story, far less credible.

3. A Romance
"The nymph of Maryland" and the Captive Bride

What happened to Deborah Sampson from the time Dr. Binney found out she was a woman sometime in the summer of 1783 until she was discharged at the end of October? If she took sick, say, in June, when there was an epidemic, and recovered in August, we still have two months to account for: September and October. Perhaps she needed a long recuperation. In his brief remembrance of Sampson, Sergeant Munn had one more thing to say, which turns out to be the only clue (aside from Mann's narrative) to what may have happened. Following her rescue in a Philadelphia hospital, he wrote, "she was after that protected by the officers who she served under, discharged and sent home to her friends."

What would "protected by the officers" mean? The simplest scenario to fit this might be as follows: General Paterson was in the Philadelphia area all summer, until late September, in charge of the trials of the mutineers. Dr. Binney informed the general in person of his discovery of the true gender of his waiter. When she recovered, she rejoined Paterson (either in Philadelphia or at West Point), who confided in a few senior officers like Colonel Jackson, who kept her secret. (Captain Webb had left the army.) She continued as his servant until he arranged for her discharge at West Point by General Knox on October 23. This may be all there is to Sergeant Munn's comment.

Something else *may* have happened: a romance. The Mann narrative filled these months with the most extravagant adventures in the entire book, for which his account is the only source and for which he does not provide enough data to test. Two and a half chapters are devoted to an affair of Robert Shurtliff with "the nymph of Maryland," followed by a long journey through Indian country in "the savage wilderness" in which one outlandish adventure is piled on top of another. The heroine is then transported back to a reunion with the maiden, after which the "two lovers" tearfully part and Sampson proceeds to West Point and a suspenseful scene of discharge.[37]

These two sets of adventures offer almost no tangible clues to probe. The woman is identified only as "a young lady of the suburbs of Baltimore" or "the nymph of Maryland," and in his 1830s manuscript, as "Elizabeth P—" or "the amiable Miss P." (a convention in eighteenth-century fiction). She is idyllic: "about seventeen," "beautiful in form with a well cultivated mind," and to top it all, heir to a fortune.[38] For the western adventures, Sampson is alleged to be in the company of "Forkson and Graham" of Philadelphia, said to be interested in "the discovery of minerals," and of a "Colonel Tupper." The first two could not be identified; Benjamin Tupper was a prominent officer at New Windsor. His land speculations in the Ohio Company were well known in postwar New England, but he did not go west to survey land until 1785. The Indians in the story are not identified, and while Mann names identifiable rivers, mountain ranges, and roads, readers are as lost in the wilderness of western Pennsylvania as were his characters.[39]

The journey through Indian country is a kaleidoscope of horrors, sheer fantasy. The Indians, nameless and tribeless, conform to all the negative stereotypes perpetuated by captivity narratives: they are cruel, warlike, treacherous, and cannibalistic. The setting is a wilderness of dense forests, fast-running rivers, mysterious caves, and Indian villages.[40] The sheer accumulation of incidents on this trip makes the tale preposterous. Natives in "warlike array" capture the travelers. The Indians are cannibals. The king threatens to eat "the *boy*" (i.e., Deborah). To win time, she pleads to be fattened first and joins in their wild ceremonies. She goes on a hunting party and kills an Indian who crawls toward her in the night with a hatchet. She saves a captive white woman from being burnt at the stake by marrying her, but foregoes the rites of marriage, preserving her "virgin purity." Miraculously, Sampson's former traveling companions reappear, and they all return to Baltimore and civilization. The adventures echo the most popular captivity narrative of the 1790s, by one "Abraham Panther," replete with a cave, a captive maiden, the threat of a sexual assault, and a rescue.[41]

The romance is as if from a picaresque novel. For the maiden, it is love at her first sight of Robert Shurtliff. When she learns he is hospitalized in Philadelphia, she sends him a letter confessing her love but concealing her identity. Later in Baltimore, when "the lovers" meet, she reveals herself and "rehearsed her plaint of love with great delicacy and refinement." Deborah wavers but "*doubtless* embraced the celestial maid," promising to return after her journey west. In the denouement of the affair, the maid reveals that "she was quickly come into the possession of an ample fortune," which could be his. Deborah "burst into tears." Unable either to confess her gender or break with her, she promises to return the following spring, "if health should permit." The maiden "made her a present of six holland shirts, twenty five guineas and an elegant silver watch. . . . Thus parted two lovers more *singular* if not more constant than perhaps ever distinguished Columbia's soil." Nothing erotic transpired between them, yet Mann teases his readers to imagine what did not occur, reassuring them that Sampson as a woman had an anatomical incapacity for sexual intercourse with another female.

Such a romance could have happened. In 1850, Elizabeth Ellet called it "another of those romances in real life which in strangeness surpass fiction." Or it could also be another example of Mann and/or Deborah borrowing a ploy from the adventures of Hannah Snell, who also had a love affair while in uniform and did not reveal her identity. A romance between two women in late-eighteenth-century America was possible, not unheard of, and not something that would have damaged a woman's reputation. Mann's Philadelphia story, however, may be more revealing of the author and his sense of his readers' expectations than of Deborah Sampson. In American society, ardent friendships between women were becoming more apparent among circles of educated literate women. Late-twentieth-century scholars who have read their letters and diaries have discovered that friendship and love between women could be intense, passionate, and seen through our eyes, sexual. Such friendships, as Carroll Smith-Rosenberg writes, were "socially acceptable and fully compatible with heterosexual marriage."[42]

A woman falling for a soldier was, of course, a cultural stereotype: soldiers flirted with women and women fell for men in uniform. In Royall Tyler's play *The Contrast,* the ingénue Maria says it is "a standing piece of raillery among the wits. A cockade, a lapell'd coat, and a feather, they tell you, are irresistible to a female heart." Moreover, "in almost every female warrior's story," Julie Wheelwright informs us, "a romantic entanglement" was common. Hannah Snell flirted, her memoir said, "to banish the least suspicion of her being a woman." Readers of Mann's memoir thus would not have been surprised at an affair between Sampson the soldier and a woman—indeed, they might have expected it.[43]

Contemporaries, however, seem to have been drawing a distinction between romantic friendships and what in England some were calling "Sapphism." Charles Brockden Brown, the prolific American novelist, made a romantic friendship between two women a central theme in *Ormond; or The Secret Witness* (1799). The greatest joy of Constantia and Sophie, friends since youth, was "in speaking their love" to each other. They spent nights together in the same bed, but the novelist felt he had to reassure his readers that nothing occurred "incompatible with purity and rectitude."[44]

Mann's portrayal of the Philadelphia romance is a perfect mirror of this dichotomy between "platonick love" and "animal love" (phrases he used). He not only insisted that an erotic exchange between the two did not happen but went out of his way to explain that it could not have happened because his heroine, as a woman, was "incapacitated" for sexual intercourse with someone of her own sex. In the 1830s, when he revised the memoir and could assume a potential readership for a sensationalized, sexualized literature, he turned the chaste romance of 1797 into a charged erotic encounter, which, had it ever been published, might have won him a place for the first American pornography depicting sex between two women. I don't believe either version of the romance. My guess is that, in the 1790s, Mrs. Gannett, from the safety of her status as a wife and mother, may have said something to Mann to the effect that women did not find her unattractive in uniform, and Mann gave himself license to fantasize the romance.[45]

4. A Discharge
"Can it be so!"

On October 25, 1783, Sampson was discharged from the army at West Point by General Henry Knox. A certificate from Colonel Henry Jackson, commander of her regiment, issued in 1786, attests that Robert Shurtliff was "honorably discharged." Sampson (as Mrs. Gannett) testified to the date in her successful petition to Massachusetts for back pay in 1792. She was "honorably discharged in writing which discharge is lost," she claimed in a petition of 1818 in which she remembered serving "until November 1783." All of this is superior evidence by standards of proof for military service at that time. Soldiers often received no discharge papers at all and it was an uncommon soldier who retained this scrap of paper, if he got one.[46]

The timing of the discharge at the tail end of the war is plausible. The war was formally over on September 25, when Congress accepted the peace treaty. At West Point, the remnant of the army was not officially disbanded until November 2, assembling the day after for the last time. The fact that in an 1818 petition Mrs. Gannett remembered serving "until November" was not a slip of memory, but rather a recollection of having lingered a week or so after her formal discharge for one of the last rituals of the war, for her an emotional event.[47] There was no question that West Point was the place of her discharge and Knox the discharging officer. Knox was the commanding officer at West Point after Washington left Newburgh late in August. She was not discharged by Washington, a claim later publicized by Elizabeth Ellet that crept into many other accounts (including an illustration of the general interviewing Sampson).[48]

Sampson's confrontation with Paterson as portrayed by Mann is melodramatic, complete with imagined dialogue. Yet an encounter of some sort between the two was likely. She was under his command. At some point he would have been told about her and he had to take some kind of action; there had to be some kind of confrontation. Judging by the fact that twenty years later she referred to him as "my old friend," in 1783 he was sympathetic and solicitous. But before she knew this, she had to hang in suspense waiting for his reaction. Mann's dramatized account is probably based on a kernel of emotional truth Mrs. Gannett conveyed: she was terrified about what would happen to her once her secret was revealed.

Mann did everything to heighten the suspense. On her return from Baltimore, he had her leaving Philadelphia for West Point as Robert Shurtliff with a sealed letter from Dr. Binney to Paterson revealing the realities. Crossing the Hudson, she was nearly drowned when a sudden storm swamped her vessel. She lost her baggage, money, and journal, all save the watch (a gift from the nymph), and a morocco wallet containing Binney's letter.[49]

At West Point, her appearance was a shock to her comrades, who thought she was dead. She presented Binney's letter to Paterson, withdrew, and then was summoned by him. Here the theatrical encounter ensued. The general praised her lavishly and asked, "Does that *martial attire* which now glitters on your body, conceal a *female form!*" She fainted and he revived her. "But an aspect of wildness was blended in her countenance. She prostrated herself at his feet, and begged her life." He gave her Binney's letter to read and again asked, "*Can it be so!*" And "she confessed herself—*a female.*" He then asked about her family and her reasons for enlisting. "She proceeded to give a succinct and true account," but "for the second time" asked "if her *life* would be spared!" He reassured her she was "safe while under his protection," would be rewarded for her "unrivalled achievements," and quickly discharged. If this dialogue is hard to believe, her fears are not.

This entire disclosure scene is imagined. Yet one hesitates before saying something *like* this could not have happened. The core of emotional truth in the story lies in Sampson's strong fear of dire punishment for her deception. What would happen to her if she were discovered? We can grasp her fears only in the context of army punishments. Would she be fined and jailed, the fate of Ann Bailey of Boston in 1777? Deborah may even have picked up the scuttlebutt that John Paterson at the time was colonel of the regiment that turned Bailey over to the courts.[50] Would she be whipped and humiliated? Public humiliation was at the heart of military justice. In February 1783, Private Thomas Steven was given one hundred lashes and stripped of his honorary badge for "using insulting language to Lt. Smith." In May, after the mutiny of the Connecticut line, Sergeant John Oakley was given one hundred lashes and ordered "drummed out of the army with a label on his back with the word mutiny on it." Over the summer of 1783, the benevolent General Paterson had presided over the courts-martial that sentenced two Pennsylvania mutineers to death. How many lashes would she receive? Would she be drummed out of camp? What label might be pinned on her?[51]

Women who violated military regulations were not spared. Sampson had seen a washerwoman tried for theft by Paterson (and exonerated). A prostitute might be made to run the gauntlet. In *The Female Soldier,* Hannah Snell bore up under a severe lashing, "her tender flesh cut and mangled by these scourgings," hiding her breasts even while she suffered "pains and agonies." Could Deborah do the same? Sampson's imagination must have played on such disciplinary horrors.[52]

The intensity of Sampson's year and a half in the army is hard to imagine. Lucy Flucker, who married Henry Knox early in the war and followed the young artillery officer into camp, "often remarked that she *lived* more in one year at this period of excitement, than in a dozen in ordinary life." Deborah could say the same of each week. No one could know the energy she poured into avoiding detection every moment of every day. Very early she hit on the successful strategy: her best hope of not being detected as a woman was to stand out as a soldier, a paradox. It was a strategy that required constant vigilance.[53]

How did she get away with the deception? In retrospect, it was a stroke of good fortune that she was chosen for the light infantry, the only active service at this point in the war where there was an opportunity to shine. The greater the danger from the enemy and the greater the tension, the more protected she was. Hence, it was another irony that the treacherous war of petty skirmishes in the neutral ground of Westchester—really a no-man's-land—was to her advantage. Danger evaporated distinctions of gender. The more risks she took, the less likely she would be suspect, or the more she would be exonerated if discovered.

In 1783, at New Windsor, it was another stroke of fortune that she was chosen to be a general's waiter. The more she met with the approval of her senior officers, the less cause for suspicion, or if she were caught, she might have reasoned, the greater the chance of sympathetic treatment. She achieved a measure of control over her military life, something few soldiers could boast of. The strategy worked. When she was discovered, she was "protected by the officers who she served under," as Sergeant Munn put it.

Would some soldiers have seen through her masquerade? In other armies, "passing" women occasionally became known to men, who accepted them and covered up for them. In Middleborough, the memories collected by Granville Temple Sproat included one such story: "One day while she was in the army, she was waiting on a poor, wounded soldier. She spoke to him in such terms of kindness that he started back and exclaimed 'Bob Shurtliff, you are a woman! No man ever spoke in a tone like that.' Then seeing no doubt in her face the distress his remark had occasioned, said quickly, 'But never mind, Bob, your secret is safe; I will never betray you.' He never did." The story may be a folk version of Mann's episode of Deborah nursing the wounded Richard Snow (or perhaps vice versa).[54]

Playing the traditional female role of caretaker might have given her away to a few other soldiers. Not so playing a soldier in battle. Two other stories passed down in Middleborough speak to this. After the fierce skirmish at Tarrytown, when her unit was allegedly reinforced by troops led by Colonel Ebenezer Sproat, her tall rescuer did not recognize her even though he had seen her at work in the Sproat tavern "and they had sat down at the same table together." It was also said that for three weeks she lived undetected in the same tent with a son of the Morton family, "although he had often seen her before in her female attire" weaving in the family house.[55]

After the war, would any of her comrades have "remembered" Robert

Shurtliff when they learned he was she? After the Civil War, when Jennie Hodgers who served in the Illinois 95th as "Albert Cashier" was revealed, a comrade "remembered" that Hodgers's actions "seemed a little funny," that "she never seemed to have to shave or go to the toilet, that she did not want to have a bunkmate or to participate in sports or games with the other soldiers, that she was industrious and reserved." "We sometimes called him half and half." No soldier seems to have put into words anything like this about Sampson.[56]

Would she have been known to other women of the army? More women were attached to the regiments in the Hudson Valley in the last two years of the war than at any other time, and it does not require much effort to imagine one of the women she encountered as General Paterson's messenger recognizing her and even acting as her confederate. A woman was more likely than a man to see through her disguise, although a soldier was more likely to ignore it, if she was proven in the field as his comrade-in-arms. The narrative, however, offers not a hint of accomplices or friends; then again, in a desire to emphasize her heroism, it said next to nothing about her deception.[57]

The presence of women in camp dressed in women's clothes (perhaps wearing a piece or two of army clothing) provides still another clue as to how she got away with it. As a routine presence, women were a constant reminder to men that the other gender appeared in camp, not in uniform, but in the way women usually dressed, doing the things women customarily did, cooking, washing, tending to men's needs. For soldiers, such women were a distraction, in both senses of the word, visible reminders of what a woman was supposed to look like.

For all our analysis, that Deborah Sampson got away with it arouses a sense of wonder. General Paterson had good reason to ask, "Can it be so!" So do we.

5. *Applause*
"A faithful & good soldier"

After she was "discovered," Sampson was accepted by her officers and not punished as she feared. Why? She was found out *after* she had proven herself in military action, and when she was revealed in 1783, the war was over and the mood of the country was celebratory. Had she enlisted earlier in the var and been caught *before* she saw action, she may well have suffered the same fate as Ann Bailey and Anne Smith of Massachusetts in 1777 and been jailed, fined, and punished. Indeed, General John Paterson, Sampson's protector in 1783, as Colonel John Paterson in 1777 was commander of the regiment in which Ann Bailey was discovered and prosecuted. After six years of war, had he changed or had circumstances changed? Probably both.

In civilian life, when a woman who cross-dressed was detected, authority considered her a legitimate subject of inquiry. In Massachusetts, she was in violation of the law against dressing in a man's apparel and was assumed to have broken some other law. She might be suspect as a runaway servant, a minor fleeing home, or a fugitive from the law. When a woman wearing a uniform was detected in the army, it was obvious she was trying to be a soldier. The same could be said of a woman aboard a sailing vessel dressed Jack Tar–like; she was a would-be seaman or cabin boy. In other words, there was no need to probe into ulterior reasons for her masquerade. In the army, what then happened to her depended on whether she was caught before or after her military service.

Deborah Sampson was more than accepted on her discovery. She was celebrated. The words an officer used in the tribute to her in the 1784 newspaper article were not perfunctory and give us a large clue to her success. She "always gained the admiration and applause of her officers . . . she displayed herself with activity, alertness, chastity and valour," and she "was never found in liquor, and always kept company with the most upright and temperate soldiers." All this spoke worlds about the little appreciated cultural differences among soldiers; implicit in this praise was a comparison of Sampson to enlisted men officers considered typical. In the American army of 1782–83, which melted away in a sea of discontent, insubordination, and sheer indifference to the political cause of their officers, her superiors saw her as the quintessential "faithful & good soldier."

"Never found in liquor" may have made her an exception among enlisted men. The army dispensed rum as part of the soldier's food ration and gave out extra drink after fatiguing action and on occasions of celebration. Aside from this steady flow of authorized liquor, troops were plied with drink by camp sutlers. In the boredom of a winter encampment, heavy drinking was common.[58] "Always kept company with the most upright and temperate soldiers" recognized the gulf between pious and profane soldiers. In 1776, Washington, in endorsing the recruitment of army chaplains, hoped that every man in the army would "live and act as becomes a christian soldier." A year later, however, John Adams, with his customary candor, warned that "the Prevalence of Dissipation, Debauchery, Gambling, Profaneness and Blasphemy terrified the best people upon the continent from trusting their Sons and Relations" to the army. By 1782–83, very few recruits were sons of "the best people," and "christian soldiers" may have had to swim against the tide.[59]

A soldier who was temperate, chaste, and did not swear could not share the common rituals of enlisted men. Drinking, whoring, and swearing were exercised communally; they were ways in which soldiers bonded, and for the sixteen-, seventeen-, and eighteen-year-olds so numerous in the army in '82 and '83, they were rituals of manhood into which they were initiated by veterans in their twenties. Drinking in the army was an extension of the camaraderie of men who lifted a tankard in public houses in small towns or big cities. Deborah, who would have observed this way of life in Sproat's tavern in Middleborough, would have shunned drinking because it could lead to a loss of control. It was too dangerous.[60]

The same can be said of the implication in the word "upright" that she abstained from profanity. "Hell and damnation," a military doctor commented, "is in almost every ones mouth from the time they awake until they fall asleep again." Swearing was "the horrible national vice," which Washington lambasted as "foolish, unmeaning, scandalous, shocking, disgusting, wicked and abominable," but its very condemnation by their betters is what gave swearing its vitality among plebeians, and always has. "To both officers and soldiers," as the military historian Charles Royster remarks, "curses were a mark of toughness and bravado."[61]

No one spoke of Deborah Sampson, as they did of some other "women warriors," as surviving by imitating men's most macho behavior. Margaret Corbin, the wounded American artillery veteran who became a member of the Invalid Corps at West Point, was said to swear like a trooper, Mary McCauley, one of the claimants to the title "Molly Pitcher," was remembered in later years as "a very masculine person, alike rough in appearance and character . . . [who] could both drink whiskey and swear." No one said anything of the sort about Sampson, young or old.[62]

In identifying "chastity" as one of Sampson's virtues, contemporaries drew still another distinction among soldiers. It was not customary to single out a heroic young man of the army for this virtue. Army chaplains held it ut as an ideal, but they had to know they were fighting an uphill battle. Underlying the comment were several assumptions about the expression of sexuality in the Continental Army. One was that soldiers took sex whenever and wherever they could, patronizing prostitutes ("camp followers" in the invidious sense of the term). Sexually transmitted disease was considered a serious medical problem, especially when the army was stationed in or near cities. A second assumption was that soldiers were sexual predators who would have "ravished" Deborah Sampson had they found out she was a woman, especially as someone who implicitly mocked their masculinity. This, too, rested on an unfounded stereotype. Among several thousand soldiers who were court-martialed, a very small number were charged with rape. Civilian women did not live in fear of Continental soldiers the way they dreaded Redcoats or Hessians. Nowhere in Mann's account (or any other) is there a hint of a sexual advance against Deborah from a male.[63]

If everything her officers said about Deborah Sampson was true, she was a pious soldier who would have been alienated from her profane fellow soldiers. Perhaps the proof is negative. She could not tell her amanuensis, as Joseph Plumb Martin wrote in his memoir, "we had lived together as a family of brothers." Robert Shurtliff never became "one of the boys." If anything, she seems to have identified with her officers.[64]

Which brings us back to her officer's encomium, "she gained the applause and admiration of her officers." This is unusually strong praise. Colonel Jackson distilled what lay behind it when he summed up Robert Shurtliff as "a faithful & good soldier." "Faithful" had a special ring in the army because desertion was so common. In late August 1782, the Fourth Massachusetts compiled a list of about 110 men in the regiment who had deserted. Mutiny was also a given. In May 1782, General William Heath referred to the informer who betrayed his fellow soldiers at the mutiny in the Connecticut line as "a faithful soldier who was a waiter to an officer." Perhaps officers just took it for granted that their waiters were faithful, in the same way southern plantation owners assumed their household slaves were faithful. "Faithful" meant trustworthy, obedient, and deferential. Heath referred to the "eleven trusty sergeants" (among them Calvin Munn) who traveled to Massachusetts in 1782 to round up the last batch of recruits. To Washington, the veteran soldiers who did not mutiny in 1783 showed "fidelity," while their opposite numbers were "of mutinous disposition." In this dichotomy there was no place for a seven-year veteran like Joseph

Plumb Martin, who was devoted to the cause yet irreverent toward authority, bitter at the army's cruel inequities, and furious with a government that failed to make good its promises.[65]

Deborah Sampson never fell asleep on sentry duty, stole a chicken from a neighboring farmer, or went absent without leave. Indeed, Mann tells us, when "one of her company having been severely chastised for stealing poultry, importuned her to desert with him and two others," she "used all the eloquence of which she was the mistress" to dissuade him. If true, she was something of an officer's soldier—a bootlicker. What's more, she followed her general to Philadelphia to suppress a mutiny against injustice. The memoir breathes not a word of sympathy for her fellow soldiers protesting the cynical "furloughs," which sent them home without a settlement. Perhaps she had such feelings and Mann felt that to portray them would cast the glorious Revolution in too dark a light.[66]

She was one of the soldiers Washington praised who went home "without . . . a farthing of money" and without a murmur. A rebel against the constraints of gender, as a soldier she was a conservative who sided with authority. She could not afford to side with the rebels. Women serving openly in modern armies under the compulsion to prove themselves know what it means to avoid identifying with dissenters who rock the boat.

What does all this reveal? Deborah Sampson loved the army. After all, she was a success in the army; the army fed and housed her; it clothed her in the uniform of distinction of a much-valorized branch of service. The army recognized and rewarded her, if not with a badge of honor, with a sense of acceptance for her achievement. To her, becoming a waiter was a promotion. She was in an officer's family where she had more family than she had with her parents in Plympton or the Thomases in Middleborough. She probably had more of a sense of mutual community in her company than in the Baptist congregation that expelled her. Whatever mixture of motives impelled her into the army—and they were as mixed as they were for thousands of other poor recruits who were drafted or pocketed bounties to join up—she had as good a claim as any man to call herself a patriot. A patriot soldier can be defined, not by what gets a person into the army, but by what he or she does once there.

All soldiers were apprehensive about returning to civilian life, many with little more than a worn uniform and a musket. There was no GI Bill of Rights in 1783. Nor were veterans of the Continental Army received as heroes—on the contrary, there was a long-standing bias against regulars as "mercenaries" in favor of the citizen militia. Sampson had her own reasons to be anxious. Who would approve of her audacious exploit? To whom could she return?

Had she proven herself as a soldier a few years earlier and been discovered when the outcome of the war hung in doubt, she might have been used to fan the flames of patriotism. Thomas Paine, who in 1776 had appealed for "some Jersey maid" to rally "summer soldiers and sunshine patriots," would have lauded her. Preachers might have hailed her as the biblical Deborah incarnate. Recruiting officers might have held her up to shame men into enlisting. Recall Colonel Huntington, who, in 1782, said that women "appear to be more zealous for recruiting & keeping up the Army than the men." Would Washington have considered Huntington's half-joking proposal to recruit women? Seven years of scraping the bottom of the recruitment barrel had led the Virginia aristocrat to accept men considered the "dregs" of white society, as well as to change his mind about the importance of "the Women of the army." But women as soldiers? Probably not.

Sampson became known only after the war was over and then only to a handful of people. In fact, at the time, very few soldiers would even have heard about her. After her disclosure, according to the Mann account, she asked General Paterson to make inquiries about her among her old messmates. "And the effect was a panic of surprise with every soldier. Groups of them now crowded" around her, "but many turned inward and few had faith." Perhaps. But, if she was not revealed until October 1783, very few soldiers were left at West Point to see her or hear about her. Most had gone home, including her regiment. It was not as if thousands of soldiers had witnessed Joan of Arc on the battlefield.

Deborah Sampson was not noticed until she herself came forward in the 1790s, and the rest of her life is in good part the story of her long fight to win the due to which she believed she was entitled.

PART THREE

"THE CELEBRATED
MRS. GANNETT"

Chapter Six

A Gannett in Sharon

In 1827, when the Dedham *Village Register* reported Deborah Gannett's death, it framed her life after the army in a way that has been followed by almost every commentator since, as a redeeming conventional coda to an unconventional transgression.

> At the disbanding of the army she received an honorable discharge and returned to her relatives in Massachusetts, still in her regimentals. . . . Soon after she resumed the sphere of her own sex, she was married to Mr. Gannett, an industrious respectable farmer. She has borne and reared him a reputable family of children, and to the close of life, she has merited the character of an amiable wife, a tender mother, a kind and exemplary neighbor, and a friend of her country.

Written either by Herman Mann or by his son, it was an obituary that obscured more than it revealed, skipping over her return to civilian life and her marriage, and ignoring her campaign for recognition—the memoir, the petitioning, the lecture tour—that began in the 1790s and was the warp and woof of her life for three decades. It drew a curtain over her nonconformity.[1]

1. *In Between*
"Our Heroine leaped from the masculine, to the feminine sphere"

The final chapter in Mann's memoir carried her up to the point of her marriage, but we hardly know what to make of it. He claimed she returned not as Deborah Sampson, but as her brother. That would have been the winter of 1783–84. Then, in the spring of 1785, to use Mann's ornate language, "our Heroine leaped from the masculine, to the feminine sphere."[2] This year and a half is a puzzle for which we have only Mann's elliptical sentences, followed by the bare bones of the town's vital records of engagements, marriages, and births. How do we make sense of it?

Lingering at West Point for the ceremonial disbanding of her regiment, in November 1783, Deborah Sampson would have been in a quandary as to where to go. Consider her alternatives. Middleborough was out of the question; there was no way she was going to give "Christian satisfaction" to the Baptist elders or face old friends she had deceived. So was Plympton. Never close to her mother, she could not be certain how she would be received by her. The family was "not at all proud of her escapade," according to a descendant, "but did respect her for keeping her secret intact and retaining her virtue. . . ." Perhaps so. She told her officers she was going to Medundock, a small town on the Maine coast where she had relatives on her mother's side; but something changed her mind. She ended up with her mother's sister in Sharon in Norfolk County, due north of Plymouth County, a good many miles away from Middleborough or Plympton.[3]

The Mann/Gannett narrative tried to create a mystique about her ties to her family during the war. She had entered the army allegedly to avoid an unwanted engagement with "a young gentleman of fortune" arranged by her "parents." Her family, anxious about her whereabouts, allegedly sent her brother to find her, and in a Hudson Valley army camp she saw him, but he did not see her. Deborah was a dutiful daughter who, Mann claimed, wrote her mother reassuring her she was safe. And when she was lost in the western wilds, he said, she wrote still another letter, regretting that she had ever left her family—the prodigal daughter repenting. All this family devotion was "moonshine," to borrow a word from the iconoclastic editor John Adams Vinton. There were no "parents" to provide a suitor; the prospect of a wealthy suitor was ludicrous; and she had not kept close ties with her mother. The fact that after the war she did not return to her mother in Plympton says it all. She was, once again, on her own.[4]

The usually confident Mann seemed flummoxed by this interlude, and possibly we can read her through his anxiety. His outline at the head of his final chapter is clear: "Goes to her relations in Massachusetts—Intrigues with her sex—Censured—Resumes the female attire and economy." It is also tantalizing. The reader flounders for facts in the sea of genteel anglicized rhetoric that follows. From West Point, "she took a few strides to some sequestered hamlet in Massachusetts; where she found some relations: and assuming the name of her youngest brother, she passed the winter as a man of the world, and was not awkward in the common business of a farmer." Hold on. The "sequestered hamlet" was Stoughton (adjacent to Sharon; eventually the two were one town); the "relations" were her aunt, Alice Bradford Waters (her mother's sister), and her uncle, Zebulon Waters, and her older brother, Nehemiah, at the time single. The "youngest brother" whose identity she could have assumed had to be Ephraim, a year or so younger, a Continental Army veteran, who, in July 1783, had married in Middleborough, conveniently far enough away for Deborah to risk pretending to be him. Both were tall.[5]

"Passed the winter as a man of the world" and "intrigues with her sex" are the actions that disturbed Mann. To use John Adams Vinton's candid translation of Mann's prose, which beat around the bush, "she passed the winter doing farm work and flirting with the girls of the neighborhood." Vinton, a former minister, didn't bat an eyelash at this, but Mann seemed to be in a near panic as he brought his book to a close. He was an inept writer, never fully in command of his narrative. Now, at the end of his thirteenth and final chapter, racing to complete a manuscript the Dedham printer was literally setting in type as he wrote, it almost seemed as if a desperate, harried author had lost control of his heroine. If she came back as her brother, her aunt and uncle must have been in on the act; she could be Ephraim Sampson to strangers, but hardly to them in a small farmhouse. Then again, Mann, of course, could have invented the entire episode—one never really knows with this author—but somehow, judging by the tone he adopted toward her, part critical, part apologetic, it seems not completely made up.[6]

Earlier, Mann had portrayed Robert Shurtliff's affair with the Baltimore heiress as a chaste romance between "two lovers" in which Deborah was the pursued, not the pursuer. "But her correspondence with her sister sex!" he exclaimed about the flirtations with country girls. "Surely it must have been that of sentiment, taste, purity; as animal love, on her part, was out of the question." This sounds as if he were trying to reassure himself as much as his readers. Now Deborah seemed to be encouraging her "sister sex." To have "correspondence" with a person could mean no more than to have a relationship, which has no sexual innuendo. But the "animal love" he denied had a vivid implication of physical sexuality. The usually verbose Mann begs leave "not to specify every particular," which, of course, only kindles the reader's imagination. Indeed, that may have been the point: one last titillating episode of his own invention.

Here, however, Mann did something he had not done in the entire book: he scolded his heroine. Her uncle "often reprehended her for her freedom with the girls of his villa." Mann chastised the girls for "their violent presumption with the young *Continental.*" Then he criticized her. "To be plain I am an enemy to intrigues of all kinds. . . . Why did she not . . . preach to them the necessity of the prudence and instructions of sage Urania?" he asked. (Urania was a classical symbol of chastity.) In other words, why didn't she chase the girls away? He seemed petulant. It was almost as if she were spoiling his book.[7]

Finally, spring arrived, and "our Heroine leaped from the masculine, to the feminine sphere"—much to our author's relief. The final sentences in the book were enigmatic: "Throwing off her martial attire . . . she recommenced her former occupation; and I know not, that she found difficulty in its performance. Whether this was done voluntarily, or compulsively, is to me an enigma. But she continues a phenomenon among the revolutions of her sex." What did it mean to say he did not know whether Deborah returned to the female sphere voluntarily or compulsively? One implication is that she did not want to return but had no choice. All in all, it was a curious way to end a book, by casting doubts on the heroine.

Mann clearly was anxious about his heroine's reputation. So he added a lengthy appendix, the aim of which was both to offer proof of her military service and to clear up any misconceptions about how she exercised her sexuality.[8] He offered a long cautionary tale, warning women of the perils of surrendering to sexual passion. In a "pathetic history" lifted from *Constantius and Pulchera*—an erotic American novella popular in the 1790s—the beautiful but unprudent Fatima fell in love with Philander, a handsome shepherd, a "peasant" who soon "possessed her virginal love" and "whose warm embraces kindled new fires in [her] bosom." Then, her "brutal ravisher" shunned her, and she departed for a "cloistered convent" to hide her shame—all because she had become a "slave to passion."[9]

The point of this erotically charged affair between the two sexes was to offer a contrast with "the intercourse of our Heroine with her sex." Deborah was a soldier, and "it must be supposed she acted more from necessity, than a voluntary impulse of passion; and no doubt succeeded beyond her expectations, or desires. Harmless thing!" In other words: as Robert Shurtliff, Deborah played the part of a lover in order to keep up her masquerade (her *necessity*); things went further than she intended but never became sexual. As a woman, Deborah had an "incapacity" to engage in sex with another woman.[10]

The next act in this postwar interlude also leaves us guessing. Here, bereft of Mann, we have only the town records to go on. Deborah had arrived in town perhaps in mid-November 1783. After a year or so as a single woman (some months possibly spent as a single man), on October 14, 1784, she and Benjamin Gannett, Jr., posted their marriage banns with the town clerk, the formal notice of their intent to marry. After an interval of six months, they were wed, on April 7, 1785; seven months later, on November 8, 1785, Deborah gave birth to a son, Earl Bradford Gannett.[11]

Looking at the timing of Deborah's actions in the year and a half from her appearance in town late in 1783 to her marriage in the spring of 1785, several things stand out. She took her time to make up her mind. She stayed unattached for almost a year, once again a "masterless woman." Then she and Benjamin Gannett, Jr., became engaged, after which they waited a very long time, as engagements then went, between posting the banns, in October 1784, and marrying in April 1785. An interval of a few weeks was common, at most a few months. Evidently, she needed time to make up her mind as to what she wanted to do with her life. Not a passive person who accepted what life dealt her, she was calculating her options. So she stayed in "her regimentals" and did farmwork. After this, however, does the long interval between her engagement and her wedding hint at something else: an uncertainty about marrying Benjamin Gannett? an uncertainty about marrying?[12]

Was it possible that Hannah Snell was again a real-life influence on Deborah Sampson (and/or Mann)? Once more there is a parallel between the narratives of the two lives. Snell played at romancing women as part of keeping up her disguise, we are told, and after she returned to civilian life, she was undecided as to what course to take. She turned down an offer of marriage—she had one "bad husband," she remarked, who was the cause of her misfortunes, and "she resolved in the mind she was then in never to engage with any Man living." "She still continues to wear her regimentals," the author of *The Female Soldier* wrote at the conclusion of his narrative, "but how she intends to dispose of herself, or when, if ever, to change her Dress, is more than what she at present seems certain of"—an uncertainty echoed in the closing sentences in Mann's *The Female Review* in a somewhat similar cadence.[13]

Why did Deborah Sampson marry, as opposed to staying a single woman? She was twenty-five in 1785. At the end of the century, single women were more numerous than in colonial days and their numbers would grow. But they continued to be stigmatized as "old maids" at an early age. There were very few mothers to say to their daughters, as would Jo's mother in Louisa May Alcott's *Little Women* (1868), "better to be happy old maids than unhappy wives." And few women to call "Liberty a better husband," as would Alcott. Stigma aside, there was almost no economic way for single women to flourish in the New England countryside unless they inherited wealth. They usually lived in their family of origin or with the family of a sibling or relative. I suspect, however, that Deborah was not so inclined and had set her sights on a way of life that required a husband. Why then did she marry Benjamin Gannett, Jr.?[14]

Herman Mann had an odd way of blurting out embarrassing personal information about the Gannetts. In 1802, in the preface to Mrs. Gannett's address on her tour, he wrote that "after the Revolution, she retired to an obscure part of Massachusetts, selected, or rather was selected a partner of an industrious farmer." Which was it: she "selected" him? Or she "was selected" by him? Was this one of those slips of the pen where someone is right the first time? His first thought ("selected") was understandable: this strong-willed woman took the initiative; his second ("was selected") was that this was not the proper thing to say: a young man was supposed to ask for the hand of his intended. It left an innuendo offensive to Benjamin.[15]

If we assume she did select Benjamin Gannett, what would have been the attraction? In the army, she had studied a wide array of men at close range because she had to draw distinctions among them in order to survive. She also came to appreciate a class of men among the officers the likes of whom she had never met before: enlightened professional men with a liberal education, as well as men on the make who had climbed through the ranks. Given that she had taken the measure of more men in a year and a half in the army than the average woman would know (or read about in novels) in a lifetime, what did she see in her fiancé?

There is not much to say about Benjamin Gannett as a young man. A twenty-seven-year-old farmer, he seems to have labored all his working years for his father, had a limited education, and had not seen much of the world outside his hometown. During the war he had served in the militia a few days and no more. Twenty years later, in 1804, Paul Revere took his measure as a man "of small force in business." Did this mean that as a young man he was an unaggressive, passive fellow, possibly attracted to Deborah because of her strength? And could she have been drawn to him for just that, a man who would accept her for the strong-willed woman that she was? Very likely her choice was limited. In her first year in Sharon, she must have discovered that her boldness had disqualified her with many men who did not want a wife as willful and unpredictable as she. In the marriage market she was still as disadvantaged as she was before the war: without connections, a dowry, or property. And if she was to win recognition for her achievement and silence the gossip, she would need the safety of a respectable marriage.[16]

Who courted whom? Or who seduced whom? She was obviously skilled in pretending to be someone other than she was. If she was trying to land Benjamin Gannett, might she have masked her emotions, playing the lover? What is the next question: She chose to be engaged to him, but did she marry him because she became pregnant? Or, did she become pregnant in order to force a marriage about which he had second thoughts? She was, to say the least, a woman who took risks. Both she, at twenty-five or so, and he, at twenty-seven, might have been eager for sexual experiences, and she became pregnant toward the end of an unusually long engagement. She may have gambled that if she became pregnant then he would have no other choice than marriage. Is this the sort of thing Mann had in mind when he condemned the "intrigues" of single country girls who risked pregnancy in order to land husbands?

Premarital sex by a betrothed couple was so common in late-eighteenth-century Massachusetts that as long as the couple married, they ran little risk of secular punishment for the crime of fornication and might get away with only a minimum of censure by the church. Judging by the scholarly finger-counting we have for eighteenth-century Massachusetts towns, where as many as 30 or 40 percent of children were conceived before wedlock, little shame was attached to it. Deborah and Benjamin hardly had a shotgun wedding. After all, they announced their intention to marry six months before.[17]

We are, like Deborah's neighbors, reduced to gossip disguised as historical speculation. Once she married, Mrs. Gannett never set down her version of her affections or her marriage, and on this subject we can only infer from family lore. There are many silences in what the family passed on about their ancestor and obvious embarrassments. An "early baby," as people called a child born seven months after marriage, was not then a source of shame, but it was to become one. Decades later, the family set back the date of the marriage from April 1785 to April 1784, which gave Earl a birth nineteen rather than seven months after the wedding.[18]

After exploring this postwar interlude—the allegation of same-sex flirtations, the reality of a very long engagement, the premarital pregnancy—we return with some skepticism to Herman Mann's optimistic epigram: "Our Heroine leaped from the masculine, to the feminine sphere." Perhaps she leaped, and did so joyfully, into a new life. But perhaps it was not so much a leap as a reluctant turn down a road for which at the time no alternative paths were available.[19]

2. A Marriage
A "taste for an elegant stile of living"

Deborah Sampson was married in a pretty, ankle-length dress, styled in the latest fashion of the mid-1780s, made from an imported cotton fabric: a bold blue print of pinecones, seashells, and flowers on an écru background. We know the dress because it survives, passed down in the Gannett family to Beatrice Bostock, Deborah's great-great-granddaughter, born in 1907.[20]

The dress, too expensive for an ex-soldier sent home "without a farthing" to have bought herself, most likely was a wedding gift from her father-in-law-to-be. And since it shows unmistakable signs of being altered from an earlier style to meet the fashions of the mid-1780s, my guess is that Benjamin Gannett, Sr., took a dress that belonged to his first wife, Mary, who had died in 1781 (he remarried in 1782) and arranged to have it altered for Deborah. It was the kind of dress that a countrywoman might have worn for her wedding, and wedding dresses, as we know, are saved. The fact that all signs point to it as being in fashion in the mid-1780s but very soon out of fashion makes it even more likely that this was the dress she wore in 1785 at her wedding party. Nancy Rexford, a skilled historian of American costumes, was able to date it by comparing the style, fabric, and alterations to other dresses of its day.[21]

The dress is evidence that Deborah Sampson married up—or that she thought she was doing so—which sheds some light on why she married Benjamin Gannett, Jr. (or why she married at all). He was the son of one of the most prosperous and respected men in town, a leading patriot. In 1784–85, she may well have calculated that, in marrying Benjamin Gannett, Sr.'s firstborn son, she was entering the class of prosperous middling sort of farmers and might fulfill what Mann called her "taste for an elegant stile of living." The fashionable dress of 1785 thus can be read as testimony both to her transition to femininity and her expectations for the new status her marriage might bring.

According to family lore passed on by Patience Payson, the longtime family "helper," who was about eighteen at the time, the couple was married in the Gannett house in Sharon. What Payson may be remembering is the wedding celebration. According to the town records, the couple was married in Stoughton, where Deborah's aunt and uncle lived, by Dr. George Crossman, justice of the peace, a resident of nearby Canton. Crossman, who had previously registered their "intention" to marry October 14, 1784, dutifully recorded: "Married by George Crossman, Esq'r . . . Benj'a Gannett Jr of Sharon & Deborough Samson of Stoughton," along with the names of two other couples, "all maried April ye 17 1785."[22]

Benjamin Gannett, Sr. (1728–1813), had come to Stoughton in the 1750s and prospered as a farmer and tanner, the owner of a large farm and a tan yard, all of which he doubtless worked with the labor of his two sons, Benjamin (1757–1837) and Joseph (1759–1846). By the early 1770s, he had accumulated 300 acres of land in the northeast end of town around what became East Street, some of it in woodland lots scattered through the town. We get some idea of what his farm was like from the remarkably explicit Massachusetts tax valuation list for 1771. He owned six acres of tillage, which produced 60 bushels of grain a year, three cattle, two oxen, two horses, and two swine. To feed them, he had eight acres of pasture, which would keep four cows; three acres of English and upland mowing land, which produced 1 ton of hay

Nancy Rexford, an experienced costume historian, has "absolutely no doubt" that the dress passed down in the family that she examined at the home of Beatrice Bostock, Sampson's descendant, dates from the 1780s. The clues lie in the style, alterations, and fabric.

At the time, the dress was called "a round gown." Originally an open robe, "it was remade in the 1780s from an earlier style in which the skirt was open in front to display an underskirt." When Rexford let down the hem to its original length, "you could see where the front corners of the open robe had been turned up." Altered to fit the style of the 1780s, it had no significant alterations dating after 1790.

The three-quarter-length sleeves are also "typical of the 1780s." The "bodice back" showed a style that was then superseding the older so-called forreau back. The original ankle length would have fit a woman of five feet seven inches. The dress was worn with *sleeve ruffles and a square of fine linen or cotton called a kerchief (later a fichu), both here reproductions.*

The fabric is cotton, "identified after a microscopic examination of the threads." The pattern—a bold blue print of pinecones, seashells, and flowers on an off-white background—marks it as an imported fabric, most likely from England. The fabric "may date as early as 1765, or possibly as late as the early 1770s, say 1765–1785."

Could this have been Deborah Sampson's wedding dress of 1785? Rexford thinks it is possible. "The dress was certainly being worn in the 1780s, and wedding dresses are the garments most likely to be saved." A dress like this "for a wealthy woman would have been an informal summer day dress, attractive in its unpretentiousness. For a less affluent woman it might very well have been her best dress."

—Nancy Rexford, reports prepared for the author,
November 12, 1994, and July 11, 1995.
Photographs by Nancy Rexford.

a year; and three acres of fresh meadow, which produced 3 tons of meadow hay. This was a thriving farm, producing surpluses.[23]

Stoughton (embracing an area called Stoughtonham that became Sharon) had been a solidly patriot town. In March 1776, Stoughtonham petitioned the legislature to change its name to Washington but was beaten to the punch by a town in Berkshire County. In 1783, the year of peace, the name Sharon was an apt second choice. It was a very small town, even by Massachusetts standards, its population hovering around 1,000 for decades. There were about two hundred taxpayers, sixty-seven of whom came out to vote in 1780. And it was a consensual town. It had no Tories to suppress.

In the war, Benjamin Senior and his sons did short militia stints (the father for twenty-nine days, Benjamin Junior for nine) but no service in the regular army, typical of men in New England towns. The father paid for a substitute in the draft. A half century later, however, Benjamin Senior was the only person the town annalist singled out for his patriotism. "I will digress here," wrote sometime selectman Jeremiah Gould in 1831,

> to pay a just tribute to Mr. Benjamin Gannett, a wealthy farmer, whose liberality and zeal in the cause of liberty was unparalleled in this town. Whenever an order was received for beef and clothing for the army, Mr. Gannett was always foremost in procuring it. Many times he bought cattle, killed them, and furnished the quantity of beef required; and when the money was raised and paid

him, it would hardly reimburse the tenth part of the cost. He usually raised an abundance of grain, but so liberal was he of it, that scarcely a year passed during the war but he would be obliged to buy for his own family before the end of the season.[24]

Benjamin Senior was a pillar of the community. The town meeting elected him selectman, and the Congregational Church trusted him to draw up a plan for a new meetinghouse and to auction off the pews. He did not come out of the war poor, as the annalist implied. In 1783, the tax assessor listed him for an assessment of £600 in real estate and £110 in personal property, a total of £710, which put him literally at the top of a list of about 218 taxpayers. There was even a slight touch of class in the family. Benjamin's first daughter, Hannah, married Edmund Quincy, Jr., of Boston, whose sister, Dorothy Quincy, married no less a patrician than John Hancock. Quincy bought land in Sharon and invested in an iron furnace, turning out cannon for the American army in partnership with Colonel Richard Gridley, the army's chief engineer. Quincy died in 1782, and it is interesting that his partner Gridley's diary for 1776 (entered in an almanac) was passed down in the Gannett family to Deborah's descendants along with her wedding dress. They were clearly a patriot family, and Benjamin Senior probably welcomed "the female soldier" into his family.[25]

The "wealthy farmer" took care of his sons in the New England way. In 1781, when Benjamin Junior was twenty-four, his father deeded him a parcel of his own land for the token sum of 6 shillings, "out of the good will and affection I have and do bear" him, reserving for himself the use of the tannery. He also deeded Joseph part of his "homestead" land. The three farms of father and sons were contiguous. In 1785, the year Benjamin Junior married, the assessor listed him for a total of £132 (£110 in real property and £22 in personal property) and Joseph for about the same, while he listed Benjamin Senior for five times as much. In the federal tax assessments of 1798, another measure of wealth, Benjamin Senior was listed as owning 202 acres of land valued at $1,892 compared to 49 acres worth $424 for Benjamin Junior.[26]

None of this would have escaped Deborah's vigilant eye. The final legal paperwork on Benjamin Junior's land took place in June 1785, two months after they were married. If, however, she anticipated life as the wife of a prosperous yeoman, she must have been deeply disappointed. Forty-nine acres made for a very small farm, and it stayed small. In 1805, Benjamin Junior's tax assessment was the same as it was in 1785, putting him in the lowest group of town property holders. Only one sixth the size of his father's 300 acres of 1771, his land supported just a few head of livestock. Benjamin and Deborah eked out a living on this farm.[27]

Such farmers got by with a constant exchange of labor called "neighboring." A townsman who reminisced about Sharon in the mid-nineteenth century could have been talking about earlier generations: "The inhabitants obtained their living mostly by the cultivation of their farms and the occasional sale of a load or two of wood. Every farmer owned one or more oxen and a yoke of yearling steers for the boys to train. Whenever a farmer had a new parcel of land to break up or that which had become overgrown with bushes, the neighbors were ever ready to lend a helping hand." The sole surviving entry from an account book kept by Benjamin Junior attests both to neighboring and to timber as a cash crop: "June 1802, Joseph Gannet Dr. [debtor] to a hand and 3 cattle. Drawing logs from Rattle Snake hill to Leonard & Kingsleys Forg." Benjamin was recording an exchange of labor with his brother, dragging timber with his oxen from the 10 acres on Rattle Snake Hill his father had given him to a forge, very likely a blacksmith's. Joseph also turned his wood into charcoal, which on occasion he hauled to Paul Revere's copper mill and brass foundry in nearby Canton. We know this from a receipt that survives.[28]

After years of working this land, Benjamin and Deborah Gannett had little to show for it. Herman Mann, visiting Mrs. Gannett in the 1790s, painted a romanticized pastoral scene: "And while she discovers a taste for an elegant stile of living; she exhibits, perhaps, an unusual degree of contentment, with an honest farmer, and three endearing children, confined to a homely cot, and a hard earned little farm." This softened all the hard edges. In 1804, Paul Revere, after visiting the Gannetts, made a stark observation: "They have a few acres of poor land, which they cultivate, but they are really poor." Either Mann had on rose-colored spectacles or in ten years the Gannetts had made a very rapid descent downhill.[29]

The farmhouse Deborah and Benjamin lived in with their three children and a servant seems to be the small building described in 1901 by Rhoda Monk, Deborah's granddaughter: "The house was a one story house with two front rooms, the one on the south corner was the 'living' room, it was 16 ft. × 16 ft. and had a fire place in it. There were two bedrooms on the back part and a butry. There was an el on the south part that had a kitchen in it. This was an old home 70 years ago." It was worth so little that after the family moved into a new, bigger house across the road, it was carted off to Canton for the use of a couple of butchers.[30]

What had happened to the promise of life for the newlyweds of 1785? Revere said no more about Benjamin Junior than that he "is a good sort of man" but "of small force in business." Coming from a successful entrepreneur, the former artisan now prospering as the owner of a brass foundry, Revere's language suggests Benjamin was a genial soul who was not very enterprising. But there probably was no way even a Yankee go-getter could wrest a good living out of "a few acres of poor land." A year or so after Revere wrote, Joseph, whose farm was no bigger, migrated with his large family to Pompey in western New York, where he squatted on Indian land he eventually acquired from the government. "He travelled with a yoke of oxen hitched into a covered wagon," Rhoda Monk recalled. Benjamin would have stayed in Sharon out of hope of inheriting his father's land. It wasn't that the Gannett sons lacked capitalist acquisitiveness. In the early 1800s, tens of thousands of New England families migrated from 50-acre farms on worn-out land, lured by the fertile soil of New York and the old Northwest. The population of Sharon hovered around 1,000 at every census from 1790 to 1840 because the outmigration canceled the normal population growth.[31]

A farmer in this neck of the woods usually had to pursue a second occupation to bring in a cash income. Benjamin Senior had been a tanner; Earl, Benjamin Junior's son, eventually became a stonecutter. Even so, at the time of his death in a quarry accident, Earl was deeply in debt. It was not until late in the nineteenth century, when Earl's son, the third Benjamin, took to dealing in horses and real estate, that a Gannett on East Street would prosper as had the old patriarch and regain his status.[32]

What did Deborah do in these early years of her marriage in Sharon? What did any member of "the female yeomanry" do on a hardscrabble farm? In the first decade after her marriage in 1785, besides the unceasing rounds of woman's work on a farm, she would have had her hands full with children: Earl, born November 8, 1785; Polly, born December 19, 1787; and Patience, born November 25, 1790. She expressed love for them. On the eve of her tour in 1802, her "heart filled with pain" when she realized she was parting with them. When she was deathly sick on the tour, she recorded in her diary, "to think myself so far from my dear children, no opportunity of hearing from them, and God only knows when I shall be so happy as to see them."[33]

What was Deborah's frame of mind these years? The naming of her children is a clue that she had drifted from the biblical traditions of her parents. She gave none of the three children an Old Testament name. Patience, a Puritan-meaningful name (like Charity or Mercy) suggested the New Testament and John Bunyan's *Pilgrim's Progress,* but neither Earl nor Polly had a religious meaning. At the same time, she clearly wanted to perpetuate a link to her Pilgrim ancestry: Bradford, the middle name she gave Earl, of course was for William Bradford, the first governor of the Plymouth colony. Her mother was a Bradford; her Aunt Alice Waters owned the Bradford family Bible. Patriotism had rekindled public memory of the Pilgrims, reinforcing family tradition. In 1785, a printer reissued an edition of Reverend Robert Cushman's sermon delivered in 1621 at the landing of the Pilgrims, the first sermon preached in America, an event that had achieved iconic status. A copy of this 1785 Plymouth imprint inscribed in two places with the autograph: "Deborah Sampson, Her book, 1785," conceivably belonged to our Deborah before she became a Gannett in April 1785.[34]

She had a servant to help with the farm chores that often overwhelmed a woman with small children. Patience Payson, an orphaned child born in 1767 who had been adopted by the Gannett, Sr., family and came to work for the young Gannetts in the 1780s, stayed with them more than forty-five years, in itself a sign that the family appreciated her. She identified herself as "helper," as did most servants of that democratizing era. There were signs of real family affection for her. Deborah named her second daughter Patience. Earl topped this, naming his second daughter Patience Payson Gannett, suggesting how devoted he was to her. She would be buried in the family plot.[35]

A servant gave Deborah Gannett some freedom. "She is sometimes employed in a school in her neighborhood," Mann wrote after a visit late in 1796. Indeed, Sharon's east district one-room schoolhouse was only a stone's throw down the road from her farm. How long she taught there we do not know—probably a few seasons. "Her first maxim of the government of children," Mann reported, "is *implicit obedience,*" which is believable. Deborah may also have gone back to spinning, a necessity in a farm household, although not to weaving. Mann pointedly said she showed him some pieces of cloth she had woven in Middleborough before she went into the army. Her return to teaching may be a token of how anxious she was for something more than farmwork and of the family's need for extra income, however small.[36]

In truth, there was little else in Sharon to engage a woman like Mrs. Gannett. It was a very small town.[37] The Gannett farms were on the outskirts, not that the center would have been much more lively. If she had a mind to it, Deborah could walk or ride a horse from her home on present-day East Street, turn west onto the Saw Mill Road, pass a gristmill and sawmill, and then make her way to the town center. There she would encounter the meetinghouse, the parsonage, and a cluster of houses around the green. A tavern was down the road from the center, a general store was at the south end of town. Five one-room schoolhouses boxed the compass. Scattered here and there were artisan shops: a few tanneries, a handful of farmer/shoemakers, a few small forges. And that was Sharon.[38]

No one called Sharon a bustling place. It was isolated. A road to Boston, about eighteen miles away, ran through the center of town but was not a major travel route. It did not get a post office until 1818, located at Cobb's Tavern on the eastern outskirts of town (not far from the Gannetts). Sharon was not Dedham, the Norfolk County seat, which had a weekly newspaper, court days, market days, and a cluster of shops, including a bookstore and a circulating library. Some farmers clearly were more affluent than others, but it would be a stretch to call them "gentry." In fact, it is hard to imagine many social occasions in Sharon on which Mrs. Gannett might have worn one of her pretty dresses cut to the latest fashion. Perhaps to someone else's wedding celebration.[39]

As to religion and politics, in the 1790s Sharon was in a lull before a storm. The "political and religious controversies" which produced "much bitterness," the town annalist wrote, were about two decades ahead. There was one Congregational meetinghouse and no other churches. Politically, the town was cool to innovation. In 1778, the town meeting opposed the proposed new Massachusetts constitution; in 1788, it opposed the proposed new federal Constitution. Benjamin Junior and Joseph filled such workaday town assignments as hog reeve, field driver, and surveyor of roads, never rising to the offices of greater trust held by their father.[40]

The woman who had gotten a big taste of a wider world landed in a sleepy rural town that was something of a backwater. Sharon, although only a short trip to the Dedham center and a day's trip to Boston, was not as much of a crossroads town as Middleborough, and for a woman it was just as much of a "contracted" sphere. Did she show "an unusual degree of contentment," as Mann wrote in 1797? Five years later, Mann exploded this sunny comment in explaining her reasons for embarking on a lecture tour. Mrs. Gannett "had a naturally ambitious disposition"; she had a "taste for a more elevated stile of life"; she hoped "to wipe off any aspersions" on her name; and she wanted to "enhance the pecuniary interest of her family." He was uncommonly frank about what she wanted: recognition, reputation, refinement. In truth, Deborah Gannett, then in her late thirties, was not unlike young Deborah Sampson in Middleborough in her early twenties. She was poor, ambitious, and anxious about what people were saying about her—far more discontented than contented. Any expectations she may have had of rising up by marrying into the Gannett family had been shattered.[41]

Unwittingly, Mann revealed that Mrs. Gannett had set her sights on something more than being a farm housewife and mother. At the end of his appendix, written after a visit to Sharon late in 1796 or early in 1797, he bluntly reported the neighborhood "hearsay" that Mrs. Gannett "refuses her husband the rites of the marriage-bed." He offered a gratuitous defense: the couple showed a "mutual harmony" and there was "a child that has scarcely left its cradle." What Mann did not bother to find out was that Deborah had adopted the baby he saw, Susanna Shephard, when her mother died after childbirth in September 1796, and her father most likely took off. The baby was born only two months after the couple was wed, which obviously made no difference to Deborah.[42]

Deborah bore three children over the first six years of her marriage from 1785 to late in 1790, when Patience, the third child, was born. Why she had no more is beyond recovery. The adoption of Susanna six years later (aside from suggesting that her heart went out to an orphaned child as she herself in effect had been) hints that either she was not able to have any more children of her own or she did not want to. This was a time when it was still common for a woman to bear seven or eight children and when one who bore only three and stopped when she was thirty-one was in a distinct minority, and therefore subject to gossip. Whatever the reason, having so few children (and having a servant to help care for them) meant that Deborah enjoyed an uncommon freedom. Had she followed the normal pattern of bearing a child every two years or so, she might have had four more children in the 1790s, which meant that she would have had a suckling child at her breast, a toddler underfoot, and a brood to take care of (even with a "helper"). Whether the "hearsay" Mann tactlessly spread was true or not, the fact that she had limited the size of her family gave her a freedom to pursue a public quest for recognition she would otherwise not have had.[43]

3. The Quest for Recognition
"Being a Female . . . has hitherto not receiv'd one farthing"

Far from being in a state of pastoral "contentment" after her third child was born in 1790, Deborah Gannett embarked on an angry campaign for reward that would absorb her until she met success in 1805, and, intermittently after that, until 1820. In 1792, she successfully petitioned the state legislature for the back pay due her as a Continental soldier in the Massachusetts line. She next cooperated with Herman Mann on the book that made her a celebrity. Then, in November 1797, two months after the book appeared, she took to the road, traveling to New York City to seek political support for a petition to the U.S. Congress. The petition failed, but it capped a heady decade of aggressive public action.

In her petition to the Massachusetts General Court, she spoke of having made "some Application to receive pay" earlier. This may have been in 1786, when she began assembling the necessary documents. From Henry Jackson, the former colonel of her regiment, now prominent in business and politics in Boston, she collected a certificate attesting to her service. In 1791, Captain Eliphalet Thorp, her mustering officer, attested to the date of her enlistment. She enclosed the two documents with her petition to the General Court, dated January 11, 1792.[44]

In the Massachusetts petition, an angry voice breaks through the formalities of deference required of a lowly supplicant to an august body. She began with the formulaic "The memorial of Deborah Gannet [*sic*] humbly showeth that your memorialist from Zeal for the good of her Country was induc'd" to serve in the army as Robert Shurtliff. She laid out the dates and place of her enlistment, mustering, and discharge, and the names of her officers. The sole military action she mentioned was that she was "engag'd with the Enemy at Tary Town New York & was wounded there by the Enemy."

Then she let down the mask of humility. She had applied before, but "being a Female, and not knowing the proper steps to take to get pay for her services, has hitherto not receiv'd one farthing for her services." She lashed out, uncertain whom to blame. "Whether it has been occasioned by the fault of Officers in making up the Rolls or whether Effrican Hamlin paymaster in the 4th regiment has carried off the papers, etc, your memorialist cannot say." (Africa Hamlin was indeed the regiment's paymaster and quartermaster.) Her military name, it would appear, was not on whatever rolls she had tracked down. In her conclusion, she fell back as a supplicant. "She hoped the House would consider the Justness of her Claim and Grant her pay as a good soldier." Here, in her first petition, was a sense of a double entitlement: as a soldier entitled to pay and as a woman disadvantaged because she lacked the knowledge common to male veterans. It was a plea for justice and equal treatment, expressed with the kind of seething anger she had shown on occasion as a younger woman.[45]

The response of the Assembly was fast and favorable. The claim was referred to a committee which included two unusually knowledgeable members, James Sproat of the Middleborough family and Dr. William Eustis of Boston, the physician in charge of the army hospital at West Point. If they had any questions, they could talk to Colonel Jackson in Boston. The committee "corroborated the facts," Isaiah Thomas's *Massachusetts Spy* reported; the Assembly acted within a week; the Senate the next day, and on the following day Governor John Hancock signed the resolution. Judging by this speed, there was no debate and the vote was unanimous. There was apparently no question about the legitimacy of her claim. Mrs. Gannett was awarded £34 in back pay, which came to £2 a month for her seventeen months, in addition to interest from the date of discharge.[46]

The recognition was handsome. She was a "faithful, gallant *soldier*," who had preserved "the virtue & chastity of her sex unsuspected & unblemished," and was discharged "with a fair & honorable character." Boston newspapers ran short paragraphs reporting the action, which a number of other papers and magazines picked up. Thomas's *Massachusetts Spy*, in Worcester, under the heading "Female Heroism," reported it as "a very extraordinary circumstance [which] arrested the attention of the house." This "extraordinary woman" enlisted as a male and "did her duty without a stain on her virtue or honor." Insofar as print is the measure, however, the award seems to have generated no other public comment. She had acquired a small fame.[47]

Soon after this recognition, Herman Mann entered Deborah Gannett's life, and she began a collaboration with him that lasted more than thirty years. Years later, he dated beginning work on the memoir to a time "directly after my marriage, while at the seminary and teach[ing] a public school." He was married in January 1792, was visiting her as late as the fall of 1796, and the book came off the press in the fall of 1797, which means he worked on the manuscript in the mid-1790s over a four-year period. He lived in neighboring Walpole and came over to talk with her in her farmhouse. In 1797, while he was apologizing to subscribers for the book being late, he was in the midst of moving his family to Dedham, where he began a partnership with the printers of the town's newspaper, soon to be his alone.[48]

Thirty years later, Mann confessed how incomplete his research was: "I wanted [lacked] the facts I have since obtained," claiming his friends rushed him into print. In the preface to the revised manuscript, Mann said that "each sheet went to press as soon as written, without scarcely a review," which is believable, given how opaque some passages were. In a prospectus soliciting subscriptions for a second edition, he stated that the first "was written with only a few leading facts and traits of this woman," but "since then she has been induced to unbosom to the author of this work all the particulars of her life," as well as the "minutiae attending her sexual trials."[49] This was an exaggeration, a puff for the revised book. In reality, she had "unbosomed" herself a good deal to him in the 1790s—an apt phrase for a woman who literally told him that she had drawn a tight bandage around her breasts. She would cooperate with him again in 1802, allowing him to write her oration, and in the 1820s would talk to him once again for the revision.

What did she see in Mann? One historian of this family of printers calls him "a learned, bookish, and somewhat poetic man." He was educated in a half-baked sort of way, but at what "seminary" is not clear; he was associated in some way with Rhode Island College, a Baptist-affiliated institution, later Brown University, which then could have been called a seminary. The clue to a link of some sort is that some thirty or so students from the college subscribed to his book. He was also a young man on the make, out to establish his reputation. Born in 1771, he was barely past twenty-one and untested as a writer when he met Deborah. He was in search of a vocation and, over the years he was struggling with the Gannett manuscript, he found himself making the decision to become an editor and printer.[50]

Mrs. Gannett, in her early thirties, saw an idealistic young man in his early twenties with pretensions to learning. In religion, he clearly had "liberal principles," which in the 1790s meant he was a deist of sorts and somewhat anticlerical, a Unitarian-to-be. Politically, he later looked back on himself as an editor "espousing the republican or democratic cause of his country," although this erased his earlier opportunism. He began editing the *Dedham Minerva* when the national political passions of 1798–99 created a storm in Dedham, and he trimmed his sails. As is apparent from the memoir, he was conscious of the inequality in the condition of women. He later carried Mary Wollstonecraft's *Vindication* in his circulating library and published a work by Hannah Adams of nearby Medfield, one of the first histories by an American woman. He never became an advocate of "the rights of women," however. Like many printers who had to attune themselves to clashing points of view, he was a straddler.[51]

While Deborah may have been attracted by Mann's liberalism (or his adulation), she may also have seen an opportunity in his inexperience. His father died when he was six, and he was raised by his mother, a schoolteacher. Although his father had served at Lexington, the son knew next to nothing about the war firsthand—he would have been eleven and twelve at the time she was in the army. He also knew very little of the real world and may have reminded her of the other green young men in the army she had been able to deceive. He clearly was taken by her, and at times, as we have seen, he was taken in.[52]

It took him a long time to put together the memoir. He took notes as she talked, copying down names, some carelessly. He talked to a few other people, but he was not at all of a skeptical frame of mind. To shape his narrative, he went home and ransacked his reading—whether the adventures of Hannah Snell or Indian captivity narratives—forever straining for a lofty style. The revised manuscript years later shows how fussy a writer he was, constantly scratching out words and inserting new lines. It is unlikely she ever saw the manuscript or proofs. She went along because she wanted to be considered a heroine, knowing that he had to present her in adventures that would sell the book. She may have passed herself off as a veteran of Yorktown, or she may have consented to be depicted there, helping him reconstruct the scene from what veterans of the battle had told her. He may have sold her on the double genre of the book—memoir and novel—which gave her an out to disavow what he made up. It was a collaboration that served them both.

Being the subject of a book was more than simply flattering. In late-eighteenth-century America, a woman was rarely the subject of a biography or memoir, which is why novels had such a large female audience. There were narratives of American women held captive by Indians, tales of English warrior women, and chapbooks about famous women of history or legend. Quaker women missionaries wrote about their experiences; women's "relations of faith" about their conversion experiences were sometimes published. Narratives of slave women or bold women who crossed into male spheres, however, were yet to come. And autobiographies of common soldiers or sailors would not appear until the 1820s.[53]

Furthermore, the book carried her likeness. More shades of Hannah Snell. Mann commissioned a portrait. The legend under her name reads: "Drawn by Joseph Stone, Framingham 1797." Either she traveled the twenty miles to sit for him, or he came down to Sharon. A self-trained artist who may have painted tavern signs and likenesses of other country people, Stone painted a small oval portrait of Deborah in oil on paper, and Mann then arranged for a copperplate engraving to be made from it, the common practice. Today, Stone is considered a "folk artist." He was not terribly skilled as a portrait painter, but there is no reason to disparage the likeness because it is indeed so close to Mann's description of her.[54]

In the painting and engraving, she is posed in a stylish dress in the latest fashion. The dress, the costume historian Nancy Rexford assures us, is "unambiguously in the style of the period of 1794–1800," when "waistlines were rising and more and more dresses were being made with bodices adjusted on drawstrings"—all features of the dress in the painting. The "low round neckline of the dress is filled with a kind of scarf often called a handkerchief in the eighteenth century or a fichu in the nineteenth." This was a "stylish accessory," which "made the neckline more modest," an indispensable component of Deborah's persona. For the period, the dress is unusual "compared to surviving dresses in having a scalloped and pointed edging around the low neckline," a detail which "may be real evidence of [Deborah's] interest in the minor shifting details of fashion, as opposed to her dressing in the generally prevailing style."[55] Unmistakably, Mrs. Gannett was style-conscious.

The total impression made by the image fit her dual persona as a feminine patriot. She was feminine: long curly hair falling to her shoulders, a choker around her neck, a small bosom modestly covered yet accented by the tight sash. Flowers trim one side of the oval frame. A stern, determined

The frontispiece of The Female Review, *published in Dedham 1797, commissioned by Herman Mann. The engraving by George Graham was from a drawing by William Beastall, in turn based on Joseph Stone's painting (reproduced as the frontispiece to this book), which it closely resembled. Courtesy American Antiquarian Society.*

DEBORAH SAMPSON.
Published by H. Mann, 1797.

woman, she is nothing if not the patriot: at the top are masculine military symbols, a musket, sword, and battle flags, and at the bottom patriotic symbols, an eagle and a medallion with the Stars and Stripes. She was a competitor with "Liberty," a frequently copied female image of the 1790s, which became a symbol of a woman of the new republic, an Americanized Greek goddess trampling the symbols of tyranny.[56]

The book was guaranteed a respectable local readership by an advance subscription, the printer's custom of the day. It was offered for 92 cents (reduced to 87½ cents after publication), with a seventh copy free if you bought six. Mann accumulated about two hundred advance subscribers, quite good for a book of its kind. Most were from nearby towns in eastern or central Massachusetts, typical of the local markets to which small-town printers catered. The list printed at the back was sprinkled with reverends, doctors, deacons, and captains (and included some thirty men identified as "R.I. College"). The turnout from her hometowns was not exactly a stampede: seven subscribers from Stoughton, four from Sharon, one from Middleborough. But these included a tavern keeper and Captain John Soule, Deborah's in-law, who took six copies. Six women subscribers were listed (five as "Miss," one as "Mrs."), although doubtless many men were ordering copies for the women in their families.[57]

The book sold out. Booksellers, Mann later recalled, "quickly devoured" 1,500 copies, suggesting a rapid word-of-mouth for reprints above the initial run for subscribers. Still, it was a small printing at a time when an annual almanac easily reached 10,000 or 20,000 copies, and a popular novel could go into numerous reprints. Mann bellyached that he had not made a cent because of his inexperience in the book trade. A few booksellers or circulating libraries advertised the book, but as Mann later recalled, there were no reviews.[58]

William Ellis's comment in 1837, that "this book was not well written in several respects and did not at the time of its publication meet the general approbation of the public," was only half true—it was badly written, but it did sell out and could have sold more. His comment about Mrs. Gannett's reaction was equivocal: Mann "collected stories and published" a "narrative . . . some part of which was not approved by Mrs. Gannett, tho many things therein stated appear to have been obtained from her." Actually, her response to the book was more complex. She allowed Mann to write the "address" she delivered on her tour; she remained on friendly terms with him and his family, visiting them in Dedham. She was ambivalent about the book, and in the 1820s her attitude to a second edition expressed this; she gave it her blessing on the condition Mann would not publish it until after her death.[59]

The book, after all, lifted her from local notoriety to the status of a regional celebrity. She was indebted to Mann for fleshing out the persona she had created. She was stuck with his tales about her outlandish adventures among the Indians and his innuendos about her sexual life, but the fact that the memoir could be read as a novel gave her a way out. Whether or not people read the book, whether or not they liked it, its very publication made it possible to speak of her as "the celebrated Mrs Gannett," opening up new possibilities in her campaign for public reward.

4. *A Petition to Congress*
"Reward this gallant Amazon"

Sometime after she won back pay from Massachusetts, Mrs. Gannett decided to petition the U.S. Congress, which probably lay behind her decision to collaborate on a memoir. After many delays, Herman Mann announced *The Female Review* as finally available in September 1797. In November, Deborah Gannett traveled to New York City, where she enlisted the support of no less a person than Philip Freneau, the nationally known editor and poet, who helped her frame a petition to the House of Representatives and published a poem in tribute to her. It was in many ways a remarkable trip: bold, ambitious, somewhat confused as to goals. Once more, she had taken to the road.

It was difficult for a veteran to get a pension in the 1790s. Congress had taken care of officers, granting half-pay pensions in response to the campaign Sampson had witnessed at New Windsor in 1783. For rank-and-file soldiers, however, Congress did not pass a general pension act for thirty-five years, not until 1818, and then restricted it to veterans who could prove they were "in reduced circumstances"—a means test. Not until 1832 did Congress provide for a pension for any veteran who could prove he had served a minimum of six months. Meanwhile, up to 1818, "invalid" soldiers were the only category of veterans eligible for pensions, but they had to prove what was called "decisive disability."

According to the law of 1793, a disabled veteran had to assemble affidavits from all of the following: his officers, or an army surgeon, testifying to the onset of his disability during the war; three "reputable" freeholders in the town in which he lived who could describe the degree to which he had been disabled; two witnesses, to verify the disability at the time of his application; and two physicians who examined him. All this testimony had to be submitted to a federal judge, who would transfer the documents to the secretary of war, who in turn had to verify the service record before submitting a recommendation to Congress. An experienced lawyer might balk at jumping ver such hurdles. In 1796, Congress began to pass private acts, possibly because the War Department route was so tied up in red tape. Mrs. Gannett may have been informed about these elaborate procedures and chose instead to petition Congress directly. The petition submitted in her name, however, was unclear as to what she was asking for, suggesting that she and/or Freneau, her guide, were ill-informed about the law.[60]

Philip Freneau was a logical person for Deborah to seek out: he was known as "the poet of the Revolution" and as an ardent Democratic Republican editor. He edited first the *National Gazette,* set up in Philadelphia in 1791 with the help of Jefferson and James Madison, Freneau's Princeton classmate, and then *The Time Piece,* established in March 1797, with the patronage of New York City Republicans. To Federalists, he was "that rascal Freneau," President Washington's epithet. Herman Mann, would-be poet, would-be editor, probably knew who Freneau was and may have told Mrs. Gannett about him. Freneau had "a number of lady contributors" to his paper, and if Mrs. Gannett simply arrived in New York City without an introduction, she could have been referred to him by a woman familiar with his openness to female writers. Conceivably, she presented him with a copy of Mann's new book as proof of her claims.[61]

Freneau's tribute to Deborah Gannett has long been known; not so the extent of his role in her campaign. The poem appeared in his paper, *The Time Piece and Literary Companion,* and in 1815, Freneau reprinted it in an edition of his collected poems with a short footnote indicating that it was written on the occasion of Mrs. Gannett's petition, "at the request of the heroine." A later note by his daughter claimed it was after an interview with her in New York City. I was skeptical about the interview, but after tracking down the manuscript notes of Helena, the daughter, I changed my mind. She is the only source for this event involving her father: his interview with Deborah, his role in writing the petition, and his public support. Furthermore, the reports in his newspaper inadvertently confirm his role.[62]

Helena Freneau Hammell, born in 1791 and married in 1816, was too young in 1797 to have known the episode firsthand. She acknowledged that the information came from her mother. Her notes, put down some years later, have a ring of authenticity, even though they have the kind of overlay of anachronistic information and telescoping of events that creeps into recollections set down long after an event. Helena wrote:

While editor [illegible word] his office was throng[ed] with Visitors mostly wanting favors of one kind or another[.] one day he [came?] in to dinner and told Mrs. Freneau that there had been rather an accentric [*sic*] character in the office that morning telling him that she had served through the revolutionary war in man's attire and had received several wounds and shoed [showed] the scars, all he could do was send her to Washington with a Petition which he did, her name was Deborah Gannet, she went to Congress presented her petition and received her pension, tho he put not his name to [it] it was immediately known as there were many of the members were his correspondents[,] also Thomas Jefferson the President.

The memory lapses in Helena's account are not disqualifying: Philadelphia, not Washington, was the capital from 1791 to 1801; the president was John Adams, not Jefferson, whom she knew as Freneau's patron; and Deborah did not get her pension until a second effort in 1805. Yet the story is credible. "Shoed [him] the scars" is possible. Freneau in a revised version of his poem in 1815 referred to Mrs. Gannett as "marked with many a scar." Her wounds, it will be recalled, were to her head and most likely her shoulder or breast. "She went to Congress [and] presented her petition" probably means that Freneau directed her to Congress rather than that she literally went to Philadelphia to present it; "tho he put not his name to [it]" clearly implies he wrote the petition, which is supported by the evidence in his own paper showing he had prior knowledge of its contents.

The original petition has not survived. We have two summaries of it, however, one from a congressional source, the other from the newspapers. According to the brief summary read to the House on November 28, 1797, she stated that "though a *female* [she] enlisted as a continental soldier, for the term of three years, that she faithfully performed the duties of a soldier . . . and received a wound while in the actual service of the United States, in consequence of which she is subjected to pain and infirmities; and praying that she may receive the *pay and emoluments* granted to other wounded and disabled soldiers" (emphasis added).[63]

Freneau's account of the petition in his own paper was slightly different, supporting his daughter's recollection that he had a hand in writing it. On December 1, he summarized a petition as "from" Deborah Gannett. "She stated that she had been wounded in the service, and therefore prayed a pension, as being unable any longer to support herself, and being compelled to ask assistance from that country which she had sacrificed many delicate considerations to serve, in the hour of its distress and danger." In Freneau's summary, she clearly asked for a "pension," not "pay and emoluments." A summary of the House actions in a Philadelphia paper, however, had it that she asked for "compensation for her services as a soldier." That her request could be reported as either for pay ("compensation") or a pension did not bode well for its success.[64]

On December 4, 1797, a week after Congress received the petition, Freneau published his ode, "A Soldier Should Be Made of Sterner Stuff. On Deborah Gannett who on Tuesday last presented a petition in Congress." His paper followed the petition until it was introduced; after that, it had no news to report until mid-March 1798, when it was clear the petition had failed. It was referred to the Committee on Claims, where it ended up with three other claimants for "supplies," "services," and "losses," in the war—which indicates the petition was viewed as a claim for compensation. On March 9, 1798, the chairman reported that the Committee had rejected all the claims under review because there was "no reason whatever for exemption from the operation of the acts of limitation" Congress had set for war claims. In other words, the Committee did not even take up her case. A request for a pension as an invalid soldier, on the other hand, would not have been too late but should not have gone to the Committee on Claims. Her petition was not well framed, which explains why it was so easy to shoot down.[65]

Deborah's petition was introduced by Congressman Harrison Gray Otis of Boston (nephew of Mercy Otis Warren, the poet and historian), who represented Suffolk County. Otis spoke of the petition as requesting "compensation for her services as a soldier," stating, "she is able to produce certificates not only of her having served but of having been wounded," which makes it appear as a request both for back pay and a pension. There is no sign of "golden-tongued Harry" coming to her defense after the Committee on Claims made its negative report. Nor did any other congressman speak for her—not Fisher Ames from Dedham, who represented her county, Norfolk, nor Colonel William Shepard, the former commander of her regiment, elected from western Massachusetts.

All three were Federalists, and the issue came before the House in the spring of 1798, when Otis and Ames were feeding the Federalist frenzy about the menace of a French invasion that led to an undeclared war with France and the political hysteria of the Alien and Sedition Acts. Federalists were in no mood to entertain a petition supported by a poem from a "Jacobin" editor portraying a feminist heroine who reminded them of the radical women of the French Revolution. Freneau's "Ode" to Mrs. Gannett actually was one of a series skewering Federalist war hawks and rich American politicians who had deserted their republican principles. He was the object of a new wave of poison-pen barbs by Federalist editors; William Cobbett called him "a little miserable filthy thing." He was probably the last editor Deborah Gannett should have been associated with politically.[66]

Freneau's poem was a democratic encomium to a woman he placed in the tradition of women warriors, the first writer to do so.[67] Freneau's four stanzas began by twitting powerful men in high office: "Ye Congress-men, and men of weight / Who fill the public chairs . . ." As he turned to her achievement, he compared her to Joan of Arc, beseeching Congress to "Reward this gallant Amazon,"

> *Who for no splendid pension sues,*
> *She asks no proud triumphal car . . .*
> *But something in the wane of days*
> *To cheer her heart and keep her warm;*

Freneau ended with a warm appeal for Gannett as a woman who had defied the barriers of "custom" and now challenged male prejudices:

> *How many bars has nature plac'd,*
> *And custom many more*
> *That women never should be grac'd*
> *With honours won from war.*
> *All these she nobly overcame,*
> *And taught by reason sage,*
> *Check'd not her military flame,*
> *But scorn'd a censuring age,*
> *And men that with contracted mind,*
> *All arrogant, condemn*
> *And make disgrace in woman kind,*
> *What honour is to them.*

The ode, it is safe to say, had no political impact; it was reprinted in only a few papers. What else happened to Mrs. Gannett on her trip we do not know. Possibly she went to Philadelphia to press her claim in person. She left no record of this trip at all. Back home in Sharon in the spring of 1798, when she received the news that Congress had turned down her plea, we can conjecture from the events that followed that she drew a political lesson: she would have to be more precise in her goals and clearer about the law. And she would need the support of "men of weight / Who fill the public chairs" if she was going to overcome the scorn of a "censuring age." She had been politicized by her failure, a fitting climax to her first years in the public sphere.[68] Implicit in the phrase Freneau used, "being unable any longer to support herself," was a striking principle: an invalid female veteran was as entitled to aid from the government as much as an invalid male, even if she had a husband whose earnings presumably contributed to her support. It was an assertion of the right of a woman to equal treatment regardless of her marital status.

Chapter Seven

A Gannett on Tour

FOR FOUR NIGHTS in March 1802, Mrs. Gannett delivered an address in the Federal Street Theatre in Boston, after which she donned a soldier's uniform and performed the soldier's manual exercise of arms. She brought down the house. From June 1802 to April 1803 she went on a tour of New England and New York that must be reckoned the first lecture tour by an American woman. She was on the road continually for almost a year, traveling by herself. There was no precedent for it. In her address (written by Herman Mann) she reinvented herself, retreating from the bold persona in the memoir (also written by Mann). Her new narrative was at once an apology for her transgression and an assertion of pride in her achievement that might have astonished as well as alienated advocates of the "rights of women."

1. *The Tour*
"An handsome ordience of Gentlemen and Ladies"

"If her health admits," Herman Mann wrote in his paper, now renamed the *Columbian Minerva*, her intent is "to revisit the principal capitals of the U. States." After Boston, she went to Providence for a successful evening in May, and then after a month's rest at home set out from Sharon in June. During the

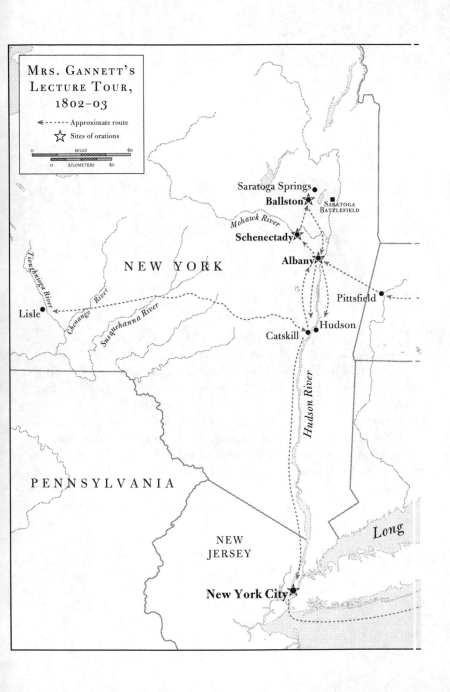

MRS. GANNETT'S
LECTURE TOUR,
1802–03

⟵~~~~ Approximate route
☆ Sites of orations

0   MILES   40
0   KILOMETERS   40

Saratoga Springs
Ballston ☆ ◼ SARATOGA
              BATTLEFIELD

Mohawk River
Schenectady ☆

Albany ☆

NEW YORK

Tioughnioga River
Chenango River   Pittsfield
Lisle
Susquehanna River   Hudson
                Catskill

                Hudson River

PENNSYLVANIA

NEW
JERSEY   Long

New York City ☆

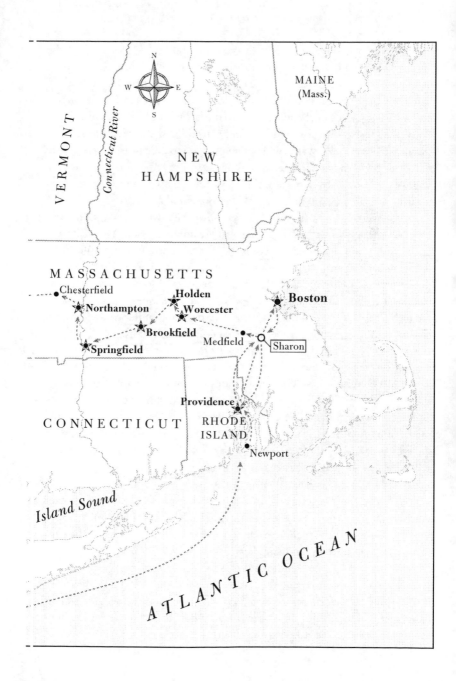

summer and fall of 1802, she "delivered an oration" or "exhibed"—the spelling she used in her diary for "exhibited"—in eight more towns, five in central or western Massachusetts (Holden, Worcester, Brookfield, Springfield, Northampton) and three in New York in the upper Hudson–Mohawk Valley (Albany, Ballston, Schenectady). In the late fall and winter, she traveled down the Hudson River to Hudson and Catskill and went west to Lisle in frontier Broome County, after which she returned to the Hudson Valley early in 1803 to perform again in Albany in February. In April, she appeared on the stage of the Park Theatre in New York City. She gave as many as twenty performances in all, perhaps more, in a dozen towns and cities.[1]

She covered a lot of ground. A direct journey west across Massachusetts to Albany was about 175 miles, from Albany south to New York City 155 miles, and from Catskill on the Hudson west to Lisle easily 160 miles (and the same back again). The last route was so infrequently traveled that it was not even listed in the mileage tables that almanacs ran for travelers. She probably went by boat from Albany to New York, and we know she returned by sea to Newport. Given all the side trips and retracing of her route, she covered upward of 1,000 miles, perhaps several hundred more, whether measured in mileages listed in the almanacs or in modern computerized travel guides. The trip was remarkable as a physical achievement alone.[2]

Mann could not have been more blunt in enumerating her motives for the tour in his preface to the "Address" he published in 1802. A "naturally ambitious" woman wanted money to fulfill her "taste for a more elevated stile of life," and to overcome "aspersions" on her character. The combination of motives in taking to the road in 1802 was not much different than that of 1782. Once again, she wanted to break out of a confining sphere.[3]

Another goal may have opened up as the tour progressed: to win the support of her former officers in her stalled campaign for a pension. Her very first stop in central Massachusetts was Holden, next door to Worcester, home to George Webb, where for three weeks she was the guest of the captain of her light infantry company. Later, she traveled for nineteen days from Catskill into the distant southwestern New York frontier to visit General John Paterson, "my old friend," where for a month she enjoyed the hospitality of the officer she had served as waiter. She would have known the whereabouts of Webb before she started, but most likely she learned about Paterson's removal from Lenox in western Massachusetts to western New York from Webb or one of several army officers she encountered.

The venture was daunting. In Sharon, as she contemplated it, she was "much agitated in mind," she wrote in her diary late in May, "anxious to persevere in my journey—tho a heart filled with pain when I realized parting with my three dear children and other friends." Her own children—now seventeen, fifteen, and twelve—were no longer youngsters, but Susanna, her adopted child, age seven, was a concern, even if left under the care of her husband and Patience Payson. She simply had "much anxiety of mind which is natural to sore disappointments."[4]

Once again she collaborated with Herman Mann, whatever her reservations about the memoir. He wrote her address—it's in his style with entire sentences taken from the book—and within a few weeks of its delivery in Boston, he published it in Dedham (at 20 cents a copy). He may have made the contact with the managers of Boston's Federal Street Theatre where she made her debut. He attended her opening performance and wrote it up for his paper. Mann's wife, Sarah, was her companion, recording in her diary that she "spent most of a week at Boston, [and] went to the Theatre to hear Mrs. Gannett speak her address two evenings." (Later, in May, Sarah "rode to Sharon" with her, "tarried all night, returned the next day," and then "rode to Boston with her one day.") In all, Mrs. Gannett spent three weeks in Boston boarding at $4 a week, presumably for rehearsals with the theatre company and instruction in oratory. On her way to Providence, she befriended a couple who helped her; but after that she was on her own, making all the arrangements herself for each leg of her journey and each appearance. Over the year she was away, she did not keep Mann abreast and his paper did not track her.[5]

The tour was her own achievement. The lines were Mann's, but, as he put it, she "remarkably soon committed [them] verbatim to memory except an addition since of three pages," which presumably he wrote and inserted in the published version, where, we cannot say. She recited the lines, probably varying a few of them after she left Boston, to recast a number of local references. One senses more of her in the address than in the book. The social triumph of the tour was entirely hers, her reception by genteel hosts and her long stays with Captain Webb and General Paterson suggesting her social graces as well as their cordiality. The tour gave her a heightened sense of herself, for which the best evidence is that she kept a journal, literally taking the blank book her husband used to keep track of his labor exchanges as a farmer to record her own experiences. It was at the same time an account book keeping track of expenses, a diary with day-by-day reports (sometimes entered a while after the event), and a journal offering an occasional reflection. The pity is that it is so short and incomplete, the gaps, silences, and abrupt ending adding to the mysteries about her adventures on the road.[6]

Where did the idea of a stage performance and a tour come from? Should we be surprised that the narrative of Hannah Snell reported that since her discharge, the British cross-dressing soldier "has at sundry times appeared upon a public Stage . . . and diverted the Auditors with a Song or two, in order to procure a little money"? Or that later, Snell "perform[ed] the military exercise" at the Sadler's Wells Theatre in London, where she "went through a number of military exercises in her regimentals"? Such exhibitions became a standby on the London stage. "The woman warrior figure," Sandra Gustafson points out, "reached the zenith of her popularity in both England and America in the 1790s." On the American stage, Joan of Arc was portrayed in theatrical pantomimes and in 1798 was the heroine of a play, *Female Patriotism, or, the Death of Joan D'Arc,* performed in New York and Boston.[7]

In 1802, however, there were almost no precedents in the United States for a woman as an itinerant lecturer. Increasingly in the 1790s, women were a presence in public celebrations. But the flourishing Democratic-Republican movement did not especially enlarge public space for women. Indeed, Thomas Jefferson believed that if women were allowed to "mix promiscuously in the public meetings of men," it would cause a "depravation of morals." Here and there a woman spoke to the local militia at a flag presentation ceremony or at a Fourth of July observance. A woman might sing a song or recite an ode on a public occasion, but deliver an address, generally no. The intoxicating celebration of "the Rights of Man" in the 1790s did not automatically spill over into a celebration of "the Rights of Woman." In church congregations, the historian Catherine Brekus observes, "only the Quakers fully recognized women's right to speak in public." In 1806, it was a first when a celebrated English woman preacher delivered a sermon in the chamber of the House of Representatives. In the first years of the nineteenth century, an itinerant woman speaker was an oddity.[8]

On the other hand, young women at the growing number of female academies, or in the boys' private schools newly opened to girls, were commonly instructed in elocution and often gave commencement orations. The much-reprinted *Columbian Orator,* for example, included a commencement address by a Boston girl who had a sense of a new age dawning as "children of both sexes" acquired an education. Girls speaking to audiences that might have included their fathers and brothers thus may have prepared the way for an adult woman being received as a public speaker by "promiscuous" audiences.[9]

Although Mrs. Gannett was not the first woman to give an oration in public, she performed years before the women usually given credit as the first, either Maria Stewart, a black woman, or the radical English feminist Frances Wright, both of whom appeared in the late 1820s. A lecture tour for a woman, however, was without precedent. The lyceum movement, which institutionalized traveling lecturers, was not in full swing until the 1830s. On the other hand, if Deborah Gannett's appearance is thought of as "an exhibition," there were precedents in touring actresses or entertainers. Still, there was nothing quite like it. For towns where there was a printer, an advertisement appeared in the paper or circulated on handbills announcing that "Mrs. Gannett (Late Deborah Sampson) The American Heroine," who "served three years as a private soldier in the Continental Army," would "make her appearance on the Stage for the purpose of relating her narrative."[10]

Nothing in the long tour came close to the theatricality of her opening appearances in Boston late in March 1802, where for four nights spread over a week she was the star attraction at the Federal Street Theatre. The theatre was the most respectable in town, catering to a genteel audience. Housed in an imposing building (100 by 60 feet and some 40 feet high) designed by Charles Bulfinch, architect to Boston's elite, and managed by a Federalist, it was in competition with the Haymarket Theatre, which had a "Jacobinical" reputation. Three of the papers running ads for Gannett's performance were Federalist and one was Republican. Only the Federalist *Boston Gazette* ran an advance "Theatrical Notice" promoting her: "The appearance of the American Heroine is at least a subject of great curiosity," adding that "Madame D'Ens herself was not so great a phenomenon in character as this *Female Soldier*." "Madame D'Ens" was a misspelling of "d'Eon" (also referred to as Mademoiselle d'Eon or the Chevalier d'Eon), a French nobleman and diplomat residing in England, who for several decades had presented himself as a woman and whose true gender was a subject of intense public speculation until his death in 1810.[11]

Each evening was carefully staged to pave the way for Mrs. Gannett's appearance. Or, as the notice in the *Gazette* put it, "the dramatic olio [mis-

cellany] in which she appears we hear was compiled for the express purpose of introducing *her narrative* to the public with every advantage which scene and situation could give it." The large company of a dozen men and three or four women set the mood with a popular play touching on a theme of her address: *The Will, or a School for Daughters,* the first night, March 22; *King Henry the IVth with the Humors of Sir John Falstaff* the second; *The Way to Get Married* the third; and on the fourth, March 29, *The Grand Historical Drama of Columbus; or, America Discovered.* Shakespeare's *Henry IV,* of course, lauded a military hero, and *Columbus* the discoverer of America, both icons of patriotism. *The Will* featured a cross-dressing theme: Albina, the heroine, follows her loved one into the navy, masquerading as a naval officer, wielding both gun and sword. In *The Grand Historical Drama of Columbus,* Nelti, a Native American woman, fights alongside her lover, saving his life. Both plays thus helped to universalize the woman warrior and then show her returned reassuringly to a feminine role.[12]

Each night, the play was followed by "The Soldier's Festival On the Eve of Battle in which Mrs. Gannett will deliver her Narrative," as the handbills put it. She delivered her address, followed by four songs by the ensemble, sung as if by soldiers in camp. Then the climax: "Mrs Gannett, Equipt in complete uniform will go through The Manual Exercise, the whole to conclude with the New Song and Chorus of God Save the Sixteen States." Each evening thus bathed her transgression in waves of patriotism.

The Boston papers carried neither accounts of the performance nor comment. But "Theatrical," the heading for a short report in Mann's Dedham paper, caught the fervor of the first night:

> During an ingenious performance of a Comedy called *The Will or a School for Daughters* . . . she rehearsed to a crowded and brilliant assembly, a remarkably pathetic sketch of her achievements during the time she personated a soldier. At the close of the farce, Mrs GANNET [*sic*], equipped in complete uniform, went through the *Manual Exercises,* attended by a company of officers. The whole concluded with the song and chorus, *God Save the Sixteen States.* On her entering the Stage an universal acclamation of joy involuntarily escaped the audience, and was repeated during the exhibition.[13]

Even allowing for Mann's bias, the evening crackled with theatricality: a play, her address (delivered in her female clothes), a round of military songs by the chorus, her withdrawal from the stage, then her return in uniform as a soldier—a transformation invariably breathtaking for an audience. She presented arms to the brisk commands of not one but "a company of officers," the whole evening ending with a rousing choral singing of a patriotic anthem. The manual exercises alone, if performed in their entirety, would have been spectacular: twenty-seven maneuvers that began with "Poise— Firelock! Cock—Firelock! Take Aim! Fire!" and included "Charge Bayonet!" (Recall Sergeant Munn's comment on how quickly Sampson had learned the drill in the army.) The fourth night was "for Mrs Gannett's benefit," that is, the proceeds went to her, a custom for the stars of theatrical companies. How much she took in we don't know—she began her account

TAKE NOTICE,

The soldier's manual exercise of arms, which Mrs. Gannett performed in Boston and Providence in 1802 and possibly elsewhere. The drawing is from a patriotic recruiting poster issued in 1799 in the quasi-war with France. Library of Congress.

book later—but the week was enough of a success financially and emotionally to allow her to raise her sights for a tour.[14]

In Providence, she advertised that she would appear "equipped in complete uniform" and "go through the MANUAL EXERCISE." Elsewhere, she usually seems to have done no more than "deliver an address." She wore a dress and did not appear in uniform to present the soldier's drill, or so it seems from her diary and the public advertisements. Her most common diary entry was "delivered an oration," and less frequently "exhibed," which may possibly have meant in uniform. To perform the manual exercise required lining up an ex-officer locally who could bark out the commands, which entailed finding a former sergeant. She performed in public halls, hotels (once in a Masonic hall), and in courthouses, but not in meetinghouses, which pious members of a congregation might have considered sacrilegious (an impersonator in the pulpit!). Only in New York City, at the tail end of her tour, did she appear again in a theatre and on the same bill with a play.[15]

In her advertisements, she showed she was a master of self-promotion. In the towns where there was a newspaper, she arranged for a genteel notice stressing her modesty, respectability, and local sponsorship, as in this notice of July 21, 1802, in the *Massachusetts Spy or Worcester Gazette,* Isaiah Thomas's paper:

Mrs. Gannett's Exhibition. The Ladies and Gentlemen of Worcester are respectfully informed that Mrs. Gannett, the celebrated American Heroine, who served nearly three years with great reputation in our Revolutionary Army—will at the request of a number of respectable characters, deliver an Address to the inhabitants of this town at the Courthouse, Tomorrow at 5 o'clock PM. Tickets may be had of I. Thomas, Jun., Price 25 cents, children half price.

In Albany, after two successful performances in 1802, she published "a card" in the paper, offering "unfeigned thanks to the Citizens of Albany for the liberal patronage" and "orderly and polite behavior" at her "exhibitions." Five months later, on her second visit, she advertised herself as "now returned from a tour of the western country." She had become a showman. The price of admission was generally the same, 25 cents (lowered to 15 cents in Providence to produce a turnout after she was unable to appear as scheduled), with half-price for children. If the theatres in Boston and New York followed their custom, tickets could have ranged from 25 cents for the gallery to a dollar for choice box seats.[16]

Travel in 1802 in an era with a rapidly increasing number of passable post roads and turnpikes would have been easier than in 1782. A journey by an unescorted woman, however, was still not quite proper. As late as 1816, when young Maria Ward Tracy, for example, traveled from Worcester, Massachusetts, to Middletown, Connecticut, "by stage and all alone at so late an hour," she reported that her friends and neighbors "were surprised that I should come alone . . . and think I had more courage than they should."[17]

After her son drove her in a carriage on the first leg of her journey from Sharon to Worcester, Mrs. Gannett traveled alone. She went either by "stage" or "hired a carriage," occasionally enjoying a vehicle offered by a generous host. Sometimes, she recorded, she went by "mail," which meant in a stagecoach carrying the mail. She made the near-three-week trip to General Paterson beyond the Susquehanna River in a wagon. On her return, she retraced her steps and probably came down the Hudson later from Albany to New York City on a sloop. In all this time on the road she recorded no threatening experiences. No doubt it was safer for a matron in her forties to travel unescorted than for a woman in her twenties. If she was menaced on the road or at a public house, it might have been enough for the lady to say she had been a soldier in the Continental Army and knew how to wield a gun.

When she went from Sharon to Providence with William Billings, a "polite gentleman and [his] Lady," she brought with her "the bill of performance" from Boston, which she gave to the local printer, who arranged to print and post handbills "in the most public places in the town." After this she was her own manager, choosing the hall, getting the notices and tickets printed and posted, and making all arrangements. At Albany, the expenses she recorded showed what she had to arrange: for printing notices and tickets, for "an old key keeper," for a ticket taker, for sweeping the courthouse, for brushing the seats, and for cleaning the candlesticks. She also paid a woman "for dressing my hair" before each performance. She was a one-person touring company, performer, and manager, and she was all business. In Hudson, after she was "quite unwell," she regretted, "I have Done no business for this long time," or entered, "Done no business to advantage," meaning she had not brought in a cent while her living expenses piled up. She kept good accounts, recording the dollars and cents of daily expenditures. The trip marked her arrival as a businesswoman as well as a breadwinner in the family.[18]

Her accommodations were a source of pleasure to her. She stayed for the most part in private homes, or "took boarding and lodging" in a boarding-house and less frequently at a public house. At Mrs. Keeler's in Albany, "a very good family and but 3 Boarders," she was delighted with "a parler chamber to myself without the least interruption except the city noise." (In Sharon, she had no parlor in her old house and no room of her own.) Only once, in the scrubby country west of Albany, did she voice the usual gripe of travelers in the backcountry about a public house: "a log house which is called a tavern," apparently run by a German or Dutch family. "I could understand very little of their conversation. all was gloominess." She identified the owners of half a dozen homes where she stayed as being captains—a former servant to a general would be sensitive to rank. At times it almost seems as if she were being passed on by a network of army officers.[19]

Travel took a terrible physical toll. In the east she was sick occasionally: "very sick of a dysentary" or "indisposition." On the New York leg of her trip, she was ill for long stretches and, after September, often miserable: "a great distance from my native home among entire strangers." For more than a month she was able to make only the barest entries in her diary: "tooth ake and ague in my face"; "in extreem pain"; "quite unwell"; and then, after a slight improvement, "very unwell yet, but am better." On her return from western New York late in December 1802, when she was stuck at a Susquehanna River crossing for three weeks because of "the badness of the weather," she came down with "the fever, violent pain in my left side," and required a doctor. Each time, however, she recovered; the first time enough to travel west, then on her return enough to make a second appearance in Albany in February 1803, and in March to swing down the Hudson to New York City. The hardships she bore amidst all this pain show how much the tour meant to her. She was driven, no less than she had been in the army. A good soldier did not turn tail and flee.[20]

How did audiences respond to her performance? Clearly, people turned out—some in tribute, many out of curiosity. There were men, women, and children. In Boston, by her reckoning 250 people attended the four performances; in Albany, she had the printer run off 300 handbills and 100 tickets, suggesting the latter number as a hoped-for audience. In smaller towns—all the others were smaller than Albany—the turnout would have been proportionately less. Midway into the tour, before she got to Albany, she sent home $110 (by way of a Sharon neighbor), which at 25 cents a head represented another 450 paying customers in the small Massachusetts towns. There may have been a few hundred more in the three upstate New York towns, and she obviously drummed up enough interest at Albany for a return engagement. She had only an indifferent turnout, however, in New York City. All told, from Boston through New York City, easily 1,500 people, perhaps as many as 2,000, paid to see and hear "the celebrated" Mrs. Gannett.[21]

We wish we knew more about the response of her audiences. Decades later, John Adams Vinton, Mann's editor, wrote of her Boston appearance: "Those who witnessed the performance, said that 'she would almost make the gun talk' every time it came to the ground from her hand." Among the witnesses Vinton talked to was Amos Sampson, at the time an apprentice printer (possibly a nephew or cousin). Local newspapers carried advertisements, but in the issues that followed there usually were no descriptions or comment.[22]

The only account to come to light is in the *Hampshire Gazette* of Northampton, in which "A Correspondent" who signed himself "Gill Blass" offered "a panygyric" to her. He reported with unbounded enthusiasm on "the numerous respectable and admiring audience (comprised of both sexes)," which "showed their regard to merit by their respectful attention during the performance." He was "at a loss which most to admire," Mrs. Gannett's achievement as a soldier, or that her "chastity [was] never called into question." He applauded her performance: "the elegant dection [diction], the manly elocution, and the correct pronunciation of the truly singular woman." And then he went on to offer one of the very few observations we have of her public appearance. She confounded the expectations of her audience: "Persons who have never seen Mrs. Gannett have figured to their imagination a large masculine frame rendered disagreeable by coarseness of manners. . . . Yet it is impossible for the most prejudiced observer to deny that she is beautiful in an eminent degree. Her form is such as 'Sir Joshua' [Joshua Reynolds, the English painter] might delight to draw—her manners easy, her eyes acute. And when she smiles a beautiful row of Chinese teeth are displayed." He went on to enumerate other qualities: "the fairness of her complexion, the harmony of her voice, the modest blushes which at times suffused her countenance." She was, in sum, a person of "charms." Would that we had more such impressions.[23]

In Mrs. Gannett's only commentary on her audiences, written about the one in Providence where she performed in uniform, she was struck by the skepticism of her viewers, which gradually melted. "When I entered the Hall, I must say I was much pleased with the appearance of the audience. It appeared from almost every countenence that they were full of unblieff—I mean in regard to my being a person that served in the Revolutionary Army. Some of them which I happened to overhear Swore that I was a lad of not more than Eighteen years of age." But she held her audience and then won them over. "I sat some time in my chair before I rose to deliver my Address. When I did, I think I may with much candor aplaud the people for their Serious attention and peculiar Respect, especily the Ladies." This may have been the pattern in other audiences: curiosity, skepticism, attentiveness, then acceptance (or at least once, harsh rejection).[24]

Judging by her diary entries, she felt that she was well received. What stands out in her brief comments about both her audiences and the hosts with whom she stayed was her sense of their quality. Gannett was consistently pleased by the respectability of her "ordience" (spelling the word phonetically as she pronounced it, with an "r," as she did "cultervation" and "invertation"—a Yankee speech pattern). She referred to them as "a very respectable ordience" (Springfield), "an handsome ordience of Gentlemen and Ladies" (Brookfield), and "a very respectable circle" (Holden), all references implying gentility more than size. She delighted in how "very polite" and "very agreeable" people were to her. Her hosts were "fine people" or "a fine family." She spoke of a "genuine friendship" with Mr. Billings and his wife, her traveling companions to Providence, who "invited me to take tea with them at our arrival." The former bound servant, the weaver, the infantry private, the officer's waiter, the farm housewife, savored every moment of such refinement and respectability. She crossed a line of class distinctions, enjoying everything she was missing in Sharon.[25]

She was overwhelmed by the reception by her two senior officers. Captain Webb had become Holden's leading citizen and a large landholder. Known for the sword Lafayette had given him as a light infantry captain, in local lore he had a reputation as "a fearless soldier and high spirited officer." He might have shown her the muster rolls and other company records he had taken home with him. (One daughter practiced her ABC's on them and wrote "Betty Webb Her Book.") She "taried" at the Webbs from July 10 to August 3, 1802, became friends with his daughter, Sally, to whom she later sent books, and impressed the family enough to borrow money from his two nephews and, it seems, from Webb. Later, she wrote warmly to him.[26]

At General Paterson's home from November 11 to December 11, 1802, she was deeply moved by the hospitality of her "old friend" and his neighbors. The general had moved in 1791 from Lenox in the Berkshires to Lisle in what was then a frontier: Tioga County (later Broome), where he again became a major landholder and leading citizen. Lisle was named for Lafayette's birthplace in France. Paterson was one of sixty proprietors of the "Boston Purchase" of some 230,400 acres. "Paterson's Settlement" at the junction of two rivers was later known as Whitney Point. Appointed the presiding judge of the county, he was elected to the state legislature and, in 1802, to Congress. A Federalist in Massachusetts, he became a Republican, a process of adaptation many conservative leaders found necessary for political survival on the frontier. (William Cooper, a Federalist land magnate in nearby Otsego County, learned from bitter experience that he had to bend to the democratic ways of Yankee yeomen.)[27]

"This respectable family," Gannett wrote, "treated me with every mark of Distinction and friendship and likewise all the people did the same. I really want for words to express my gratitude." She described frontier conviviality. "They often met together in the Neighborhood and had the most Social meetings. They seemed to unite in hearty Congratulations with my old friend Judge Paterson on our happy meeting." She made no mention, however, of delivering her address, suggesting that she did not do so. What was the upshot of her visit? Paterson would serve in the Eighth Congress from October 1803 to March 3, 1805. This was the Congress that made a change in the requirements for pension eligibility for invalid veterans that allowed Gannett to receive a pension from the War Department in March 1805. No correspondence between the two survives, and there is nothing in the printed record to indicate what he did on her behalf, if anything; but he had a reputation as a friend of the veteran, and it would have been out of character had he not taken up her cause.[28]

Her attraction to the world of gentility stands out in other entries in her journal. She was fascinated by the medicinal springs at Ballston, eight miles from Saratoga, already a fashionable spa. She "delivered an oration" there, and she beheld "a great Numbr of people here at these Springs from all Quarters. they give great credit to the waters." She tasted a drink "whose sparkles are full of animition [animation]" and found it "very disagreeable," and no better than common salts. At the "pool at Bethlehem," another spa, a parade of coaches, chaises, and wagons put her in mind of a passage in the Bible. The people were "going as it were to the pool of Siloam to be cleansed. I observed among the rest the Impotent man which we read of in Scripture, one of the greatest cripples I ever saw. however he was put into the pool, and that was the last I saw of him." She was remembering the New Testament, John 5:1–9.[29]

In Albany, she indulged her passion for clothes. The woman who in 1785 was married in one fashionable dress and in 1797 had her portrait painted in another, bought clothes, accessories, and fabrics galore on both stays in town. On the first shopping binge, in 1802, she kept careful track of the cost: "one umbrilla, $6.00, one cloak and trimming $6.39, one handkerchief, $1; cost of my bonnet, $2.17, Moroco shoes, $1.36; 1 shade 1.17, ½ yard sattin riband, .20, 1 scane [skein] black sewing silk, 8 cents, 1 ivory comb .34." On her return trip in February 1803, she went on another spree in which she did not even bother to list prices. "I have bought 1 pair of silk gloves, 1 silk shall [shawl], 1 pair moroco shoes, 1 neck handkerchieff, lace 3 yards, yard wide. [illegible word] 3 scanes of thread, 5 scanes sewing silk." She was rewarding herself with money she had earned twice over, once in the army and once on tour. She was celebrating not only her success but her expectations of moving into other fashionable circles. In her diary she seems exhilarated.[30]

The diary/journal shows sides of Deborah Sampson Gannett revealed nowhere else. With a little help from a friend, she could easily have written her own memoir. Her spelling was indifferent. She spelled some words as she heard them and may have been putting down others for the first time. But she had a sophisticated vocabulary ("anxiety," "animation," "persevere," "consolation," "advantageous"), indicating a person who read and conversed with other literate people. She could write clear, forceful prose, describing sites vividly. Moreover, she had an excellent memory, listing at the end of her account book two dozen persons not entered previously with whom she had stayed, and the cost of travel for each leg of the journey over a year's time. She remembered things in sequence, located places geographically, and had a good eye for detail—all of which lends credence to her recall in the 1790s of her military adventures. (If she could retain all these names in 1802–03, she probably remembered the names of her fellow soldiers correctly, and it was Mann who garbled them in the memoir.)

Most important, she expressed her feelings in her diary—whether her sense of pain and gloom, her elation at her social acceptance, or her love for her children. The bond to her children was unmistakable. She cried out to them in moments of despair. In sending back money, it was with the hope that "my family will make good use of" it. (She mentions her husband not at all, a silence that alerts us to ask questions about their relationship.) The diary reveals a woman brimming with emotion—if only she had kept a similar record of her seventeen months in the army.

And yet, doesn't the diary of 1802–03 reveal something about her in 1782–83? Would the woman who at age forty-two to forty-three went on an arduous lecture tour have been that different from the woman who, at twenty-two to twenty-three, went on a formidable tour of military duty? Can we not say that she showed in her diary, reporting her success as a lecturer, some of the secrets of her success as a soldier which have been so difficult to reconstruct? The diary reveals a physical stamina, a willingness to take risks, a capacity to be on her own, a perseverance, a resourcefulness, and an attention to minute detail, as well as her social skills, befriending and charming strangers. I long lamented the absence of a diary for her time in the army, but I believe we are entitled to read back to her army experience the qualities she shows in the diary on her tour.

The lecture tour, given the goals Mann claimed for her, was a success, even if devastating to her health. She made some money, although probably not much beyond the $110 she recorded sending home (plus whatever she cleared in Boston). Her expenses ran high: in March 1803, she summed them up as "one hundred dollars. another ninety-two. another ninety two," which can be read as a total of $284, and this was before she got to New York City. Boardinghouses and carriages were expensive, to say nothing of clothes. But acquiring the stuff to rise socially was, after all, one of her aims. She also overcame the "aspersions" on her character by showing people she was neither a fraud, a virago, nor an eccentric. And, judging by the results, she won political support for a pension.[31]

The tour was a triumph—until she came to New York City, where her single performance was a fiasco. She arrived in the city from Albany late in March 1803, judging by a short newspaper item reporting that Mrs. Deborah Gannett was "in this city on her way Southward." She was identified as "this extraordinary woman . . . [who] was at the storming of Yorktown under Gen. [Alexander] Hamilton," linking her to a still famous New Yorker. Her performance was managed (or mismanaged) by no less than William Dunlap, the reigning impresario of the New York theatre, and was held at the Park, the city's principal theatre. Colonel William Smith, John and Abigail Adams's son-in-law, recommended her to Dunlap; he "wished that she could have an opportunity for delivering an oration from the stage. . . ." Smith may have seen her in Boston. Dunlap had enlightened views about women; he was an early reader of his friend Charles Brockden Brown's *Alcuin; A Dialogue* (New York, 1798), a biting indictment of gender inequality. Dunlap scheduled her as the added attraction for three performances of a new play, *The Blind Boy*, a comedy in five acts, followed by a farce in two acts. He may have chosen the main play because it featured his leading lady, Mrs. Johnson, cross-dressing as Pedro, a blind boy whose sight a doctor restored.[32]

A newspaper account of her first and only performance April 13 was brutal: "Mrs Gannet, the female who is distinguished for having served three years in the American army as a soldier in the late war, delivered an oration yesterday evening at the Theater. Her talents do not appear calculated for theatrical exhibitions, and we are informed that she is not to appear again." As an afterthought, the writer made a plea for her as a charity case. "We understand that her character is irreproachable and her situation such as merits sympathy and aid from the generosity of the public." Dunlap probably wrote the piece.[33]

What had happened? It was not that New York audiences were unpatriotic. Two months later, on the Fourth of July, Dunlap put on a flag-waving potboiler, which took in the largest sum he ever made on a single play. The problem may have been that he did not give Mrs. Gannett the dramatic buildup Boston's theatre manager had done. New York's audiences, moreover, were unusually demonstrative. Washington Irving, writing in 1802 as "Jonathan Oldstyle," reported that the gallery at the Park often sounded like Noah's Ark, "with an imitation of the whistles and yells of every kind of animal." Gallery denizens called the tunes for the orchestra, "stamping, hissing, roaring, whistling, and when the musicians are refractory, groaning in cadence." A crowd like this may have hissed and catcalled Mrs. Gannett off the stage. Judging by the newspapers, she gave only the oration and did not do the more exciting exercise of arms. The Park was a huge theatre; an oration would have required a high energy level; exhausted from her long trip and illness, she may simply not have projected herself. The play was also a dud; it was "never popular," Dunlap wrote. He said of Mrs. Gannett's performance, "It was an ill judged exhibition and failed accordingly." For whatever reason, her appearance was a humiliating flop.[34]

The experience was so traumatic that she took no note of it at all in her diary (unless she did so and someone excised the pages). Nor did she make any entries for her travel to New York, her days in the city, or where she was later. The editor Philip Freneau, so cordial five years before, was no longer there. If she was headed "Southward," as the newspaper had it, we know not where. We lose track of her from mid-April, the time of her performance, to June, when she records a return by sea to Newport without a specific date or place of departure. "Very sea sick" is all she wrote. If she went on to Philadelphia, as she may have contemplated the year before, there is no obvious sign of her public presence there. My guess is she was holed up in a boarding-house in New York, sick and miserable. When she arrived home in June 1803, she was not well. Half a year later, early in 1804, Paul Revere found her "much out of health."[35]

The year on the road, rewarding and exhilarating, was also harrowing and debilitating, a combination much like the year and a half in the army. The New York City disaster may have colored her attitude to the tour as a whole. I think she buried it in her memory. Mann said nothing about the tour in his revised manuscript, nor did Vinton, even though he had picked up faded memories of her performance in Boston. Her tour was not listed among her achievements in the notices of her death—perhaps because in 1827 a woman lecturing was even less in fashion. When Frances Wright, the English feminist, lectured in American cities in the late 1820s, one paper railed that she had "waived all claims" to courtesy because, by speaking in public, "she ceased to be a woman" and had become "a female monster." To her family and friends, Gannett talked about her army exploits but not at all, it seems, about the tour. In 1902, when the town of Sharon sponsored a dinner celebrating the 100th anniversary of the Boston address, it was news to her descendants. Yet, as America's first itinerant woman orator, Deborah Sampson Gannett was even more of a pioneer than she was as a woman soldier.[36]

2. The Address
". . . my high respect and veneration for my own SEX"

What did she say? Mrs. Gannett delivered her address in a climate of opinion shaped by the conservative backlash against "the Rights of Woman" that actually reached new heights between 1797, when her memoir appeared, and 1802–03, when she appeared in public. Because her appearance alone on a public stage violated the norms for her sex, she had to make clear in her address that she was not the threat she appeared to be. It was a challenge, for which she assumed a new persona.

In the 1790s, Mary Wollstonecraft's *Vindication of the Rights of Woman* (1792) had found a welcoming audience in the United States. Twenty years after Abigail Adams's plea to her husband in the spring of 1776 to "remember the ladies" in recasting the nation's laws, men had not repealed their "masculine systems," as John Adams put it. The changes in the legal and political status of women in the Revolutionary era were minimal. The American common law accepted the dictum of William Blackstone, the English codifier, that "the legal existence of the woman is suspended in marriage." New Jersey alone granted single women of property the vote, but took it back in 1807. More girls and young women were going to school than ever before, yet education also heightened the disparity between promises and possibilities. As Priscilla Mason asked in her commencement address at the Young Ladies Academy of Philadelphia, "where shall we find a theatre for the display" of oratory? "The Church, the Bar, and the Senate are shut against us." The author of *The Female Advocate,* who identified herself as an "aged matron," wrote in 1801, "Men engross all the emoluments, offices and merits of church and state." Clearly, there were changes in the expectations of many women but not in their basic status.[37]

It is not surprising, therefore, that by the mid-1790s many women shared the opinion of Elizabeth Drinker, a well-read, well-to-do Philadelphia Quaker matron, about Wollstonecraft that "in very many of her sentiments, she as some of our friends say, *speaks my mind.* In some others I do not always coincide with her. I am not for quite so much independence." Wollstonecraft's plea for women to take personal action on their own—"it is time to effect a revolution in female manners—time to restore to them their lost dignity"—was in many ways more threatening to men than her appeal to reform laws. Her admonitions to women to throw off "slavish dependence" and "slavish obedience" made it the kind of book that inspired women to change their own behavior. In Philadelphia in 1796, for example, Elizabeth Hewson, a single woman in her mid-twenties, was emboldened to take passage on a stagecoach without a male escort. When a friend expressed alarm, Hewson snapped that she had not "profited much by the reading of Mrs. Wollstonecraft . . . I thought the Rights of Woman would have cured her of such ridiculous notions." Wollstonecraft, in short, was an inspiration to make the personal political.[38]

Her American counterpart, Judith Sargent Murray, also found an audience in the 1790s for her essays on "the equality of the sexes" in Massachusetts magazines. The essays were published in Boston in three volumes in 1798 as *The Gleaner* for a list of seven hundred subscribers, headed by George Washington and John and Abigail Adams, half of whom were women. To prove the equal capacities of women, she offered lengthy historical catalogues of the achievements of individual women, demonstrating they could be as ingenious, heroic, brave, eloquent, and patriotic as men. Murray argued that women "should be enabled to procure for themselves the necessaries of life; independence should be placed within their grasp."[39] By the 1790s, enlightened opinion about women had settled at an accommodation the historian Linda Kerber has called "republican motherhood," in which mothers were endowed with a patriotic responsibility for raising their sons and daughters as citizens. It was a radical concept, staking out a claim for women as citizens performing a vital public role and elevating the importance of education for women. Yet it played "a conservative stabilizing" role in confining women's exercise of citizenship to the domestic sphere.[40]

At the turn of the century, a wave of misogyny put even such moderate feminism under siege. In 1802, to orthodox Federalist New Englanders, Wollstonecraft was as much anathema as was Thomas Paine for *The Rights of Man* and *The Age of Reason,* or President Jefferson for his deism. The revelations about her personal life in the memoir by her husband William Godwin (1798) were a godsend to conservatives—a child born out of wedlock, attempts at suicide, a second child conceived before their marriage, her own death in childbirth—as proof that female independence led to immorality and self-destruction. Wollstonecraft was a "strumpet" to Timothy Dwight, president of Yale, who completed an eight-article diatribe against her in a Boston paper only a few weeks before Mrs. Gannett appeared on the stage there. Professor Benjamin Silliman, another Yale worthy, claimed that Wollstonecraft "wishes to introduce the [female] sex into the Camp, the Rostrum and the Cabinet," envisioning "Amazon legions" in battle. "The Female Advocate" was furious with this din: every attempt to prove "female worth," she wrote, met with an intimidating scarecrow about "masculine women," "women of masculine minds," and "manly women."[41]

In this atmosphere, the Massachusetts women advocates of the "equal worth of women"—Murray, Adams, Mercy Otis Warren—avoided the vocabulary of "the rights of women," disassociating themselves from women who pushed the boundaries further than they wanted to go, like warrior women. In 1784, Warren had written a play, *The Ladies of Castille,* in which Maria, the heroine, led troops into battle in seventeenth-century Spain; in 1805, in her two-volume history of the American Revolution, she had not a word to say about women in the Revolutionary War. Mrs. Murray, after parading long lists to prove women capable of the military virtues, made crystal clear "we are not desirous to array THE SEX in martial habiliments; we do not wish to enlist our women as soldiers." For that matter, Wollstonecraft herself, who compared the slavishness society fostered in women to the blind obedience armies fostered in soldiers, made clear she was not going to advise women "to turn their distaff into a musket."[42]

This was the climate of opinion when Mrs. Gannett stepped onto the lecture platform. Thus, a hypothetical audience might include a fairly broad range of opinion: on the left, disciples of Wollstonecraft like the defiant young Elizabeth Hewson and the matronly author of *The Female Advocate;* in the center, older women of the Revolutionary generation, halfway admirers of Wollstonecraft like Elizabeth Drinker and Abigail Adams; and on the right, misogynist readers of Dwight in Boston's Federalist newspapers (the men perhaps dragged to the theatre by their wives). The Mann/Gannett oration showed an exquisite sensitivity to this array, especially to the prejudices of conservatives. Actually, since 1797 both of them had honed their skills of adapting to audiences. Mann as an editor had learned how to trim his sails politically. Mrs. Gannett had learned from the ceaseless gossip about her and from her failed pension campaign that she had to overcome hostility to "masculine" women.[43]

In important ways, the address retreated from the book. Recall that in the memoir, Deborah was an impoverished daughter of "the female yeomanry," a near-orphan girl, a bound servant with a thirst for knowledge trying to break out of a contracted female sphere. Along with coarse descriptions of her life as a soldier there were sexually bold scenes. The oration erased every bit of this. She was a lady of classless origins, the war was sanitized and any sexual innuendo banished. Once again, Mann helped Deborah reinvent herself.[44]

The words in the address are Mann's. Judith Hiltner, who has made a close study of his career, has traced a third of the oration to the book and finds much of the rest repeated in his later writings. Yet Deborah's voice seems to break through Mann's florid oratory. The wording is grandiloquent, but the requirements of an oratorical style forced a directness in the rhetoric missing in the rambling book. Mann had also gotten to know Mrs. Gannett better, so that as a ghostwriter he could write lines that fit her assertive personality. It is not hard to imagine hearing this feisty, strong-willed woman coming down on certain passages with greater force than others.[45]

We do not know in what style she delivered the address and whether she used gestures. Oratory with gestures was in fashion and went with the grand Ciceronian literary style. Mann said she memorized the talk verbatim, which meant—because she did not need to hold a script in front of her—that her arms were free. Besides, she was not speaking from behind a pulpit or lectern she could grasp. It is interesting that her shorthand diary entry for her performance is "exhibed" or "exhibited." In these years when young ladies and gentlemen trained in elocution delivered dialogues, plays, and addresses at schools and academies, they performed at what were often called "exhibitions." Gestures were taught. The elocution handbooks appearing some years later prescribed and illustrated a range of gestures (separate for women and men) codifying what was probably common practice in the early 1800s. Recall, too, that Mrs. Gannett, who stayed for several weeks in Boston before her first performances, was very likely coached by members of the Federal Street company in a theatrical style.

Given this context, it is possible that she delivered her address with numerous gestures: spreading her arms wide, crossing them over her chest, pointing with her right hand to the heavens, or clasping hands in front when pleading. We can't be sure, but this may be what the correspondent to the *Hampshire Gazette* had in mind when he referred to her "manly elocution." "Manly elocution" by preachers or politicians was accompanied by gestures. He said almost nothing about the content of her address, but he remembered the style—another clue that she did more than just speak her lines.[46]

The address was skillfully balanced. It went back and forth from the apologetic to the assertive and from the patriotic to the conservative republican protofeminist. Mrs. Gannett began—we can say Mrs. Gannett, aware that the words were Mann's—with a string of "preliminary apologies," in effect, a ploy. She portrayed herself as the modest woman awakened "from the tranquil slumbers of retirement" to speak by "the solicitations of a number of worthy characters and friends." (This from the aggressive petitioner who had pushed herself onto Philip Freneau.) She granted what she did was "a breach in the decorum of my sex unquestionably," which "ought to expel me from the enjoyment of society, from the acknowledgement of my own sex." Her action was "a foible, an error and presumption." After seven paragraphs in this vein, she abruptly shifted tone. "And, yet, I must frankly confess, I recollect it with a kind of satisfaction"—there it was—and then, as if too bold, came a slight retreat, "recollecting the good intentions of a bad deed" as someone who "lives to see and to correct any indecorum in his life."[47]

Having appeased her audience, she moved quickly to justify her transgression on the grounds of youthful patriotism. Her "juvenile mind" responded to events—"the massacres in our streets, in the very streets which encompass this edifice—in yonder adjacent villas [Lexington and Concord, wrote Mann in a footnote], on yonder memorable eminence [Breed's Hill, said Mann]. My mind became agitated with the enquiry— why a nation separated from us by an ocean more than three thousands miles in extent should endeavor to force on us plans of subjugation." Perhaps "the critical juncture of the times could have excused such a philosophical disquisition of politics in woman."[48]

Protected by this cloak of patriotism, she then turned the flowery rhetoric Mann took from his book into what might be heard as a forceful protofeminist statement. "Wrought upon . . . by an enthusiasm and phrenzy, that could brook no control—I burst the tyrant bands which *held my sex in awe,* and clandestinely, or by stealth, grasped an opportunity which custom and the world seemed to deny as a natural privilege." She did not rebel against a "contracted" female sphere, as in the book. Yet she linked her personal quest with the nation's quest for "FREEDOM and INDEPEN-DENCE," as did countless other people in the Revolutionary era. To magnify the importance of her enlistment, she exaggerated the low state of the American cause. "And whilst poverty, hunger, nakedness, cold and diseases had dwindled the American armies to a handful," while "even *Washington* himself" was "tottering over the abyss of destruction," she decided to "throw off the soft habiliments of *my sex* and assume those of the *warrior.*" In capitalizing on this misleading "Valley Forge" image of the war, she was obscuring both the date of her enlistment and the state of the American cause. Her listeners might think she enlisted in 1777 rather than in 1782.[49]

Then she delivered a few simple lines that melted Mann's bombast and asserted her agency: "Thus I became an actor in that important drama," and "a new scene, and as it were, a new world, now opened to my view." At this point, about halfway into the oration, she resorted to another ploy, which avoided spelling out the details about her military experience. "The curtain is now up. A scene opens to your view. . . . What shall I say further? Shall I not stop short and leave to your imagination to portray the tragic deeds of war?" And she did just this, leaving it to her audience to imagine "the hardships, the anxieties, the dangers even of the best life of soldier," and leaving her female listeners to imagine "the perils and sexual inconveniences of a girl in her teens," because "only one of my own sex . . . can conceive of my situation."[50]

She then devoted a few meager passages to evoke four wartime episodes, each pinned to a person, a battle, or a site that had won a place in patriotic memory. The Westchester skirmishes became: "Hence you can behold the parched soil of White Plains drink insatiate the blood of her most peaceful and industrious proprietors—of freemen and of slaves. I was there! The recollection makes me shudder." Of Yorktown, she said only that there was "the havoc, carnage and death," and "three successive weeks, after a long and rapid march, found me amidst this storm," and let the battle go with that. Cornwallis gave his sword to "the illustrious, the immortal WASHING-TON." Her expedition into northern New York became: "I will not even portray an attempt to reinforce the brave SCHUYLER, then on the borders of Canada; where if the *war-whoop* of infernals should not strike you with dismay, the *tomahawk* would soon follow!" And for her escape from death in

Philadelphia: "Nor need I point you to the death-like doors of the hospital in Philadelphia . . . though I myself made one of the unhappy crowd" of the sick and dying. All but the last were inventions: she was not at the battles of Yorktown or White Plains, and General Schuyler had retired from active service.[51]

"You have now but the shade [shadow?] of a picture which neither time nor my abilities will permit me to show you to the life," she concluded. Thus, after devoting no more than a few minutes to these episodes, she could say, "But we will now hasten from the field." She referred to her wound evasively ("A dislocated limb draws fresh anguish from my heart"). She offered no vivid detail, only symbolic evocations. In moving so rapidly over her experiences, she encouraged her listeners to take them for granted, discouraging them from asking questions.

Having brushed lightly over what she did, she returned to the question of "what particular inducements" brought her "to elope from the soft sphere of her own sex," answering with a long hortatory poem (composed by Mann):

> And dost thou ask what fairy hand inspired
> A nymph to be with martial glory fired?
> Or, what from art, or yet from nature's laws,
> Had joined a Female to her country's cause?

She then threw the question back to her audience.

> Then ask—why Cincinattus left his farm?
> Why science did old PLATO'S bosom warm?
> Why HECTOR in the Trojan war should dare?
> Or why should HOMER trace his actions there?

She did the same with Newton, Charles I, Locke, Jove, and Vulcan, in effect challenging a double standard for women.[52]

In her peroration, Mrs. Gannett moved from a personal defense to a claim for the importance of women in society. Once again, she began with apologies—"I swerved from the accustomed flowry paths of female delicacy"—and with disavowals: she yielded "every claim of honor to the hero and patriot who met the foe in his own name." She was like "a bewildered star traversing out of its accustomed orbit." Then she reversed herself, veering into another protofeminist assertion that put down the contemporary derogation of women: "I cannot contentedly quit this subject or this place," she said, "without expressing, more emphatically my high respect and veneration for my own SEX." She offered her "most sincere declaration of friendship for that sex," which "neither in adversity or prosperity could I ever learn to forget or degrade."[53]

Before doing this, however, she felt she had to disassociate herself from the "extremes" of "vice" (male and female) her appearance may have conjured up. She condemned "the prodigal from the time of his revelry with harlots" (because parents may have thought of her as the proverbial prodigal daughter); "the libertine, the bacchanalian, the debauchee" (because some may have compared her to Mary Wollstonecraft, demonized as a libertine); "and what is more wretched than all, of the emaciated form of modern baggage in the streets" (because camp followers were commonly equated with prostitutes, a growing presence in American cities).[54]

Speaking directly to the women in her audience, she was bold: "The rank you hold in the scale of beings is, in many respects superior to that of man." Then she fell back to the conservative cliché of women as molders of men. "Nurses of his growth and invariable models of his habits, he becomes suppliant at your shrine, emulous to please." This permitted her to end on the relatively safe ground of separate but equal spheres: "On the whole, as we readily acquiesce in the acknowledgement, that the *field* and the *cabinet* are the proper spheres assigned to our MASTERS and our LORDS; may we, also desire the dignified title and encomium of MISTRESS AND LADY, in our *kitchens* and in our *parlours.*" In her final note, she thus accepted the role of women as republican mothers: "and as an over ruling providence may succeed our wishes—let us rear an offspring in every respect worthy to fill the most illustrious stations of their predecessors."[55]

The address, however conservative in doctrine, may have had a more ambiguous effect on those who were hearing it and watching her. It had a back-and-forth thrust. She apologized, yet she did not apologize. She asserted pride in her military achievement so aggressively—"I was there"—as to preempt any challenges. She explained herself but rejected the very idea that she had to explain herself—men who did great deeds were not asked to account for their motives, why must a woman? She ended up affirming separate spheres, but the entire performance—a woman speaking in public—invaded the male sphere. She advocated republican motherhood while demonstrating republican citizenship. For many, the medium of the performance overpowered the message.

How might women in her "promiscuous" audience have responded? If we can return to our imagined assemblage of representative women attending an "exhibition," say, in Boston, there would have been a range of responses. Youthful disciples of Wollstonecraft might have cheered. The graduate of the Boston public school who in her commencement oration said, "here on our western shores we can justly boast of a [Mercy] WARREN, a [Sarah Wentworth] MORTON and an [Abigail] ADAMS," might have added "a GANNETT" to her list of Massachusetts luminaries, as proof that "the mists of superstition and bigotry are vanishing." Elizabeth Hewson, the young woman empowered by reading Wollstonecraft to travel without a male escort, would have pointed to Gannett as a model for female travelers, although she would have chided her for retreating to a pose of feminine humility from which Wollstonecraft was trying to free women. So, too, the "aged matron" writing as "The Female Advocate" would have hailed her as worthy of the biblical Deborah in breaking the taboo that denied women the right to speak in public.[56]

The older women of the Revolutionary generation might have been ambivalent. For Abigail Adams, who in 1776 had pledged that women would "become a Race of Amazons" if need be, Deborah Gannett was more of an Amazon than she had in mind. So, too, Mercy Otis Warren might have considered the former servant from Middleborough parading on a Boston stage the epitome of the world turned "topsy turvey" she deplored. Judith Sargent Murray might have been especially conflicted. "We are not desirous to array THE SEX in martial habiliments," she had written. Yet Deborah was living proof of the capacities of women who were "in every respect equal to men."

As to the conservative women who distanced themselves from Murray or Wollstonecraft, Mrs. Gannett's acknowledgment of woman's proper role ("in our *kitchens* and in our *parlours*") made it easier for them to accept her, but her actions—as soldier and performer—spoke louder to them than her words. No matter that some men might perceive her as feminine and even beautiful, very different from the coarse virago they expected, she was the "masculine woman" their fathers had warned them about. Her audiences may have heard in her address what they wanted to hear and have seen in her what they wanted to see, in itself a tribute. Yet how remarkable it was that she was there before them to be seen and heard.

PART FOUR

"OLD SOLDIER"

Chapter Eight
Public Woman

DEBORAH GANNETT was not the first woman who saw service in
the Revolution to receive a disability pension from Congress—that was
Margaret Corbin in 1779—and other women were rewarded by state govern-
ments. But she clearly was the woman who conducted the longest and most
persistent battle for a pension. She was hardly the first American woman to
hold forth in private circles expressing opinions on public affairs—women
whose husbands were men of affluence or influence had long done that in
salons. But she was unusual as a self-educated farm woman who, as her
admirer William Ellis put it, "conversed with such ease on the subjects of
theology, political subjects and military tactics, etc." that she reminded him
of the style of an "able diplomat." She was a unique kind of public woman in
the young republic.

1. A Petitioner, 1803–21
A Quest for Equal Treatment

Late in 1803, some months after she returned from her tour, Deborah Gannett again petitioned Congress for a pension, the first time since her failure in
1797–98. She wrote to her congressman, William Eustis of Boston. In Febru-

ary 1804, Paul Revere, after coming over from his home and brassworks in nearby Canton to visit her in Sharon on her farm, wrote Eustis a compassionate letter of support. He reported that "she is now much out of health," and that "she has told me that she has no doubt that her ill health is in consequence of her being exposed when she did a soldier's duty & that while in the army she was wounded." It was in this letter, quoted earlier, that Revere referred to her husband as "a good sort of man, though of small force in business," and said that "they have a few acres of poor land, which they cultivate, but they are really poor." Whatever money the tour brought in probably went either to pay family debts or to doctors. Revere said nothing about the tour, and she may have said nothing about it to him. After all, if she was claiming ill health stemming from war wounds and military service, it was hardly politic to bring up a tour which demonstrated her capacity to endure an arduous, year-long journey. And perhaps this was still another reason why the tour went into oblivion in family memory.[1]

This time, unlike in 1797–98, she had effective political support: two congressmen who knew about her could plead her cause—Eustis and John Paterson. William Eustis, representing a district that included her own county, Norfolk, as well as Boston's Suffolk, had been a member of the Massachusetts legislative committee in 1792 that approved her petition for back pay. In the previous Congress, he "strenuously presented" claims for another veteran's pension barred by a statute of limitation. General Paterson was also known for "supporting and defending the claims of the Revolutionary soldiers." In 1798, she may have had nominal support from her own congressman, Harrison Gray Otis, a Federalist. This time she had bipartisan support. While Revere was an influential Federalist, Eustis and Paterson were members of the Democratic-Republican majority in the Eighth Congress.[2]

In the years after her return from her tour, she was sick, poor, and in debt. She had borrowed money from Captain Webb's two nephews, from Revere many times, and probably from others. In fact, the only letters by Deborah Sampson Gannett over her long life which have survived are two plaintive pleas from these years—one to Webb to stave off creditors and a second to Revere beseeching him for another loan. In June 1804, in her apology to Webb, while her petition was making its slow way through channels, she was optimistic as to her prospects: "I flatter myself that I shall see better days than ever I have done heretofore. I hope to be able to Satisfy every demand against me." Would he inform his nephews, she asked, that she still felt "under the greatest obligation to them—I will make remittances to them as soon as I possibly can but must beg their patience a while longer."[3]

The exact process by which Mrs. Gannett got her pension is a small mystery because the documents have not survived—lost, it was said, in a fire in Washington, D.C., during the British invasion in the War of 1812. In the early 1790s, as we saw in describing her failed first petition, Congress gave authority to the Department of War to issue pensions to invalid veterans, prescribing an intricate array of proofs which few veterans could assemble. The disability had to have occurred *during* and not *since* the war. On March 4, 1805, the last day of the session, the Eighth Congress amended this law, extending it to "all persons who, in consequence of known wounds received in the active service of the United States . . . *have at any period since* become and continue disabled, in such manner as to render them unable to procure a subsistence by manual labor." This fit perfectly the claim Mrs. Gannett was making. The revision made her eligible. The Congress passed an enabling measure permitting the secretary of war to consider petitions from individuals in her category. Eustis and/or Paterson probably played a role pushing this bill through Congress; one or both may also have intervened on her behalf at the War Department.[4]

One week after Congress amended the act, on March 11, 1805, Secretary of War Henry Dearborn placed Mrs. Gannett on the rolls of invalid pensioners, telling Benjamin Austin, the Massachusetts pension agent, to "enter her name in your books." She was placed on the rolls at the rate of $4 a month, or 80 percent of the $5 allowed for a full pension for someone with "decisive disability." Her pension was made retroactive to January 1, 1803, the year she applied. The swiftness with which she was placed on the rolls indicates that she had already submitted papers, that they had been processed, and that somebody was following her case. Surely, a clerk in the War Department would pay attention to a request from a former general or a former army surgeon, both Republican congressmen. Secretary Dearborn, in his letter to Austin, wrote that Mrs. Gannett had been "severely wounded." The law still required the testimony of doctors and other proof of disability. So the fact that she received a sum for partial disability suggests she had submitted at least some of the medical testimony the law required. In April 1805, Benjamin Austin made out a bank draft for Mrs. Gannett for $104.53, a payment for two back years (at $48 a year) and two current months prorated. Subsequently, every six months she received a payment of $24 from Boston's old

Jeffersonian Republican warhorse, her signature on the receipt suggesting that she may have taken the occasion for a trip to Boston. She was not one to miss a chance to travel.[5]

The pension of $48 was possibly more cash than the Gannett farm brought in over a year. It was enough, for example, to buy a horse, albeit an old one. And $104.53 would have been a real windfall, the total valuation the tax assessor would put on several "neat cattle" the Gannetts owned some years later. What it went for we don't know.[6] In any case, the payments Mrs. Gannett began receiving in 1805 did not stretch very far. On February 22, 1806 (after receiving one or two payments), she turned again to Revere, imploring him for the loan of a paltry $10:

> Honoured Sir—After my unfeigned regards to you and family, I would inform you that I and my son have been very sick—though in some measure better—I hope Sir that you and your family are all in the injoyment of helth which is one of the greatest of blessings.—My own indisposition and that of my sons causes me again to solicit your goodness in our favour though I with Gratitude confess it rouses every tender feeling and I blush at the thought that after receiving ninety and nine good turns as it were—my circumstances require that I should ask the Hundredth—the favour that I ask is the loan of ten Dollars for a Short time—as soon as I am able to ride to Boston I will make my remittance to you with my humble thanks for the distinguished favour—from your Humble Servent—Deborah Gannett.[7]

Her short letter showed she had become a master in the art of supplication. It was skillfully composed, the sentences well constructed, the vocabulary sophisticated (her wishes were "unfeigned"), and had a literary flavor (she blushed "at the thought" of asking another good turn). All of this reinforces the sense conveyed by her diary that she was a reader of books and adept in conversation. One historian, who has read several thousand letters of men and women in all walks of life in early America, was struck by the sophistication shown by her two extant letters, as well as by the accomplished handwriting. Somewhere along the line she had benefited from the example of formal letters by others—perhaps by her army officers—and she may have received some instruction.[8]

Revere doubtless responded as generously as he had before—"ninety and nine good turns" suggests this. Local lore has it that on occasion he

Honoured Sir —

After my unfeigned regards to you and
Family, I would inform you that, I and my Son
have been very Sick — though in Some measure
better, I hope Sir — that you and your family
are all in the inoyment of helth — which
is one of the greatest of blessings — my own
Indisposition and that of my Son causes me again
to Sollicet your goodness in our favour — though
I with Gratitude confess it rouses every tender
feeling and I blush at the thought — that
after receiving ninety and nine good turns
as it were — my circumstances require that
I should ask the Hundredth — the favour
that I ask is the loan of ten Dollars for a
Short time — as Soon as I am able to ride
to Boston I will make my remitance to you
With my humble thanks, for the distinguished
favour — from your Humble Servent —
                                    Deborah Gannett
February 22d 1806 —

In 1806, in one of her two surviving letters, Mrs. Gannett artfully asks Paul Revere for "the loan of ten Dollars for a Short time." Courtesy Massachusetts Historical Society.

A petition from Mrs. Gannett to Congress, December 26, 1809, asking that her pension as an invalid soldier awarded in 1803 commence from the time of her discharge in 1783. The petition was denied. Courtesy Massachusetts Historical Society.

came down from Canton to have a drink with Mrs. Gannett in the tavern room at the public house at Cobb's Corner in Sharon, a few miles from her house. The tavern, which also served as the town post office, is still intact: a long, low, dark room, more or less as it was two centuries ago, with a bar, a few shelves behind it for liquor, and a few tables and benches. The letter also suggests she looked forward to seeing Revere in his home in the metropolis ("as soon as I am able to ride to Boston"). Any excuse to get out of Sharon, perhaps.[9]

Mrs. Gannett was not done with her campaign. In 1809, she sent another petition to Congress asking for a retroactive lump-sum payment on her pension, to "commence from her discharge from the army in 1783." She claimed that she had "received Wounds by which she has been disabled from performing the common occupations of life as otherwise she might have done," asserting as she had in 1797 the principle that a woman was entitled to compensation even if her husband presumably had an income. She now prayed that "she may be entitled to the further consideration of having her pension-pay commence at the time of others pensions belonging to the said American army, as the law has made and provided." How common it was for other invalid pensioners to receive such retroactive sums is not clear. In any case, she wanted equal treatment.

The Committee on Claims interpreted this request to mean "a sum equal to her pension from the conclusion of the war up to the time when she was placed on the pension list" that is, from 1783 to 1803. If approved, this could have given her $960 ($48 a year for twenty years), a small fortune. In 1810, the Committee rejected her plea on the grounds that Congress had established a principle "only to allow pensions to commence from the time when proof of disability of the party" was shown. In other words, even if she was wounded in the war, she had not offered proof until twenty years later. Congress supported the Committee.[10]

She would return to this issue. Meanwhile, in 1816, her pension went up automatically when Congress in its generosity increased the monthly stipend for invalid veterans of her class from $4.00 to $6.40 a month, which came to $76.80 a year. Then, after 1818, she had a chance to benefit from the country's liberality to veterans in the wake of the patriotism following the War of 1812, coupled with a compassion for what one scholar has called "the image of the suffering soldier" of the Revolution. In March 1818, Congress passed the first general pension act, providing stipends for any veteran who could prove he was in "reduced circumstances" and had served at least nine months. The pension for enlisted men would be $8 a month, or $96 a year, for life. The *Dedham Gazette* cheered the act but lamented "the humiliating condition" imposed by this means test. Lawyers offered to help veterans prepare their applications gratis.[11]

On September 14, 1818, when Mrs. Gannett filed an application to qualify under the new act, she fell into yet another battle in her long pension war. She recited her army bona fides (her officers and unit), relinquished her invalid veteran's pension, and ended with the assertion that "she is in such reduced circumstances as to require the aid of her country for her support." It was in this deposition that she added gratuitously that "she was at the capture of Lord Cornwallis"—a claim she does not seem to have made in earlier petitions—and "was wounded at Tarrytown."[12]

She was immediately caught up in the conservative backlash against the cost and corruption of the new pension program. The War Department was swamped with more than 28,000 applications amidst the "Panic of 1819," a depression that threatened to eliminate the Treasury surplus. Some applicants had no proof they had served, others clearly were far from poor. By the fall of 1818, department clerks were furiously screening out the unworthy. Mrs. Gannett's application either did not go through, or it went through and was held up.[13]

Six months after her initial deposition, on March 16, 1819, Judge John Davis of the federal court signed a printed form amending her application: "I am satisfied that Deborah Gannett by reason of his [*sic*] reduced circumstances in life, is in need of assistance from his country for support," enclosing documents. Then he had second thoughts. On March 20, he attached a short letter of transmittal to no less than the Hon. John C. Calhoun, secretary of war, who had taken on the role of Grand Inquisitor rooting out frauds and imposters. Her declaration, Davis explained, "was made in September last but has been delayed for evidence respecting her circumstances." Whether "circumstances" referred to her economic status, her military record, or her gender is ambiguous. He went on: "there is no accompanying proof of her services. This was supposed to be unnecessary as she was already on the pension list under a preceding act." The judge was playing it safe.[14]

The records show that Deborah Gannett was issued "certificate No. 13434 July 31, 1819 at the Massachusetts Agency," entitling her to a pension, which suggests her application went through initially and then was suspended, like thousands of others. In December 1819, Secretary Calhoun could crow to Congress that of 28,555 applications, his department had rejected 11,881 and had 404 under review, which may have included Gannett's. In Dedham, in July 1820, 120 "of the old Revolutionary Worthies" appeared at a special session of the Norfolk county court to "renew their claims." The *Village Register* ran an angry editorial. "If we may judge by appearances," they were entitled to pensions. Many of "these frosted veterans" had lost limbs or "were bowed down with age & infirmities, pinched with poverty and worn out with the labors of their life." The new law "operates with cruel and oppressive weight" on individuals forced to travel "in some instances from 20 to 30 miles" to make good their claims. "The government might have employed their time in legislating on matters of more consequence."[15]

Once more, on December 19, 1820, Mrs. Gannett appeared in court in Dedham and "presented for *renewal* her claims," as the local paper put it, indicating that her prior documentation was flawed. The paper, under the heading "Female Pensioner," ran a glowing review of her military career, obviously intended to boost the application. The impression locally was that her military record was being challenged, because the paper reported that "there are many living witnesses in this county who recognized her on her appearance at the Court, and were ready to attest to her services."[16]

It seems, however, that authority had decided she simply had not filed the required proof of poverty. Gannett now filled in a printed form, dated December 20, 1820, attesting to her military service in a single sentence (without making a claim to having been at the Battle of Yorktown) and referred to "my former certificate 13434" by which she had been placed on the rolls and "my former application of 14 September, 1818." On another printed form she attested that she did not have "any property, or securities, contracts or debts due me; nor have I any income, other than what is contained in the schedule hereto attached." To this she attached a small piece of paper with a one-sentence handwritten statement: "Schedule of property belong [*sic*] to Deborah Gannett. Wearing Apparel—$20.00. Deborah Gannett." This new declaration did the trick in Washington and put the pension into effect. When she received her first payment is not clear—not before the early months of 1821, which means that from the time she had first applied in September 1818, the government had taken two and a half years to make sure it had avoided the menace of an imposter, a sixty-year-old grandmother, defrauding the United States of an extra $17 a year beyond her invalid pension.[17]

It would be hard to find a more poignant document by Deborah Gannett than this "Schedule of Property": testimony to her poverty; to the inequality of the common law that made a woman's husband the sole proprietor of land they jointly farmed and the house they jointly occupied; as well as to her lifelong passion for clothing. Twenty dollars might have been a conservative reckoning of the worth of a wardrobe that in 1820 could have included the wedding dress of 1785, the dress in the portrait of 1797, the dresses she wore on her tour in 1802–03, and clothing bought since. Perhaps it would not do for someone claiming to be "in reduced circumstances" to say she had garments of greater value. Then again, as a fashion-conscious woman, she was very aware that dresses quickly went out of fashion and lost their value.

Meanwhile, before all this red tape was unsnarled and before she was transferred to the new pension roll, Mrs. Gannett made a last-ditch effort for a retroactive lump-sum payment on the *invalid* veteran's pension she was relinquishing. This was a woman with a desperate need for money and a sense of justice denied who would not give up. On January 25, 1820, she submitted a brief petition to Congress, claiming that "while others were on the list of pensioners and received their pension soon after the termination of the war she was not on the list of pensioners until the first of January, 1803, owing to the great disadvantage she was under to procure sufficient credentials which were necessary to lay before Congress." This is a reference to the difficult requirement in the unamended law for proof of disability incurred during the war; to her predicament as a soldier discharged without credentials; and, by implication, to her status as a woman unfamiliar with the procedures of the political system. On March 31, 1820, Congress turned down her plea, as it had done a decade before.[18]

As a recipient of a general pension, Gannett differed only in gender from the twenty thousand or so other aged veterans eventually pensioned under the 1818 law, just as she was like the young recruits she joined in 1782. "By 1820," according to the historian John Resch, "most claimants were laborers, artisans or farmers in their mid-sixties. Most no longer owned real property and they were unable to work at full capacity. Based on the means test, they were either destitute, poor or propertyless. Eight of ten attested to less than $100 in property," and about five in ten to less than $50. Deborah Gannett could have been any and all of the above. The pension rolls were shocking testimony to American poverty in a land of plenty, thirty-five years after the end of the Revolution.[19]

The nineteenth-century accounts of Deborah Sampson Gannett's life celebrated the government granting her a pension but not the obstacle-strewn path by which she obtained it, and did so invariably with a smug air of self-congratulation, as if to say a grateful nation had sought her out and bestowed its largesse upon her. It was cut from the same cloth as the stories that George Washington discharged her, gave her a reward, and later received her in the nation's capital, not one of which was true. All this reinforced a larger belief comforting Americans that the country always took care of its veterans. In reality, from the time of her discharge late in 1783, it had taken her eight years to win back pay (1792), twenty-two to get a pension as an invalid veteran (1805), and thirty-eight to get a general service pension (1821). It was only after repeated, angry appeals that she had gotten anywhere, and for several years she was needlessly suspended from the general pension rolls. She received a pension because she fought for it; no one handed it to her, and at that it was paltry. Moreover, she was turned down twice for the large retroactive sum that might have made a real difference in her life.

Deborah Gannett had a sense of entitlement that included the right of a woman no less than a man to support from a country she had served. In standing up for herself, she had fought for a principle: that as a woman she had a right to a living when she "was unable any longer to support herself."

2. *Masculine/Feminine*
". . . a woman of uncommon native intellect and fortitude"

The woman who over a span of thirty years petitioned, sought support from politicians, publicized herself through a memoir, and appeared on public platforms, in all save petitioning, invaded the male "public sphere."[20] In the process, she showed she was the equal of men with formal education. She spoke in public, even if the words were not her own. She was articulate in private, where the words were hers. She also usurped male functions within the family. She left home to make money, keeping meticulous accounts; she borrowed money, warding off creditors and pleading for loans. She won a pension which kept going up, bringing in more cash than the farm. In all of this, she was acting not as a deputy for her husband, long an accepted role for New England wives, but on her own. If her husband was, as Revere put it, "of small force in business," she was of large force.[21]

How in the last two decades of her life was this woman perceived by contemporaries? Among the three men who set down their observations of Deborah Gannett as an older woman—Paul Revere, Herman Mann, Jr., and William Ellis—there was a near consensus as to her abilities and personal qualities. There was disagreement only as to how masculine or feminine she appeared, which reflected the expectations each man brought to viewing her.

In 1804, Revere, who lived and worked "but a short distance from the neighborhood where she lives," traveled down to her farm and saw Mrs. Gannett for the first time. He was in his seventies and she was about forty-five. He had been "induced to inquire her situation & character," he wrote Congressman Eustis, "since she quitted the Male habit & soldier's uniform for the most decent apparel of her own sex, & since she has been married and become a mother." He reported first what others said about her. "Humanity & Justice obliges me to say, that every person with whom I have conversed about Her, & it is not a few, speak of her as a woman of handsome talents, good morals, a dutiful wife, and an affectionate parent. She is now much out of health. She has several children," and it was in this context that he made his observation already cited about her husband and their poverty.[22]

Revere was uncommonly frank in saying how much she differed from what he expected, in effect, the common stereotype of a woman who crossed over into a male occupation. "We commonly form our ideas of a person whom we hear spoken of whom we have never seen, according as how their actions are described. When I heard her spoken of as a Soldier, I formed the idea of a tall, masculine female, who had a small share of understanding, without education & one of the meanest of her sex—When I saw her & discussed with her I was agreeably surprised to find a small affeminate conversable Woman, whose education entitled her to a better situation in life." The stereotype itself is interesting. Revere, who had served in the war for a while as a militia officer, had lived most of his life as an artisan in Boston's North End, long the center of laboring-class life. He may have seen women doing "men's work" on the city's docks and streets. "Mean" in the eighteenth century was common usage for the lowest class. "Meanest of her sex" suggests his prior image of her was as a coarse masculine woman eking out a living at physical work. Relative to the person he anticipated, he found Mrs. Gannett "small" and "affeminate." His reaction is similar to the contrast between expectations and perceptions in the correspondent who reported with such enthusiasm on her performance in western Massachusetts.[23]

Herman Mann, Jr. (1795–1851), son of the author, set down his impressions of Mrs. Gannett in his journal as he remembered her about 1820, when he was twenty-five and she was past fifty. He had "often seen her and heard her converse of her campaigns at my father's house in my early days," he wrote, "where she was a frequent and welcome visitor." He also "visited her at her house in Sharon and soon after my marriage about 1820 she paid me a short visit in my house in Dedham." Thus, he knew her over a fairly long period and had seen her frequently in social situations.

"The extraordinary woman," he wrote, borrowing from an article he had written for the *Dedham Register* in 1820, "is now in the sixty-second year of her age. She possesses a clear understanding, and a general knowledge of passing events, is fluent in speech, and delivers her sentiments in correct language, with deliberate and measured accent, is easy in deportment, affable in her manners, robust and masculine in her appearance." Mann, Jr., who grew up hearing about her military exploits, unlike Revere, took it for granted that she was "robust and masculine."[24]

The third observer, William Ellis of Dedham, a former selectman, state representative, and state senator, a pension agent with lawyerlike skills, set down his observations in 1837, ten years after Mrs. Gannett died. He was reviewing her history for a congressman on the occasion of Benjamin Gannett's petition to transfer her pension to him. A man in his late fifties, Ellis was the most analytical observer of the three. He could speak "from what I have seen of Mrs. Gannett myself." Although his own acquaintance with her was "somewhat limited," he stated, "It happens I have several connections who reside in [her] immediate neighborhood."[25]

"I can truly say," Ellis wrote, "that she was a woman of uncommon native intellect and fortitude. . . . Her stature was erect, a little taller than the average height of females, her countenance and voice was feminine but she conversed with such ease on the subjects of theology, political subjects and military tactics, etc. that her manner seemed masculine. I recollect that it once occurred to my mind that her manner of conversation on any subject embraced that kind of demonstrative, Elustrative Style which we admire in the able diplomat."

Among these observers—a mix of men in age, status, and vantage point, all three worldly enough to make comparative judgments—there was agreement on two major points. She was an articulate conversationalist: "conversable" (Revere), "fluent in speech" (Mann, Jr.), and "conversed with ease" (Ellis). Second, she was knowledgeable and well informed: a person with an "education" (Revere) and a "general knowledge" (Mann, Jr.), who could hold forth with ease "on a variety of subjects" (Ellis). There was disagreement among the three only as to her gender qualities. To Revere, who expected to see "a tall, masculine female . . . one of the meanest of her sex," she seemed "small" and "affeminate." To young Mann, who grew up with Deborah's tales about herself as a soldier, she seemed "robust and masculine." Ellis, perhaps the most astute of the three, drew a distinction between her inherited and acquired traits. Her face and voice were "feminine," but her conversation, he wrote, was so able that "her manner seemed masculine."

These were the observations of men; if any contemporary women set down their impressions, they have not survived. Some left evidence of how they felt about Mrs. Gannett by the unending barrage of gossip they kept up about her, a subject to which we will return.

3. Her Conversations
A "style which we admire in the able diplomat"

We would like to be a fly upon the wall when Mrs. Gannett conversed on subjects of public interest. William Ellis would have heard her when she visited Dedham, very likely at the house of the Manns. In his novel *Alcuin; A Dialogue* (1798), Charles Brockden Brown portrayed a Mrs. Carter, an educated Philadelphia widow with whom Brown's alter ego engages in numerous conversations on topics of the day. She held forth in what he called "Mrs. Carter's Lyceum." Had Mrs. Carter or Mrs. Gannett been the wife of a well-to-do merchant or an influential politician in Boston or Philadelphia, New York or Washington, she would have been the kind of woman who might have presided over a salon. Given what we know of contemporary public controversies in Sharon and eastern Massachusetts in the first two decades of the nineteenth century, it is not hard to suggest the range of topics Mrs. Gannett very likely discussed.[26]

Military tactics: This is the easiest to intuit. Like other old soldiers, she talked about her "campaigns," as Mann, Jr., said, which meant the ones she took part in in the Hudson Valley (and the ones Mann, Sr., claimed she was in, like Yorktown), and about the famous generals she had known, like Knox or Paterson (or claimed to have encountered, like Washington, Lafayette, and Schuyler). As the veteran of a successful war, she would have felt qualified to offer opinions on the disasters and blunders of the very unsuccessful War of 1812. In New England the war was controversial, but among Republicans and veterans of the Revolution, it rekindled the "Spirit of '76." It was a second War for Independence. In fact, 120 Sharon men traveled up to Boston to work on the harbor forts, and Earl, Deborah's son, became a captain in the militia.[27]

Politics: The national conflict between Republicans and Federalists divided Sharon. In the early 1790s, Sharon voters supported Federalists; after 1796, they voted Republican by slight majorities for Congress and presidential electors and split more evenly in gubernatorial elections. By the 1810s, the town selectmen were usually Republican. Turnouts varied, from 80 to about 160 voters, but the trend was up, indicating the politicization of the citizenry.[28] By 1815–16 the town was completely polarized, as illustrated during a terrifying epidemic of "la grippe," in which eighteen of the first twenty-four victims died. Daniel Stone, the town physician, "a gentleman of the old school" and a Federalist, was unable to stem the tide. The selectmen then called in a Dr. Mann of Boston, a Republican, "with whom they were long conversant . . . as a citizen and physician," who ministered to more than sixty patients, only three of whom died. The selectmen and nine others—all Republicans—sent a letter to the Boston paper lauding Dr. Mann, prompting Federalists to rush into print with a defense of Dr. Stone.[29]

Where Mrs. Gannett stood politically is guesswork. If gratitude influenced her politics, she would have been loyal to the Republicans. The two editors who pleaded her cause, Mann, Sr., and Freneau, were Republicans. She received her pension from administrations presided over successively by Jefferson, Madison, and Monroe. She owed her invalid pension to a reform voted by a Republican Congress in which her benefactors were Eustis and Paterson, both Republicans.[30] On the other hand, there was a tendency for educated, genteel women to be Federalist. Mrs. Gannett, as a woman exercising the rights of petition and speech yet denied the right to vote, may have rejected both political parties. She may well have been like Mrs. Carter in Brown's *Alcuin,* who when asked "Are you a Federalist?" replies caustically: "What have I, as a woman, to do with politics? . . . We are excluded from all political rights without the least ceremony."[31]

Theology: We can say more about her religious views. The denominational storms that racked Massachusetts early in the nineteenth century broke with full fury in Sharon after 1810. The town annalist, writing in 1830, could say that "for many years much bitterness has been manifested in political and religious controversies in the community." In fact, differences in politics did not become acrimonious until they were intertwined with the religious splits between Unitarians-to-be and orthodox Calvinists.[32]

The controversy broke up the First Parish Congregational Church. In 1799, the town settled as its new minister Jonathan Whitaker, a Harvard graduate, a Unitarian in his principles and a Federalist in politics, who, as one church historian put it, "was bitter in his denunciations of the Democratic Party. Unfortunately for him, the majority of his parishioners were Democrats." At the funeral of an opponent, Whitaker sang a verse from Isaac Watts's hymn "Behold the Aged Sinner Go." In retaliation, a Democratic Republican parishioner "marched into the meeting house one Sunday morning armed with a hammer and horse-shoe and proceeded to nail up his pew door, and fasten the horse-shoe on the outside." He left singing a popular Democratic song, "All Haughty Tyrants We Disdain."[33]

In this charged atmosphere, orthodox trinitarian Calvinists peeled off from Whitaker's church. In 1813, a small group of twenty-six formed a Baptist society, the town meeting began maneuvers to oust Whitaker, and in 1816 he resigned. In 1821, when the congregation finally agreed on a successor, a second orthodox minority of forty-two withdrew to form the Christian Society, leaving a Unitarian majority in control of the original church. From here on, there were three churches in Sharon: Congregational, Unitarian, and Baptist, all at loggerheads with one another. This ongoing religious conflict would have provided endless subjects of conversation about theology, church governance, and the politics and personalities of ministers.[34]

Where was Mrs. Gannett in all this? Her family was enmeshed in a controversy as tricornered as the hat of a colonial gentleman. Her father-in-law remained faithful to his ancestral Congregational faith (he died in 1813); her husband became a founding member of the Baptist Society; and she became an advocate of liberal Christianity—in effect, a Unitarian-to-be. Mann, talking to her in the mid-1790s, dwelt at length on the evolution of her religious views, and while he may have projected his own liberalism onto her, since he reported her adhering to views he disapproved of, his report deserves credence.

First, she had gone through a process of questioning her own religious beliefs, and in the 1790s may still have been on a religious quest. Mann did not approve of how far she had gone: "She considered herself in a state of probation, and a free agent; and consequently at liberty to select her own religion," he wrote, "and in this she was, in a measure mistaken."

Second, as part of this, she seems to have moved from one denomination to another. She made "researches in Christianity . . . finding herself almost an infinite variety of sects. . . . Thus when she would attach herself to *one* the sentiments of a *second* would prevail, and those of a *third* would stagnate her choice and for a while she was tempted to reject the whole." She even considered the wisdom of "being bound to any set of religion," a path also unacceptable to Mann.

Third, she rejected the gloomiest tenets of orthodox Calvinism, which Mann summed up as "the doctrines of *total depravity, election* and a few others." He offered as a "summary" of the "genuine religion" that she "now" believed (in the 1790s): "THAT religion, which has a tendency to give us the greatest and most direct knowledge of DEITY, of his attributes and works, and of our duty to HIM, to ourselves and to all the human race, is the truest and best. . . ." Thus, by the mid-1790s, Mrs. Gannett had arrived at a kind of rational religion that pointed toward Unitarianism.[35]

We have proof that her husband, Benjamin, became a Baptist, and that their son, Earl, was a Unitarian.[36] We have no church records for Deborah, but given the outlook Mann summarized, she seems to have remained a member of Sharon's Congregational Church as it moved toward Unitarianism.[37] In so doing, she would have been torn by her sympathy for Reverend Whitaker's theological liberalism and a possible distaste for his crotchety, divisive Federalism. If I am right, the exchanges in the Gannett household could have been hot and heavy: Deborah's liberal Christianity vs. the evangelical orthodoxy of her husband vs. the old-fashioned orthodoxy of her aged father-in-law. Deborah Sampson Gannett's religious trajectory, in her youth from Congregationalist to evangelical Baptist, then back to the Congregationalists and toward Unitarianism in her later years, was not typical of women who became Baptists, but neither was it unusual. Women who had the mettle to break with one church obviously were fortified to break with another. She had a mind of her own.[38]

As impressive as Mrs. Gannett's ability to converse on a range of subjects—she was not simply a garrulous veteran reliving moments of glory—is what Ellis called her "manner of conversation." Recall his words: "it imbraced that kind of demonstrative, Elustrative Style which we admire in the able diplomat." The impression she made on Revere was similar: "a woman whose education entitled her to a better situation in life." Implicit in both observations was that she drew from a fund of knowledge she could have gotten only from her reading.

Once again, as in her youth, we know that Deborah read, but we do not know precisely what. We have a few small clues (aside from the vocabulary in her diary and letters) that books were part of her life: she sent books to the Webbs in Holden after her visit; she lent her name to a subscription list for an English conduct book Herman Mann reprinted; there were a few books in the probate inventory of her son's estate. But we also have a large clue in her long-term association with Herman Mann, at whose home, as his son reported, she was "a frequent and welcome visitor." Besides publishing a succession of newspapers, Mann printed books and pamphlets, maintained a bookstore and a circulating library, and ran a bindery in which he bound books in a marbled paper of the family's invention. The career of Mann and his three sons was an epitome of the explosion of American print culture in the first quarter of the century.[39]

Dedham center was only eight or nine miles from Sharon, and as her pension increased, Mrs. Gannett had spending money. But the point is she did not have to buy books; she could borrow them from Mann's circulating library at 6 cents to 12½ cents a week per book (with "out of town" subscribers allowed three books "returnable at leisure"). Among the books Mann printed, sold, or stocked in his circulating library (600 titles by 1823) there were works in every field of her interest: political classics, pamphlets, religious tracts galore, biographies of leaders of the Revolution, and memoirs of Massachusetts officers. His library catalogue also listed scores of titles marked "R" for romance or "N" for novels, as well as works of travel and description.[40]

In Middleborough, old-timers spoke of young Deborah Sampson as stern, inward, and often angry. In her later years, judging by the men who wrote about her, she was talkative, outgoing, and agreeable. She drew people to her by her talents in conversation. In discourse she was rational rather than rancorous, accommodating rather than confrontational—in short, she was diplomatic. Thus, in conversation, as in her diary and letters, her voice seems very different from that of the person projected by Mann in either the bombastic book or the declamatory oration. She conversed in a style Benjamin Franklin had cultivated and made famous in his autobiography, in which he disavowed a "positive dogmatical Manner." But while she more than likely read Franklin, she did not need him to instruct her. Her style suggests a self-educated woman who knew that by virtue of her unusual experience as a soldier she commanded attention, yet who was aware that she could not speak with the authority of either a man of degrees (a doctor, a lawyer, a minister) or a man of affairs (a merchant, a politician, a former officer). Therefore, she had to convince people by persuasion. She had mastered the style to make her way through life, as had Franklin, as a way of rising into the respectable world she hungered to enter.[41]

Chapter Nine

Private Woman

THERE WAS GOOD REASON for the urgency in Mrs. Gannett's campaign to win and enlarge her pension. Paul Revere's comment about the Gannetts in 1804—they were "really poor"—held true for many more years. The family was in dire straits. Recall that in 1805, Joseph, Benjamin's younger brother, migrated from Sharon with his family to western New York for a new start. More than this, there was an uncertainty as to who would inherit the patriarch Benjamin's land when he passed on. In 1813, after the Gannetts achieved the prospect of a modicum of security, they moved into a new house on which Deborah could focus her aspirations for middle-class gentility. But by the time of her death in 1827, she had achieved only a few tokens of the "elegant stile of life" she had long sought.

1. A Scramble for Security
Three Generations of Gannetts

The future of Benjamin and Deborah Gannett depended on what Benjamin's father would do with his land. Their problem was that Benjamin Senior, who in 1782 at fifty-five had taken Anna Everson as his second wife, now had a third son, Warren, born 1783, Benjamin Junior's half brother, who also had to be provided for. Earl, Junior's son and Senior's grandson, born in 1785, would have grown up with Warren (who was also his uncle).[1] In 1805, when Warren was twenty-two, his father conveyed half of his estate to him for $1,500 (we assume a fictitious sale), reserving for himself and his wife when she became his widow "one half of my dwelling house . . . one half of my barn . . . and one half of my Corn barn," a common arrangement. One has to imagine the tension among the Gannetts generated by this transfer of land to Warren, the third-born son, rather than to the firstborn son, Benjamin, age fifty-one. Joseph, the second son, left for the west the same year, knowing there was now no chance for an inheritance for himself. He sold his land. Two years later, however, in 1807, Warren died, ending the tension and raising the prospect of Benjamin Junior and/or Earl acquiring the patriarch's land.[2]

After Warren's death, Earl's fortunes rose slowly with the acquisition of small parcels of land and property, a gift most likely from his grandfather. Then, in the spring of 1812, the elder Benjamin, at age eighty-one with the grim reaper in the shadows, conveyed "the whole of my homestead farm," containing "by estimation 100 acres," not to Benjamin, his oldest son, but to Earl, his grandson, and Seth Gay, husband-to-be of his granddaughter Patience, reserving his "dwelling house" for himself and his wife Anna, and for her after his death. According to the deed, he sold the land for $3,000, a sum beyond the capacities of the two young men and thus most likely a fictitious sale. A year later, in July 1813, the patriarch died.[3]

On the newly acquired land, the two young men and Benjamin Junior built a new house and a new barn, using money, we have to assume, from the estate, and timber cut from outlying Gannett woodlands. They built the kind of boxlike two-story frame house that after 1810 was going up all over New England. The style was so common that it required not an architect but a number of craftsmen in the building trades: a housewright to frame the building, a mason to build the numerous brick fireplaces and chimneys, and a glazier to install the many sash windows. If the family followed custom, they did most of the work themselves with help from their neighbors.[4]

The year the house was going up, 1812, the two young couples were wed: in July, Deborah's daughter Patience, twenty-two, to Seth Gay, twenty-seven; in September, Earl, twenty-seven, to Mary Clark, twenty-three—the age of the men being testimony to how long it could take before farmers' sons in New England had the wherewithal to start families. Mary, Earl's first child, was born in the old house in March 1813, six months after her parents married, an "early baby," as the saying went, just as Earl had been an "early baby" for young Benjamin and Deborah. ("Like father, like son," gossips would have said.)[5]

The patriarch's deeding of his land to Earl and Seth, rather than to his son, was very likely a source of humiliation to Benjamin Junior, but for the family it was a prudent act. At fifty-five in 1812, the son was reckoned old and economically a failure. Later, there would have been a transaction (for which no document survives) whereby Benjamin and his son, Earl, amalgamated their land and became joint owners of the new house and farm. There would also have been some sort of document assuring that the family would take care of Anna, their father's second wife. (She died in 1817.) Afterward, Patience and Seth Gay and their children moved out, he selling his share of the land.

Together, the two remaining families headed by father and son would have a chance of making a go of it on the larger farm they would work jointly. What the Gannetts who stayed in Sharon did was what other non-migrating New England farm families did in this bleak agricultural region: they consolidated their land rather than divide it further.[6] In effect, the patriarch was attempting to provide for the security of his unsuccessful son and his daughter-in-law Deborah by transferring his land to their offspring. Benjamin Junior must have been a disappointment to his father. But the old patriot may well have had a soft spot for Deborah, who had proven her mettle. She had more get-up-and-go than his son.[7]

This two-generation family never became well-to-do. Benjamin and Earl, as joint owners of the new house and farm, between them owned a 14-acre home lot, 22 acres of meadow and pasture, and 44 acres of unimproved land. To the tax assessor, the value of Benjamin's portion was $781 and Earl's $1,013. The house and barn were worth all told $400. It was a small dairy farm with a few cows and a few hogs.[8] Such a living arrangement—two generations of a family under one roof—while not as common as it once had been, was not unusual. With his father aging, Earl must have done the lion's share of the farmwork, and with Deborah in her later years intermittently sick, Mary Gannett would have had the burden of the woman's work.[9]

From 1813 to 1827—the last fourteen years of Deborah's life, spent in the new house—the Gannetts hardly prospered. Compare this farm with the elder Benjamin's prosperous farm in the 1771 tax assessment (described in chapter 6), which enabled him to supply beef and grain to the Continental

Army. It was a farm that over the decades might have fed the family, between the milk, butter, cheese, and eggs from the dairy, the vegetables from the garden, and fruit from the orchard, but did not produce enough surplus to allow its owners to rise to great comfort, let alone gentility. Timber from the outlying lands would still have been the cash crop. All this gives meaning to the comment that Daniel Arguimbau, the present farm owner, made to me in the 1990s: that 175 years ago it was "a hardscrabble farm, just as it is today."

In 1836, when Benjamin petitioned Congress to transfer his wife's pension to himself, he represented himself as "infirm in health and [in] indigent circumstances," with "two daughters dependent on charity for support" (Patience, we know, by then was widowed). On his death in 1837, Benjamin's estate was pitiful. In his will he left $50 to Mary (Polly), $100 to Patience, and all of his property and land to his son.[10]

Earl, unable to make a living solely as a farmer, became a stonecutter as well. In 1845, at age sixty, while working in a quarry at Quincy, he was fatally injured in an accident; he died without a will and in debt. The probate inventory of his estate reveals how little wealth two generations of Gannetts had accumulated since 1813. He owned a homestead farm of 88 acres plus 33 acres of "out lands" in four parcels scattered about town. The real estate came to $2,585 and the household property and farm equipment to $220—a meager sum. There was a huge pile of debt. Earl owed about $850 to thirty-eight creditors in Sharon and surrounding towns for "notes" and "accounts," all for small sums. He had been borrowing for years, $10 here, $25 there, for how long is not clear, but it's no wonder that Deborah had petitioned so insistently in 1820 for a lump-sum retroactive pension payment. To meet this debt, the court mercifully put only the "out lands" up for auction, bringing in just enough to pay Earl's creditors and enable Mary, his widow, to keep the farm and house.[11]

The probate inventory reveals a working capital of four cows, a pair of oxen, a horse, and two swine, about the same quantity of livestock that Earl had owned jointly with his father twenty years before. The farm tools were a plow and a few rakes and pitchforks; the vehicles were an old farm cart, a wagon, and a sleigh. There was no carriage. After Earl died, his wife, Mary, according to their daughter Rhoda, "lived alone in the mansion, kept four cows, made butter, did all her own work and some farm work." In other words, she was a poor widow, raising a large brood of children. She died in

1873. And this was the state of the farm until late in the century, when her son, the third Benjamin, rose to affluence, not as a farmer but as a trader in horses and town real estate.[12]

By virtue of the bounty of the patriarch Benjamin Gannett, Sr., and the merging of family lands, the Gannett family of Sharon survived—in itself no small achievement in New England in those years. Benjamin and Deborah Gannett did not have to join the exodus to the west. But they struggled to keep their heads above water. Deborah Gannett was better off after she became a celebrity than before—thanks to the largesse not of Uncle Sam but of her father-in-law—but fame had not brought her fortune.

2. A Quest for Gentility
The Willow Tree and the Cup Plate

The move from the "old" to the "new" house in 1813 was a landmark in Gannett family history. In the "new" house, Deborah Gannett could attempt to fulfill her aspirations for what people then spoke of as "refinement." Neither the farm nor the pension, however, ever allowed her to acquire more than a few tokens of such status.

In their reminiscences, the grown grandchildren were insistent on the distinction between the "old" and the "new" houses, which for them marked crossing one of those divides in social class to which Americans have ever been attuned. Some descendants referred to the new house as "the mansion," or as "Earl's mansion," which of course has present-day overtones of an imposing, luxurious residence. What they had in mind was the house they knew around the turn of the twentieth century, when it had acquired a Victorian makeover by Earl's successful son, the third Benjamin. In 1813, when it was built, the "new" house was a "mansion" only by comparison with the cramped "old" house, which was worth so little that some years after Deborah and Benjamin died, it was sold to butchers who moved it to Canton.[13]

The old house was something like the average small house, which the federal inventory of 1798 shows was one and a half stories high, had two rooms on one floor, and averaged no more than 465 square feet of space. In such a small house, the large room on the first floor was multipurpose. Such rooms typically were cramped, and with so much work equipment, furniture often had to

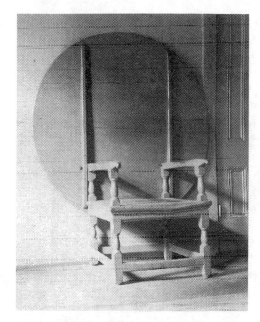

This hutch table (a combination table/chair) is one of two pieces of furniture handed down from the Gannett farmhouse. Courtesy Muriel Nelson.

be collapsible.[14] For this reason, the hutch table—the combination chair and table passed down by descendants (which Muriel Nelson showed me in her house in Sharon)—very likely was originally from the old house, mute testimony to its lack of space. It can be moved to the center of a room and folded down for dining or as a worktable, and then folded up and pushed against a wall out of the way, where it becomes a chair. In 1901, a reporter called it a "curious old relic." It looked to me like the chair tables pictured in a handbook of the furniture of the "Pilgrim century," the seventeenth.[15]

By contrast, the new house was spacious—40 by 32 feet, or 1,280 square feet on one floor, with a total of 2,560 square feet on two floors—roomy even when occupied by two families. In 1798, such a house was typical for only one white family in ten; after 1810, it was typical for perhaps one family in three. The house, even today, just about fits the guidebook description for a "simple box" Adam-style wood frame house of that day: "two rooms wide, two rooms deep and two stories high" with a central doorway opening to a wide central entryway and staircase. Today's house is probably much like the farmhouse Deborah lived in before the Victorian additions of the late nineteenth century, which made it a "mansion" in the eyes of the family.[16]

Within, one has to guess how space might have been allocated among three generations: grandparents, parents, children, and servant. Between 1813 and 1831, Earl and Mary had nine children, seven of whom survived. The present-day house has four rooms on the first floor, four on the second, an unfinished basement, and no attic. Then, upstairs rooms were probably all bedrooms, and three of them were enough to sleep Earl and his wife and their children in an age when children invariably all slept together. Patience Payson, the beloved family helper for forty-five years, one assumes had her own room.[17] The first floor, following the trend in a house of this size, could have been divided into rooms with single functions, the goal of refined living. The room with the hearth was still multipurpose as kitchen, dining room, and workroom.

With four rooms downstairs, there could have been a separate parlor. The parlor, writes Richard Bushman, a historian of the culture of refinement that absorbed early America, was "the crucial characteristic of a refined house," a room "free of work paraphernalia and beds, and dedicated to formal entertainment and the presentation of the family's most decorative possessions." Would a room in the Gannett house have been set aside as a parlor? Very likely. Recall how on her tour in Albany, Mrs. Gannett relished the luxury of "a parler chamber to myself," and how in her lecture she claimed that women "deserve the encomium of MISTRESS and LADY in our *kitchens* and in our *parlours.*"[18]

Upstairs, by family lore, she had a room of her own, or rather one she shared with her husband. She occupied the front bedroom on the second floor on the right (facing outward), at once bedroom, dressing room, and sitting room, with its own fireplace, a great improvement over commonly unheated bedrooms. Benjamin, her grandson, remembered his grandmother thanking him for bringing a few sticks of wood to her fireplace, or so he said (he was two when she died).[19]

On the grounds, there were unmistakable signs of refinement which could be attributed to Mrs. Gannett. There was a conscious effort to mark the house off from the surrounding workhouses, woodland, and meadowland. It was set on a slight rise, the front facing the nearby road, unlike many farmhouses whose side faced the road or which looked as if they had been scattered over a field. And there was a yard, with landscaping. Fashion,

*The "new" house on East Street, Sharon, built by the Gannett family in
1812–13, in which Deborah and Benjamin Gannett lived with their son,
Earl, and his family. It was passed down in the family until World War I.
There is no image of the early house, but the unadorned building of the
late twentieth century (top), in a photo of 2002 by the present owners,
looks more like the original plain farmhouse than the Victorian mansion
improved by a later generation pictured early in the 1900s (bottom).*

 *The original house had a different roof and many chimneys. Late in
the nineteenth century, a more prosperous Gannett family altered the roof
and added bay windows at both ends, a front porch with railings, and a
portico with a balcony. The owners who turned the house into a speakeasy
in the 1920s removed these Victorian refinements from the front. The
father of the present owners acquired the house and farm in 1934.
Photographs (top) courtesy Daniel and Peggy Arguimbau; (bottom)
courtesy Muriel Nelson.*

writes Bushman, dictated that front yards "were required to present shrubs and trees." In the 1850s, when Reverend Stillman Pratt, Deborah's Middleborough biographer, came up to visit, he wrote: "The western portion [of the house] is literally embowered with willow-trees, one of which was set out by Deborah herself and now measures twelve feet in circumference, and almost constitutes a grove in itself. The eastern portion is covered by a woodbine. . . . Rose-bushes and other flowering shrubs are interspersed with perennial plants." Such planting would have been Deborah's doing, probably with the help of Patience Payson.[20]

Trees often took on symbolic meaning in early America, such as the religious "Tree of Life," or the political "Tree of Liberty" of the Revolution, the memory of which was revived in the 1820s in Boston. The giant willow tree became a source of legends associated with Deborah. One grandchild said her grandmother planted it from "a stick," that is, a slip, brought from Plympton, suggesting she was trying to root herself in her ancestral past. A grandson later made a cutting from the tree, which he said he was giving to the Daughters of the American Revolution in Washington to plant on their grounds. In the mid-1890s, after the willow was blown down in a gale, delegates from a nearby D.A.R. chapter, who were inaugurating an annual pilgrimage to the house, carved a gavel from its wood. Deborah's gravestone was decorated with a willow tree.[21]

This successful effort to set a refined tone on the grounds implies a similar attempt inside, although after a succession of owners, it is not possible to say what the interior was like for its first occupants. There are good clues, however, as to how the house was furnished in the probate inventory taken at Earl's death in 1845, even though eighteen years had lapsed since Deborah died.[22] Allowing for a bias of undervaluation of appraisals made at market value, the furniture and furnishings were sparse and inexpensive. There were three tables worth altogether $2.25, eighteen chairs worth $3.35, one armchair and one rocking chair (55¢), fireplace andirons and tongs (15¢), and a clock ($1.50). Piece these together, and one can imagine Deborah in her declining years sitting in a rocking chair near her own fireplace, poking logs on the andirons with the tongs, listening to the tick of the clock. Doubtless she was reading, but the fact that the unlisted books in the inventory came to all of 75 cents (less than the cost of one new book) meant that whatever books she may have accumulated earlier, only a handful were left. There was an unstated number of "beds, bedsteads and bedding" ($14.00), three chests ($8.50), and three bureaus ($3.00), indicating three or four bedrooms. And there were two looking glasses ($1.10). In one's mind's eye one can see Deborah preparing for a trip to Dedham or Boston, taking out a dress from her chest (closets came later), adding accessories from her bureau, and sitting in front of her mirror to comb her hair. Rhoda Monk remembers combing her grandmother's hair; a woman who made so much of her appearance throughout her life hardly lost her vanity in old age.

In the inventory of food utensils, only silver spoons valued at $1.25 offer a hint of luxury. On a separate printed form for "Household Goods, Furniture & Wearing Apparel," the appraisers left blank the categories of sofa, pianoforte, bookcase, desk, jewelry, stoves, carpets and rugs, which suggests there were no such items. They allowed $10 for wearing apparel. All told, the household property was valued at around $85. The house was thinly furnished, with only the plainest utilitarian objects. Nothing within bespeaks affluence. By 1845, not even the mirrors and clocks would have been considered luxuries.

In this context, the handful of possessions Deborah Gannett gave to her children and grandchildren, which they in turn passed on to their descendants, provides bittersweet testimony to her aspirations for gentility. Of the items that can be accounted for, she bequeathed two teacups, two tea plates (then called "cup plates"), two pewter porringers, and one mirror.[23] Descendants prized these mementos: the clue is the vivid family memories of the way they were passed down. Rhoda Monk (1820–1904), Earl's daughter, was explicit in 1901 about the transmission. Rhoda's grandson Rodney Monk reported her saying, "My grandmother . . . had 2 china cups made without handles[,] and a small pewter porringer that Deborah gave her. After my grandmother died, these 3 articles were given to her 3 children." Rodney then reported the second transmission of this inheritance. "After grandmother's death[,] to divide these things fairly among her children, my two sisters, Edythe and Helen, and I put the three items under bowls on the kitchen table. When my father, his sister and brother came from the sitting room, Aunt Abbie found a teacup under the bowl she chose. The other went to Uncle Gus, and my father had the porringer. The cups cannot be found, the porringer is intact." And, he added, "those cups were marked as having belonged to Deborah."[24]

The porringer was passed on to Rodney Monk's daughter. The teacups seem to have disappeared, but of the two cup plates (which passed down via

This porcelain china cup plate of a kind imported from England c. 1810–20 marked the gentility to which Deborah Gannett aspired. Photograph by Ann Gilbert, courtesy Susan Goldstone.

another daughter), one has survived. Gilbert Thompson, grandson of Mary (Polly) Gannett, wrote in 1905, "my mother once had a small porcelain plate she [Deborah] purchased with her pension money; but I lost it when my goods and furniture were burned several years ago." This accounts for one of the two cup plates. The other, descended via Mary Monk, Earl's daughter, ended up with Beatrice Bostock, together with the 1785 dress and other memorabilia.[25]

The surviving cup plate thus turns out to be a rich clue to Mrs. Gannett's search for gentility. Authenticated by museum curators as the kind of Staffordshire ware called pearlware, it was manufactured in England about 1810–20 for export to the United States. In the center of the plate, on an oval-shaped blue-and-white-transfer print, there is a very English landscape depicting a small manor house (or perhaps the ruin of a castle) in the background, and in the foreground a well-dressed gentleman on a farm. The manor house was to the English countryside what Deborah may have imagined her "new" house was to the New England landscape: a building that stood out as belonging to a person of quality. Deborah could have splurged on the cups and plates on one of her trips to Boston, especially after 1821, when her pension went up to $96 a year. Such a dish could have been part of a larger tea set, but more likely was just one of several pieces of china that caught her fancy.[26]

The cup plate, then, bespoke a genteel pretension. It is a flat dish, not a saucer indented to nestle a cup. Among the well-to-do, the full-blown tea ritual required a lavish array of dishes and utensils, including cup plates. "It was the custom of the day," wrote Caroline King, reminiscing about the tea ritual in Salem in the 1830s, "to cool your tea before drinking it by pouring it [from the tea cup] into your saucer, and these small plates were used to hold the cup." She called them "pretty little 'cup plates.'" Susan Blunt, describing a supper she attended in the same era at which a country woman set out her "best dishes," reported that "at every plate she put a little cup plate about the size of a dollar to put our cups in when we poured out our tea into the saucer to drink."[27]

It is hard to conceive of Deborah hosting a large tea party in the sparsely furnished parlor of the Sharon farmhouse, but it is not hard to imagine her offering tea as a sign of hospitality to a few neighbors or to the families of a sister or brother who came to visit. Imagine the scene in the parlor. The round hutch table would have been turned down onto its chair base and covered with a cloth. She would have poured hot water from a teakettle taken from the hearth, steeped the tea in a pewter teapot, and then poured it into the cups. Her guests either sipped the hot tea from a cup or poured it into a saucer and drank from the saucer. Then they would have turned the teacup over onto the cup plate. She might have served cakes, cookies, or sweets on a pewter platter or in a porringer. Almost all these artifacts can be accounted for as Gannett possessions.

By the time of the American Revolution, Bushman tells us, tea services, like knives and forks, glassware and silver spoons, were "little indicators of genteel living . . . touching people at every economic level." Deborah did not acquire these until almost forty years after the Revolution. Earlier, she had splurged on clothing, a very visible sign of status she could display when she went out; later, as her physical mobility declined, she indulged in the kind of objects she might show off to a visitor. The surviving cup plate is a wonderful "little indicator," just as the eight-room two-story "new" house and the giant willow tree are very large indicators, of Mrs. Gannett's aspirations for a touch of class in her last decade.[28]

3. Letting Go
". . . Some unmerited taunts and jeers from a few of her own sex"

Sometime when she was in her sixties, probably after she had given up winning a retroactive pension payment, Deborah Gannett chose to take off her mask. William Ellis, the veterans' agent, writing in 1837, said: "it is evident from what I have seen of Mrs. Gannett myself and what I have long since heard from her son and others that she was rather inclined after she had passed through her military enterprize that act should rather sleep, than be kept alive during her lifetime."[29]

Not quite. While she no longer wanted to publicize her exploits, she wanted to be remembered for them. The memories passed down by her grandchildren and friends at the end of the nineteenth century suggest this process occurred late in her life. She died in 1827. All the grandchildren who lived in the new house were born in 1813 or after, and therefore knew their grandmother only when she was in her last years and they were very young, or else knew about her through the memories adults agreed upon and transmitted after she died. The same could be said of grandchildren born elsewhere who visited. Years later, Anna Holmes, a granddaughter, said that "during all the years" that she knew Deborah, "she was very sensitive to any allusions even to her life as a soldier, and was very unwilling to speak of it." The family, as mentioned, also blocked out her extraordinary achievement as a lecturer (as she herself had done). George Washington Gay (1817–1889), son of Patience and Seth, who was ten when his grandmother died, and who "was fond of her and provided in his will for a permanent memorial to her" in the Sharon cemetery, had never even heard that she had given public lectures.[30]

In her last years, the otherwise "conversable" Mrs. Gannett had ceased to be a teller of tales. The few grandchildren who set down fragments of childhood memories remembered themselves *with* Deborah, not stories about her or by her. Benjamin remembered bringing wood for her fireplace. Rhoda talked about combing her grandmother's hair, about the "old" house and the "new" house, and little more. Benjamin, when interviewed by a reporter in the 1890s, remembered her as a stern disciplinarian. He said a whip hung on the wall and, as the reporter painted the scene, "generally the vision of the tall dignified grandmarm, sternly pointing to the whip was sufficient to subdue the most exuberant."[31]

Yet, while she wanted her military adventures "to sleep," she still wanted to be spoken of as "the old soldier." Rodney Monk, who took down *his* grandmother Rhoda's recollections of Deborah, reported that "when I was a boy, she always spoke of her grandmother as 'The Old Soldier,' never as her grandmother." Benjamin remembered her as "old Deborah." The neighborhood children who passed the house on the way to the nearby one-room schoolhouse called her "the soldier." Daniel Johnson, born in Sharon in 1820, who recalled that as a boy of six or seven, "He not infrequently entered the house to see his schoolmates living there," also "remembers her as a person of plain features," but could say no more about her. Elisha Horton, a mill foreman in Canton, also remembered her as "old Mrs Gannett of Sharon (called old Souldier)." In a way, it was an honorific title—after all, long after they served, army and militia officers were addressed by the highest rank they held—but it could also sting. Some of the grandchildren remembered being taunted, "Your grandmother is a soldier," which sounds akin to the modern kids' gibe "Your mother wears army boots." She must have grown weary of this burden.

For these years, few images of her at home have been put down, save one which calls up a scene of work. A cotton textile mill had come to Canton in 1804, importing raw cotton from the South, which had to be farmed out to be cleaned by hand before it could be processed. Horton, the foreman, remembered Mrs. Gannett as "one of the old & young Ladies, Children & old Men of every Class & Station who took the packages [of cotton] to their several places of abode & with there hands & fingers separated the bad cotton, Dirt, Seeds & c." While he spoke of women "of every Class & Station," it is hard to believe that this was something that, say, Mrs. Rachel Revere of Canton, wife of the wealthy owner of the brass foundry, would have done in her old age.[32]

I think Deborah let go of her public persona as a heroine because she was tired of fending off the gossip it evoked. There was the gossip passed down by the denominational descendants of the Middleborough Baptists who, in 1782, had condemned her "loose and unChristian ways." Long after she died, Sharon's Baptist minister was happy to attribute to Deborah (claiming it came from her grandchildren) the view that "in her later years she did not regard her disguising herself as a man as a womanly or truthful act." Perhaps so. An act of deception even in a heroic cause must weigh heavily unless the world continues to honor you for what it enabled you to accomplish.[33]

The wartime masquerade aside, folks in Sharon had an unbroken string of events in Deborah's personal life to rehash. In 1829, two years after her death, Mann was still writing that she had "lived to see . . . herself" condemned "by the lips of candor and charity, of envy, jealousy, sarcasm and caprice."[34] She was probably aware she confronted a problem without a remedy. "Reputation is like a glass [looking glass] which being once cracked will never be perfect again." This was an aphorism in *Human Prudence* by William De Britaine, a book we may be fairly certain Mrs. Gannett owned because she was listed in the back as a subscriber. It was a version of a classic seventeenth-century English conduct book that Herman Mann edited and published in 1806. It laid out in thirty-five chapters Benjamin Franklin–like mottos on how to succeed in life. The chapter "Reputation" spoke to her. "It is easy to get an ill name because evil is so willingly believed by the vulgar." The book offered no solutions, however, only admonitions to preserve one's good name and to pursue a policy of stoic forbearance to detractors: "Never speak ill of any man." She expressed the same philosophy in a letter to Captain Webb: "it is my real wishes never to injure anyone, neither in name or property."[35]

Deborah's attitude to a second edition of her memoir is the strongest testimony that the gossip was painful. In the 1820s, Herman Mann, Jr., confided to his journal that Mrs. Gannett "gave my father a more full and minute account of her extraordinary life than was obtained in the published memoirs. . . . But there was an express understanding between Mrs. Gannett and my father . . . that no public disclosure of them should be made until after her decease." Why? The younger Mann was explicit. "One of the principal reasons for this delay," he wrote, "I have always understood and believe to be, was she was subjected to some unmerited taunts and jeers from a few of her own sex on the appearance of the published memoirs [1797] . . . and was averse to undergoing the ordeal again unnecessarily in her declining years." Dedham's William Ellis confirmed this.[36]

Deborah Gannett thus did not recant her famous deception. On the contrary, by talking to Mann again, she was trying to secure her place in history. She was willing to enlighten him, blissfully hopeful, perhaps, that he might correct some embarrassing stories, but she was not willing to see old coals stoked while she was alive. Mann let her down. Two years after she died, he opened a subscription for the book; he fussed with his revisions for several years, but left a sprawling, incomplete manuscript on his death in 1833. His son, Herman, reopened the subscription but got nowhere. He then condensed the manuscript, submitting it to Harper's, the New York publisher, who in 1850 turned it down.[37]

Gossip, as Mary Beth Norton makes clear in her luminous study of gender relations in early America, was "a crucial mechanism of social control—one used especially by women, who lacked easy access to courtrooms and other forums of the formal public." It was "above all a women's weapon although men too employed it. Women were both major wielders of gossip and its frequent targets." From the second half of the eighteenth century on, as laws punishing immorality were liberalized or less enforced, gossip assumed an even more important function, namely, to punish those who in the eyes of the community were engaged in immoral behavior but were beyond the reach of the law. "The most damaging gossip aimed at women was necessarily sexual in nature," Norton points out, "for most women had complete control over few other aspects of their lives." Much of what Deborah Sampson Gannett did or was alleged to have done was sexually charged.[38]

The gossip was hard on Deborah because it cut her off from people locally. On her lecture tour, as her diary makes so clear, she savored her social acceptance in "respectable" circles. Her letter of 1804 to George Webb is testimony to a hunger for the sociability she had found in his family. "I take the liberty of writing to you," she began, "not for mere compliments—but real esteem—I hope sincerely that these [lines? words?] may find you and every branch of your Family enjoying health and happiness—I should be extremely happy to see you all again—I hope I shall have the gratification before many months—I present my love and acknowledge my gratitude to all my friends in this place."

After a paragraph reassuring Webb that she would soon be able to repay her debts, she closed with an aside to his daughter: "Sally, I believe you may have forgot me or you Would have wrote me long before now—do some of you write—I long to hear from you." She added, "in your letter let me know if your Father has received those books I sent him and Mr Pratt—adieu my friends." The letter conveys a feeling of reaching out to hoped-for friends. Was there anyone in Sharon to whom she could offer such warm expressions of friendship and gratitude?[39]

This well-composed letter hints she may easily have written others. It also reveals her isolation; she had to seek friends outside her hometown. She found a small welcoming circle in Dedham around the Manns. After 1813, her quest for refinement in the new house may have been fed by a desire for respectability that might breach the fences local gossip had erected. Conceivably, her displays of refinement had the opposite effect, giving the impression she was putting on airs.

It was not only that Deborah never silenced the wagging tongues, but as living memories of the war faded, her achievements as a soldier became harder to believe because they seemed so anachronistic. As conceptions of what was proper behavior for a middle-class woman narrowed, it was more difficult to conceive of the military exploits of the tough women of the Revolutionary era. In "Victorian" America, genteel women did not do such things; in retrospect, such deeds became incredible.[40] The creeping "cult of domesticity" also narrowed what was permissible for a proper woman to do in public—like drinking. Deborah seems to have had a taste for rum, possibly acquired in the army and perhaps necessary for medicinal purposes. Thomas Adams, brother of a Boston publisher, recalled having seen her when he was a small boy in a store where she "asked for rum, took the bottle & drank of a glass in manly style." That would have been a time when even grocery stores dispensed liquor. Lore also placed Deborah in Cobb's Tavern, lifting a glass with Paul Revere. At a time when a national crusade against demon rum was bubbling up—in 1832 little Sharon would have its own temperance society— a woman who drank in a public place had another cross to bear.[41]

In her later years, she seems to have been as cut off from her parents as she had been earlier. Both parents became paupers. From 1807 through 1810 (and perhaps at other times), the town of Plympton boarded out "the widow Deborah Sampson" to a string of lowest bidders and then tried to shift the burden to Fayette, Maine, where her husband had ended up. Fayette "set up" Jonathan Sampson and Martha (Patty), his common-law wife, as paupers. He seems to have died in 1811 in Maine, and Deborah Bradford Sampson sometime thereafter in Plympton. There is no hint of a reconciliation of the two with each other or of either with Deborah.[42]

Deborah's siblings, judging by several who proved trackable, do not seem to have climbed any rungs on the social ladder. Nehemiah, her younger brother, moved from Sharon in 1799 with a family of four children to Readfield, Maine, where he became some kind of a doctor. When he died in 1818, the family was so poor his wife scattered their children. Ephraim, the brother, who after the army settled in Middleborough, became a worker in an iron mine, and died in 1810. His second wife applied for his pension under the law providing for impoverished veterans. Sylvia, Deborah's younger sister, married into the Cushman family of Plympton, and for a while was paid by the town to board their mother. Sylvia, Ephraim's daughter, married Jeremiah Thomas, the grandson of Deborah's former master in Middleborough. It was a small world.[43]

What was the response of the siblings and their families to their transgressing sister and aunt? If we can rely on recollections passed on by Zilpah Tolman of Middleborough, it was mixed. They "were not at all proud of her escapade," but respected her "retaining her virtue." Tolman, born in 1830, was passing on conversations of the late 1840s in the family of Sylvia Thomas, Deborah's niece. However, the siblings did not break off contact with her. Irene Soule, another niece, said, "I well remember Deborah Sampson, my mother's sister, her visiting us and I and my brothers visiting her when she lived in Sharon."[44]

In her final years, Mrs. Gannett seems to have been intermittently sick and then constantly so. Patience Payson, testifying later on behalf of a pension for Benjamin, said that "she well knew that Deborah was unable to perform any labor a great part of the time in consequence of a wound she received in the American army." Mrs. Gannett's claim was that the wound was "from a musket ball lodged in her body which was never extracted," the story the family had agreed upon. The family, engaged for a decade in transferring her pension first to the father, and then to the children, wanted to be doubly sure no one questioned that her disability was the result of a wartime wound.[45]

Whatever the source of her ill health, Mrs. Gannett required extensive medical care. In his petition to Congress, Benjamin Gannett claimed medical expenses of $600 for his wife over the course of her life. Earl reported bills of $386.78 from 1784 to 1804 from Dr. George Craftsmen, while Benjamin spoke of bills of $300 from 1804 to 1827 from Dr. Daniel Stone. These were huge costs. It is hard to translate them into doctor's visits, medications, and procedures, but this was at a time when the fee schedule of the Boston Medical Association allowed $6 for a consultation on the first visit and $4 for each subsequent visit. Country doctors doubtless charged less, but at the end of her life doctors' bills probably ate up Deborah's pension of $96 a year.[46] The semiannual pension payment of $48 on March 3, 1827, signed for in Boston by Willard Gould, attorney, would be her last.

When Deborah Gannett died on April 29, 1827, the country did not make much of it. There was a short obituary in the local Dedham paper, reprinted in *Niles Weekly Register* in Washington, a prominent national paper, and per-functory notices in a few Boston papers. A few magazines picked up the news: "Another Revolutionary Character Gone" . . . "Another Revolutionary Soldier No More." Neither newspapers nor family memories reported a memorial service. Was there none? Was there no eulogy? One would like to have heard what a Sharon minister—whether Unitarian, Congregationalist, or Baptist—had to say, especially if Deborah's religious odyssey had taken her beyond all "sects," as Mann had hinted. These silences are strange.[47]

Nor is there even a remembrance by the town historian. Selectman Gould, who in his annals of Sharon in 1830 had digressed to laud Benjamin Senior for his wartime patriotism, said nothing about the female soldier. This was at a time when public consciousness of the suffering soldiers of the Revolution was at its height. In 1824, at Lafayette's visit to New England, and in 1825, at the mammoth fiftieth-anniversary celebrations of the battles of Bunker Hill, Lexington, and Concord, the "hoary headed" veterans were rounded up and trotted out for display. No one ever said Deborah Gannett was honored at a Fourth of July celebration. She died less than a year after July 4, 1826, the fiftieth anniversary of the Declaration of Independence, the day on which Thomas Jefferson and John Adams both died, the timing leaving the country awe-stricken. Patriarchs of the Revolution were celebrated; matriarchs, it would seem, were not, at least not those who had transgressed.[48]

The obituary in the Dedham *Village Register* by one of the Manns was an exercise in the tribute of erasure. It excised from the record as it extolled, comforting the reader. Her life was "extraordinary," her military service "extraordinary," although at what risk to her was not spelled out. The country had rewarded her with back wages, a bounty, and a pension—as if all this fell from heaven. Not a word about her thirty-year campaign for the pension or her daring lecture tour. The woman "of uncommon intellect and fortitude" resonant of Deborah, the biblical judge in Israel, had disappeared. She was transmuted into a safe American heroine.

4. *Benjamin Gannett, Jr.*
The Unhappy Husband of an American Heroine

After her death, a patriarchal society continued to put Deborah Gannett back in her place. The family, partly because it was just too down and out, was slow to give her her due in the graveyard. She was buried in a family plot in the Rock Ridge Cemetery, about a mile from the house on East Street, but for several decades after her death in 1827, her grave went unmarked, even though Earl, her son, became a stonecutter. Benjamin Junior's will provided for "decent grave stones for myself and wife," after his death. The two were buried alongside each other. Earl died in 1845, debt-ridden.

When gravestones finally went up, it was for all three. The family identified the father as "Benjamin Gannett/Died Jan. 3, 1838/Aged 80 Years," the mother as "Deborah, Wife of Benjamin Gannett/Died April 29, 1827/Aged 68," and "Capt. Earl B. Gannett/Died June 9, 1845/aged 59 Years." These stones probably went up in the 1850s or early 1860s, about thirty years after her death. (At about this time, the town named a lane near her house after Deborah Sampson.) The family honored Earl for his rank in the militia, but Deborah (once Private Shurtliff) only as Benjamin's wife. Years later, on the other side of her headstone, a stonecutter with a different lettering style carved: "Deborah Sampson Gannett/Robert Shurtliff/The Female Soldier/Service 1781 to 1783." The year 1781 was fixed in family mythology.[49]

Benjamin Gannett's near indifference to honoring his wife is a good point of departure to attempt to understand him. It is hard to bring him out from under the shadow of his wife or father. Indeed, that may have been his problem. He was less than a success, a pale shadow of his prosperous, eminent father or his celebrated wife. His father deeded the family land not to him, but to his son and son-in-law. When the family moved onto the consolidated farm, Benjamin owned the buildings and land jointly with his son. This was the end of the farmboy's dream of someday inheriting his father's land. He may have been nursing a bitterness to his father since 1805, when the old man deeded half his own farm to Benjamin's half brother Warren, thirty years his junior. Then, from 1813 on, he was dependent on his son for labor. Meanwhile, his wife had an income of her own (which went from $48 a year in 1805 to $96 in 1821), which hardly made her independent but gave her the authority to make her own decisions as to what she bought.

In the context of these major blows to his ego, all confirming his dependence, Benjamin Junior's decision in 1813 to join Sharon's new Baptist Society takes on meaning as a hollow effort to assert some kind of independence in defiance of his wife, his father, and his son.

Long before this, he probably chafed as the husband of a transgressing celebrity. Mann had an uncanny way of denigrating Benjamin: she "selected" him as her husband, he wrote, and she "refuses her husband the rites of the marriage-bed." True or not, as no children appeared after the three born in the first five years of their marriage, since she had proven her fertility, the rumor impugned his manhood. One could infer he was either infertile, impotent, or henpecked. She took off for a year without an escort on a wild tour to God knows where, "exhibiting," and became the breadwinner. All these actions challenged Benjamin's capacity to control his wife. At the end of the appendix to the memoir, Mann wrote: "I cannot learn, she has the least wish to usurp the prerogatives of our sex. For she has often said, that nothing appears more beautiful in the *domestic round* than when the husband takes the lead, with discretion, and is followed by his consort, with an amiable acquiescence." Perhaps she did say so. But was it possible that the man Paul Revere said was "of little force" in business took the lead in family affairs? The fact that Deborah felt she had to make clear that her husband "takes the lead" suggests that more than one man in Cobb's Tavern wanted to know, "Who wears the breeches in the family?"[50]

One searches in vain for signs of love or affection between the two. Revere spoke of Deborah as a "dutiful wife," the obituary of "an amiable wife." And doubtless she was. Was she a loving wife? On her tour in 1802, when she thought she was at death's door and expressed an anguished love in her diary for her four children (berating herself at first for omitting Susanna, her adopted child), she expressed none for her husband. Indeed, she did not mention him at all in the diary, or even list him on the inside cover where she inscribed the names of her children.[51]

Was Benjamin a loving husband? In 1813, when he became a Baptist, it is hard to conceive of an act less supportive of his wife of almost three decades. He must have known that the Baptist Church in Middleborough had cast her out, yet he embraced the church that rejected her. At age fifty-five Benjamin Gannett, Jr., along with ten other men and seven women, became a founder of Sharon's Baptist Society, so tiny that it met for years in a private home. He took no role as a leader, but testified to his convictions by filing a certificate of exemption from the church tax Massachusetts still required of members of dissenting churches. To be a Baptist in Sharon was to be an outsider. The choleric Reverend Whitaker ranted against them—"I will exterminate those Baptists," he said. The personal rebuke to his wife aside, Benjamin and Deborah would have been at opposite theological poles, and if he was as full of the Holy Spirit as other born-again Christians, he would have had a lot to say to her about her liberal religious beliefs and sinful ways.

Benjamin's joining the Baptists in 1813, the same year the family moved into the "new" house, can also be taken as an expression of Puritanical contempt for the gentility she yearned for. The woman who loved fashionable clothing, had her portrait painted, and bought imported porcelain cup plates was not the Baptist ideal of a Godly woman. In this context, one other little episode suggests a tension between the two explicitly over her efforts at refinement. This is the only way to give meaning to a puzzling story about the willow tree Deborah planted, volunteered in 1902 by Florence Moody, Deborah's great-granddaughter. "The first tree," she wrote, "was brought from Plympton," Deborah's birthplace, "and planted in the yard of her Sharon home. She watched the growth of this tree carefully and finding it was not making the desired progress, examined the roots only to find they were obstructed by stones. The stones, it was after learned, were placed there secretly by her husband, whose favorite tree was evidently not a willow. The stones being removed the tree again took root and flourished for over a century. Its massive branches were finally torn asunder by the since storms."[52]

There is no reason to doubt the story, because it was not set down in malice but was offered by a bewildered family member to the new Sharon Historical Society assembling memorabilia about the Gannetts. This was hardly a boyish prank; Benjamin would have been in his late fifties. I read it as an expression of hostility, attempting to kill the tree that, like the roses and shrubs and woodbine, stood for his wife's aspirations for refinement.

Benjamin Gannett could not even establish a separate identity after his wife's death. True, he won a moment of fame as the only man claiming a pension as the widower of a Revolutionary War veteran, but it was posthumous. It is a sad story. Deborah died in 1827. He began his campaign for a pension in 1831, but had no prospect of success until 1836, when Congress amended the law to permit the widows of veterans to apply, if they had married their partner *before* his wartime military service. Legally, Benjamin Gannett did not qualify. With the help of William Ellis, he submitted to the House a pathetic petition reviewing his wife's military record, her long pension history, and her medical condition, enclosing the doctors' bills, Patience Payson's testimony, and the selectmen's affidavits as to his own character and indigence. The House Committee on Revolutionary Pensions reported in his favor. Benjamin Gannett, who had married a veteran *after* the war, they said, did not come within the spirit of the recent amendment, "but they believe they are warranted in saying that the whole history of the American Revolution records no case like this." It "furnishes no other similar example of female heroism, fidelity and courage."[53]

The Committee then paid tribute to Benjamin: "He has sustained her through a long life of sickness and suffering . . . occasioned by the wounds she received and the hardships she endured in defense of the country and as there cannot be a parallel case in all time to come," it acceded to his request, bending the law. Congress approved a bill in December 1837, granting Benjamin $80 per year retroactive to March 4, 1831, "for and during his natural life." Unfortunately, he died on January 3, 1838. The news arrived after his life was over. The three children then petitioned to transfer their father's pension to them, and later in the year Congress approved a payment to them of $466.66, the total Benjamin would have received from 1831 to his death.[54]

While the children profited from association with their famous mother, for the longest time they, as well as the grandchildren, lost hold of her memory, the price Deborah paid for letting go of her own history. One clue to this neglect is the gravestone. More revealing is the family naming pattern. She was born in 1760. Before then, Deborah was a common name in the Sampson family. In the last quarter of the eighteenth century, there were a half dozen other "Deborah Samsons" or "Deborah Sampsons" in Plymouth County and thereabouts. But in the Gannett family after 1818, although Earl named his third daughter Deborah (she died at age three), thereafter neither he nor his two sisters named another daughter Deborah, nor did any of their numerous children. Not until the 1930s, when her great-great-grandson Rodney Monk named a daughter Deborah, did a Gannett descendant so honor her.[55]

As to Benjamin Gannett, he rattled down the halls of history in his grim success as the only widower of a Revolutionary War veteran awarded a federal pension (and at that, notified after his death). But, unintentionally, his petition provoked a formal tribute from Congress to his wife, bringing her to the attention of no less a public figure than John Quincy Adams. The former president of the United States, then serving as a member of the House of Representatives, chose to make a remarkable speech about her, which was an auspicious way for her to begin her passage into American history.[56]

PART FIVE

PASSING INTO HISTORY

Chapter Ten

Genteel and Plebeian

W HAT DOES IT TAKE for an ordinary person to win a place in
American history, especially for a woman as unconventional as Deborah Sampson Gannett? In her own lifetime, Mrs. Gannett, as we have seen,
won only limited public recognition. At her death, while notices could refer
to the "famous female soldier," as fame went in the rapidly growing nation,
hers did not cut a very wide swath. The fifteen hundred copies of the memoir sold out, but by the 1830s, William Ellis could not find a copy, even in
Dedham. Perhaps two thousand men and women across New England and
New York had paid to see and hear Mrs. Gannett deliver her address. But if
Ellis was right in 1837 in claiming veterans had a thousand stories about her,
no one set them down. In Middleborough, Granville Temple Sproat collected only a few faded memories of her from "the old folks."

Should it surprise us that Gannett's fame was fragile? Neither soldiers
nor women of the Revolution were much heralded. In personal memory,
there was the normal process of forgetting that came with old age, followed
by the difficulties of one generation passing on individual memories to
another. In public memory, however, there was a more complex and essentially political process. As conservative elites established their cultural
authority in the new nation, they chose to erase the memory of the side of the
Revolution they or their fathers had fought so hard to control: the mobs, the

hangings of effigies, the tarring and featherings, the backcountry rebellions, the mutinies of soldiers, all those insurgencies of runaway apprentices, slave insurrections, and women like Abigail Adams who threatened to "foment a rebellion." When elites did allow the "popular" side into the historical narrative of the Revolution, they often sanitized it. The destruction of the tea, as it was known at the time, an electrifying act of defiance, thus became in the 1830s "the Boston Tea Party," with overtones of a comic masquerade or child's play.[1]

When Thomas Paine died in 1809, no more than ten people attended the funeral of the author of the three most widely read pamphlets of the Revolutionary era, *Common Sense, The Rights of Man,* and *The Age of Reason.* He had been demonized by conservatives as a "Jacobin" and an "infidel." More astonishing, major political leaders associated with organizing popular resistance were eclipsed. That same year, John Adams was alarmed that Samuel Adams and John Hancock were "almost buried in oblivion." There was, he said, "a very extraordinary and unaccountable Inattention in our countrymen to the History of our own country," which may have given Adams himself a premonition of his own long decline in public memory. If it could happen to men as famous as these, should it surprise us that it happened to a person of lesser fame like Deborah Sampson?[2]

It took Americans a very long time to honor the ordinary soldiers of the Revolution. The country erected statues to its generals but none to 250,000 enlisted men and ordinary seamen. It took even longer to recover the women of the Revolution; Mann's memoir of a woman stood almost alone until Elizabeth Ellet's collection of sketches appeared in 1848–50.[3] We are only beginning to understand this process of selective remembering and willful forgetting of the Revolution. There were "dominant" or "mainstream" public memories, as opposed to "alternative (usually subordinate) memories," the historian Michael Kammen concludes. These correspond more or less to the contrast between "official" and "popular" memory.[4]

To trace the public remembering of Sampson over two centuries, we have to create our own road map. She illustrates what Gloria Steinem calls the general fate of women's history: "to be lost and discovered, lost again and re-discovered, re-lost and *re*-re-discovered."[5] There is no clear pattern. We often have to go hunting for her as for a needle in a haystack. There are long silences, sudden recognitions in unexpected places, class variations. What shapes such bewildering ups and downs? Deborah Sampson seems to rise in public memory when particular currents in American life waft her to the fore. Awareness has gone up, first, when women were venturing into new roles and women's movements for equality were searching for their own past; second, in times of war and an increased presence of the military in American life and of women within the military; third, when public consciousness of the American Revolution has increased, particularly during the centennial and bicentennial celebrations; fourth, when academic history has expanded its scope to include the people left out of the traditional narrative; and, lastly, when changes in sexual mores have made an unconventional woman more acceptable. Nothing has been automatic about this process. Changing tides of opinion may have created publics more receptive to Deborah Sampson, but there always had to be individuals to claim a place for her.

Untangling her in public memory is almost as challenging as reconstructing her life; indeed, the two projects contribute to each other. We may understand her history better when we understand what "history" has made of her.

1. *Congressman John Quincy Adams*
She "rushed into the vortex of politics"

The female soldier was not recognized by the genteel, articulate women of Massachusetts of the Revolutionary era, the advocates of a "blue-stocking" kind of feminism. It was not only that John Adams chose not to "remember the ladies" in recasting the laws of the new nation, but when it came to writing the history of the Revolution, neither did Adams's contemporaries, the historians Mercy Otis Warren and Judith Sargent Murray.

It is not surprising that Mrs. Warren made no mention of Mrs. Gannett in her 1,298-page, three-volume history of the Revolution in 1805. She evaded almost all military history; it was "the peculiar province of masculine strength . . . [to] describe the bloodstained field and relate the story of slaughtered armies." While she took note of "the barbarous abuses of the hapless females" and of "the feebler sex" by British soldiers, the strong, tough women who served in army camps or who took over their husbands' farms were not in her ken. Her history, like her poetic plays, celebrated women who mobilized men to resist tyranny, but not women who fought.[6]

It is surprising, however, that Mrs. Murray, advocate of "the equality of the sexes," found no space for Deborah in two hefty volumes of *The Gleaner* in 1798, the object of which, she wrote, was "to prove by examples, that the minds of women are *naturally* as susceptible of every improvement as those of men." To prove women "in every respect equal to men," she piled one historical example on top of another in ten categories. But among her long catalogues of accomplished women in Western European history, she excluded women warriors. "We are not desirous to array THE SEX in martial habiliments; we do not wish to enlist our women as soldiers."[7]

If neither John nor Abigail Adams (nor their friends) could "remember the ladies" of the Revolution, their son, John Quincy Adams (1767–1848), did, in an astonishing speech in the last phase of his long political career as a member of Congress, when, in June 1838, he gave Deborah Gannett an encomium on the floor of Congress that she could not have imagined in her wildest dreams. John Quincy Adams, former president of the United States (1825–29), former secretary of state and senator, had been a member of the House of Representatives since 1831—the only ex-president before or since to serve in that body after a term in the White House. In a lengthy oration that was the high point of his militant defense of the right of women to petition, Adams invoked Gannett's record in the Revolution, and then defended her from the attack it provoked. His marathon speech was the first anyone had made about Deborah Gannett in a public body.[8]

Adams's tribute took place at the conjunction of several events, the first local. In 1837, as we have seen, in response to Benjamin Gannett's petition, the House voted him a pension as Deborah's widower. In the spring of 1838, a petition from the three Gannett children asking to transfer their father's pension to them was making its way through the House.[9] The second event was national. The antislavery movement, in full bloom in the late 1830s, rained petitions on Congress calling for the abolition of slavery in the District of Columbia. Beginning in 1836, the House adopted a rule that all petitions "relative in any way to the subject of slavery or the abolition of slavery, shall without being either printed or referred be laid on the table," without "further action"—the gag rule. In 1837–38, the antislavery forces responded with petitions containing about 200,000 signatures asking for either abolition in the capital, the repeal of the gag rule, a ban on the slave trade between states, or a ban on slavery in the territories. A large proportion of the signers were women.[10]

In 1838, a third event, the "Texas Question," raised the ante. After Texas won independence from Mexico and demands for annexation welled up from the South and West, anti-annexation petitions flooded Congress, like the one from Plymouth signed by 238 women whose one-sentence case against annexation rested on "the sinfulness of slavery." Benjamin Chew Howard of Maryland, chairman of the Committee on Foreign Affairs, in refusing to report the petitions out of committee, attacked the woman signers as "discreditable" for their "departure from their proper sphere." Adams, by adroit parliamentary maneuvering, forced a vote on the Committee's negative report. "At last the issue was joined in Congress," Adams's biographer writes, "for or against the annexation of Texas. This meant a debate for or against slavery, despite the 'gag rule.' " Beginning in June 1838, Adams "got the floor of the House during the morning hour" and "held it each day until Congress adjourned three weeks later." It was a filibuster: against annexation, against slavery, for the right of petition—and for the right of women to participate in public life, the first such speech in Congress.[11]

Adams began with the obligation of the House to receive petitions whatever the origin, even from "the meanest petition of the lowest and poorest individual in this country." The House, he contended, simply had no right to reject a petition a priori without a hearing.[12] As his speech unfolded, Adams shifted his focus from class to gender. On June 26, he presented a petition against annexation from the women of Plymouth, "every one . . . a mother, a wife, a daughter or a sister of some constituent of mine," and another from Hanover, signed by 153 women and 192 men. Caustically, he asked whether "the right of petition itself is to be denied the female sex? to WOMEN? . . . Are women to have no opinions or action on subjects relating to the general welfare?"

And here Adams began an amazing voyage through history, reviewing the public achievements of women from biblical times through ancient Greece and Rome up to his time. He taunted his southern Bible-quoting colleagues with a parade of strong women from the Bible: Miriam, Abigail, Huldah, Judith, Esther, and Deborah, who summoned Israel to battle. "Has he [the congressman] never read that inspiring cry—'Awake, awake, Deborah; awake, awake, utter a song; arise Barak and lead thy captivity captive, thou son of Abinoam'?"[13]

Two days later, Adams shifted to "the innumerable instances recorded by the profane historians where women immortalized their names by the part they took in the affairs of their country." No sooner did he come to the

American Revolution than he was into the story of Deborah Gannett, to whose husband the House "recently voted" a pension "on the merits of his deceased wife."[14] "The Chairman of the Committee [Howard] thinks it is a reproach to a woman even to petition on a matter of politics," said Adams, "but this Deborah Gannett not only did as much as this but rushed into the vortex of politics to the extent of exposing her person down to the close of the Revolutionary War. And what says the report of the Committee on her?" Here, he quoted from the report: " 'the whole history of the American Revolution records no case like this,' and 'furnishes no other similar episode of female heroism, fidelity, and courage.' " "Where I ask, again, is the Chairman of the Committee on Foreign Affairs?" (A laugh from the House, the congressional stenographer recorded.) "Does this report declare that heroism, that fidelity in the case of a woman is a reproach to her and to her country? No; it is a virtue of supererogation of the very highest and noblest order," in other words, more than duty required.[15]

The day after, Congressman Howard responded sarcastically. He hoped Adams "might find more appropriate models to hold up for imitation to the modest and virtuous girls of New England than the two which he had selected . . . one of which, Aspasia, was notorious for the profligacy of her life; and the other a woman who had usurped the habiliments of the other sex, and in man's dress, associated with men for years." (Aspasia was a Greek adventuress who, as Pericles' consort, supposedly exerted great influence over him.)

In his retort, Adams referred Howard to the committee report on Mrs. Gannett "as conveying a principle directly the reverse" of his. In the next breath he returned to the larger issue, pushing the argument a notch higher, asking whether "the right to petition . . . is to be denied to women because they have no right to vote! Is it so clear that they have no such right as this last?" And with this, he ended his remarks and Congress adjourned for the morning. In the same way that Adams's defense of the right to petition against the extension of slavery took him into the more radical terrain of the abolition of slavery itself, in his defense of the right of women to petition, he gestured toward the more radical ground of the right of women to vote.[16]

So ended the remarks on Deborah Gannett by John Quincy Adams, clearly the best-known figure in Congress. Public attention was riveted on the debate. It was a time when many newspapers ran daily transcripts of congressional debates. Adams soon published his remarks in a 131-page pamphlet. For a brief moment, Deborah had emerged as a symbol of women's citizenship. Congressman Adams received testimonials from all over, especially from women. Miss Anna Quincy Thaxter of Hingham thanked him for his "just, generous and Christian defense of the character and claims of her sex." Adams's touching response was that he was only doing his duty to the memory of his mother. In truth, in recognizing Deborah Gannett as an epitome of women in the Revolution, he was acknowledging what his mother and father could not.[17]

2. *The Plebeian Tradition of Passing Women*
From Chapbooks to Beadle's Dime Tales

Unbeknownst to patricians, in the first half of the nineteenth century Deborah Sampson passed into plebeian consciousness via a genre of literature about adventurous cross-dressing women. An indigenous American sensational literature now replaced the chapbooks and memoirs imported from England. Surprising as it may seem, Sampson became an icon in this literature. Just as young Deborah may have learned about her predecessors from narratives about Hannah Snell, so some nineteenth-century women became aware of her.

Cross-dressing among young working women seems to have become, if not more common in the early nineteenth century than in the colonial era, more publicized. As the cult of domesticity narrowed their already contracted sphere, young women had much more to rebel against. There was a world of tomboys trying to break out of the confines of "Victorian" conceptions of what was proper for young women. There were more opportunities beckoning them to factory towns and seaport cities and a greater migration of people: "The whole population is in motion," a Boston writer observed in 1818. More anonymity awaited the migrants to huge metropolitan hives. Wondrous new means of transportation—canal boats, steamboats, railroads—made travel easier for women. What's more, ready-to-wear clothing made men's cheap clothing more available.[18]

We don't know much about such passing women; historians bump into them in the course of other research. Here are some samples taken down by one historian, Shane White, while turning the pages of early-nineteenth-century American newspapers. 1817: Eliza Bennett of Vermont, a driver of a hack in New York City, drove over 1,200 miles dressed as a man before being detected by the police after a theft. 1820: A New England women of nineteen, "in neat boys attire," an apprentice to a carpenter for three years accompanied the master carpenter, in reality her lover, until his wife caught up with them. 1832: "A scotch lass" of sixteen or eighteen, "being unable to find employment in New York," shipped out as a cabin boy, and after she was discovered was placed in domestic service by a humane captain. 1836: Jane Walker, age thirty, voyaged from Ireland to Montreal to Brooklyn in search of her lover, dressed as a man to be "better protected from insult," working on the Brooklyn docks as James Walker. We know these instances only by serendipity.[19]

Such an array of anecdotes, random as it is, hints at patterns. The women were young; most seem to have been in the laboring classes; some were immigrants; and all took to the road. Some headed west, more gravitated toward large cities. Their stated goals, as much as they can be untangled, were for freedom or opportunity. (There were also runaway slaves.) For some women, cross-dressing enabled them to pursue amorous attachments, most, it would seem, to the other sex. The patterns seem not very different from those suggested by eighteenth-century examples.[20]

American readers were still interested in English and European cross-dressers. By the early 1800s, however, the narratives and ballads about warrior women had peaked; as armies and navies modernized, such women became far less common. The genre had seen its day.[21] In the American pulp literature about adventure-seeking women, disguised or undisguised, there were tales of female soldiers and sailors, among them *The Female Warrior* (1843) by Leonara Siddons; *Life and Sufferings* (1844) by Emma Cole; *The Female Officer* (1851) by Madeline Moore. There were even more tales about women in occupations gendered male, such as *Fanny Campbell, The Female Pirate Captain* (1845), *The Female Land Pirate* (1847), and *The Female Bandit of the Southwest* (1852).[22]

In this literature, the fame of Deborah Sampson was sometimes taken for granted. Take the narrative *The Female Marine,* which had no less than nineteen printings in Boston circulating among sailors, "juveniles," and the "Ann Street population," slang for patrons of pornography.[23] The heroine, Lucy Brewer, an innocent young woman from Plymouth (Deborah's home county), tells a story of being seduced (or raped) at sixteen, betrayed by her lover, and recruited into a Boston brothel. This took place in 1812, when the war with Britain began. An "acquaintance," the first lieutenant of a privateer, to whom she expressed an interest in travel, advised her to dress as a man. To convince her, he said, "History furnished us with many instances. Here my friend referred to the remarkable instance of Miss Sampson, who during the Revolutionary War disguised herself like a male by the name of Robert Shurtliff, and as such, by the most scrupulous concealment of her sex, served her country as a private soldier. . . ." Brewer said she "thoroughly studied the memoirs of Miss Sampson," after which she enlisted in the navy on a frigate, "encouraged by the active part which one of my sex had taken in the late American war, without exposing her sex."[24]

Two decades later, Sampson was still alive in this genre. *The Cabin-Boy's Life,* published in New York City in 1840, told the story of Ellen Stephens, who in the 1830s deserted an adulterous husband she had married against her will, and spent eight months disguised as a cabin boy on a Mississippi riverboat. At the end of her short tale, her amanuensis wrote, "there have been many such instances of females, thus disguised . . . among which our readers will doubtless recollect the instance of Miss Deborah Sampson, a native of the State of Massachusetts, who in male attire" served in the army and received a pension.[25] A year later, in *The Friendless Orphan,* also published in New York City, Sophia Johnson narrated her affecting adventures as a disguised soldier in the War of 1812, when she lost an arm at the Battle of Bridgewater in upstate New York. The "concluding remarks" paid tribute to "the still more remarkable instance of female valor and achievement . . . the celebrated Mrs. Gannett of Sharon, Norfolk County, Massachusetts." Johnson, writing in 1841, "doubted not but at that moment there were many females, travelling by both sea and land in semblance of males."[26]

Deborah Sampson may also have been the inspiration for the character of a woman soldier in several patriotic plays in the New York theatre. In 1803, the year he sponsored Mrs. Gannett's ill-fated performance, William Dunlap wrote "Sally Williams" into a comic interlude in *The Glory of Columbia, Her Yeomanry!* as the sister of one of the three captors of Major André. Dressed in boy's clothes, she says, "I'm a good mind to 'list for a soldier." In *She Would Be a Soldier* (1819), Mordecai Noah, a Jacksonian Democratic politician, created a character, Christine, who in the War of 1812, like Deborah in Mann's memoir, joins the army to avoid a marriage with an unwanted suitor. For thirty years it was one of the city's most popular plays.[27]

Given Sampson's presence in this subterranean popular culture, it is not surprising that she herself made a literary appearance in the Civil War, when it was said some four hundred women in both armies were disguised as men. Mary Livermore, who as a leader of the U.S. Sanitary Commission made several tours of Union military hospitals, reported that "some startling histories of these military women were current in the gossip of army life; and extravagant and unreal as were many of the narrations, one always felt they had a foundation in fact."[28] Deborah appeared in the "Beadle Dime Novel" series, issued monthly between 1860 and 1865, which sold from 35,000 to 80,000 copies for each issue, 4 million copies in all. In a subseries of short stories, *Beadle's Dime Tales,* a volume featured "Deborah the Maiden Warrior," with an illustration of her in uniform standing alongside a cannon.[29]

The author offered an abbreviated version of Deborah's adventures (drawn entirely from Elizabeth Ellet's account discussed below), stressing how the indentured servant improved herself and became a schoolteacher, how she was wounded in battle and saved from death's door, how twice "the affections of fair maidens were laid at her feet," and how she was discharged by General Washington and later visited him as president when Congress awarded her a pension for life, leaving her "in comfortable circumstances." Deborah Sampson, the author predicted, might "become invested with a glory like that which encircles the memory of the Maid of Orleans."

To soldiers, this Beadle tale would have been credible in light of what they had seen or heard. In 1866, John Adams Vinton introduced his reprint of Mann's book with the observation that "many remarkable instances of female courage and heroism occurred in our late civil war" on both sides. The narratives of such cross-dressing soldiers would in turn replace Sampson's, but she would reappear, either in time of war or in the wake of a war in which women were participants.[30]

3. *The Genteel Tradition of Women's History*
The Apologia of Elizabeth Ellet

In 1840, two years after John Quincy Adams eulogized Deborah Gannett in Congress, his son Charles Francis Adams wrote as if it had never happened. In introducing his edited two-volume collection of the letters of his grandmother Abigail, Adams wrote that "the heroism of the females of the Revolu-

Deborah Sampson, the Maiden Warrior, *illustrates a short narrative in the best-selling* Beadle's Dime Tales *issued during the Civil War. By portraying her guarding a cannon, the artist associated Sampson with "Molly Pitcher," already legendary for replacing her fallen husband at his gun at the Battle of Monmouth. Courtesy Northern Illinois University Library.*

tion has gone from memory" and "nothing, absolutely nothing remains upon the ear of the young of the present day." It was a foolish thing to say: the deeds of many women of the Revolution lived on in the memory of their descendants, just as his grandmother Abigail lived on in his memory and in her letters. This is exactly what Elizabeth Ellet found in the 1840s when she compiled the biographical sketches for what became the first history of women in the Revolution. Ellet, as her biographer writes, "searched out and examined numerous unpublished letters written by women during the Revolution and talked with their descendants." She compiled what was in good part an oral history, often oblivious to the limitations of her sources.[31]

The appearance of Ellet's three-volume *Women of the American Revolution* in 1848–50 was an event, enabling a new generation of women to discover the lost heroines of the Revolution. While Elizabeth Ellet (1818–1877) was not the first American woman to write about the contributions of women to history, she was the first historian to write about women in the Revolution, the first to recover Sampson, and actually the first woman to comment about her in print. Sampson was lost to the great white male historians who produced the monumental multivolume tomes on the Revolution in the nineteenth century, whether George Bancroft, Jacksonian Democratic celebrant of the common people, or the caustic Federalist Richard Hildreth. Peter Force, the avid collector of Americana, requested documents about her from the pension office, and the antiquarian Benjamin Lossing took notes on her, but neither found space for her in their publications.[32]

Dates can be misleading. Although Ellet published her first volume in 1848, the year of the pathbreaking convention at Seneca Falls, New York, her impulses were more conservative than those of the advocates of women's rights. Her aim was to recover "the vast influence of women's patriotism" exercised within women's traditional sphere, not to argue for equal rights. She singled out those "matrons" whose names "deserve to live in remembrance." Engravings of genteel women adorned the first two volumes; but, as the historian Linda Kerber points out, there were also accounts of brave young farm women riding through the night as couriers and as spies, and she devoted a third volume in 1850 to obscure women, making for an amazing total of 160 biographical sketches.[33]

"Deborah Samson"—Ellet reverted to the original family spelling—was the subject of chapter 32 in volume 2. Ellet had mixed feelings about her: "it cannot be denied that this romantic girl exhibited something of the same spirit" as Joan of Arc, but she wished she had shown this "enthusiasm . . . in a more becoming manner." Her career "cannot be commended as example," but her chaste behavior in the army perhaps excused her initial transgression.[34]

While Ellet was not able to find a copy of Mann's book, she did not regret it, she said, because she understood that "it was not in any measure reliable," and that Mrs. Gannett had repudiated it. Ellet claimed she "received her facts from a person who knew her [Deborah] personally and has often listened with thrilling interest to the animated description given by herself of her exploits and adventures." Her source had a likely connection to Mrs. Gannett, but it does not make the tales she passed on especially credible.[35]

Ellet offered a sentimental tale. She was all apologies for her deed. Deborah was the youngest child of poor parents whose "poverty was rendered hopeless by pernicious habits," presumably her father's. She was indentured as a servant to "a respectable farmer," but she was "alone in the world" and "felt herself accountable to no human being." Her enlistment, Ellet was confident, was the result of the "purest patriotism—her disguise made it a secret, so she could not expect applause—but was also prompted by her imagination, curiosity and restlessness." Ellet wrote next to nothing about Deborah's military service. She dwelt instead on her romances, devoting two pages to an alleged "love passage" with "a young girl" at the home of Captain Nathan Thayer and two pages to the alleged Philadelphia affair with a woman she was told was Dr. Barnabas Binney's niece. In the mid-nineteenth century, same-gender romances obviously were not taboo to a very proper Mrs. Ellet.[36]

In the mid-nineteenth century, the historian Elizabeth Ellet popularized the myth that Deborah Sampson was discharged from the army by General Washington. In this engraving, Sampson is shown presenting a letter to the commander in chief revealing her true identity. Of unknown origin, the drawing reappeared every now and then in twentieth-century newspapers. Library of Congress.

Ellet ended her sketch with a dramatic account of an invented interview of Deborah with General Washington in 1783, who discharged her without a word of reproach. "How thankful—she has often said 'was I to that great and good man who so kindly spared my feelings!' " Ellet followed this with the other fantasy about an invitation from Washington to visit the capital, after which Congress immediately granted her a pension and land. "She was invited to the houses of several officers, and to parties given in the city." In 1805, "she was living in comfortable circumstances"—every part of this story the opposite of what actually happened.[37]

Ellet thus offered a version of Deborah's life that was thoroughly romanticized (in both senses), in which a poverty-stricken girl was rewarded by the father of her country. Almost all subsequent accounts of Sampson well into the present drew on Ellet rather than Mann, or else blended the two. The very fact that Ellet's version sanitized Deborah, however, made it possible for her to be embraced by as mainstream a woman as Sarah J. Hale, editor of *Godey's Lady's Book,* the most popular woman's magazine of the day, in which Ellet's sketch first appeared. Afterward, Hale's encyclopedia, which included Sampson among 2,400 "distinguished women," further legitimized her. Before long, the Boston Brahmin Dr. Oliver Wendell Holmes was citing her in a novel. In portraying her as an unthreatening romantic heroine, Ellet had opened a path for Sampson into genteel culture.[38]

4. *Local Heroine*
Sharon discovers its "most famous citizen"

Strange to say, Deborah Sampson's reputation was national before it was local, probably the reverse of most military heroes of the Revolution. From the closing decade or so of the nineteenth century through World War I, this changed as the Gannett family and the town of Sharon rediscovered her, acclaiming her as they had never done in her life. And the way it happened begins to give another answer to our question: What does it take to recognize an ordinary person who did extraordinary things? The popularity of Ellet suggests it takes a women's movement interested in recovering its forerunners to provide an audience for women's history, but that a life has to be romanticized to be acceptable. The Civil War, in which it was common knowledge that women were disguised as soldiers, suggests that it takes contemporary experience to make similar things in the past credible. The local revival at the end of the nineteenth century was made possible by a confluence of a national celebration of the history of the colonial and Revolutionary eras, a renewal of the women's movement, and a rampant local boosterism.

The local recovery of Sampson owed much to a wave of patriotism in the last quarter of the century which attempted to restore the colonial era, the "founding fathers," and New England to a sacred place in American history. Filial piety abounded. This was the formative era of the Sons of the American Revolution, the Daughters of the American Revolution, local historical societies, and movements for the preservation of New England "antiquities." The observance of the centennials of the Revolutionary era—the Declaration of Independence in 1876, the Constitution in 1887, and the inauguration of Washington in 1889—contributed to this process. Many avowedly conservative currents fed the stream.[39]

The rediscovery was fed, secondly, by a renewal of the women's movement. Typically, Mary Livermore, who after the Civil War became a crusader for woman's suffrage and temperance, crisscrossing the country, offering as one of her lectures "Woman's Place in the Early History of the Country."[40] The memory of Sampson was refurbished as a feminist. A novel in 1891 by the American Jane Austin portrayed young Deborah bursting bonds: "I want no good man taking me to wife, and I want no petticoat, nor apron nor dish-clout, not to be tied by a leg in the barn-yard. I've borne it all for twenty years and I'll have no more of it." In 1900, the *Ladies' Home Journal,* whose editors were trying to expand the "traditional areas of interest" of middle-class women, profiled Deborah Sampson as a soldier. Livermore and Frances Willard, the temperance crusader, put her in a new biographical compendium. To a Boston paper she was "A Yankee Jeanne D'Arc."[41]

In this climate, the rise of a new generation of the Gannett family to prosperity and prominence in Sharon made it easier for them to take their prodigal ancestor back into the fold. The family was no longer down and out. Benjamin Gannett (1825–1901), the third Benjamin (Earl's son and Deborah's grandson), served as selectman for nineteen years and was a pillar of the now respectable Baptist Church. As he gentrified the house and landscaped the grounds, it became known as the "Gannett mansion," while enlarged cleared land supported a thriving dairy farm producing for a market.[42]

The patriotic societies gave Sampson cachet. A few descendants became members of the D.A.R. or S.A.R. In nearby Brockton, Chapter 323 of the D.A.R., founded in 1897, took Deborah Sampson's name, as did a lodge of the International Order of Odd Fellows. These societies nurtured her memory through relics. Members of the D.A.R. made a pilgrimage to the East Street house, where Benjamin Gannett donated a door from a cupboard by tradition crafted by Deborah to be used in framing the chapter's charter. In later years, Helen Monk Weeks, Deborah's great-granddaughter, an officer of the D.A.R., appeared in Deborah's 1785 dress on ceremonial occasions.[43]

To achieve local fame it takes local enthusiasts. Earlier, Herman Mann, his son Herman Junior, and William Ellis, all of Dedham, played this role. Sharon owed its turn-of-the-century Sampson revival to a boosterism personified by Eugene Tappan, a lawyer and assistant registrar in the probate court in Boston, who had moved to the town in 1897. Tappan "quickly discerned the dramatic features" in Sampson's career and became the "chief spirit" behind a dinner in April 1902, observing the centennial of her address in Boston.[44]

The dinner at the town hall caught up all the currents flowing into the Sampson revival: patriotism, women's rights, and local and family pride. It was a bang-up affair, attended by one hundred people, most of them local, with a sprinkling of luminaries coming in from Boston and other cities by train or the new interurban electric trolley car. Fourteen people stood up as descendants or "married to descendants" of Deborah, nine of them women. As Rodney Monk set down his memories of the event sixty years later, it stuck in his mind that "my grandmother [Rhoda Gannett Monk] a granddaughter [of Deborah] age 82 years would not attend"—suggesting a willful act, perhaps for religious reasons. The Congregational pastor and the wife of the Unitarian minister were present, but the Baptist Church was unrepresented, consistent with Sharon's former Baptist minister insisting that Mrs. Gannett did not regard "disguising herself" as a "truthful act."[45]

Shrewdly, Tappan shifted attention from the controversial career of Deborah Sampson as a soldier to Mrs. Gannett "as an early woman lecturer." As toastmaster, he hailed her "among the first of her sex in the field and on the platform." In 1802, a woman lecturing was a radical action, but by 1902 women had long since been accepted as public speakers; Deborah therefore could be portrayed as a pioneer of a right already won. This switch also shifted attention from any gossip lingering from *The Female Review,* a book Tappan dismissed as "a kind of romance." The arrangements committee reprinted her Boston address and struck engravings from the same copperplate Mann had used. At the dinner, Susan Moody, a great-granddaughter, read excerpts from both the address and the tour diary. The main speaker, Mary Livermore, legendary at eighty-two, was the incarnation of the woman crusader. Known as the "Queen of the Lecture Platform," for a quarter of a century she had averaged 150 lectures a year, or almost 3,000 in all. As past president of both the Massachusetts Women's Suffrage Association and the Massachusetts Woman's Christian Temperance Union, she embodied the two leading women's movements of the day.

The pictures, "conspicuously displayed," connected Sampson to other crusading women: Anne Hutchinson, Hannah Duston, and Mary Lyon, as well as to the obligatory heroines of the Revolution, Martha Washington and Betsy Ross. The head of the Grand Army of the Republic spoke of these crusaders as "women who dared": Hutchinson, who "suffered for her determination and pointed speech"; Duston, who in killing her Indian captors, "took retributive justice into her own hands"; while Lyon, as founder of Mount Holyoke College, "opened the way to higher education" for women.[46]

Livermore gave the main history lesson. "Of all the public women of the past, Deborah Sampson has a fascination for me that none other ever had," she began. One reason was her patriotism. "The call was for men, men, men. . . . Deborah was fired in her own soul . . . and in those years was fighting, fighting, fighting with the bravest." She also admired her, she half-joked, because throughout her disguise she was "close mouthed. I tell you I admire a woman who can hold her tongue." (Sixty years later, Rodney Monk remembered this remark, after which there was "great laughter.") Finally, said Livermore, she admired Deborah as a lecturer because "it was a hard battle to become a public speaker."[47]

Livermore linked Sampson to women reformers. "But one woman before Deborah Sampson had ever spoken on a public platform, Anne Hutchinson, who was a reformer, and reformers are never very welcome." Referring to the 1802 address, Livermore said, "one thing only I feel sorry for, and that was that Deborah Sampson saw fit to apologize for what she had done when she came to tell the story of her war experiences. If war is right, then a woman has a right to engage in it. It is not a question whether women have a right to fight, but whether or not war is right. That is the question that must be decided first." When Livermore left after her speech, "all the company rose and remained standing and cheering" until she was out of the hall. It took a contemporary crusader to bring a historic one to life, as it often does.[48] Sharon's Congregationalist pastor, the closing speaker, cited Judges and the prophetess Deborah. The diners, who earlier had joined the three-piece orchestra to sing "My Country 'Tis of Thee," ended the evening with "Auld Lang Syne."[49]

She had arrived. The Sharon Historical Society came into existence and flourished. Tappan collected stories about Deborah and the town, which eventually filled five scrapbooks. Descendants donated objects belonging to Deborah to the town. A picture postcard of the Gannett house was issued (part of a national craze to memorialize local sites that by 1920 produced some 20 million picture postcards). The Brockton D.A.R. mounted bronze plaques commemorating Deborah: in Sharon, Plympton, and Brockton. Middleborough alone was bereft of recognition, save for a picture postcard of the Thomas house.[50]

In 1908, the local Sampson revival reached a peak with the dedication of a plaque in Sharon's Rock Ridge Cemetery at a ceremony attended by twelve hundred people, undoubtedly the largest public event in the town's history. A grandson, George Washington Gay, a shoemaker, had provided in his will for a double memorial: to the town's Civil War dead, who included his son, and to Deborah. After twenty years, when his bequest reached $8,000, the town commissioned a statue of a male Civil War soldier flanked by a bronze tablet with a bas-relief of Deborah. The crowd, which came from all over (some in newfangled automobiles), included officers of the G.A.R. and D.A.R., linking the nation's two epochal wars. The town selectman said Gay's aim was "to perpetuate the name of Sharon's most famous citizen." After Edythe Monk, Deborah's great-granddaughter, unveiled the plaque, the band struck up "The Spirit of '76."[51]

The bas-relief plaque gave Sampson a faint touch of Marianne, the symbol of female militance in France's revolutions. The carriage of her head and upper torso was adapted from the 1797 engraving, but in feeling it could not have been more different: she wears what might be taken for a uniform, and her straight hair is somewhat wild, as if windblown. The face, with a prominent nose, is stern and strong. The inscription navigated the disputed issues about her service:

Deborah Sampson Gannett • Woman Soldier in the War of the Revolution • Enlisted under the name of Robert Shurtleff • Several years in active service • Wounded at the Battle of Tarrytown • Honorably discharged in 1783 • Pensioned by Congress in 1803 • This tablet is placed here by request of her grandson, George Washington Gay

For all this restraint, she finally received the due that family and town had withheld.

For the family, the years before World War I were a golden era. Muriel Nelson, born in the homestead in 1910, the last Gannett to be born there, remembered her childhood glowingly when she talked to me in the mid-1990s. She had fond memories of her chores on the farm, her father's milk wagon, and the horse Molly. She was, and still is, a member of the Baptist Church (although for a while she had been a Quaker), showing me the hymnal imprinted with her grandfather Benjamin's name.[52] It was a time of celebrating Deborah Sampson Gannett. She remembers a stream of visitors to the house, and she and her mother taking them to see the memorial in the cemetery. Looking at a picture postcard of the fashionable house on East Street draped with flag bunting, two horsedrawn carriages in front and family members assembled on the porch, she remembers it as the family's annual Fourth of July observance.[53]

And then the golden era of Sampson's rise to fame faded. During World War I, the family sold the farm and house and moved into town. Deborah remained "A Sharon Celebrity," as one paper put it, but nationally her fame lacked staying power. National recognition, like that in the past—from John Quincy Adams's speech, Elizabeth Ellet's sketch, the *Beadle's Dime Tale,* Mary Livermore's oration—was ephemeral. It would remain so until the last quarter of the twentieth century.

Chapter Eleven
Lost and Found

Bronze plaques in a local cemetery or on a boulder on a village green fame doth not sustain. Nationally, for the half century from the end of World War I through the depression era, through World War II, and for most of the postwar era, Deborah Sampson received no more than occasional recognition. And then, in the last quarter of the twentieth century, the national context changed and Deborah Sampson arrived.

1. *An Occasional Heroine*
The Twentieth Century to 1970

From the 1920s until the early 1970s, the institutions that usually pass on the memory of Americans with a claim to fame failed Deborah Sampson. In Sharon in the era of Prohibition, the Gannett house and farm passed into the hands of bootleggers, until it was bought in 1934 by the father of the present owner, Daniel Arguimbau, who turned the property into a chicken farm. The Sharon Historical Society lost its live wire, and the town "lost" the relics donated by descendants.[1]

Deborah became fair game for anyone who wanted to spin a wild yarn about her. In 1918, a Worcester paper garbled her life in a Sunday feature:

"Only Girl to Fight British, Priv[ate] Deborah Sampson Loves Holden Man Who Proves Traitor." In the reporter's fantasy, Deborah enlisted at sixteen to be with her lover, David Potter of Holden, a soldier later court-martialed for desertion who was saved only when Deborah pleaded for his life with Martha Washington. Potter, indeed, went AWOL many times, but the story was sheer invention. The New Deal WPA Federal Writers Project, zealous to honor the unsung, perpetuated it in its published guide to Massachusetts. The Historic American Buildings Survey, another federal project recovering lost history, identified the wrong house in Middleborough as the "Deborah Sampson house." The problem was that there were no keepers of the flame to guard her legacy.[2]

Nationally, she was little more than a curiosity. Robert Ripley's syndicated newspaper cartoon about oddities offered a drawing of Benjamin Gannett as the only man who ever received a pension as the widower of a veteran—"Believe It or Not!" She was the subject of a play, *Damn Deborah,* billed as "A Comedy of Female Presumption" when first produced in summer stock on Cape Cod in 1937. Deborah in disguise was a vivacious soldier, and Sergeant Ben Gannett, her handsome male army buddy, pulled off scenes a local reviewer found "riotously funny." Some years later the piece was turned into a musical. In 1937, the snobbish *New Yorker* ran a condescending profile of Deborah, proving only that its articles could be as underresearched as the Sunday supplements. In books, she appeared mostly in collections of essays about eccentrics, like *Forgotten Ladies* or, ironically, *Lost Men of American History.* She was also in a comic book.[3]

Obviously, she had not disappeared in public memory. She was thus available when the country needed a symbol to mobilize women. In World War II, when women were beckoned by Uncle Sam to replace men on the assembly lines or serve as WACS and WAVES, the government named Liberty Ship Number 2620 the *Deborah Gannett.* The ship was christened by Sally Gannett, daughter of Frank R. Gannett (1876–1957) of Rochester, descended from Joseph Gannett, Deborah's brother-in-law, who had migrated to western New York in 1805. Frank R. Gannett was founder of the chain of newspapers that bore his name and a contender for the Republican nomination as president and vice president in 1936 and 1940. At the christening, he saluted his great-great-aunt as "a pioneer in breaking down the restrictions and conventions which bound women at the time."[4]

In the early years of the Cold War, the government paraded Sampson as proof of the recognition a democracy has always given women and veterans. In 1947, the "Freedom Train," which crisscrossed the country with a walk-through exhibit of one hundred "basic documents" of American freedom, included Mrs. Gannett's petition to Congress of 1818. The documents were chosen by a conservative "approval" committee that included John Foster Dulles, soon to be Dwight Eisenhower's secretary of state.[5]

In the 1950s and early 1960s, Deborah was generally out of fashion, as Daniel Arguimbau, owner of the Gannett farm, recalls those years. The books about her were accessible only in research libraries, and there was not much in writing for children or young adults. Muriel Nelson remembers Sharon schoolchildren performing pageants and writing tributes, but the family scrapbook has only a few clippings for these decades. There was an occasional feature about "America's First WAC," and a gladiola was named for her. Arguimbau remembers only one devoted descendant who visited the Gannett farm, Rodney Monk. In the 1960s, when Michael Gannett, then an officer in the Department of State, began a family genealogy, he recalls that the few descendants who knew about Deborah were not especially proud of her. In the early 1970s, when Charles Bricknell, Plympton's champion of Sampson, began his research, "people in Plympton and Middleborough claimed she was a tramp and a camp follower." When he expressed his frustration to a Middleborough librarian, she told him, "We are somewhat ashamed of Deborah here."[6]

With the hindsight of the changes in the last quarter of the twentieth century, one can see what was missing in the fifty years before. After World War II, the WAC was disbanded and the number of enlisted women in the army plummeted. Rosie the Riveter was sent back to the kitchen, albeit sometimes to a suburban house. High school history textbooks were dull and bland. Historians of the American Revolution kept it a "safe," consensual revolution. There was no feminist movement looking for forerunners. Famous founding fathers came into fashion—but founding mothers? Women's history was not an academic field, and the talented women biographers who wrote the readable books about the Revolution wrote about men. Esther Forbes, for example, who brought Paul Revere to life, took note of his political support for the "curious and picturesque" Mrs. Gannett. Note, too, that these were years when the medical and psychiatric establishment made a cross-dressing woman suspect for "the love that dared not speak its name."

In sum, the stage was not set for a woman soldier, however dressed, to be received with applause.[7]

2. *Arrival*
No Trivial Pursuit

What does it take for a person whose reputation has gone through as many ups and downs as Sampson's to secure a place in public memory, "official" and "popular," and move from "subordinate" to "mainstream" memory? The Deborah Sampson revival that began in the 1970s was wafted by tidal waves changing American life.

First, women were establishing an extraordinary presence in the American military. By 1994, there were about 200,000 women in the combined services, and by mid-1999, there were 1,239,500 female veterans.[8] Second, in the wake of the civil rights movement, which placed racial equality on the national agenda, a new women's movement in the 1970s and 1980s did the same for "women's liberation." As more and more women entered the labor force, comprising half of all workers by the 1990s, they were in a wide range of very visible hitherto "male" jobs.[9] Third, the bicentennial celebrations of the Revolution stimulated, as had those of the centennial, a renewed interest in the founding era, save now they were honed by a new sensitivity to the issues raised by the movements for racial and gender equality. Finally, a new generation of historians, dissatisfied with the textbook version of the American past, began to explore the Revolution "from the bottom up." As women entered the historical profession—by 2000, two out of five Ph.D.'s in history were going to women—the field of women's history bloomed.[10]

The presence of women in the military launched a sea change in American opinion about woman soldiers. Women holding down occupations gendered "male" gave proof of the capacity of a woman to do "a man's work." The movements for equality hunted for their pathbreakers, while the bicentennial celebrations stimulated a search for forgotten local heroes. The new academic history recovered groups previously seen only as victims as shapers of their own history. Then, as gays began to come out of the closet, a search began for gays and lesbians hidden from history.[11]

For all these trends, the rediscovery of Deborah Sampson was not the result of knowledge discovered by professional historians trickling down to the public, a vanity of academics. Just as Deborah had been brought to the public earlier by amateurs, she was now recovered by a handful of enthusiasts from several towns in eastern Massachusetts who found one another in a campaign to win recognition for her as an act of justice. The core included Patrick Leonard, a former Pinkerton detective of Braintree; Charles Bricknell, a retired appliance repairman of Plympton; Emil Guba, a former professor of plant pathology; and Jan Lewis Nelson, who grew up in Middleborough.

Leonard dates his "infatuation" with Deborah "to a spring day in 1924 at St. John's school in Canton, Mass. when our second grade teacher, Sister St. Agatha" told him about her. Bricknell "started the project as a hobby when I had to retire after a heart attack." Guba also took up the subject in retirement, completing a book about Deborah when he was in his nineties, deaf and legally blind. Nelson learned about Deborah from her high school teacher, became caretaker of her Plympton house, and ended up writing a novel about her. In 1982–83, the group achieved one of their major goals when the legislature and governors proclaimed "Deborah Samson" (spelled without a "p") the official heroine of Massachusetts, and May 23 (the date she was mustered into the army) as "Deborah Samson Day," an observance still on the books. Meanwhile, one Gannett produced a short anecdotal biography and another the first modern genealogy of the Gannett clan.[12]

The road to recognition at times was rocky with controversy. Her Massachusetts enthusiasts took issue with a cantankerous archivist, Julia Ward Stickley, who was unrelenting in her conviction that Sampson enlisted in 1781 and fought at Yorktown, insisting that the Massachusetts state document attesting to 1782 had been doctored. Advocates of black pride who claimed that Deborah was black—a subject we will return to—provoked endless refutations from her white fans.[13]

How widespread is recognition of Sampson? Locally, she is well known. In Plympton, her birthplace, her image is on the town flag and on patches on policemen's uniforms, and the historical society devotes a room to her. In 1989, Sharon commemorated her with a statue, about which more at the end of this chapter. In Middleborough, which once scorned the erring youth, she has any number of devoted, knowledgeable admirers.[14] During the bicentennial of the Revolution, she became accessible to a national public. *National*

Geographic ran a dramatic illustration of her charging with bayonet at the Battle of Yorktown. A traveling exhibit, *Remember the Ladies,* broke the ice for museums.[15] Deborah became increasingly known to schoolchildren: the subject of biographies, fiction and non-fiction, and a workbook of primary sources. There are Deborah Sampson reenactors in Massachusetts, New York, and California.[16] Belatedly, academic scholars have been catching up, tracking facets of her life. Ignored by the *Dictionary of American Biography* (1928–36), she was recognized in *Notable American Women* (1971). She is one of 17,450 Americans in the new *American National Biography* (1999), inclusion in which, as two historians observe, "will come to constitute formal recognition of a person's national significance."[17]

While military historians have found a place for Sampson, military institutions have not quite reached a level of tokenism.[18] At West Point, where a plaque marks Margaret Corbin's grave, an illustration of Sampson commissioned for a temporary exhibit in 1954 has been retired to storage. At the Pentagon's "Corridor of Military Women," installed in 1983, one can find her picture and an engraving of "Molly Pitcher" in an exhibit somewhat the worse for wear. The privately managed New Windsor encampment, on the other hand, marks the site of the hut in which Sampson might have lived, and a woman in uniform reenacts her on annual Deborah Sampson Days.[19] Women veterans have a growing sense of Deborah Sampson. Witness The Women's Memorial, a museum sponsored by women veterans at the entrance to Arlington National Cemetery in Washington. At its dedication in 1997, attended by some 36,000 veterans, the biblical "Song of Deborah" followed the invocation.[20]

This array of recognition at many levels of American life is impressive. How much staying power does it give her? Shapers of "official" memory know her. The *Chicago Tribune,* in a Memorial Day tribute to veterans, for example, chose her as the emblematic woman soldier in an editorial that began: "But don't think for a minute that they [women] haven't been there from the start." For Women's History Month, March 1999, a presidential proclamation by William Jefferson Clinton singled out Sampson as one of "the countless women" who "have shaped our destiny and enriched our society."[21]

How does one measure whether she has arrived in "popular" memory? By a coloring book on the Revolution for children available at historic sites?

By a counterfeit folk song in the style of the women warrior ballads of the eighteenth century? By articles in the *National Enquirer,* mother of all scandal sheets? Or a novel in which Sampson is depicted as "a cross-dressing whore"? Or a question in the parlor game Trivial Pursuit? Deborah Sampson is in all of these. Movie and television projects are on the way.[22]

And, yes, she can be tracked on the Internet, perhaps the ultimate measure of popularity in the electronic age. Early in my research, there were a number of scholarly research engines to locate manuscripts, books, and articles about Sampson. In mid-2001, when my wife and I sat down at the computer to search via Google and entered "Deborah Sampson," we were not prepared for what we found: more than two thousand entries. Some were no more than her name on a list or a passing mention. But the sheer volume of material was mind-boggling: biographical essays, lists of books, book reviews, lesson plans, school assignments, course syllabi, excerpts from encyclopedias, dictionaries. There was nothing like this five years before.[23]

The range of this vast mishmash on the Internet is dazzling: a college professor gives students in her course "Warriors and Equality" an excerpt from Herman Mann and asks, "What fears does he allay?"; a kid expresses her admiration for a heroine in an essay that begins: "I am Deborah Sampson." There is an endless array of essays by elementary school pupils. Her fame does not at all approach that of the three female icons of the Revolution: Betsy Ross, Martha Washington, and "Molly Pitcher," but is it catching up?[24]

The public Internet is also disheartening. Web sites offer mounds of misinformation, recycling the same myths. And she is usually profiled only as Deborah Sampson, rarely as Deborah Gannett, which erases her equally pathbreaking life after the army. You can find everything on the Internet except bodies of original sources or some guidance in sorting out fact from fiction. The Internet is a great deceiver, all the more so because most users are unaware of its serious limitations.[25] Representing neither official memory nor academic memory, the Internet is popular memory, celebrating a newfound heroine with all the garbling common to storytelling. It is chaotic and unreliable. But here are ordinary people recovering, constructing, and celebrating another ordinary person. May we not say Deborah Sampson has arrived?

3. *Enlisting Deborah Sampson*
Americans Claim a Forerunner

We have still another measure of when a historical figure is popular: when he or she is appropriated by groups who seek to validate their claims to a historic lineage. Among Revolutionary era leaders, Thomas Jefferson is a good example. "He could be quoted on every side of every question, it was often said," observes Merrill Peterson, who devoted a pathbreaking book to "what history made of Thomas Jefferson." In the twentieth century, Jefferson was claimed politically by southern states' rightists and racists as well as Roosevelt New Dealers, foes of big government and foes of big business, conservative libertarians and radical activists.[26]

Something like this has happened to Deborah Sampson on the spectrum of the recent movements for equal rights. She has been claimed as a person of color, as a lesbian, and as a feminist. Should we be surprised? This process has been accelerated by the Internet, but has been going on for years. It is part of a time-honored quest of groups trying to legitimize themselves by establishing their forerunners, especially if they can be connected to the founding period. It is as American as it is inevitable. Indeed, the ups and downs of Sampson's reputation over two centuries suggest that she has been recovered only when movements have discovered her or created a climate of opinion for others to take her up. At the same time, this claiming reveals the pitfalls of appropriating for a modern cause someone who lived two hundred years ago.

All three claims involve an uncertainty in definition and a carelessness in weighing evidence. They are based either on imposing a modern concept on another era (that she was a feminist); or on a misreading of a single source (that she was a person of color); or on a wishful, uncritical reading of dubious sources (that she was a lesbian). I don't believe one claim is as good as another, but because they are of concern to a wide range of people, I have taken them seriously. Discussing them helps to clarify the way historic figures are often refracted through prisms of our own making.

Was Deborah Sampson a person of color? Many people seem to think so. In mid-2001, when we entered "Deborah Sampson and black" as keywords on Google, there were about five hundred entries (of which perhaps four hundred actually make this link). She is in books and articles about famous black

Americans and military heroes and in two encyclopedias of black women in American history published in the 1990s.[27]

There is no credible evidence, in my opinion, for this claim. The assertion that Sampson was colored, Negro, black, African-American, or a woman of color (the terms changed over the decades as blacks chose different names to identify themselves) has never been presented with any clarity. Does it mean that she was visibly a person of color? Or that she was a person of African ancestry who passed as "white"? In any case, so far as I can make out, the claim has its origin in making too much of a passage in William Nell's *The Colored Patriots of the American Revolution* (1855), one of the first books by an African American enlisting black history in the struggle for equality. Nell (1816–1874) was a leading figure in Boston's African-American community, a co-worker of the abolitionists William Lloyd Garrison and Frederick Douglass, who led one crusade to desegregate Boston's public schools and another to erect a statue to Crispus Attucks of Boston Massacre fame.[28]

In his anecdotal history, Nell did not say that Gannett was black, but left readers with this inference in a one-sentence account of the recollections of Lemuel Burr, a contemporary of Nell, about the conversations his *grandfather*, Seymour Burr, had with Jeremy Jonah, both black soldiers. "Lemuel Burr often speaks of their reminiscences of Deborah Gannett," is all Nell wrote. His story is thus twice removed from the source, and exactly what Lemuel Burr passed down from his grandfather's conversations, we do not know. After this sentence, to identify Gannett, Nell reprinted the 1792 resolve of the Massachusetts legislature, which recognized Mrs. Gannett's "extraordinary instance of female heroism" (but said absolutely nothing about her as a person of color). Nell made no reference to her skin color, race, or origin, so my guess is that he and/or the grandson simply *assumed* she was a person of color because two black soldiers talked about her.

What do we know of the two soldiers who held the conversation? Seymour Burr very likely did hear tell about Sampson and may have seen her in the war: he was a soldier in her regiment, who, like her, was discharged at West Point late in 1783. Until his death in 1835 he lived in Canton, a stone's throw from Sharon, so he also may have seen her or heard about her in later life. Jeremiah Jones or Jonas (a name close enough to be Nell's Jeremy Jonah) was in another Massachusetts regiment and also served in the Hudson Valley until the end of the war. Possibly the two men were familiar with light-skinned blacks who passed, and especially with stories of fugitive slaves who escaped by pretending to be white and by cross-dressing, and simply took it for granted that a woman who passed as a man in the Revolutionary War had to be black. Another possibility is that in Canton the soldiers heard that Sampson had once been an indentured servant and assumed this meant she had been a slave.[29]

When Nell wrote in the 1850s, stories of slave women cross-dressing to escape were in the air. As a Bostonian, he would have been familiar with the spectacular flight in 1848 of Ellen Craft, a light-skinned slave who disguised herself as a white man and came to the city. In *Uncle Tom's Cabin* (1852), Harriet Beecher Stowe's runaway best-seller, Eliza Harris, another near-white slave, also cross-dressed to escape. Nell would have known the book, as Stowe wrote the introduction to his own history. But nowhere in Nell's text do either of the two reminiscing veterans, the grandson or Nell, claim that Sampson was passing.[30]

After Nell, the claim had little currency. Then, from the 1950s on, the authors of some of the first books and articles recovering Negro history assumed she was a Negro. Interestingly, when publishers were challenged, several withdrew the claim. She appeared in 1956 in the first edition of *The Pictorial History of the Negro in America*—co-authored by Langston Hughes, the well-known African-American poet, and Milton Meltzer, a white journalist—but was removed by the fourth edition. "The indications now," Meltzer wrote in 1983, "are that Deborah was not black." Benjamin Quarles, a black scholar, then the leading authority on blacks in the Revolution, wrote in the introduction to a reprint of Nell's book that "Nell does make the mistake repeated by later historians, that Deborah Sampson Gannett who impersonated a man was a Negro." In the preface to his own book, Quarles was emphatic: "The female combatant, Deborah Sampson, was not a Negro." John Hope Franklin, later the dean of African-American historians, concurred. Seemingly, as far as scholarship went, this laid the claim to rest.[31]

When the movement for civil rights shaded into a movement for black power, however, the claim resurfaced in a variety of black publications ranging from *Ebony,* the popular picture magazine, to *The Crisis,* the NAACP organ, to a ten-volume compendium on the achievements of black women. White Gannett enthusiasts, who had spent years researching her, challenged the claimants, mobilizing a stream of negative evidence: about her ancestors (on both sides of English stock); about her descendants (all considered white); or from the visual depictions of 1797. These refutations went unanswered or were merely acknowledged with the comment that the question was in dispute.[32]

In my research, I have been struck by the absence of so much as a hint about color in contemporary references to Sampson. In the army it was a time when even New England officers were extremely color-conscious in identifying enlisted men on descriptive muster rolls, commonly filling in a column for "complexion" as "colored," "black," or "mulatto." (We have such descriptions for some 750 Massachusetts soldiers.) I have never found "Robert Shurtliff" described on any roll, but there is no suggestion that anyone in the army took him for a person of color. And, although the Plympton town clerk routinely referred to the color of the recipients of town charity (Walter Blake was "a colored person," as was "Rose, the black woman"), in his several comments on the Sampsons, he never made any such annotation for any member of the family. Recall that Deborah's mother was in his records as a ward of the town.[33]

None of the first commentators on Deborah made any sort of racial identification, neither her contemporaries who knew her, Mann, Sr., Mann, Jr., or Ellis, nor the mid-nineteenth-century writers, Vinton, Ellet, or Pratt, at a time when race-consciousness was unusually high. The twentieth-century researchers who ransacked local and genealogical records found nothing. Nor have I found any such innuendos at moments when her gender deception was the object of scrutiny—in legislative bodies, in newspapers, by audiences on her tour, by her former officers and political supporters. It is hard to believe that General Paterson, a slaveholder who brought his slave Agrippa Hull with him into the army, would have received his former waiter so warmly after the war had he thought she was a person of color, or that Paul Revere, who observed her so closely in her home, would have ignored color in his letter to a congressman endorsing her petition.

Herman Mann dwelt on his heroine's complexion twice. In the 1797 book describing the woman who sat before him in the mid-1790s, he wrote: "She has a skin naturally clear and flushed with a blooming carnation," which meant she had rosy cheeks. And in the 1830s, writing as if he were Deborah, he constructed his description around negatives: "My nose is rather of the Roman cast; not perfectly straight, nor aquiline. My mouth is of the middling size; lips not nigh so thick as a negro's, sometimes like my cheeks, white, but generally of a carnation glow." At the conclusion, he wrote: "My complexion was not olive, nor lilly-white. It is now somewhat sun-burnt, powder-burnt, and weather-beaten." I read none of this as implying he saw her as a woman of color. The sole newspaper report on her appearance delivering a lecture singled out "the fairness of her complexion" and "the modest blushes which suffused her countenance."[34]

Only one small piece of the family record has given me pause. Deborah had a younger brother, Nehemiah, born four years after her, around 1764. A Nehemiah Sampson who enlisted in the Continental Army for a six-month term from the town of Scituate, Massachusetts, on July 20, 1780, was identified on a descriptive muster as age sixteen; stature five feet; and complexion "molatto." Judging by his name and age, this could have been Deborah's younger brother; genealogists later claim this military service for him. He is not identified as a person of color, however, in any other military record or in a wide range of local records of his later life. Nehemiah was living in Sharon when Deborah married into the Gannett family; he married in 1789, and around 1799 moved to Readfield, Maine, where he acquired local fame as a doctor, apparently self-trained. He died impoverished in New Hampshire.

If Nehemiah was indeed mulatto, and if he was the son of Deborah Bradford Sampson (none of whose other children were ever rumored to be of color), the father would have been a person of color, and, in 1763–64, either a slave or a free black, and such miscegenation by a married woman would have been a disgrace. There is no hint of such a scandal. The color-conscious, gossipy Plympton village clerk, who volunteered to the family of Ephraim Sampson (Deborah's brother) that his father and mother "quarreled," never offered any chatter about race mixture in the family. There is an outside chance that this was one of the things the couple quarreled about. Of course, even if the identification of Nehemiah in 1780 as mulatto is correct, and if this Nehemiah was her brother, it does not follow that his sister Deborah, born four years earlier, was a person of color.[35]

The origins of tales about heroes are one thing; why tales live on or reappear is another. Almost always they fill some need in both the tellers and their audiences. This one pops up like a jack-in-the-box. The sentence by Langston Hughes and Milton Meltzer in their 1956 history says it all: "The first American woman ever to enroll in the armed services was a Negro, Deborah Sampson Gannett. . . ." What a proud claim at a time when blacks were still struggling for the most elementary rights in the army.[36]

In neither of two recent encyclopedias of black women in American history do the authors of the entries for Sampson confront the controversy. The most recent one acknowledges, "While it is generally accepted that Deborah was a Black American, there are those who question the authenticity of this claim." But both authors seem oblivious to the problem of evidence and to the enormous implications for the story of her life, if she were a person of color. It is understandable that Nell's story should have reemerged in the early stage of rediscovering black history, but puzzling that it should persist when the rich encyclopedias are themselves evidence of the recovery of so many hitherto unknown heroic black women.[37]

It is a sign of the changing attitudes toward race in America, however, that Gannett descendants are of several minds about the claim. I have talked to family members who take for granted that it is false and are irritated, to Gannetts with an open mind waiting for the case to be made, and to still others for whom it is a ho-hum matter. One younger family member who assumes the claim is true expresses a sense of pride in her ancestry. My conclusion is that Deborah Sampson was not black: there is no credible evidence that she was, and after many years of sifting contemporary sources, there comes a point when the absence of evidence itself becomes compelling.[38]

Was Deborah Sampson a lesbian? Yes, according to another set of "hits" on the Internet (some 377, one night in mid-2001) in response to the keywords "Deborah Sampson and lesbian." She appeared on a half dozen lists of "Notable Lesbians" sponsored by American reference centers in gay and lesbian history, and on still others in Canada, Brazil, and Croatia. Indeed, as a "lesbian," her fame is international. Meanwhile, she is so identified in entries in a variety of printed compendia. A well-researched exhibit, *Improper Bostonians,* displayed a large blowup of the 1797 engraving of Sampson. For the founding era, for some gay people, she may have become a poster girl.[39]

Should she be? Aside from the fact that in the America of Sampson's day people would not have known the terms "lesbian" or "homosexual," in general they did not assign sexual identities to others. New Englanders were quite aware of biblical injunctions condemning sex between men and sex between women and of statute law which punished homosexual acts by men as sodomy. In the eighteenth century, while cases were occasionally brought against men (usually for attempted sodomy), legal action against women for "lewde behavior" with another woman were rare. The law did not recognize or punish sexual "orientation." In several cases of recurrent acts by a man, community opinion, as opposed to the law, was ready to assign an identity to him.[40] But romantic friendships between women were taken for granted. As to cross-dressing, colonial Americans would not have made the assumption that a woman discovered to be disguised as a man was doing so to attract or woo other women. They might have assumed she was up to no good, but not necessarily up to something sexual.[41]

The claims about Deborah Sampson's sexuality, needless to say, originate with Herman Mann. Mann's portrayal of Robert Shurtliff in a romance, I suggested in the Prologue in introducing the problem of reading his memoir, was most likely a product of his literary imagination. The fact that in his 1797 account he was at pains to deny there was even a physical possibility of sexual intercourse between two women does not mean that he was covering up for his heroine. Rather, he was fashioning her to conform to the values of those late-eighteenth-century readers who were drawing a distinction between sentimental love between women and an eroticism some were calling Sapphism. The fact that in his revised manuscript thirty-some years later Mann switched his story, making the affair a highly sexualized encounter, does not mean he was at last revealing the truth. Rather, this author-printer-editor-publisher, who was ever attuned to finding readers, believed there was an audience for such soft pornography. In the mid-nineteenth century in her sketch of Sampson, the very proper Elizabeth Ellet, as we have seen, dwelt on the Philadelphia romance (and added another), but after that the subject was ignored, until the modern gay and lesbian movement discovered Sampson.[42]

She was put on the map for students of sexuality by Jonathan Ned Katz, who in his massively researched collection of documents of the gay experience in America (1976) reprinted "several suggestive and curious passages" from Mann's 1797 book about her wartime romance, postwar flirtations, and the hearsay about her denying her husband sexual relations. Aware that the biography was "semi-fictionalized," he placed a warning flag on the evidence. He grouped Sampson in a section with other "Passing Women, 1782–1920" to whom he was unwilling to assign a sexual identity, warning that "categorizing these women as lesbian transvestites tends to narrow understanding rather than expand it." They "can be understood not as imitation men, but as real women, women who refused to accept the traditional socially assigned fate of their sex. . . . A basic feminist protest is a recurring theme in all these lives." Others have ignored such warnings.[43]

The pioneer scholars of gay and lesbian history have taken exception to the unending effort to find sexual pigeonholes for historical figures. Martha Vicinus, after researching a large number of passing women, criticizes the tendency "to categorize and define women's sexual behaviors too hastily," observing that most of us "understand that sexual behavior is unpredictable, various, and strikingly influenced by both same sex and opposite sex desires and influences."[44] Martin Duberman, addressing gays, writes, "We can never confirm our present images by citing lengthy lineages in the past. . . . Gay people long for some proof—some legitimatizing evidence, that we have always existed and in pretty much the same form as we currently do. . . ." "Alas," he reflects, "we can never find *exact* precursors in the past, and any search for them is doomed to disappointment." He suggests instead "reclaiming the history of gender non-conformity." Gender nonconformist fits Deborah Sampson well. Do we deepen our understanding of her by trying to give her an identity any more specific than this?[45]

Was Deborah Sampson a feminist? Not, for example, the way the term is used by two authors of a biography who, after calling Sampson "America's first official woman soldier, America's first heroine, America's first feminist," claim that "she volunteered to fight as the nation's first feminist, to prove women had the courage to wage war on behalf of their country by the side of men." Overkill aside—she was none of these firsts—the passage assigns to her a motive not on her mind: going into the army on behalf of a cause to prove a principle. Aside from using another term that did not come into use until much later, it attributes to her a consciousness the evidence does not support.[46]

"Feminist consciousness," as defined by Gerda Lerner, a historian who has long reflected on the subject, includes: "the awareness of women that they belong to a subordinate group; that they have suffered wrongs as a group; that their condition of subordination is not natural but is societally determined; that they must join with other women to remedy these wrongs." Sampson never really explained herself, and Mann attributed one set of ideas to her in his memoir, another in the address. On the basis of her behavior, one can deduce that she was aware she was doing things most women did not do and that women suffered wrongs. There is no evidence, however, to say that she joined with other women to remedy these wrongs. In the long run, one can argue that she contributed to feminism, but by what she did rather than by what she said.[47]

Historically, it is often lost that advocates of women's rights have not been allies of women in the military. From Mary Wollstonecraft and Judith Sargent Murray to Jane Addams through the Vietnam era, "pacifism remained a strong part of the feminist social critique," Linda Kerber reminds us. Recently, as the number of women in the armed forces expanded, the women's movements lagged in taking up their unequal treatment.[48] For their part, women in the modern military have not commonly seen themselves as feminists. In a discussion on the Internet, a captain at the U.S. Air Force Academy who freely labels herself a feminist writes that she has found only a few women in the military "willing to call themselves feminists . . . a woman doing a 'male' job can be threatening enough to men around her: why should she further that alienation to the point that she can be dismissed as a 'femi-nazi'?"[49] If my analysis of Sampson's wartime success holds, she, too, was a "conservative" in the Revolutionary army, one who survived the same way that women in today's military do, by becoming a crack soldier. She *was* a feminist, like so many women who broke barriers, in spite of herself.

Deborah Sampson has deservedly inspired present-day women, old and young, however they identify themselves. Cora Cheyney Partridge, author of the first biography of Sampson for young adults (1959), went on at sixty-eight to be ordained as one of the first woman priests in the Episcopal Church, serving a parish in Vermont. "I have always felt such an affinity with Deborah," she wrote, "some of her rubbed off on me of course." Jan Lewis Nelson, crusader for recognition of Deborah in Massachusetts, remembers using her as an example in the 1970s at women's "consciousness-raising" groups. Even Beatrice Bostock, the feisty descendant who in her eighties welcomed me to her house on Cape Cod to show me Deborah's dress, greeted me with a twinkle in her eye: "I'll bet you are one of those women's-libbers." Decades later, women wear the term flung at them in derision as a badge of honor.[50]

Deborah continues to inspire a young generation. Theresa Ramppen Gaydos, who has reenacted Sampson in uniform at the New Windsor encampment, writes: "She has shown me a side of myself I never knew existed. . . . While portraying Deborah I present a strong and determined sense of self worth. By taking Deborah's part I draw a part of her strength and courage as my own." Salima Khan, of Public School 94 in the Bronx, New York, ends her essay on the Internet with: "I thought that Deborah Sampson was a brave and special person. She made me believe that I can do anything I want to do and be anyone I want to be." Present-day women, young and old, who take inspiration from Deborah Sampson have not made a mistake. How important is it what we call her?[51]

4. Masculine/Feminine
A Statue in Sharon

As one of her officers predicted in 1784, Deborah Sampson is now "noticed by the compilers of the history of our grand revolution," as well as by her countrymen. The question left us is not whether she should be recognized, but how and for what? In the late 1980s, this question came to a head dramatically when the town of Sharon commissioned a sculptor to create the statue that since 1989 has stood in front of its public library. It is an arresting, life-size figure in blackened bronze, clearly in an appropriate place for a girl who was hungry for books and as an adult whose self-education Paul Revere thought "entitled her to a better situation in life."

Public statues commemorating soldiers arouse contention when the wars they took part in were controversial. Witness the statues to Confederate generals in the public squares of southern cities, which have become objects of criticism for honoring leaders of a war fought in defense of slavery. Witness the initial furor over the Vietnam War Memorial in Washington, Maya Lin's haunting wall of names listing the 58,000 dead American combatants, which now brings tears to visitors' eyes. There was also a debate over the accompanying memorial to the 265,000 women who served in that war.[52] The controversy in Sharon over a statue to Deborah Sampson was muted— no one questioned that she deserved recognition—yet it revealed some of the undercurrents that have affected the way she has been represented visually from the beginning. At the heart of the problem is how to depict a woman who crossed boundaries of gender.

Not surprisingly, the country has erected so few statues to women soldiers for any war that there is no firm tradition to draw upon. For that matter, almost no statues were erected to ordinary *male* soldiers of the Revolution. For the Revolutionary War, soldiers were long symbolized in Massachusetts by the bleak obelisk at Bunker Hill, and when a statue honoring a soldier was erected in Lexington in 1875, it was to a generic "Minute Man" of the militia who left his plow, the citizen soldier, rather than a "regular" in the Continental Army.

It is forgotten, however, that previous generations did not hesitate to depict women warriors as bellicose. For Hannah Duston, who, after she was captured by Indians in King William's War (1697), killed and scalped her captors, there are two statues—one of which depicts her with a tomahawk in one hand, scalps in the other. The few women of the Revolution celebrated in public art have usually been presented in military action. The mythical Molly Pitcher is depicted at the Monmouth, New Jersey, battlefield on a bas-relief brass plaque furiously jamming a ramrod into a cannon, while a statue in Carlisle, Pennsylvania, portrays her as a tough, heavyset woman gripping the ramrod, ready for action. At West Point, on a gravesite plaque, Margaret Corbin, known as "Captain Molly," also loads a cannon. At Carmel, New York, Sybil Luddington, the teenage girl who rode through the night in 1777 to rouse the militia, is appropriately mounted on a horse, brandishing the stick she used to knock on doors.[53]

Public statues, of course, are the work of artists, and in the case of Sharon, she is Lu Stubbs, an accomplished sculptor whose works grace other public places in Massachusetts. But public art, unlike works created on artistic impulses alone, is created with the expectations of a host of people in mind: the local public, official sponsors, financial contributors, family, tourists with no knowledge at all of the subject, and so on. In this case, the statue was created by a longtime resident who had to win over fellow townsfolk. Stubbs, who describes herself as "one of the original women's-libbers," said she admired Sampson for "her patriotism, her will and her bravery."[54]

The process by which Stubbs brought the sculpture to fruition guaranteed that she would have to accommodate community opinion. She proposed the statue and appeared before the town board and historic groups; consulted with Muriel Nelson, Deborah's great-great-granddaughter, living in Sharon; and invited public comment on a half-size model. Eventually, a twenty-one-person committee raised $40,000 from some five hundred contributors (among them the Gannett Foundation set up by the family of the

In this watercolor of Deborah Sampson commissioned for an exhibit at West Point in 1954 honoring women in the military, Deborah Sampson is tall and thin, like the men in conventional drawings of the light infantry, as well as feminine, coy, and cute. The painting is by the prominent German military illustrator Herbert Knotel. West Point Museum Art Collection, U.S. Military Academy.

publisher Frank E. Gannett, which donated $10,000). Stubbs, anxious for approval from potential critics, explained her decisions in interviews, in an article, and, since then, in a conversation with me in her studio.[55]

Stubbs defined the questions confronting her as at what point in Sampson's life should she portray her, what her clothing should be, and how she should look. These subjects reflected two larger unarticulated issues: What should she be celebrated for? And how masculine or feminine should she appear? The questions are not very different from those facing the other depicters of Sampson who had to meet the expectations of their sponsors. In 1797, when Joseph Stone painted Mrs. Gannett, he had to satisfy both his subject and Herman Mann, who commissioned the portrait as the basis of an engraving in his book. Both wanted a patriotic but feminine heroine and a likeness that contemporaries could say resembled her. In 1954, Herbert Knotel, a well-known German military illustrator commissioned by the West Point Academy to do a drawing for an exhibit, had to meet the unstated expectations of army brass. So he simply adapted the time-honored drawings of the uniformed soldiers of the Massachusetts Light Infantry—all tall, thin, handsome, square-jawed men. Deborah came out tall, thin, impossibly long-limbed, with a smiling face, pouting lips, and well-coiffed hair—a cute but ridiculous figure, compatible with the army's expectations for women.

Stubbs's solutions, like Stone's, straddled the alternatives, but in a different way. She decided "against portraying her as a soldier," she writes, "because the viewer would then think the sculpture depicted a man. My plan was to depict her as a plain young woman at about the time she was discharged from the service." The choice of clothing then became crucial. Imaginatively, Stubbs "played with ideas of dressing her as male on one side of her body and as a female on the other, then as one in front and the other in back." But on Cape Cod, Stubbs had an epiphany when she saw Deborah's dress that was inherited by Beatrice Bostock, held it up against herself, and realized that it would fit her. She "rejected both thoughts" of a masculine/feminine Deborah, "and decided that since she *was* a woman I'd put her in the dress I'd seen and have her hold the uniform." She borrowed a replica of a uniform from a local Sampson reenactor. However, this didn't "read clearly"; but "when I draped the coat over one shoulder, I started getting excited because I realized that was it."

The result is a life-size figure of a fairly tall woman, standing erect, looking resolutely ahead, who wears a plain dress that comes down to her ankles (not the pretty wedding dress) and has the coat of a Continental soldier draped over her shoulder, covering her right side. Her left arm steadies an upright musket, which leans against her; her left hand holds a tricornered hat, her right hand a powderhorn. Her weapon is at rest. The war, presumably, is over.

Stubbs's solution to Deborah's looks breaks with the 1797 likeness of a long-faced, lantern-jawed woman with a strong Roman nose. Early on, during consultations, two Sharon residents had "questioned whether it would be necessary to make her as ugly" as the Stone portrait. Stubbs reassured them it was not; she rejected Stone as a "primitive artist," whose portrait was "out of proportion and exaggerated." Instead, she turned to old photographs of the Sharon great-great-granddaughters as young women and their mother, all decidedly "attractive," attempting a composite face rather

This statue of Deborah Sampson by the sculptor Lu Stubbs stands at the entrance to the Sharon Public Library. Commissioned by the town and dedicated in 1989, it is a life-size figure in blackened bronze depicting Sampson, not in battle but at a point after her return from the army. She wears a dress, and a soldier's coat is draped over her shoulder; her musket is at rest at her side; her right hand holds a powderhorn, her left a man's colonial tricornered hat. The face departs from all previous representations of Sampson. Courtesy Lu Stubbs.

than a likeness. "I was trying to express her spirit," Stubbs wrote. Then, after she unveiled a model, sure enough, she was asked by some townspeople, "Don't you think she's too pretty?" "This time," said Stubbs, "I made her a little stronger."[56]

The result of this give-and-take is that Stubbs's Sampson, with her round face, pert nose, and a firm but short jaw, is decidedly more "pretty" than "ugly." Yet, with her long hair pulled back taut and tied in a queue, she retains the earlier determined look. If you know Sampson's story, the total effect is of a feminine woman possibly at the end of her stint as a soldier. This is not the woman in the smart uniform of the light infantry, tensely stalking the roads of Westchester, praised by her officers as a "vigilant" soldier. There is not a whiff of combat about her.

Stubbs's enigmatic statue can be read in different ways. I read it, in its own way, as a masquerade. Stone's painting in the late 1790s, when masculine women were suspect, had to cover up Deborah's masculine side. Stubbs's statue, created in an era of growing acceptance of women in the military and in combat, did not have to evade the puzzle of masculine/feminine and depict her safely returned to the female sphere. She is clearly a strong, determined woman, but determined to do what? For the girls and young women walking into the library, it is a safe, unthreatening figure; it raises neither the terror faced by a woman who had to disguise herself as a man nor the prospect of crossing a boundary into a new life. It can be read as a reassuring image, saying that a woman can be a soldier with a gun and remain a woman in a dress—in other words, that she can "have it all."

Yet, because the statue is not up on a lofty pedestal (traditional for political leaders), or on a high horse (a requisite for generals), it is a provocative figure. She is one of us. You can have your photograph taken while you stand alongside her. And, by depicting Deborah on the way home from war, the statue refuses to celebrate war, which is understandable for a work of public art shaped in the 1980s, still close to the wrenching turmoil within America over the Vietnam War. She is not the Lexington Minute Man poised to spring to arms, or Molly Pitcher blowing up people with her cannon, or Hannah Duston exultantly displaying scalps. The statue celebrates the achievement of a woman who dared to be a soldier; it does not glorify war.

The statue does what public statues of heroes rarely do. Instead of intimidating us, it raises questions: "What did you do to deserve this place of honor?" and "Why are you wearing the dress of a woman and half-wearing the military coat of a man while holding a gun?" Possibly we can find the answers within the library. She also asks the viewers questions: "Do you have to disguise yourself as someone other than who you are to do what you want to do in life? Do you have to pretend in order to cross a forbidden boundary?" For such questions we have to seek an answer within ourselves. The statue, like the story of Deborah's life, gives us something to ponder.

Epilogue

The Seagull

IN THE OPENING PAGES of *Little Women,* Louisa May Alcott's all-time best-selling novel set during the Civil War, Jo, her heroine, announces after her father has gone to war as a chaplain: "I can't get over my disappointment in not being a boy, and it's worse than ever now, for I'm dying to go and fight with Papa." Jo would have seen a kindred spirit in Deborah Sampson. Near the end of the novel, Jo sits on the New England seashore watching the birds with Beth, her shy, sick sister, who tells her: "You are the gull, Jo, strong and wild, fond of the storm and the wind, flying far out to sea, and happy all alone." She likened herself to the sand-bird, "always near the shore." Sampson was like Alcott's gull, "flying far out to sea" in an attempt to escape the constraints on women, yet forced to fly back to shore and the conventions of a society she could not forever fly above or escape from to reach another shore.[1]

While Deborah Sampson Gannett clearly led an unconventional life, this book suggests that, set in context, she was less unique than we might at first think today. She was like other women of the laboring classes who passed as men to pursue opportunities not open to women, or to escape servitude or take flight from the law. She was hardly the only disguised woman in an eighteenth-century army. If she was a romantic friend to another woman, so were countless others. In conceiving a child after she was

313

engaged but before she was wed, she had lots of company. Even as a woman who limited the size of her family, she fits the profile of a small but growing minority of New England women.

For her transgression as a soldier, moreover, her contemporaries honored her. Her former officers lauded her (her general and captain later welcomed her to their homes), and soldiers passed on lore about her. The legislators of Massachusetts valorized her. In time, the U.S. Department of War granted her a pension. People bought her memoir, paid to hear her speak, and applauded her address. Locally, others were attentive to her opinions on public subjects expressed in private conversations. Some young women who heard tell of her may have taken her as a model: "If Deborah Sampson could . . . then why shouldn't I . . . ?"

Why, then, was she subjected to "taunts and jeers"? In the sermons still being preached at public hangings in New England in her day, the minister warned the vast sea of faces before him that small vices led step by step to the larger crime that had brought the criminal before them to the gallows. For Deborah, this stereotype was reversed: if initially she was capable of such an enormous "abomination" against the "natural" order as wearing "that which pertaineth unto a man" (Deuteronomy 22:5), some may have reasoned, then she was capable of all the other sins of which she was accused. And in exhibiting herself on a tour twenty years later, she flaunted her original transgression.

More than that: She took a defiant stance throughout her life. She left one church for another, and then fled the church of her rebellion. She conducted an aggressive public campaign for her due as a veteran. She was a woman who did not stay in her place and did not hold her tongue. In marriage, she could be taken as the ultimate threat: a woman "who wore the breeches." In these actions she was far more threatening to the status quo than in anything she did in her sexual life, real, rumored, or imagined. Some village Puritans old enough to have witnessed shaming punishments might have liked to pin a letter on her outer garment, but what would it be? "I" for imposter? "C" for cheat or counterfeit? (Earlier, such letters were meted out by the courts.) Or they might have wished for a band of "regulators" to take this uppity woman for a skimmington ride and teach her a lesson. But no such thing happened, which is why her critics resorted to gossip.

If some of her detractors assumed that once a woman broke one taboo, she was capable of breaking all the others, should we? Did it really work that way for her? Sampson defied convention, yet she repeatedly sought shelter by attempting to conform to convention. There was a compelling social pressure on her to justify her initial transgression, and the way she did so brings us a step closer to understanding her as a person. To survive in the army, the nonconformist became a conformist, a model soldier. From the time she was "discovered," she adopted a persona in which she apologized for what she had done. If she had flirtations with women, she then took the traditional path by becoming a wife and a mother. Her "early" baby was not a disgrace (because she married), but she then flew in the face of convention by bearing no more children after she had had three.

And so it went. She collaborated with an author who made her the subject of a book, exceptional for a woman, but in it she was portrayed more or less with traditional values. A woman performing as an orator was new, but her message was conservative. As a claimant before the public, she presented herself as adhering to a patriarchal system. On her tour, she was eager for the applause of respectable audiences and the approval of the genteel circles that received her. After she moved into her new house, she cultivated refinement in pursuit of the social acceptance that eluded her. In these roles, she was not defiant but hungry for approval and recognition. This swinging back and forth is not a paradox; rather, it provides a thread to pull together the strands of a life which seem to fly off in opposite directions.

The threads that run through Sampson's life, for all the elusiveness of the record, are so vivid that they are not hard to weave into patterns. The decisions she made were always within the constraints of class as well as gender. She was, indeed, in her biographer's words, a young woman "of low birth and station" who belonged to "the female yeomanry," and she stayed so. Beginning life as an unfree servant, close to the bottom of rural society in a small New England farming town, she was freed from the burdens of labor in a farm household only when she became a weaver, a teacher, and a soldier, and later, after she became a farm housewife, only when she left town for her lecture tour or was laid up in illness. She stayed poor; her pension was a pittance, and she never was awarded the lump-sum back payment that might have lifted her family to prosperity. She was, in today's language, a poor rural farm woman, albeit one with aspirations for gentility.

She launched her transgressions, however, after she became a skilled weaver and a teacher, both androgynous trades. Her status in early American society was unusual: she was a free single woman, not under the control of a master, a "masterless woman." She did not break out when she was a servant, dependent, supervised, and unfree, but in the years when she was free and on her own. The army then gave her another kind of independence.

She was, to use the words of Dedham's William Ellis, a person of "uncommon native intellect and fortitude." The girl Mann portrayed as "able to read with propriety in almost any book in her language" became the self-educated woman Paul Revere considered as someone whose learning "entitled her to a better situation" in life. Her skills expressed a high level of literacy: she was a reader; she wrote polished letters and kept an observant diary; she memorized and delivered a lengthy oration; she was fluent in discussions. She was a skilled performer, with social skills that enabled her to carry off a masquerade in the army and maintain a persona afterward. David Ramsay, the participant historian of the American Revolution, could have cited her as an example when he wrote that the war "gave a spring to the active powers of the inhabitants, and set them on thinking, speaking and acting in a line far beyond that to which they have been accustomed. . . . It seems as if the war not only required but created talents."[2]

Given her gifts, it is not surprising she was a person with ambitions, in effect, a woman in search of a career, unheard of at a time when careers were not open to most men. As a young woman, Sampson wanted more out of life than was allowed for someone of her gender and "station," probably not knowing exactly what she wanted. Her ambition unfolded. Not many servant girls defied their masters to read and write. A minority of women became weavers; as yet, few became teachers; and only a tiny handful had a fling as soldiers or sailors. After she became the subject of a biography, her ambition soared. What other farmer's wife traveled to New York City to enlist "the poet of the Revolution" in a pension campaign, appeared on the stage of the Federal Street Theatre in Boston, or took to the road for a year as a performer? She was unusual among women in her bearing: assertive rather than submissive, bold and not meek, and hardly modest. She seized life rather than accept a fate that had been dealt her.

After playing a soldier, her career in a real sense became winning recognition for her success as a soldier. In effect, she reenacted her military masquerade—in Mann's memoir, on the lecture platform, and in her petitions.

She capitalized on a unique double persona: as a woman soldier and as a woman recognized for playing a soldier, "the celebrated Mrs. Gannett." After all, she had no other capital. Later, other veterans, desperate and unrewarded, would do the same, selling their life stories to survive.

She had an extraordinary capacity for taking risks. The dream in which she conquered terrifying monsters may be read as an emblem of her life. The fact that she told it again twenty years later makes it all the more so. The abandoned child "whose sun clouded over" became a young woman who responded to a voice from the biblical Deborah commanding her to "Arise, stand on your feet, gird yourself, and prepare to encounter your enemy." Confronted with desertion by her parents and the kind of shunting about that might have broken the spirit of many children, she developed a sense of herself that enabled her not only to cope with adversity but to risk the new and unknown (and why one child can do that while another in similar circumstances cannot remains a mystery we wish we could tap into).

The risk-taker became a survivor. She slew the dragons of her dream again and again. Over her life she experienced one nightmare after another: confronting the Baptist elders at a stormy inquisition; patrolling as a soldier in Westchester, not knowing whether the enemy might appear out of thick woods; near to breathing her last in a Philadelphia hospital where undertakers were carting away the dead; turning her back on the whispered stings of gossip of Sharon neighbors; tossing in pain on her tour in some strange inn on the frontier; performing in a New York City theatre amidst the catcalls of the gallery. She survived them all.

In the context of a lifetime of taking risks, Sampson's several episodes of cross-dressing seem purposeful. Clustered as they were in a two-year period (1782–84), "passing" was not a lifetime or recurrent practice. She should not be categorized as a "cross-dresser" or "transvestite," modern terms with connotations of a condition or an obsession. We are in Bible-reading eighteenth-century Massachusetts, where it was a violation of the law as well as of Deuteronomy to dress in the apparel of the other sex. Her first escapade, her attempt to enlist in Middleborough as "Timothy Thayer"—something of a lark, as it comes down to us—seems to have been to win the bounty money and try out a disguise. The immediate purpose of her second, as "Robert Shurtliff," was to take flight from the threat of legal prosecution for the first, as well as from the threat of excommunication by the Baptists. She disguised herself as a man because it was dangerous for a young single woman to take to the road. Then, it was the only way for a woman to serve in the army, as opposed to serving in an army camp.

After the war, if she stayed in her regimentals and played at being "Ephraim Sampson," it may have been a freedom she was reluctant to give up. In Boston, when she put on a uniform to do the soldier's exercise of arms, it made her performances spectacular and lucrative. In dressing like a man to escape, she was like an uncounted number of women in early America for whom such disguise was commonly an act of desperation, not desire.

It may well be that "disguise begets desire," to borrow the phrase of a scholar steeped in the topsy-turvy world of the theatre in Shakespeare's day. Whether she had a romance with a woman from Baltimore or flirted with girls in Sharon seems beyond knowing. If she did, she may have resembled Hannah Snell, a likely model for Mann and/or Deborah, who, Snell's memoirist tells us, "endeavored to try if she could not act the Lover, as well as the Soldier, which she so well effected." There is a difference between motivation and unanticipated possibilities.[3]

In her masquerades, Sampson clearly mastered the role that clothing plays in performing gender, which, after all, is one of its functions. A uniform made her a man; a dress then made her a woman. Clothes were also indispensable in performing class, that is, in moving from one status to another, a different function. She "dressed *up*" in both senses when she went from woman to man and then from man to woman. Private was a lowly rank, but the distinctive uniform of the light infantry allowed her to bask in the status of a member of the army's elite corps and then as a general's waiter. On the stage, the uniform brought applause. Dresses, from her wedding onward, made her a would-be lady, a sign that she had married *up* (or hoped that she did). If there is a single thread in Deborah's life for which we have an abundance of proof, it is her emotional investment in clothes. Think of the array we can account for: the uniform which she brought out to show Mann and wore again in 1802; the gown she wore at her wedding celebration; the dress in which she posed for her portrait; the cape, bonnet, and shoes she bought in Albany on tour. Obviously, she saved clothing, the only property she could declare as her own in 1820. She would have been delighted that her principal personal possession that survives to this day (she was never co-owner of the new house in Sharon) is her wedding dress.

She also knew that clothes were indispensable to mask her other side.

Throughout her life she was perceived as having both masculine and feminine qualities, and she knew it. In the army she had to cover up the feminine (binding her breasts, cutting her hair, avoiding exposure of her body) and to walk, talk, and act like a soldier. When she "became" a woman again, she knew that she had to appear feminine to overcome the inevitable perception that she was masculine—inevitable because, after 1784, anyone who looked at her could have known that this was the lady who once upon a time was a Continental soldier. The portrait/engraving of 1797 sums up this tension: feminine clothing to distract from the masculinity projected by her facial features. She had to make sure people knew she was feminine.

WHAT WOULD IT have taken for Deborah Sampson Gannett to remain a nonconformist, cross another barrier, and become a champion of other women confined to a contracted sphere? After she acquired local fame and a pension, and after she moved into her new house, might "the celebrated Mrs. Gannett" have taken a different path, conforming less to the norms for respectability and middle-class refinement? She was a rebel who did not become a radical who questioned the system she had rebelled against; she never, as far as we can tell, seems to have become a public advocate of the cause of women. Rather, she aspired to a genteel life that eluded her—for which the willow tree and the cup plate were symbols. Should we be surprised that a woman who crossed as many boundaries as she did retreated?

To have become a crusader, she would have needed more recognition for her achievement as a soldier, for one thing. However, the "poor soldiers" of the Revolution "were turned adrift like old worn out horses," as the eloquent veteran Joseph Plumb Martin put it decades later. Americans have forgotten. What if Mrs. Gannett and other veterans had been sought out and given a place of honor at local Fourth of July observances while they were still in their prime, and did not have to wait until the jubilees of the battles of Bunker Hill, Lexington, and Concord to be exhibited like relics?[4]

She would also have especially needed recognition from other women. What if the articulate protofeminist women of Massachusetts had paid tribute to her for her contribution "to the sex," to use their language? Suppose Judith Sargent Murray had sung her praises in her encyclopedic lists which proved the capacities of women for courage? What if Abigail Adams, who often attended the theatre in Philadelphia while her husband was president, and knew its political impact, had made the trip from her home in Quincy to

Boston in 1802 and paid Mrs. Gannett the honor of sitting in a box at her performance at the Federal Street Theatre? Might "the celebrated Mrs. Gannett" then have ventured forth to become "the celebrated example of the equal worth of women"? And what if other feminist-minded women had not run for cover amidst the scapegoating of Mary Wollstonecraft but rather stood fast for her principles? Might Mrs. Gannett then have risked becoming "the celebrated advocate of the rights of women"?

All these "what-ifs," one might say, are ahistorical. Veterans had to wait until 1818 or 1832 to get their pensions, and women did not hold a woman's rights convention at Seneca Falls until 1848. Without a women's movement in her own day to sustain her and lift her horizons, Deborah Sampson Gannett did not become a leader of women, although others of "the sex" may, indeed, have found in her an example. She did what other isolated, non-ideological rebels do who bravely cross frontiers alone into forbidden land. She made her way as best she could in a country that was not ready for her.

Louisa May Alcott, who during the Civil War wrote, "I long to be a man; but as I can't fight, I will content myself with working for those who can" (and served as a nurse), would have understood Sampson, who did what Alcott the seagull only dreamed of doing.[5] So might countless other Americans who seek to cross boundaries, and who will not be alone, thanks to the efforts of their forerunners.

Notes

AAS	American Antiquarian Society
Address	*An Address . . . Boston,* 1802, by Deborah Gannett (Dedham, 1802)
Bricknell	Charles Bricknell Scrapbooks, PHS
DAB	*Dictionary of American Biography,* 20 vols., ed. Allen Johnson (New York, 1928–36)
Descendants	Michael Gannett, *Gannett Descendants of Matthew and Hannah Gannett of Scituate, Massachusetts* (Chevy Chase, MD, 1976)
DG	Deborah Gannett
DG, Pension	Deborah Gannett, Pension File 13232, NA
DHS	Dedham Historical Society
Diary	"Diary of Deborah Gannett, 1802–03," facsimile copy of MS by Eugene Tappan, 1901, SPL, DHS
DS	Deborah Sampson
GW, *Writings*	*The Writings of George Washington,* 39 vols., ed. John C. Fitzpatrick (Washington, DC, 1931–44)
LC	Library of Congress
MA	Massachusetts Archives
Mann, *FR*	Herman Mann, *The Female Review* (1797; 1866, ed. John Adams Vinton)
Mann, "Heroine"	Herman Mann, "The Heroine: or Memoirs of Miss Deborah Gannett" (1827–33), MS, DHS
Mass. S&S	*Massachusetts Soldiers and Sailors of the Revolutionary War,* 17 vols. (Boston, 1896–1908)
MHS	Massachusetts Historical Society

NA	National Archives
NAW	*Notable American Women: A Biographical Dictionary,* 3 vols., ed. Edward James et al. (Cambridge, MA, 1971)
OED	*Oxford English Dictionary*
PHS	Plympton Historical Society
SHS	Sharon Historical Society
SHS Scrapbooks	Sharon Historical Society Scrapbooks, 5 vols. (1904–08)
SPL	Sharon Public Library
WMQ	*William and Mary Quarterly,* 3rd series

PROLOGUE

1. DG, "Petition to Governor, Senate and House of Representatives of the Commonwealth of Massachusetts, Jan. 11, 1792," reprinted in John Adams Vinton, intro. to Mann, *FR,* xxiii–iv. In the 1860s, Vinton copied this from the original in MA, which is no longer available.
2. DG, Diary, Nov. 11, 1802, transcription from the original by Eugene Tappan, 1901, in facsimile, SPL and DHS.
3. Patrick J. Leonard, "Ann Bailey: Mystery Woman of 1777," *Minerva: Quarterly Report on Woman and the Military* 11 (1993): 1–4; *Government and People* v. *Ann Bailey,* August 1777, Mass. Bay Superior Court Judicature, MS, brought to my attention by Elizabeth Bouvier, head of Supreme Judicial Court of Massachusetts Archives; for Anne Smith: *Pennsylvania Packet,* June 25, 1782, report dated Springfield, MA, June 4, 1782.
4. William Barton [to ?], Nov. 17, 1788, Elizabethtown, NJ, Microfilm Reel 1, item 82, David Library, reprinted in Robert Fridlington, ed., " 'A Diversion in Newark': A Letter from New Jersey Continental Line, 1778," *New Jersey History* 105 (1787): 75–78.
5. [New York] *National Advocate for the Country,* March 8, 1822, brought to my attention by Shane White. For summaries of women soldiers in the Revolutionary War: Linda Grant De Pauw, *Battle Cries and Lullabies: Women in War from Prehistory to the Present* (Norman, OK, 1998), 115–31; De Pauw, "Women in Combat: The Revolutionary War Experience," *Armed Forces and Society* 7 (1981): 209–26; Janice E. McKenney, "Women in Combat: A Commentary," *Armed Forces and Society* 8 (1982). De Pauw's comment is in a letter to Alfred Young, May 27, 1994. For another summary, see Holly Mayer, "Women Soldiers," in Richard L. Blanco, ed., *The American Revolution, 1775–1783: An Encyclopedia,* 2 vols. (New York, 1993), 2:1795–97; *Women Patriots of the Revolution: A Biographical Dictionary* (Metuchen, NJ, 1991) lists numerous individuals culled from local records with the identification soldier, spy, sentinel, scout, but few details.
6. Arlette Farge, "Protesters Plain to See," in Farge and Natalie Davis, eds., *A History of Women in the West,* vol. III: *Renaissance and Enlightenment Paradoxes* (Cambridge, MA, 1993), 499; Olwen Hufton, *The Prospect Before Her: A History of Women in Western Europe, 1500–1800* (New York, 1996), 259.

    I have profited from the discussion of cross-dressing in Europe and England in Julie Wheelwright, *Amazons and Military Maids: Women Who Dressed as Men in Pursuit of Life, Liberty and Happiness* (London, 1988); Marjorie Garber, *Vested Interests: Cross Dressing*

Notes to Pages 9–10

and *Cultural Anxiety* (New York, 1992); Vern L. Bullough and Bonnie Bullough, *Cross Dressing, Sex and Gender* (Philadelphia, 1933); and Rudolf M. Dekker and Lotte C. Van de Pol, *The Tradition of Female Transvestism in Early Modern Europe* (London, 1988). There is no comparable scholarship for early America.

For the history of sexualities, I have benefited especially from Martha Vicinus, " 'They Wonder to Which Sex I Belong': The Historical Roots of Modern Lesbian Identity," in Henry Abelove, Michele Aina Barale, and David Halperin, eds., *The Lesbian and Gay Studies Reader* (New York, 1993), 432–52, quotation at 436, and Vicinus, "Lesbian History: All Theory and No Facts or All Facts and No Theory," *Radical History Review* 60 (1994): 55–75; Terry Castle, *The Apparitional Lesbian: Female Sexuality and Modern Culture* (New York, 1993); Emma Donoghue, *Passions Between Women: British Lesbian Culture, 1688–1801* (London, 1993); and Tim Hitchcock, *English Sexualities, 1700–1800* (New York, 1997). Richard Godbeer, *Sexual Revolution in Early America* (Baltimore, 2002), provides the first map of the subject for early America.

7. *Pennsylvania Gazette,* Feb. 13, 1750, in Daniel Mendes, comp., *Eighteenth Century White Slaves: Fugitive Notices* (Greenwood, CT, 1993), vol. I: *Pennsylvania, 1729–1760,* 232–33 (Catherine Davidson); *Pennsylvania Gazette,* Sept. 5, 1776 (Maria), brought to my attention by Jonathan Prude; Carlton E. Fisher, *Supplement to Soldiers, Sailors and Patriots of the Revolutionary War Maine* (Rockport, ME), 216 (drummer); *New England Weekly Journal,* Sept. 8, 1729 (Charles), brought to my attention by Thomas E. Foster, one of half a dozen reports of cross-dressing he found in Boston papers from the mid-eighteenth century; *Pennsylvania Gazette,* July 16, 1752, and Feb. 20, 1753 (Charlotte Hamilton); Kirsten Fischer, *Suspect Relations: Sex, Race and Resistance in Colonial North Carolina* (Ithaca, NY, 2002), 98–99 (Mary Gorman); Case of Martha Kingsley, Bristol County [Mass.] General Session of the Peace, Grand Jury Presentment, April 13, 1697, brought to my attention and explained by Elizabeth C. Bouvier, Massachusetts Supreme Judicial Court Archives.

8. Dianne Dugaw, *Warrior Women and Popular Balladry, 1650–1850* (Cambridge, UK, 1989); Wheelwright, *Amazons and Military Maids;* for women at sea, see Marcus Rediker, "Liberty Beneath the Jolly Roger: The Lives of Anne Bonny and Mary Read, Pirates," in Margaret Creighton and Lisa Norling, eds., *Iron Men, Wooden Women: Gender and Seafaring in the Atlantic World, 1700–1920* (Baltimore, 1996); Linda Grant De Pauw, *Seafaring Women* (Boston, 1982); Suzanne J. Stark, *Female Tars: Women Aboard Ship in the Age of Sail* (Annapolis, MD, 1996); and David Cordingly, *Women Sailors and Sailors' Women: An Untold Maritime History* (New York, 2001).

9. Natalie Davis, "Women in Politics," in Farge and Davis, eds., *History of Women,* 168; Thomas Paine, *The American Crisis,* Dec. 23, 1776, in Philip Foner, ed., *The Complete Writings of Thomas Paine,* 2 vols. (New York, 1945), 1:51; Abigail Adams to John Adams, Sept. 20, 1776, in L. H. Butterfield, ed., *Adams Family Correspondence,* 2 vols. (Cambridge, MA, 1963), 2:129.

10. On the role of women attached to the army, see Holly A. Mayer, *Belonging to the Army: Camp Followers and Community During the American Revolution* (Columbia, SC, 1996), quotation at 7; for the context: Barton C. Hacker, "Women and Military Institutions in Early Modern Europe: A Reconnaissance," *Journal of Women in Culture and Society* 6 (1981): 643–71;

for American statistics: John Rees, " 'The Multitude of Women': An Examination of the Numbers of Female Camp Followers with the Continental Army," *Minerva* 14 (1996): 1–47; Don N. Hagist, "The Women of the British Army: A General Overview," *Brigade Dispatch* 24 (Summer 1993): 1–10; (Autumn 1993): 9–17; (Spring 1995): 11–16; for Molly Pitcher: De Pauw, *Battle Cries and Lullabies,* 126–31; for Sarah Osborn: Richard O. Eldres, "The Heroine of Yorktown," *Daughters of the American Revolution* (November 1984): 635–36.

11. Elizabeth F. Ellet, *The Women of the Revolution,* 3 vols. (New York, 1848–50), offers the first and still the fullest array of sketches of such women. Mary Beth Norton, *Liberty's Daughters: The Revolutionary Experience of American Women, 1750–1800* (Boston, 1980; Ithaca, NY, 1996), chap. 7.

12. For brief summaries of Sampson's life: Elizabeth Commetti, "Deborah Sampson," *NAW,* 3:227–28; Samuel William Crompton, "Deborah Sampson" in *American National Biography* (New York, 1999), 19:230–31; Vera O. Laska, *"Remember the Ladies": Outstanding Women of the American Revolution* (Commonwealth of Mass. Bicentennial Commission Publication, 1976), 63–100, a scholarly essay; Pauline Moody, *Massachusetts's Deborah Sampson* (North Attleborough, MA, privately printed, 1975), a labor of love by a descendant. For longer works, see Cory Cheyney, *The Incredible Deborah* (New York, 1967), an imaginative, feminist work aimed at a young adult audience; Emil F. Guba, *Deborah Samson alias Robert Shurtliff, Revolutionary War Soldier* (Kingston, MA, privately printed, 1994), a summary by a scholar in his nineties of the efforts by Gannett's champions in Massachusetts to set the record straight.

13. *Benjamin Franklin's Autobiography,* ed. J. A. Leo Lemay and P. M. Zall (New York, 1986), with an essay by John William Ward, "Who Was Benjamin Franklin?" 325–35.

14. Herman Mann, Preface to "Catalogue of the Principal Works, published and unpublished, of Herman Mann," [1827], Mann Papers, DHS.

15. Mann used the phrase "a novel based on fact" in his paper, the [Dedham] *Columbian Minerva,* in the spring of 1801 to describe his plans for a book he never wrote about the local Jason Fairbanks murder case; Calvin Munn, letter to the editor, *New York Evening Post,* June 30, 1827, brought to my attention by Shane White. For the style, see Cathy N. Davidson, *Revolution and the Word: The Rise of the Novel in America* (New York, 1986), chap. 5, who treats Mann's memoir as a novel.

16. Judith Hiltner, " 'She Bled in Secret': Deborah Sampson, Herman Mann and *The Female Review,"* *Early American Literature* 34 (1999): 190–220.

17. Carlo Ginzburg, *Clues, Myths, and the Historical Method* (Baltimore, 1986), 96–125, originally in *History Workshop* 9 (Spring 1980): 5–36. The same spirit is expressed by James Deetz, *In Small Things Forgotten: The Archeology of Early American Life* (Garden City, NY, 1977). For reading the clues in artifacts, see Laurel Thatcher Ulrich, *The Age of Homespun: Objects and Stories in the Creation of an American Myth* (New York, 2001).

18. [Herman Mann], *The Female Review: or, Memoirs of an American Young Lady . . .* By a Citizen of Massachusetts (Nathaniel and Benjamin Heaton, Dedham, MA, 1797). My citations are to a reprint of this edition. *The Female Review: Life of Deborah Sampson, the Female Soldier in the War of the Revolution* (Boston: J. K. Wiggin & Wm Parsons Lunt, 1866), with an introduction and notes by John Adams Vinton, cited hereafter as Mann, *FR.* Vinton's edited

edition had a run of 250 copies in 1866 and was reprinted from the original by Arno Press, New York, in 1972. My citations are to this 1866 edition because it is more readily available in libraries. The pagination is different from the 1797 edition because, aside from type size, it has Vinton's footnotes, which include excerpts from Mann's unpublished MS. This MS, "The American Heroine," and the condensed MS version by Herman Mann, Jr., also entitled "The American Heroine," are in DHS. The son's MS is also in typescript in Charles Bricknell Papers, PHS. The Mann Papers, DHS, include a diary by his wife, Sarah; a journal by Herman Mann, Jr.; and later correspondence over the publication of the latter's MS.

PART ONE · DEBORAH SAMSON
CHAPTER 1: DEBORAH

1. John Adams Vinton, *Genealogical Memoirs of the Sampson Family* (Boston, 1864); for the Cushman sermon, see chapter 6 below.

2. Fragment of "a letter written by a visitor to the house in 1928," in Pauline Moody Papers, SPL; Jan Lewis Nelson, letter to the author, July 24, 1995, describes the house. When Nelson lived there in 1974, it had been occupied by one owner for almost a century. My thanks to Dr. and Mrs. David Browne for a tour of the current house.

3. Emil F. Guba, *Deborah Samson alias Robert Shurtliff, Revolutionary War Soldier* (Kingston, MA, privately printed, 1994), 23–25 (on the basis of later claims about her age, Guba calculates she may have been born in April 1759); "Deborah Sampson's Brothers and Sisters," memorandum by Charles Bricknell, Bricknell, PHS. No researcher has come up with evidence of an older brother whose first name, Robert, she allegedly took for her army name. The claim first appeared in Herman Mann's 1830s MS. As Guba points out, the name was inconsistent with the biblical pattern of naming for all the other children.

4. William Jenkyn, *An Exposition of the Epistle of Jude* (London, 1656), 4, cited in John J. Waters, "Naming and Kinship in New England: Guilford Patterns and Usage, 1693–1759," *New England Historical and Genealogical Register* 138 (1984): 161–81; Daniel S. Smith, "Continuity and Discontinuity in Puritan Naming: Massachusetts, 1771," *WMQ* 51 (1994): 67–91; E. G. Withycomb, *Oxford Dictionary of Christian Names* (London, 1977), for "Sylvia" (not a biblical name).

5. Vinton, *Genealogical Memoirs*, 3; Guba, *Deborah Samson*, 21–34; "The Spelling of Deborah's Family Name," memorandum by Charles Bricknell, Bricknell, PHS; Patrick Leonard, letter to the author, April 30, 1993. I am indebted to Patrick Leonard (Braintree, MA), whose careful research convinced me that "Samson" was the proper spelling of the family name.

6. "Minutes of the Third Baptist Church of Middleboro," MS, Andover Newton Theological Seminary, entries for Nov. 12, 1780, and Sept. 3, 1782; Frederic Endicott, ed., *The Record of the Births, Marriages and Deaths and Intentions of Marriage in the Town of Stoughton from 1727 to 1800 . . .* (Canton, MA, 1896), 114, 123; *Vital Records of Sharon, Massachusetts for the Year 1850* (Sharon, MA, 1909), 97.

7. Mann, *FR*, 50–51.

8. A letter from William H. Soule, Town Clerk, Plympton, Dec. 6, 1854, in Ephraim Sampson Revolutionary War File, Mass. W 11053, Record Group 15, RG 93, Pension Files, NA.

9. "Division of Estate of Jonathan Samson, Sr., 1759," in "Registry of Deeds," Book 15, pp. 122–24, typescript of MS report to John Cushing, Judge of Probate, together with a present-day map showing the division of land, Bricknell, PHS.

10. Charles Bricknell to Pauline Moody [1972], Bricknell, PHS, passing on information from Eugene Wright, who was a child in Plympton around 1900.

11. Barbara Lambert Merrick, "The Secret Life of Jonathan Sampson," *The Mayflower Quarterly* 48:4 (November 1982): 172–77, a carefully researched article; neither Guba, *Deborah Samson,* 51–56, nor Patrick Leonard was able to find much more about Samson in Maine. *Mass. S&S* has six entries for Jonathan Samson, one of whom is identified as forty-eight years old in 1777, which would match our Jonathan's birth date of 1729. My thanks to Keri Scofield Lawson, a descendant, for passing on documents about Jonathan Samson.

12. Mann, *FR,* 52–54.

13. Lawrence W. Towner, "The Indentures of Boston's Poor Apprentices, 1734–1805," Colonial Society of Massachusetts *Publications* 43 (1966): 417–33, reprinted in Towner, *Past Imperfect: Essays on History, Libraries and the Humanities,* ed. Alfred Young and Robert Karrow (Chicago, 1993), 36–54; John Demos, *A Little Commonwealth: Family Life in Plymouth Colony* (New York, 1970), chap. 7; Middleborough Selectmen and Assessors Book, 1736–1788, Town Hall, Middleborough, 1766 (for the Marshalls, date not taken down by me); Edmund S. Morgan, *The Puritan Family* (New York, 1944, 1966), chap. 3.

14. Janet Griffith, then secretary of the Middleborough Historical Commission, and I searched the minutes of the Middleborough selectmen and the Town Records, vol. IV (1772–88), both in Town Hall, without finding any record of Deborah Samson; Mrs. Griffith, who is descended from the Thomases, believes they and the Samsons were related.

15. Albert Matthews, "Hired Man and Help," Colonial Society of Massachusetts *Publications* (1897–98), 5:225–56, still the standard work; cf. Lawrence W. Towner, *A Good Master Well Served: Masters and Servants in Colonial Massachusetts, 1620–1750* (New York, 1998), passim.

16. Thomas Weston, *History of the Town of Middleboro, Massachusetts* (Boston, 1906), 329 (Thomastown), chap. 8 (militia); *Book of the First Church of Christ in Middleborough* (Boston, 1852), 61 (Benjamin Thomas as deacon); "List of persons qualified to serve on juries, November 10, 1777," in Town Records, vol. IV (1772–88), 209–11.

17. For genealogy, John M. Raymond, *Thomas Families of Plymouth County, Massachusetts* (Thomas Family Publications, 1980), 15 (Benjamin), 17 (Jeremiah, 1735–1798), and 30 (Jeremiah, his son, 1764–1846). Mrs. Zilpah (Cyrus L.) Tolman (b. 1830, d. post-1905) claimed that Deborah "was bound to her great-grandfather Cephas Thomas" who raised a family of ten boys. Tolman to Eugene Tappan, Jan. 29, 1902, in Tappan, "Deborah Sampson Gannett Dinner . . . Sharon, April 3, 1902, MS, SPL, 71–78. This is inaccurate. Her great-grandfather would have been not Cephas but Jeremiah (1735–1798), father of Jeremiah (1764–1846), whom she rightly claims as her grandfather. And there were five boys in the family, not ten. Janet Griffith was unable to find a Cephas in the Thomas genealogy to match Tolman's claim—Griffith to the author, May 12, 1994. Charles Bricknell was also skeptical of the claim for Cephas ("Thomas Family in Middleboro," 1-page memorandum, Bricknell, PHS).

18. Mann, *FR,* 63 (for the Thomases); for Susanna Shephard and Patience Payson, see chapter 6 below.

19. Kenneth Crest, the present owner of the house, has identified two deeds in the Plymouth County Registry of Deeds in which Jeremiah Thomas, Sr., deeded land to his son, Jeremiah Junior, dated as received May 7, 1734 (Book 28, p. 202), and Nov. 10, 1736 (Book 30, p. 202). At the next deeding of the land, in 1819, Amos Thomas inherited the estate from his father, Jeremiah Junior. I am indebted to Kenneth Crest for clarifying this. The land passed to Joseph Shaw (a builder who in 1898 remodeled the house around the old structure), then to his son, Michael Collins, and eventually to the Crests. For the farm economy: Leigh D. Johnsen, "Toward Pluralism: Society and Religion in Middleborough, Massachusetts, 1741–1807" (Ph.D. diss., Univ. of California, Riverside, 1984), chap. 1.

20. Kenneth Crest to the author, Aug. 28, 1995. There is some confusion as to which house Deborah Samson lived in. One source of the confusion stems from Herman Mann, who said she was a servant to Jeremiah but gave him the title of "Deacon," which alone belonged to Benjamin, his father-in-law. Benjamin lived in a house two miles or so from the Jeremiah Thomas house on Sachem Street. Most of the descendants, however, have assumed Deborah was a servant to Jeremiah and not to Benjamin. Stillman Pratt, the Middleborough minister who wrote about Deborah in the 1850s, also understood she was a servant in the Jeremiah Thomas house. In the 1890s, when he was taking pictures of the town's historic houses, this is the one Walter Beals of Middleborough photographed as the Deborah Samson house. And this is the house on a picture postcard as the Samson house. After Joseph Shaw remodeled it, it was the subject of another postcard. Beal's glass plate of the original Thomas house is in the Middleborough Historical Association.

 A further source of confusion is the Historic American Buildings Survey (HABS), which in the 1930s identified a different house as the Deborah Samson house: a one-and-a-half-story Cape Cod building on what was then called Thompson Street (now Wareham), on what basis I have not been able to track down. HABS, *Historic Buildings of Massachusetts* (New York, c. 1976), prints a photograph of this house taken by Arthur Haskell, 1937, in a section under the name of the town. The HABS file in Prints and Photographs Division, LC, also has a careful architectural rendering and floor plan, but no further information (HABS No. 2–49, Mass 12 Midb, 6–1). A tax assessor's report on the house, c. 1993, secured by Janet Griffith in 1995, identifies the date of construction as 1886, but a carpenter who looked at the house at her request thought it was built in the early 1800s. The house now stands at 49 Wareham Street, a location outside "Thomastown." None of the knowledgeable present-day town residents had ever heard of the HABS designation, and the consensus among them was that it was an error. I am indebted to Janet Griffith for tracing the house through various official records. How HABS reached its identification is a mystery. There were other Deborah Sampsons listed in births and marriages in *Vital Records of Middleborough* I:136, 185, 296; II:66, 70, 205, and it is possible that another woman with this name was connected to this house.

21. Jack Larkin, *The Reshaping of Everyday Life, 1790–1840* (New York, 1988), 15–24. I am indebted to Larkin, director of Old Sturbridge Village, and to Nancy Gray Osterud for conversations clarifying the gendered division of labor.

22. Stillman Pratt, "The Life of Deborah Sampson," *Nemasket Gazette* [later *Middleboro Gazette*], in 16 "chapters," Aug. 7, 1857–Jan. 9, 1858, Middleborough Public Library; chap. 2, Aug. 21, 1857, is "Her Youthful Career." While Pratt drew on some material from local sources not otherwise available, he generally followed Mann. Vinton, Mann's editor, consulted Pratt.

23. Pauline Moody, *Massachusetts' Deborah Sampson* (Attleborough, MA, privately printed, 1975), 31, 33. In the 1890s Benjamin Gannett, Deborah's grandson, gave the Brockton Deborah Sampson Chapter of the Daughters of the American Revolution the door to a cupboard Sampson was said to have made, to use in framing their charter. In the 1990s, Muriel Nelson showed me this cupboard in her home in Sharon and passed on the lore.

24. Mann, *FR*, 52–54.

25. Ibid., chap. 2, 63; *Book of the First Church in Middleborough*, 61 (Benjamin Thomas).

26. Mann, *FR*, 60–62; Joseph Buckingham, Memoir, cited in David Hall, *Cultures of Print: Essays in the History of the Book* (Amherst, MA, 1996), 55.

27. The titles I list in the following paragraphs are informed by the scholarship of Elizabeth C. Reilly in "Common and Learned Readers: Shared and Separate Spheres in Mid-Eighteenth New England" (Ph.D. diss., Boston Univ., 1994), and in Reilly and David D. Hall, "Customers and the Marketplace Modalities of Reading" and "The Colonial Book in the Transatlantic World," both in Hugh Amory and David D. Hall, eds., *A History of the Book in America*, 5 vols. (Cambridge, UK, 1999), 1: chap. 11. See especially David Hall, "The Uses of Literacy in New England, 1600–1850," in his *Cultures of Print*, 36–78.

28. For the reading of another evangelical woman, see Barbara Lacey, "The World of Hannah Heaton: The Autobiography of an Eighteenth Century Connecticut Farm Woman," *WMQ*, 45 (1988): 280–304; for Conant inheriting Thacher's library, see Lawrence W. Towner, "Research Project Description," Jan. 14, 1987, MS in folder "Willard Project," Towner Papers, Newberry Library. Towner found Conant's handwritten name below Thacher's in a copy of Samuel Willard, *A Complete Body of Divinity* (Boston, 1726).

29. I have given weight to works printed or distributed by Boston printers. See, for example, "An Account of Books Read by Mr John Stevens" (1766, 1767) MS, AAS, cited in Reilly, "Common and Learned Readers," chap. 5. Stevens was the son of a Rhode Island gravestone cutter. I have profited from Victor Neuberg's scholarship: *Penny Histories* (London, 1968); *Chapbooks: A Bibliography* (London, 1972); and *Popular Literature* (Harmondsworth, UK, 1977).

30. Benjamin Colman, *Early Piety Again Inculcated* (Boston, 1720), 32–34, cited in H. Ray Hiner, "Adolescence in Early America," *History of Childhood Quarterly* 32 (1975): 258.

31. For women's status: Laurel Thatcher Ulrich, *Good Wives: Image and Reality in the Lives of Women in Northern New England, 1650–1750* (New York, 1980); Mary Beth Norton, *Liberty's Daughters: The Revolutionary Experience of American Women, 1750–1800* (Boston, 1980; Ithaca, NY, 1996), part I; for wretchedness in the cities, Gary Nash, *The Urban Crucible: Social Change, Political Consciousness, and the Origins of the American Revolution* (Cambridge, MA, 1979), chaps. 7, 9, 12.

32. Photographs of these houses are in the files of the Middleborough Historical Association

and are reproduced in Weston, *Middleboro,* 273, 278, 319. My thanks to the weaver docents at Old Sturbridge Village who demonstrated the looms.

33. Laurel Thatcher Ulrich, "Wheels, Looms, and the Gender Division of Labor in Eighteenth Century New England," *WMQ* 55 (1998): 1, 3–36, quotation at 6; Gloria Main, "Gender, Work and Wages in Colonial New England," *WMQ* 51 (1994): 39–66, quotation at 60.

34. Main, "Gender, Work and Wages," 60.

35. Abigail Foote's Journal (June 2–Sept. 17, 1775), MS, Connecticut Historical Society, entries for June and July 1775.

36. Elizabeth Foote's Journal (Jan. 1–Oct. 29, 1775), MS, Connecticut Historical Society, entry for Oct. 23, 1775; Laurel Thatcher Ulrich, " 'Daughters of Liberty': Religious Women in Revolutionary New England," in Ronald Hoffman and Peter J. Albert, eds., *Women in the Age of the American Revolution* (Charlottesville, VA, 1989), 211–43.

37. Ulrich, "Wheels, Looms, and the Gender Division of Labor," 37 ("repertoire"); for the intricacies of weaving, Ulrich, *The Age of Homespun: Objects and Stories in the Creation of an American Myth* (New York, 2001), chaps. 2, 5, and esp. 8; Weston, *Middleboro,* 222–23, reprints the selectmen's regulations of prices issued Feb. 20, 1777, which also serves as a guide to the various fabrics woven in town and the occupations pursued.

38. Granville Temple Sproat, "The Old Folks Traditions of Deborah Sampson," cited in note 44 below; Mann, *FR,* 99; Pratt "Life of Deborah Sampson," *Nemasket Gazette,* Aug. 21, 1857.

39. Jane Nylander, *Our Snug Fireside: Images of the New England Home, 1760–1860* (New York, 1993), 174–79; Elizabeth Fuller cited in Norton, *Liberty's Daughters,* 17.

40. Mann, *FR,* 100–01; Lawrence Cremin, *American Education: The Colonial Experience, 1607–1783* (New York, 1970), 499–509; Larkin, *Reshaping of Everyday Life,* 34–36.

41. Weston, *Middleboro,* 245–49; Selectmen and Assessor's Book, 1736–88 (Middleborough Town Hall); Pratt, "Life of Deborah Sampson," *Nemasket Gazette,* Sept. 18, 1857 (schools), and Jan. 2, 1858 (Hannah Perkins). Pratt claims DS boarded with Abner Bourne while teaching; this would have been while teaching near the Four Corners and what today is South Main Street. The building she taught in was "subsequently removed to Water Street [today Wareham] and is occupied as a dwelling house." Today it is referred to as the Professor Elisha Jenks house.

42. John Adams Vinton, who had taught school in Massachusetts around 1820, reported the books cited above as commonly used—Mann, *FR,* 101, note 22. He also reported that the Westminster Assembly Catechism "was taught in this as in other schools every Saturday."

43. David Fischer, *Albion's Seed: Four British Folkways in America* (New York, 1989), 72–75; Demos, *A Little Commonwealth,* 77–79; see Amy Froide, *Never Married: Singlewoman in Early Modern England* (forthcoming), for court action in Southhampton; Christopher Hill, *The World Turned Upside Down: Radical Ideas During the English Revolution* (New York, 1972), chap. 3, "Masterless Men."

44. Granville Temple Sproat's article, "The Old Folks Traditions of Deborah Sampson," I have taken from a letter to the editor by M. M. Copeland (of Middleborough) entitled "Deborah Sampson," in *Boston Evening Traveller,* Jan. 19, 1889, p. 6, col. 9, AAS, which Copeland makes clear was taken from the papers of Sproat, location unidentified. A handwritten copy

of Copeland's printed letter is in Pauline Moody's papers, SHS. Sproat, born in Middleborough in 1810 and married in 1838, went to California in the Gold Rush of 1849. He was known later as "the Shaker poet" and lived in a Shaker community in Canaan, New York. He wrote numerous historical articles in local papers. He very likely interviewed the "old folks" of Middleborough when he was in his twenties, which would date them in the 1830s. The first two thirds of Copeland's letter is based on Sproat's oral histories; the last third follows Mann. I was not able to locate Sproat's papers: for making a search, I am indebted to John Aubrey, Newberry Library; Sharon Duane Koomler, Curator, Hancock Shaker Village; and Dorothy Thayer, Middleborough Historical Association.

45. Sproat, "Old Folks Traditions"; Mann, *FR*, 134; Mann, "Heroine," 178–80; for Ephraim Sampson, see pension file W11053, NA; for average heights, see chapter 2 below on her enlistment. Mann, Jr., raises the height to five feet seven and a half inches, "The American Heroine," 89–90.

46. Mann, *FR*, 134; "A Correspondent," [Northampton] *Hampshire Gazette*, Sept. 1, 1802; Mann, "Heroine," 178–80.

47. The recollections of Daniel Johnson (b. 1820) are in Eugene Tappan's Preface to DG, Diary, MS, SPL, 5.

48. The portrait, *Deborah Sampson*, oil on paper, is in the Rhode Island Historical Society; the engraved frontispiece is in Mann, *FR*, in both the 1797 and 1866 editions; the copperplate is in DHS. Jack Larkin, director of Old Sturbridge Village, called my attention to the long lantern jaw as the look of descendants of migrants from East Anglia. For the East Anglia origins of the early migrants to New England, see Fischer, *Albion's Seed*, 13–54; Zilpah Tolman to Eugene Tappan, Feb. 11, 1902, SHS Scrapbooks, I, 110, SPL.

49. Of the descendants, the most likely claim for a resemblance I have encountered is for Pauline Monk Wise (1914–1994), daughter of Rodney Monk (1883–1975), descended from Deborah's son, Earl. Rodney Monk, who had seen many descendants, spoke of Polly, one of his four daughters, as resembling DS, a view her sisters shared. I am indebted to Rodney's daughter, Mrs. Roger Merrick (Temple, NH), for sharing family lore, documents, and photographs (conversations and correspondence, 1995, 2001). Two other descendants who have written to me about family lore that someone in their families resembles Deborah are: Keri Scofield Lawson (Fullerton, CA), July 9, 1997; and Mary Moffitt Ford (Cameron Park, CA), Aug. 22, 1997.

50. Mann, *FR*, 134; Mann, "Heroine," 180.

51. Mann, *FR*, 55, 72–73.

52. Sproat, "Old Folks Traditions"; Ulrich, "Wheels, Looms, and the Gender Division of Labor," 19.

53. Pratt, "Life of Deborah Sampson," *Nemasket Gazette*, Jan. 2, 1858 (Hannah Chapin).

54. Johnsen, "Society and Religion in Middleborough," 21–22, 112–14 (size of land transactions).

55. Weston, *Middleboro*, 139 (on number of army recruits); Johnsen, "Society and Religion," 122–23. For the general social patterns of soldiers, see chapter 2 below, sec. 3, "Enlistee."

56. Mann, "Heroine," 131; Vinton reprints this anecdote in Mann, *FR*, 121, note 32, although he doubts it ever took place.

57. Barbara Lindemann, " 'To Ravish and Carnally Know': Rape in Eighteenth-Century Massachusetts," *Signs* 10 (1984): 63–82; Mary Beth Norton, *Founding Mothers and Fathers: Gendered Power and the Forming of American Society* (New York, 1996), 66; David Konig, ed., *Plymouth Court Records, 1686–1859,* 16 vols. (Wilmington, DE, 1978–81), 3: passim; Sharon Block, "Lines of Color, Sex, and Service: Comparative Sexual Coercion in Early America," in Martha Hodes, ed., *Sex, Love, Race: Crossing Boundaries in North American History* (New York, 1999), 141–63; Cornelia Hughes Dayton, *Women Before the Bar: Gender, Law and Society in Connecticut, 1639–1789* (Chapel Hill, NC, 1995), 283.

58. For the Revere massacre engraving in its many forms, see Clarence S. Brigham, *Paul Revere's Engravings* (New York, 1969), 52–78; for a powderhorn with this theme, see Alfred F. Young, Terry J. Fife, and Mary E. Janzen, *We the People: Voices and Images of the New Nation* (Philadelphia, 1993), 64–65.

59. Sharon Block, "Coerced Sex in British North America, 1700–1820" (Ph.D. diss., Princeton Univ., 1995), chap. 6; Oliver Dickerson, ed., *Boston Under Military Rule, 1768–1769, as Revealed in "A Journal of the Times"* (Boston, 1936), passim; the Revere engraving in *Freebetter's New England Almanack for the Year 1776* (New London, CT, 1776) is reproduced in Young, Fife, and Janzen, *We the People,* 40; Mercy Otis Warren, *History of the Rise, Progress and Termination of the American Revolution,* 2 vols. (Boston, 1805; Indianapolis, 1988), 1:191; Mann, *FR,* 94–95.

60. David D. Hall, *Worlds of Wonder, Days of Judgment: Popular Religious Beliefs in Early New England* (New York, 1989), chap. 2; Keith Thomas, *Religion and the Decline of Magic* (London, 1971); Richard Godbeer, *The Devil's Dominion: Magic and Religion in Early New England* (Cambridge, MA, 1992), 24, 30–31, 34–35.

61. Mechal Sobel, letter to Alfred Young, May 2, 1994; Sobel, *Teach Me Dreams: The Search for Self in the Revolutionary Era* (Princeton, NJ, 2000), 190–96. Mann's comment on the dream occurring on "three successive nights" appears in his 1830s MS, but inasmuch as this was a common belief, it seems relevant for the time claimed for the dream.

62. Daniel L. Schachter, *Searching for Memory: The Brain, the Mind, and the Past* (New York, 1996), 196–97; Weston, *Middleboro,* 130–44 (militia "alarms").

63. Mann, *FR,* 79–84; the dream is substantially the same in the revised MS, "Heroine," 101–12, save that for the previously undecipherable letters on the serpent's tail (discussed below) Mann substitutes Democratic Republican political slogans, "The Rights of Man are at our disposal!" and "Come let us destroy the hag, Liberty . . . ," more appropriate to the 1790s.

64. My thanks to Elizabeth C. Reilly for calling my attention to the image of the snake in Dilworth's speller.

65. David Jeffrey, *Dictionary of Biblical Tradition in English Literature* (Grand Rapids, MI, 1992) ("Serpent"); Elizabeth C. Reilly, *A Dictionary of Colonial American Printers' Ornaments and Illustrations* (Worcester, MA, 1975), 302–13 (Holy Jesus).

66. The masthead engraving of the scotched snake is in Brigham, ed., *Revere's Engravings,* plate 70; Peter Linebaugh and Marcus Rediker, *The Many-Headed Hydra: Sailors, Slaves, Commoners, and the Hidden History of the Revolutionary Atlantic* (Boston, 2000), 1–7; see also Nona C. Flores, " 'Effigies Amicitae . . . Veritas Inimicitae': Antifeminism in the Iconogra-

phy of the Woman-Headed Serpent in Medieval and Renaissance Art and Literature," in Flores, ed., *Animals in the Middle Ages: A Book of Essays* (New York, 1996), 167–95. Nona Flores also pointed out to me the symbolism of the biblical Samson subduing a serpent.

67. Mann, *FR*, 225 ("animal love"); David H. Flaherty, *Privacy in Colonial New England* (Charlottesville, VA, 1972); on masturbation: Roy Porter, "Forbidden Pleasures: Enlightenment Literature of Sexual Advice," in Paula Bennett and Vernon A. Rosario II, eds., *Solitary Pleasures: The Historical, Literary, and Artistic Discourses of Autoeroticism* (New York, 1995), 75–98.

68. On the age of menarche: Malcolm Potts and Roger Short, *Ever Since Adam and Eve: The Evolution of Human Sexuality* (Cambridge, UK, 1999), 171–76; Joan Jacobs Brumberg, *The Body Project: An Intimate History of American Girls* (New York, 1997), 3–4, 23. On the image, Joseph Warren, *An Oration . . .* (Boston, 1772) and *An Oration . . .* (Boston, 1775); *The Votes and Proceedings of the freeholders . . . of . . . Boston . . .* (Boston, 1772) also has a reference to "streets stain'd with blood."

69. I consulted two English editions of *The Holy Bible* [King James version] likely to be circulating in the colonies (Oxford, 1743, and Cambridge, 1763), in both of which the wording was the same in Judges 5:12 (the earliest American printing was Philadelphia, 1782). For a modern wording, see *The New English Bible* (Oxford University Press and Cambridge University Press, 1961, 1977), 275. The scriptural Deborah has long been appropriated by the women's movement: see, e.g., Elizabeth Cady Stanton et al., *The Woman's Bible* (New York, 1898; Washington, DC, 1974), part 2: 18–23.

70. Hall, *Cultures of Print*, 55 (Buckingham); Vinton, *Genealogical Memoirs of the Sampson Family* (Jael Hobart Bradford).

71. Ulrich, *Good Wives*, 168.

72. Ibid., 169.

73. Lisa Norling, *Captain Ahab Had a Wife: New England Women and the Whale Fishery, 1720–1870* (Chapel Hill, 2000), 55–56 (Starbuck); [Anon], *The Female Advocate* (New Haven, 1801), 10, 22.

74. *The Sentiments of an American Woman*, broadside, Philadelphia, June 10, 1780; Linda K. Kerber, *Women of the Republic: Intellect and Ideology in Revolutionary America* (Chapel Hill, NC, 1980), 104–05; see also *United States Magazine* I (March 1779), 123 ("Clarissa"), cited in Jay Fliegelman, *Prodigals and Pilgrims: The American Revolution Against Patriarchal Authority, 1750–1800* (Cambridge, UK, 1982), 89.

75. Mann, *FR*, 84.

76. *Interpretation of Dreams* (24th edn, London, 1740), circulated in the colonies. The English handbook that seems to have been the basis of reprints in the United States was *Nocturnal Revels: or, Universal Interpreter of Dreams and Visions . . .* (London, 1789). The American reprints (in variant forms) with the title *Universal Interpreter of Dreams . . .* or *Universal Dream Dictionary* are Baltimore, 1795; Philadelphia, 1797; and Wilmington, 1797 (all in Evans imprints), and Philadelphia, 1826, with the title *Universal Dream Book*. My quotation is from the Baltimore, 1795, printing, 185. For the importance of this work, see Sobel, *Teach Me Dreams*, 40–41. Given the long popularity of this handbook, its use seems permissible for dreams interpreted in the 1770s, or in the 1790s, by Mann and DSG. For the importance of

Artemidorus, see S. R. F. Price, "The Future of Dreams: From Freud to Artemidorus," *Past and Present* (November 1986): 3–37. For Hannah Heaton's dream, see Lacey, "The World of Hannah Heaton," 286.

77. Mechal Sobel, "The Revolution in Selves: Black and White Inner Aliens," in Ronald Hoffman, Mechal Sobel, and Fredrika J. Teute, eds., *Through a Glass Darkly: Reflections on Personal Identity in Early America* (Chapel Hill, NC, 1997), 163–205, quotation at 199; for an enlargement of this theme, see Sobel, *Teach Me Dreams,* chap. 1.

78. Douglas Winiarski, letter to Alfred Young, May 10, 2000, after reading an earlier version of my account of the dream. I have profited from Winiarski, "All Manner of Error and Delusion: Josiah Cotton and the Religious Transformation of Southeastern New England, 1700–1770" (Ph.D. diss., Department of Religious Studies, Indiana Univ., 2000), part II, "A Scene of Enthusiastick Madness."

CHAPTER 2: THE REBEL

1. J. Franklin Jameson, *The American Revolution Considered as a Social Movement* (Princeton, NJ, 1926; Boston, 1956), 9; *Peter Oliver's Origins and Progress of the American Rebellion: A Tory View,* ed. Douglass Adair and John A. Schutz (Stanford, CA, 1961; cited hereafter as Oliver, *Origins and Progress*), 120–21.

2. Marion and Warren Whipple, "Middleborough in the American Revolution," *Middleborough Antiquarian* (May 1988): 7–13. I take the distances from John Hayward, *A Gazetteer of Massachusetts* (Boston, 1849), 200; for a traveler's description of the town in 1796, not very different from twenty years before, see Timothy Dwight, *Travels in New-England and New-York,* ed. Barbara Miller Solomon, 4 vols. (New Haven, CT, 1821; Cambridge, MA, 1969), 2:2. Richard D. Brown, *Knowledge Is Power: The Diffusion of Information in Early America, 1700–1805* (New York, 1989), chap. 10; Thomas Weston, *History of the Town of Middleboro, Massachusetts* (Boston, 1906), 110–11 (Committees); 124 (Tupper).

3. For Sproat's tavern, Weston, *Middleboro,* 318–22, and Granville Temple Sproat, "Traditions of Famous Old Houses in Middleboro: The Sproat Tavern," *Middleborough Antiquarian,* reprinted from "an old scrapbook" and published originally in the *Middleborough Gazette,* late nineteenth century; "The Necessary," *Middleborough Antiquarian* (July 1982): 7–8.

4. Edward M. Cook, *The Fathers of the Towns: Leadership and Community Structure in Eighteenth-Century New England* (Baltimore, 1976), 177–79. On Cook's commercial index on which Boston is 5646, Marblehead 293, and Lexington 18.6, Middleborough is 6.9 (Appendix, 199–212); Weston, *Middleboro,* chaps. 19–25, organizes his description by neighborhoods; for analysis, Leigh Johnsen, "Toward Pluralism: Society and Religion in Middleborough, Massachusetts, 1741–1807" (Ph.D. diss., Univ. of California, Riverside, 1984), 19.

5. Weston, *Middleboro,* 222–23, reprints the selectmen's regulation of prices in 1777, a good clue to the occupations in town.

6. Johnsen, "Society and Religion," 21, 111–14; Isaac Backus, "An Historical Account of Middleborough," Massachusetts Historical Society *Collections* 3 (1794): 175–76.

7. Clifford Shipton, "Peter Oliver," in Shipton, *Representative Biographies from Sibley's Harvard Graduates* (Cambridge, MA, 1963), 313–35, 316 (mansion).

8. Weston, *Middleboro,* 359–64; Frederick Eayrs, Jr., "An Archeological Survey of Judge Oliver's Ironworks," *Middleborough Antiquarian* (November 1964): 1–3.
9. Sylvanus Conant, *An Anniversary Oration Preached at Plymouth, December 23, 1776 . . .* (Boston, 1777). Sproat's "Memoir of Mary Norcutt," originally in *Middleborough Gazette,* is reprinted in Weston, *Middleboro,* 371–73.
10. Shipton, *Representative Biographies,* 313–35; Peter Oliver [a descendant of the judge], "Judge Oliver and the Small Oliver House in Middleborough," *Middleborough Antiquarian* (July 1970): 1–6.
11. For "A Plan of Judge Oliver's Estate and Works," Weston, *Middleboro,* 365.
12. Weston, *Middleboro,* chap. 7, "Slaves in Middleboro." Peter Oliver, Sr., owned Quassia, a slave, and had a servant Cato; his son owned slaves, 104–05. For "Black Jennie," a servant at Benjamin Leonard's, a free woman, see below in this chapter, sec. 3.
13. Weston, *Middleboro,* 517–43, lists all elected town officers and representatives. In the ten years from 1765 to 1774, the five selectmen's seats were occupied most of the time by the same five families—Leonard, Montgomery, Sprout [also Sproat], White, Wood; ibid., 450–51, for the Olivers' pews in the meetinghouse.
14. Joyce M. Jeness, "A History of the American Revolution in the Town of Middleborough, Massachusetts, 1765–1781," *Middleborough Antiquarian* (July 1972): 2–5; Marion and Warren Whipple, "Middleborough in the American Revolution," *Middleborough Antiquarian* (May 1988): 7–13. Peter Oliver, Jr.'s, letters are in Peter Orlando Hutchinson, ed., *The Diary and Letters of His Excellency Thomas Hutchinson, Esq.,* 2 vols. (Boston, 1884–86), 1:246–47, and for 1774–75 are reprinted in Weston, *Middleboro,* 148–52.
15. Bernard Bailyn, *The Ordeal of Thomas Hutchinson* (Cambridge, MA, 1974), chaps. 6, 7; Oliver, *Origins and Progress,* chaps. 7, 8.
16. The size of the mob threatening Wood grew from one account to another: Oliver, Jr.'s, letter of Sept. 14, 1774, in Weston, 150 (80 men); Oliver, *Origins and Progress,* 153 (200 or 300 men); Thomas Hutchinson to Elisha Hutchinson, Sept. 22, 1774, in Weston, *Middleboro,* 152 (500 men). See Thomas Hutchinson, *The History of the Colony and Province of Massachusetts-Bay,* ed. Lawrence Shaw Mayo, 3 vols. (Cambridge, MA, 1936), 3, for this period.
17. Peter Oliver, Jr., Oct. 27, 1774, in *Diary and Letters of Hutchinson,* 1:264, and Weston, *Middleboro,* 320n.
18. Peter Oliver, Jr., June 1, 1775, in Weston, *Middleboro,* 151.
19. Peter Oliver, Jr., Dec. 7, 1775, in ibid., 152; Peter Oliver, Sr., Diary, March 27, 1776, in ibid., 369; Oliver, "Journal of Chief Justice Peter Oliver," March 27, 1776, in *Diary and Letters of Thomas Hutchinson,* 2:48.
20. Sproat, "Memoir of Mary Norcutt," in Weston, *Middleboro,* 371–73; Charles Royster, *A Revolutionary People at War: The Continental Army and American Character, 1775–1783* (Chapel Hill, NC, 1979), 237.
21. For the resolutions, see Weston, *Middleboro,* 115–16; for popular ideology as it was refracted in the countryside, Richard Bushman, *King and People in Provincial Massachusetts* (Chapel Hill, NC, 1985), chap. 5, and Conant, *An Anniversary Oration;* for the political process, Richard Brown, *Revolutionary Politics in Massachusetts: The Boston Committee of Correspondence and the Towns, 1772–1774* (New York, 1970); for the movement for independence

from below, Pauline Maier, *American Scripture: Making the Declaration of Independence* (New York, 1997), chap. 2.

22. Weston, *Middleboro,* 329.

23. The Resolves of the Middleborough town meeting are reprinted in Oscar and Mary Handlin, eds., *The Popular Sources of Political Authority: Documents on the Massachusetts Constitution of 1780* (Cambridge, MA, 1966), 125–27, 396–97, 693–700.

24. Mann, *FR,* chap. 3; for the erasure of radicalism, see my *The Shoemaker and the Tea Party: Memory and the American Revolution* (Boston, 1999), part 2.

25. Weston, *Middleboro,* 136 (Bourne); 322–25 (Sproat); 273 (Morton); 136–37 (the patriot Leonards).

26. Ibid., 116–44 (the militia); 239–42, 344–46.

27. Isaiah Thomas, *The History of Printing in America,* ed. Marcus A. McCorison (Worcester, MA, 1810; New York, 1970), 265–74; Thomas Paine, *The American Crisis* (Philadelphia, 1776), in Philip Foner, ed., The *Complete Writings of Thomas Paine,* 2 vols. (New York, 1945), 1:51.

28. See, for example, "Roads to the Principal Towns of the Continent, &c. from Boston," and "Directions . . ." in Samuel Stearns, *The North American Almanack . . . for 1776* (Isaiah Thomas, Worcester, 1776), unpaged. A copy of this almanac was used by Richard Gridley, Chief Engineer of Arms for the Continental Army, as a diary for 1776, and ended up with the Gannett family. Gridley's partner in manufacturing in Sharon was Edmund Quincy, who married Hannah Gannett, Benjamin Gannett, Sr.'s, daughter. It was passed down in the Gannett family to Beatrice Bostock, who also acquired Deborah's wedding dress and other things—see chapter 6 below. I am indebted to David B. Ingram of Foxborough for identifying Gridley as the author of the diary interleaved in the almanac.

29. For an introduction to women in the churches, see the essays in Janet Wilson James, ed., *Women in American Religion* (Philadelphia, 1980); Mary Beth Norton, *Liberty's Daughters: The Revolutionary Experience of American Women* (Boston, 1980), chap. 5; and Laurel Thatcher Ulrich, " 'Daughters of Liberty': Religious Women in Revolutionary New England," in Ronald Hoffman and Peter Albert, eds., *Women in the Age of the American Revolution* (Charlottesville, VA, 1989), 211–43.

30. Cited in Johnsen, "Religion and Society," 55; H. L. Mencken, *The American Language* (New York, 1967, 4th edn, abridged by Raven McDavid), 233. See Elder Asa Hunt's language below.

31. "The Records of the Third Church of Christ of the Baptist Denomination of Middleborough . . . ," MS, Andover Newton Theological School, entries for Nov. 12, 1780; Sept. 8, 1782. My thanks to Diana Yount, Special Collections Librarian, for supplying a True Copy of pp. 78–89; cf. Mann, *FR,* chap. 4.

32. William G. McLoughlin, *New England Dissent 1630–1833: The Baptists and the Separation of State,* 2 vols. (Cambridge, MA, 1971), 1:438; Hamilton Hurd, *History of Plymouth County Massachusetts . . .* (Philadelphia, 1884), 981; Johnsen, "Society and Religion," 78.

33. McLoughlin, *New England Dissent,* 1:555; Weston, *Middleboro,* 469–79; McLoughlin, *Isaac Backus and the American Pietistic Tradition* (Boston, 1967), chap. 4; Johnsen, "Society and Religion," chap. 3.

34. For a description and prices of pews, Weston, *Middleboro*, 447–51, and for a "Catalogue of the Members," 640–86; for the general pattern, Robert J. Dinkin, "Seating the Meeting in Early Massachusetts," *New England Quarterly* 43 (1970): 450–64.

35. The first Baptist meetinghouses have not survived, often destroyed by fire. For the Bell School, also known as the Neck School, built in 1796 on Assawampsett Neck, which served as a Baptist church, see *Middleborough Antiquarian* (November 1962): 6; Juster, *Disorderly Women: Sexual Politics and Evangelicalism in Revolutionary New England* (Ithaca, NY, 1994), 24; for the plain structures of the Virginia Baptist churches, Rhys Isaac, *The Transformation of Virginia, 1740–1790* (Chapel Hill, NC, 1982), 314–16.

36. McLoughlin, *New England Dissent*, 1:337 (Backus quote).

37. Juster, *Disorderly Women*, 42–45, 83.

38. Backus, *Diary*, 2: Jan. 1, 1779, May 19, 1780, cited in Johnsen, "Religion and Society," 128.

39. Asa Hunt's letters are in Hurd, *History of Plymouth County*, 987–88.

40. Johnsen, "Religion and Society," 126–127, and tables 53 and 54.

41. Franklin B. Dexter, *Biographical Sketches of the Graduates of Yale College*, 6 vols. (1885–1912), 3:473–74; Backus, *Diary*, 2: Jan. 20, 1779, p. 1013.

42. Pratt, "Life of Deborah Sampson," *Nemasket Gazette*, Sept. 25, 1857.

43. For a conversion experience, see Barbara Lacey, "World of Hannah Heaton: The Autobiography of an Eighteenth-Century Connecticut Farm Woman," *WMQ* 45 (1988): 280–304.

44. Douglas Winiarski, "All Manner of Error and Delusion: Josiah Cotton and the Religious Transformation of Southeastern New England, 1700–1770" (Ph.D. diss., Dept. of Religious Studies, Indiana Univ., 2000), part 3; Winiarski to Young, May 10, 2000 (quotation).

45. Mann, *FR*, 101–06; Juster, *Disorderly Women*, 35–38; for Mrs. Gannett's religious experiences in Sharon, see chapter 9 below.

46. McLoughlin, *New England Dissent*, 1, chap. 8; McLoughlin, *Isaac Backus*, 136–57.

47. McLoughlin, *Isaac Backus*, 157–66; Backus, "An Appeal to the People" (1780) and "Truth Is Great and Will Prevail" (1781), both in McLoughlin, ed., *Isaac Backus on Church, State, and Calvinism*, 2 vols. (Cambridge, MA, 1968), 1:386–425; Walter Frederick Eayrs, "Isaac N. Backus and the Evolution of Evangelical Piety: Religious Dissent and the American Revolution" (honor's thesis, Dartmouth College, 1995).

48. Juster, *Disorderly Women*, chap. 3: 75.

49. Juster, *Disorderly Women*, 35–37, 19 (liminality); Winiarski, "All Manner of Error and Delusion," part 3.

50. Mann, *FR*, 128.

51. Pratt, "Life of Deborah Sampson," *Nemasket Gazette*, Sept. 25, 1857; Vinton's note is in Mann, *FR*, 124–25.

52. Weston, *Middleboro*, 136–37 (the Leonards), 120 (Isaac Wood), 577 (Israel Wood); "Map of the Town of Middleborough . . . surveyed by H. F. Walling, Superintendent of the State, 1855," reproduced in ibid., vii. I am indebted to Janet Griffith for help in locating families and to Marion Whipple for conversations tracking this event. Zilpah Tolman to Eugene Tappan, Jan. 29, 1902, in Tappan, "Deborah Sampson Gannett Dinner . . . Sharon, April 3, 1902," MS, 70–78, SPL, gives the family version of the event.

53. Elizabeth F. Ellet, *The Women of the American Revolution*, 3 vols. (1848–50), 2:122–35; DG,

Diary, MS, July 3, 1802. The raw data in *Mass. S&S,* 15:547–49, 562–64, reveals a connection of sorts for Captain Nathan Thayer of Medway and a Timothy Thayer. Captain Thayer was an army veteran of the northern campaigns, 1775–78. In 1780, he was captain of a militia company in Medway in a regiment commanded by Colonel Ebenezer Thayer, and was "appointed to command men detached from the militia to reinforce the Continental Army"; he saw service for three months, July 7–Oct. 9, 1780, and was stationed at West Point.

Of twenty-five entries in *Mass. S&S* for "Timothy Thayer," one was for a private (his town unidentified) in Captain Thomas Newcomb's company, in a regiment commanded by Colonel Ebenezer Thayer, the same regiment Captain Nathan Thayer was in. Timothy is also listed for three months service, Aug. 3–Oct. 31, 1780. Part of the regiment was sent to Rhode Island, part to reinforce the Continental Army, possibly at West Point. This is evidence for a real-life Timothy Thayer close to Captain Nathan Thayer. But I doubt if Timothy Thayer was Deborah Sampson in disguise because it seems so unlikely that a woman could pass herself off as a man in a militia unit organized on a town basis where everyone knew everyone else. It is possible evidence that she knew someone named Timothy Thayer.

As to Captain Tisdale of Medfield with whom she stayed in 1802, he was a veteran of the northern campaigns (1775–78) who had risen from sergeant to captain. He was at West Point from 1778 until the end of the war in 1783, where he was in the Third Massachusetts Regiment when Deborah was in the Fourth. So he clearly would have known about her. Ellet identified her informant as "A niece of Captain Tisdale upon whom Robert attended in the army for some months." "Attended" I interpret as meaning being a waiter. So there is a chance that Robert Shurtliff was a waiter for Tisdale as well as for General Paterson; it is more likely the niece garbled Mrs. Gannett's story. I am indebted to George Quintal for tracking the two officers, Tisdale and Thayer, in the pension records (Nathan Thayer, S 33199 and James Tisdale, S 33806) and in other military records.

54. John Shy, comment at the panel, "Ordinary Soldiers in the American Revolution," Conference of Omohundro Institute of Early American History, Toronto, June 2000; Jonathan Smith, "How Massachusetts Raised Her Troops in the Revolution," Massachusetts Historical Society *Proceedings* 55 (1921): 345–70; A Citizen of New York [James Hawkes], *A Retrospect of the Boston Tea Party, with a Memoir of George R. T. Hewes . . .* (New York, 1834), 74–75.

55. Middleborough "Town Records" IV (1772–88), Jan. 4–Feb. 15, 1781, 148–54, MS, Middleborough Town Hall.

56. For height of recruits as an issue at West Point, see chapter 3 below.

57. George Washington to Major General William Heath, May 13 and 22, June 22, Aug. 1, 1782, in GW, *Writings* 24:252, 275–76, 371, 452ff.

58. "Records of the Third Baptist Church," Sept. 3, 1782, MS, Andover Newton Theological Seminary. "Last Spring" has to refer to the spring of 1782. It is the common sense of the term and it fits the date of her enlistment, which is confirmed by other documentary sources. It does not seem likely that it refers to the spring of 1781, the previous year; the church would hardly have waited fifteen months to take disciplinary action. But given that she left town in April or May, an interval of three months over the summer (June, July, August) would seem to be a reasonable period for the church to have waited.

59. Susan Juster, letter to Alfred Young, July 12, 1995; for the long-drawn-out treatment of Moses Thomas, see "Records of the Third Baptist Church," 78–86. I am indebted to Juster for her analysis.

60. Mann, *FR,* 108.

61. Abigail Adams to Issac Smith, April 20, 1771, in *The Adams Papers: Adams Family Correspondence,* ed. L. H. Butterfield, 2 vols. (Cambridge, MA, 1963), 1:76.

62. For the strolling poor: Douglas L. Jones, *Village and Seaport: Migration and Society in Eighteenth-Century Massachusetts* (Hanover, NH, 1981); Ruth W. Herndon, *Unwelcome Americans: Living on the Margin in Early New England* (Philadelphia, 2001); for runaway women, Judith A. H. Meier, comp., *Runaway Women . . . As Advertised in the Pennsylvania Gazette, 1728–1789* (Apollo, PA, 1993); for runaway servants and fugitives, see the Prologue above.

63. Mann, *FR,* 115; for fortune-tellers, see the discussion of her dream in chapter 1.

64. Ibid., 123.

65. Ibid., 110, 112, 114.

66. Ibid., 126–27; a Bennett house is on the "Map of Middleborough for 1855," on the same road with the Jeremiah Thomas house.

67. Ibid., 128; James Thacher, *History of the Town of Plymouth* (Boston, 1835), 215–16 (Simeon Samson); for privateering: Abigail Adams to John Adams, Sept. 29, 1776, *Adams Family Correspondence,* 2:135; Marcus Rediker, *Between the Devil and the Deep Blue Sea: Merchant Seaman, Pirates, and the Anglo-American Maritime World, 1700–1750* (Cambridge, UK, 1987), passim. The song, "The Female Warrior" or "The Valiant Maiden," is in, among other places, "Orderly Book of Thomas Cole" (Boston, 1778), MS Division, LC, generously provided by Dianne Dugaw from her personal collection of ballads.

68. [John Lundvall], "Deborah Sampson," in Bellingham Historical Commission, *Crimpville Comments* (May 1977): 1–8; Ernest Taft, *Bellingham Historic Guide* (2001).

69. The spelling varies: Bounty Receipt issued by Noah Taft, May 23, 1782, appears to be signed by Robert Shurtlieff, MS, MA; but Emil F. Guba, *Deborah Samson alias Robert Shirtliff, Revolutionary War Soldier* (Kingston, MA, privately printed, 1994), 17, 72, points out this signature is Shurtliff, claiming that what looks like an "e" before the "f" is clearly a loop before "ff." Colonel Henry Jackson, in his certificate of 1786, also referred to her as Shurtliff. The certificate signed by Eliphalet Thorp, captain of the Seventh Massachusetts Regiment, Dec. 10, 1791, MA, refers to her as Shirtlief. In the company muster of November 1782, presumably taken orally, she was put down as Shirtlef. In the only document Mrs. Gannett submitted with this name, her petition to the Massachusetts legislature, January 1792, she was Shirtliff. *Mass. S&S,* which used this source, spelled it Shurtliff. I have used Robert Shurtliff. After she signed the bounty receipt in May 1782, Sampson herself may not have remembered what spelling she used.

70. *Mass. S&S,* 14:164ff; *Descendants of William Shurtleff of Plymouth and Marshfield, Massachusetts,* 2 vols. (Revere, MA, 1912), lists numerous Roberts in this area, including several who would have been in their twenties; "Map of Middleborough for 1855" (for a local Shurtliff); "Records of the Third Baptist Church," May 3, July 8, 1781 (for Shurtliffs admitted to the church), MS, Andover Newton Theological Seminary. Mann, in his 1830s MS,

mentioned for the first time that Deborah chose the name Robert because it belonged to her deceased older brother, but there is no evidence of such a brother in the genealogies, and given the Old Testament pattern of the names of her siblings, Robert was an unlikely choice; it is possible she may have believed she had an older brother, Robert, who died.

71. Eliphalet Thorp, Certificate, Dec. 10, 1791, in Docket for Chap. 23, House Resolves for 1791, MA; *Mass. S&S,* 15:696–97, verifies Thorp's rank and status as "Muster Master" in 1782–83; Calvin Munn, letter to the editor, *New York Evening Post,* June 30, 1827.

72. [Isaiah Thomas], *Thomas's New England Almanack, or the Massachusetts Calendar for 1775* (Boston, 1774), unpaged; "An Account of the Books Read by Mr. John Stevens" (1766–67), cited in Elizabeth Reilly, "Common and Learned Readers: Shared and Separate Spheres in Mid-Eighteenth-Century New England" (Ph.D. diss., Boston Univ., 1994); *Connecticut Courant,* April 2–9, 1771, brought to my attention by Susan Cifaldi.

73. For the use of the Indian disguise: Philip DeLoria, *Playing Indian* (New Haven, CT, 1998); Reeve Huston, *Land and Freedom: Rural Society, Popular Protest and Party Politics in Ante-Bellum New York* (New York, 2000), chap. 5; Alan Taylor, "Agrarian Independence: Northern Land Rioters after the Revolution," in Alfred F. Young, ed., *Beyond the American Revolution: Explorations in the History of American Radicalism* (Dekalb, IL, 1993), 221–45.

74. For the Yorktown tradition, see Kenneth Silverman, *Cultural History of the American Revolution* (New York, 1976), 410; a chapbook, *The World Turned Upside Down; or the Comical Metamorphoses,* reprinted often in England, 1750–1800, with variant titles is listed in Evans (Philadelphia, 1779; Boston 1780 and 179?). *Catchpenny Prints: 163 Popular Engravings from the Eighteenth Century Originally Published by Bowles and Carver* (New York, 1970) reproduces a dozen eighteenth-century English drawings of reversals on one broadsheet, including *The Wife Turned Soldier, the Husband Spinning. The Wife Acting the Soldier* (Boston, 1794), also issued as a separate engraving. For the concept in religion, see Christopher Hill, *The English Bible and the Seventeenth Century Revolution* (London, 1993), chap. 18. I am indebted to Paul Uek and Georgia Barnhill for searching for American imprints.

75. *The Continental Almanack for 1782* (Philadelphia, 1781).

PART TWO · "ROBERT SHURTLIFF"

CHAPTER 3: THE CONTINENTAL ARMY

1. DG, *Address,* 14–15. In her address of 1802, DG mentioned no dates for her service but claimed she was at the Battle of Yorktown (September–October 1781). The evidence for her enlistment in 1782, not 1781 as claimed by Herman Mann, is in the enlistment documents, discussed in chapter 2 and in DG's petition of 1792, taken up in chapter 6. The muster rolls for Captain George Webb's Light Infantry Company of the Fourth Massachusetts Regiment for 1781 and 1782 provide additional proof of service that began in 1782.

There are four complete muster rolls for this company in MA, as follows with the time covered in parenthesis: December 17, 1781 ("from the last of February to the last of November, 1781, inclusive being 10 months"); January [1782] (December 1781); Feb. 7 or 9 [1782] (January 1782); March 1782 (February, 1782). The name "Robert Shurtliff" does not appear on any of these four rolls, which together cover a period from Feb. 1, 1781, through February

1782. Her absence from the first roll, which by internal evidence covers the time the company was in Virginia and Philadelphia, is evidence that she was not at Yorktown (twenty-one members of the company she joined were). No rolls have survived (or surfaced) for March to November 1782.

"Robert Shurtlef" appears for the first time on a roll dated Nov. 17, 1782, which ended up in United States Revolution Collection MS Box, Folder 2, at the American Antiquarian Society in Worcester (next door to Holden, Webb's hometown), together with other MS papers of Webb. This seems to be a draft roll, which the compiler intended to transcribe to the official roll. It is a list of soldiers arranged by rank, not in the tabular form of the formal report. There is no reason, however, to doubt its authenticity; names of soldiers on the earlier rolls are repeated and new ones added. The first four rolls offer clear negative proof that DS was not in Webb's company in 1781 and the fifth offers positive proof that she was in the company by November 1782, leaving open when she joined the unit, which had to be sometime after May 23, 1782, the date of her enlistment, established in other documents. These muster rolls were discovered by Jan Lewis Nelson and are discussed in Nelson to Bricknell, October 3, 1975, Bricknell, PHS, and in Nelson to Michael Gannett, Jan. 20, Feb. 2, 1976, Michael Gannett Papers. I have examined photocopies of the first four rolls in Bricknell, PHS, and the original of the fifth in AAS.

2. Washington to Thomas Paine, Sept. 18, 1782, GW, *Writings,* 25:176–77; GW to Major General John Armstrong, Jan. 10, 1783; GW, *Writings,* 26; for Washington during these years, see James Thomas Flexner, *George Washington in the American Revolution, 1775–1783* (Boston, 1967), chaps. 51–54.

3. Robert K. Wright, *The Continental Army* (Washington DC: U.S. Army Center of Military History, 1983), chap. 7; Paul Sanborn, "West Point," in Richard L. Blanco, ed., *The American Revolution, 1775–1783: An Encyclopedia,* 2 vols. (New York, 1993); David R. Palmer, *The River and the Rock: The History of Fortress West Point, 1775–1783* (New York, 1969), chap. 23.

4. Mark V. Kwasny, *Washington's Partisan War, 1775–1783* (Kent, OH, 1996), chap. 11.

5. For numbers: Charles H. Lesser, ed., *The Sinews of Independence: Monthly Strength Reports of the Continental Army* (Chicago, 1976), 214–54; for New Windsor: Janet Dempsey, *Washington's Last Cantonment: "High Time for Peace"* (Monroe, NY, 1990); "Inspector's Return for Colonel William Shepard's Regiment, June, 1782" is in Fourth Regiment, 1781–83, Miscellaneous, M 246, Jacket No. 6, NA [call no. 32-4 Roll 36], Shepard Papers, LC. There were 351 men present and fit for duty, but if complete, the regiment would have had 612 men.

6. Sarah Osborn, Pension Application, in John C. Dann, ed., *The Revolution Remembered: Eyewitness Accounts of the War for Independence* (Chicago, 1980), 240–50; Washington, General Order, Sept. 8, 1782, in GW, *Writings,* 25:139, and GW to Henry Knox, March 8, 1783, in GW, *Writings,* 26:199; John Rees, " 'The Multitude of Women': An Examination of the Numbers of Female Camp Followers with the Continental Army," *Minerva: Quarterly Report on Women in the Military* 14 (1996): 1–47, esp. 28–31, a meticulous study; Holly A. Mayer, *Belonging to the Army: Camp Followers and Community During the American Revolution* (Columbia, SC, 1996), replaces all previous works on the subject.

7. James Thacher, *Military Journal of the American Revolution* (1823; 1969 from the Hartford, 1862, edn), 307–26; William Heath, *Memoirs of Major-General William Heath by Himself*

(Boston, 1798); see letters and diary of Lieutenant Benjamin Gilbert cited below, chapter 4, sec. 1.

8. Joseph Plumb Martin, *Private Yankee Doodle: Being a Narrative of Some of the Adventures, Dangers and Sufferings of a Revolutionary Soldier,* ed. George F. Scheer (Hallowell, ME, 1830; Boston, 1962), 274–75.

9. For examples of punishments in 1783, see GW, *Writings* 26: Washington, General Orders, Jan. 28 (74); Feb. 8 (109–10); Feb. 13 (129–32); March 13 (220); April 9 (310–11); for the Newburgh Conspiracy, see chapter 5 below.

10. Charles Patrick Neimeyer, *America Goes to War: A Social History of the Continental Army* (New York, 1996), chap. 7; Carl Van Doren, *Mutiny in January . . .* (New York, 1943); for the 1783 mutiny, see chapter 5 below.

11. John Shy to Alfred Young, Sept. 28, 1994; Mark M. Boatner III, *Encyclopedia of the American Revolution* (New York, 1974), 634–35; Paul Sanborn, "Light Infantry," in Blanco, ed., *Encyclopedia of the Revolution,* 935–37.

12. John Shy, ed., *Winding Down: The Revolutionary War Letters of Lieutenant Benjamin Gilbert of Massachusetts, 1780–1783* (Ann Arbor, MI, 1989), 51–52; GW to Captain John Pray, Aug. 14, Sept. 11, 1782, in GW, *Writings* 25:18–19, 125.

13. Wright, *The Continental Army,* 158; Edward C. Boynton, comp., *General Orders of George Washington Commander-in-Chief of the Army of the Revolution, Issued at Newburgh on the Hudson 1782–1783,* ed. Alan Aimone (1909; Harrison, NY, 1973), May 17, 1782, 21.

14. Marquis de Chastellux, *Travels in North America,* 2 vols. (London, 1787), 1:104; Thacher, *Military Journal,* 266; Sanborn, "Light Infantry."

15. Martin, *Private Yankee Doodle,* 136.

16. Gilbert, April 30, 1782, *Letters,* 56–57; Orders of the Day for a Light Infantry Company at Fort Montgomery, Sept. 10, Oct. 15, 1779, cited in Colonel John Womack Wright, *Some Notes on the Continental Army* (New Windsor Cantonment Publication No. 2, Vails Gate, NY, 1963), 74–75; Rees, "The Multitude of Women," 23–26.

17. The muster rolls are listed in note 1; see Colonel William Shepard Collection, 1779–83, MS, LC: vol. 3, Receipt Book for Supplies, for the receipts of Quartermaster Africa Hamlin for equipment issued to Captain George Webb's Company, May–October 1782; ibid., vol. 1, for the weekly returns and location of the units.

18. I am indebted to Jan Lewis Nelson and Michael Gannett, who generously shared their analysis of these muster rolls with me.

19. Sergeant William Fairbank, *The Surprising Life and Adventures of Maria Knowles* (Newcastle, UK, 1798), 2; John Sellers, "The Origins and Careers of the New England Soldier: Non-Commissioned Officers and Privates in the Massachusetts Continental Line" (unpublished paper, c. 1975), kindly made available to me by Sellers, Manuscript Librarian, LC. Sellers analyzed 546 men drawn from four regiments, including two complete companies from the Fourth Massachusetts for 1781–83, Robert Shurtliff's regiment. Mayer, *Belonging to the Army,* 58 (for von Steuben).

20. I have not been able to identify an army height requirement in standard collections of military laws. I have concluded (a) that the requirement was set by the chief commanding officer of the army from which recruiting officers were dispatched; (b) that it changed over time;

and (c) that recruiting officers had fairly wide discretionary authority in accepting or rejecting individuals brought in by bounty agents. I appreciate the efforts of several military historians, Holly Mayer in particular, to run down this elusive requirement.

21. Ebenezer Huntington to Samuel B. Webb, June 2, 20, 1782, in Worthington C. Ford, ed., *The Correspondence and Journals of Samuel Blachly Webb,* 3 vols. (New York, 1893–94), 2:401–02, 405. I deduce a prior regulation of five feet five inches from this letter; GW to Captain Henry Sewall, June 11, 1782, in GW, *Writings,* 24:331–32 (five feet two inches).

22. Sanborn, "Light Infantry," 935–37; for Washington's expectations of height for the light infantry in 1780, see John W. Hawkins, Orderly Book, No. 2, April 23–July 26, 1780, 2nd Canadian Regiment, Historical Society of Pennsylvania, MS, AM649, entries for July 16, 17, 18, 1780—brought to my attention by Holly Mayer.

23. Sellers, "The New England Soldier." There is more or less a consensus among scholars as to the social origins of the soldiers; they disagree as to the significance of the data. For a summary of the discussion, see Richard H. Kohn, "A Social History of the American Soldier: A Review and Prospectus for Research," *American Historical Review* 86 (1981): 553–67, and Charles Royster, *A Revolutionary People at War: The Continental Army and American Character, 1775–1783* (Chapel Hill, NC, 1979), "A Note on Statistics and Continental Soldiers' Motivation," 373–78. For the most recent overall analysis, see Neimeyer, *America Goes to War;* for a variant analysis for Peterborough, New Hampshire, John Resch, *Suffering Soldiers: Revolutionary War Veterans, Moral Sentiment, and Political Culture in the Early Republic* (Amherst, MA, 1999). The incisive remarks of John Shy are in a comment at the panel "Ordinary Soldiers in the American Revolution," Conference of Omohundro Institute of Early American History, Toronto, June 2000.

24. Wright, *Some Notes on the Continental Army,* chap. 8; Harold L. Peterson, *The Book of the Continental Soldier: Uniforms, Weapons, and Equipment with Which He Lived and Fought* (Harrisburg, PA, 1968). I have profited from the exhibit *The Continental Soldier in Camp: Life at New Windsor Encampment, 1782–83,* at New Windsor Cantonment, New York State Historic Site, and from the reconstruction by the National Temple Hill Association at the cantonment. Mann, *FR,* 134, writes that her "military apparatus" included a "hanger with white belts." A hanger was a type of sword, an uncommon piece of equipment for an enlisted man at this stage of the war, although possible for one in the light infantry. In January 2003, a sword attributed to Deborah Sampson was sold on eBay, the Internet auction site. Held in a private collection since the 1970s, on the basis of photographs it was appraised in 1975 as a sword of the 1770s–80s by George C. Neumann, an authority on the weaponry of the Revolution. The claim is that the sword was discovered in the mid-1970s stuffed in the basement brickwork of the chimney in the Plympton house of Jonathan and Deborah Bradford Samson, Deborah's grandparents. The sword, unknown to previous researchers, came to light after research on this book was closed.

25. It may well be that Deborah stood out in handling a musket because she had so little competition among the army recruits of the last few years of the war, the vast majority of whom were drawn from those classes in society least likely to own guns and be skilled in their use. See Michael Bellesiles, *Arming America: The Origins of a National Gun Culture* (New York, 2000), 202–07.

26. *Independent Gazette; or the New-York Journal,* Feb. 9, 1784 [reprinted in the Prologue]; Calvin Munn, letter to the editor, *New York Evening Post,* June 30, 1827; Mann, *FR,* 134–35 (emphasis added in these quotations).

27. On 1777 clothing: Lieutenant Colonel John Brooks cited in Royster, *A Revolutionary People at War,* 142; Martin, *Private Yankee Doodle,* 101; General Order, March 3, 1783, GW, *Writings,* 26:181.

28. Mann, *FR,* 134–35; for the use of Mann's description, see Company of Military Historians, *Military Uniforms in America: The Era of the American Revolution, 1755–1795,* ed. John R. Elting (San Rafael, CA, 1974), article by H. Charles McBarron, Frederick P. Todd, and John R. Elting; illustration by McBarron, 82, and plate 601, "Fourth Massachusetts Regiment of the Continental Line Battalion Companies, 1782–1783," description by Alan Archambault and Marko Zlatich, illustration by Archambault. See Prints Division, LC vertical file, for other similar engravings of light infantry officers and privates.

29. Description from Company of Military Historians, *Military Uniforms in America,* 82.

30. On how other disguised women carried out their deception, I have benefited especially from Julie Wheelwright, *Amazons and Military Maids: Women Who Dressed as Men in Pursuit of Life, Liberty and Happiness* (London, 1989). For clues from women soldiers in the Civil War, see Elizabeth D. Leonard, *All the Daring of the Soldier: Women of the Civil War Armies* (New York, 1999), and DeAnn Blanton and Laura M. Cooke, *They Fought Like Demons: Women Soldiers in the Civil War* (Baton Rouge, LA, 2002), chaps. 3, 9.

31. My thanks to Henry Marshall Cooke IV, a modern-day historical tailor of uniforms, for conversations about uniforms and for sharing his study, "Communities in Uniform: The Social Evolution of the Tenth Massachusetts Regiment, 1776–1780" (master's thesis, Tufts Univ., 1984); Elizabeth Schafer, "Clothier General," in Blanco, ed., *Encyclopedia of the Revolution.*

32. Mann, *FR,* 134n; Mann, "Heroine," 179; [Anon.], *The Life and Adventures of Mrs. Christian Davies, the British Amazon, Commonly Called Mother Ross* (2nd edn, London, 1741), 20.

33. John Murphy, Jr., "Uniforms," in Blanco, ed., *Encyclopedia of the Revolution;* Meredith Wright with illustrations by Nancy E. Rexford, *Everyday Dress in Rural America, 1783–1800* (New York, 1990), 60–70 (shirts); *Life of Christian Davies,* Appendix (urinary instrument); Linda Bird Francke, *Ground Zero: The Gender Wars in the Military* (New York, 1997), 80–82 (the experiences of women pilots in survival training). In Lara Cardella's novel, *Good Girls Don't Wear Trousers* (1994), which sold more than 2 million copies, Annetta, the tomboy heroine in Sicily, is taught by Antonio "how to strut like a boy and shake hands like a man." "Standing shoulder to shoulder," the heroine writes, "we peed together" (excerpt reprinted in Christian McEwen, ed., *Jo's Girls: Tomboy Tales of High Adventure. True Grit and Real Life* [Boston, 1997], 26–32). My thanks to Dr. Dennis Pessis, a urologist affiliated with Rush Presbyterian–St. Luke's Hospital, Chicago, for a conversation on the subject, clarifying the physical possibilities.

34. Mann, *FR,* 134 (voice), 155, 157 ("blooming boy"), 183 ("smock-faced boy"); Howard L. Applegate, "Constitutions Like Iron: The Life of the American Revolutionary War Soldiers in the Middle Department, 1775–1783" (Ph.D. diss., Syracuse Univ., 1966), chap. 10 (hazing); Malcolm Potts and Roger Short, *Ever Since Adam and Eve: The Evolution of Human Sexuality* (Cambridge, UK, 1999), 161, 171–73 (changing ages of puberty, historically).

35. Mann, *FR*, did not use "molly"; the first usage I find applied to Sampson is in Elizabeth F. Ellet, *The Women of the American Revolution*, 3 vols. (New York, 1848–50), 2:130; *OED*, s.v. "Molly"; for England in the eighteenth century, see Frances Grose, *A Classical Dictionary of the Vulgar Tongue* (London, 1785; reprinted as *A Dictionary of Buckish Slang* . . . , London 1811, 1971), has this entry: "MOLLY. A Miss Molly; an effeminate fellow, a sodomite." See also Rector Norton, *Mother Clap's Molly House: The Gay Subculture in England, 1700–1830* (London, 1992); *Adventures of Hannah Snell* (London, 1750), 19, and in the longer version reprinted in Menie Muriel Dowie, ed., *Woman Adventurers* (London, 1893), 95. The historian John Demos told me that he recalls a use of "molly" in late-seventeenth-century Massachusetts. For migration of Londoners, Bernard Bailyn, *Voyagers to the West: A Passage in the Peopling of America on the Eve of the Revolution* (New York, 1986).

36. GW, *Writings*, 25:8–9: GW, General Orders, Aug. 12, 1782; Wright, *Some Notes on the Continental Army*, 74.

37. GW, *Writings*, 25:102: GW, General Orders, Sept. 1, 1782 (bathing); see von Steuben's manual cited below in note 40.

38. GW, *Writings*, 26:68: Order of the Day, Jan. 25, Feb. 10, 1783, 111–12; Wright, *Some Notes on the Continental Army*, 38.

39. Betty Friedan, *The Second Stage* (New York, 1981), 166–67 (on women at West Point); "Amenorrhea" in Christine Ammer, *The New A-to-Z of Women's Health: A Concise Encyclopedia* (New York, 1990), 18–20; Dr. Anne B. Loucks, a biologist quoted in Linda Villarosa, "Tri-Fold Ailment Stalks Female Athletes," *New York Times* (Science section), June 22, 1999, D-7; Mayer, *Belonging to the Army*, 140–42 (washerwomen). I am indebted to the late Dr. Alex Tulsky, professor of obstetrics and gynecology, University of Illinois Medical School, for a conversation on this subject.

40. Baron von Steuben, *Regulations for the Order and Discipline of the Troops of the United States* (Boston, 1794), chap. 20. The "Blue Book," as the manual was called, was originally approved by Congress in 1779 and was reprinted in many editions, often issued by the Inspector General.

41. My thanks to Alan Aimone, Librarian, West Point Academy, for his suggestion about the prevalence of "spooning."

42. Wayne Franklin, introduction to James Fenimore Cooper, *The Spy: A Tale of the Neutral Ground* (New York, 1821, 1997), vii–xxx; quotation from Cooper at 10. My thanks to Wayne Franklin for pointing out these passages and for conversations about Cooper.

43. Otto Hufeland, *Westchester County During the American Revolution, 1775–1783* (White Plains, NY, 1926), chap. 14; Joseph Scharf, *History of Westchester County* . . . , 2 vols. (Philadelphia, 1886), vol. 2.

44. Palmer, *The River and the Rock*, chap. 23.

45. Sung Bok Kim, "The Limits of Politicization in the American Revolution: The Experiences of Westchester County, New York," *Journal of American History* 80 (1993): 868–89.

46. Catherine S. Crary, "Guerrilla Activities of James DeLancey's Cowboys in Westchester County: Conventional Warfare or Self-Interested Freebooting," in Robert A. East and Jacob Judd, eds., *The Loyalist Americans: A Focus on Greater New York* (Tarrytown, NY, 1975),

14–24; Crary, ed., *The Price of Loyalty: Tory Writings from the Revolutionary Era* (New York, 1973), 173–77, 181–85; Kwasny, *Washington's Partisan War*, chap. 11.

47. Edward Countryman, *A People in Revolution: The American Revolution and Political Society in New York, 1760–1790* (Baltimore, 1981); Sung Bok Kim, *Landlord and Tenant in Colonial New York: Manorial Society, 1664–1775* (Chapel Hill, NC, 1978); Kim, "Impact of Class Relations and Warfare in the American Revolution: The New York Experience," *Journal of American History* 69 (1982): 326–46.

48. Kwasny, *Washington's Partisan War*, 313–28, quotations at 316, 324, 325; this overall picture was long held by the local historian, Hufeland, *Westchester County*, chap. 14.

49. Washington Irving cited in Crary, "Guerrilla Activities of James DeLancey's Cowboys," 15; Timothy Dwight, *Travels in New England and New York*, ed. Barbara M. Solomon, 4 vols. (Cambridge, MA, 1969), 3:345–46.

50. Kwasny, *Washington's Partisan War*, xii, citing Captaine De Jenney, *The Partisans: or, The Art of Making War in Detachment* (London, 1760), 1–2.

51. For the capture of Major André, see Franklin, intro. to Cooper, *The Spy*, vii–x; Robert E. Cray, Jr., "Major John André and His Three Captors: Class Dynamics and Revolutionary Memory Wars in the Early Republic," *Journal of the Early Republic* 17 (1997): 371–97.

52. Stuart Goulding, "The McDonald Interviews," *History Today* 29 (1979): 429–40. I went through the McDonald Papers, 6 vols., MS, Thomas Paine Library, New Rochelle, NY, with the kind assistance of Catherine T. Goulding, Librarian. In these oral histories of the 1840s that covered 1782–83, I found no memories of Deborah Sampson but many vivid memories of the horrors of the chaotic warfare. Jeremiah Anderson's remembrance is in 6:855–73. My thanks to Mary Beth Norton for calling this source to my attention.

CHAPTER 4: THE LIGHT INFANTRYMAN

1. For the identification and location of these petitions, see chapters 6 and 8 below.
2. Mann's account of DS at Yorktown, *FR*, 143–53, is the only source for her presence at the battle, and there is little in it that can be construed as proof. For his 1797 book he drew on such published histories as William Gordon, *The History of the Rise, Progress, and Establishment of the Independence of the United States*, 4 vols. (London, 1788), 4:186, which has a number of passages very similar to Mann for Yorktown and the Battle of Bunker Hill. In his much-enlarged MS of the 1830s he plagiarized heavily from the military journal of Dr. James Thacher, *Military Journal During the American Revolutionary War, from 1775 to 1783* (Boston, 1823). In his 1797 account, he placed his heroine close to famous military leaders: she was under the command of Lafayette and she was so near General Washington, "she heard distinctly what he said." He included winning coarse detail: as a result of the rolling motion of the transport boat, "she puked for several hours without much intermission"; after working twenty-four hours building a battery, "her hands were so blistered that she could scarcely open or shut them." All such detail I take as testimony to Mann's artfulness. He could have gotten the stories from other soldiers or she could have gotten them from other soldiers in her company who were at Yorktown.

3. Jane Keiter, "Deborah Sampson, Continental Soldier," *Westchester Historian* 76 (Winter 2000): 4–13; (Spring 2000): 52–60; (Summer 2000): 84–93; (Fall 2000): 116–25. Keiter's painstaking reconstruction of Sampson's wartime experiences in Westchester is based on the assumption that she enlisted in May 1781 and that Herman Mann's revised post-1827 MS is reliable. I disagree with her dating several episodes in 1781 but respect her identification of places and people.

4. For the muster rolls in Captain George Webb's company, see chapter 3. For the regiment: Colonel William Shepard Collection (1779–83), MS, 5 vols., and Colonel Henry Jackson Papers, 1777–82, MS, 4 vols., both in Manuscript Division, LC, also on microfilm. For General John Paterson, I was unable to locate any papers for these years, although Thomas Egleston, *The Life of John Paterson, Major General of the Revolutionary Army* (New York, 1898), seems to have had access to papers. For the correspondence of the commander of the light infantry camp at Peekskill, see Worthington C. Ford, ed., *Correspondence of Samuel B. Webb,* 3 vols. (New York, 1893–94).

5. I have found useful Dr. James Thacher, *Military Journal,* and William Heath, *Memoirs of Major-General William Heath by Himself* (Boston, 1798), two of the earliest first-person sources covering the Hudson Valley to be published.

6. For this and the following paragraph: Washington's orders to (or about) the light infantry in 1782 are in GW, *Writings,* 24: General Orders, May 17 (262), June 4 (309), Aug. 5 (466), GW, *Writings,* 25: Captain John Pray, Aug. 14 (18–19); to General William Heath, Aug. 18 (34); General Orders, Aug. 19 (43); Aug. 21 (46); General Orders, Aug. 31 (98); to Captain John Pray, Sept. 11 (125); to Colonel Samuel B. Webb, Sept. 20 (209); General Orders, Oct. 25 (294–95), Nov. 19 (353–54), Dec. 2 (386–87). Selected general orders are in Edward C. Boynton, comp., *General Orders of George Washington. Issued at Newburgh on the Hudson, 1782–1783,* ed. Alan Aimone (1883; Harrison, NY, 1973). The letters to and from Samuel B. Webb, commander of a light infantry brigade in 1782, are in Ford, ed., *Correspondence of S. B. Webb,* 2:412ff., Webb to Joseph Barrell, Oct. 8, 1782, 426–28 (claim of five battalions and 1,200 men). GW, *Writings,* 24: General Orders, May 17 (262), June 4 (309), Aug. 5 (466); GW, *Writings,* 25.

7. GW, *Writings,* 26: General Order, June 20, 1783 (31); Heath, *Memoirs,* Sept. 25, 1782, May 2, 1783 ("covered by the Light Infantry").

8. For an overview, see John C. Dann, ed., *The Revolution Remembered: Eyewitness Accounts of the War for Independence* (Chicago, 1980), intro.; the petitions are in Record Group 15 of the Veterans Administration, NA, and are available on microfilm (898 reels) in regional NA offices.

9. I followed this line of research on the suggestion of John Shy, one of the few historians to make major use of the pension records for military history and to deal with this last phase of the war in Westchester. I used the "Roll of Muster for Captain Webb's Light Infantry Company for Nov. 17 1782." (A search of the rolls taken earlier in 1782 might turn up a few more petitioners.) I searched for these men in the compiled service records: *Mass. S&S,* then in *Index of Revolutionary War Pension Applications* (Washington, DC, 1976) and in Virgil D. White, comp., *Genealogical Abstracts of Revolutionary War Pension Files,* 4 vols. (Waynesboro, TN, 1991). After I identified company members who had applied for pensions, Jon

Parmenter, then a graduate student at the University of Michigan, searched for the applications in Microfilm Publication M 805, NA 898, Clements Library, University of Michigan. I worked from photocopies of these applications.

10. Roger Barrett, Pension No. W 21648, NA. Barrett, at the time a resident of Washington County, New York, was inscribed on the pension rolls (New York 14974) and issued a pension of $52 a year. He is listed on Captain Webb's company muster for Nov. 17, 1782. For the strength of retention of memories of youth, see Daniel Schacter, *Searching for Memory: The Brain, the Mind and the Past* (New York, 1996), chap. 3.

11. Moses Hall, Pension Application W 19723. Hall, who also joined Webb's company in May 1782, wrote that "the summer succeeding the enlistment the regiment were on the lines or near the North River in the vicinity of New York." He marched with the company to winter quarters in December, and served in a reorganized company in the winter of 1782–83.

12. Solomon Beebe, Pension S 38531, cited in Keiter, "Deborah Sampson," part 1, 12; William Jeffords, Mass. S 47339. Jeffords filed under the 1818 law; Benjamin Hobbs S 32846, NA.

13. GW, *Writings*, 25:242–43: GW to Colonel Samuel B. Webb, Oct. 7, 1782, reporting that Captain George Webb "might have left camp" before GW had so ordered. Captain George Webb's report is in Samuel B. Webb to GW, Oct. 8, 1782, Ford, ed., *Correspondence of S. B. Webb*, 2:425–26, in which Colonel Webb endorses Captain Webb's report but says there was "an impropriety." The outcome of this disciplinary action is not clear. Captain Webb may have been reprimanded. It is conceivable that this action near Tarrytown was the one in which Sampson was wounded; in any case, Captain Webb's report is clear evidence that her company saw service near Tarrytown in the fall of 1782, the most likely time that she was wounded.

14. John Shy, ed., *Winding Down: The Revolutionary War Letters of Lieutenant Benjamin Gilbert of Massachusetts, 1780–1783* (Ann Arbor, MI, 1989); Rebecca D. Symmes, ed., *A Citizen Soldier in the American Revolution: The Diary of Benjamin Gilbert in Massachusetts and New York* (Cooperstown, NY, 1980), which I have supplemented with Benjamin Gilbert, Diary, 1778–86, MS on microfilm 88/7, New York State Historical Association, Cooperstown. The generalizations in the following paragraphs draw on these three sources.

15. Ford, ed., *Correspondence of S. B. Webb*, 2:427; Rowena Buell, comp., *The Memoirs of Rufus Putnam* (Boston, 1903), 86, cited in Keiter, "Deborah Sampson," part 4, *Westchester Historian* 76 (Fall 2000): 125.

16. Mann, *FR*, 138, 165.

17. Jane Keiter is convinced that this skirmish took place in 1781, following Mann in dating Sampson's enlistment as May 1781. In "Deborah Sampson," part 1, *Westchester Historian* 76 (Winter 2000): 4–13, she concludes that the soldiers killed were Solomon Beebe, John Sperrin, and James Battles (not John). Therefore she accepts the name "James Battles," who in the muster roll for December 1781 is reported as having died Dec. 1, 1781.

Keiter is also convinced that Mann's reference to Jacob Towne as "Ensign" is another indication that the skirmish occurred in 1781, because Towne was appointed a lieutenant in 1782, and had the engagement been in 1782, she argues, Sampson would have identified him as "Lieutenant." Her source for officers is Francis B. Heitman, *Historical Register of Officers of the Continental Army* (Washington, DC, 1914), which lists Towne as lieutenant as of May

27, 1782. I find, however, in *Mass. S&S* 15:910–11, that Colonel Henry Jackson recommended Ensign Towne for promotion to Governor John Hancock June 20, 1782, and that the Massachusetts Council was advised that Hancock had issued a warrant for the appointment July 3, 1782, which news might have taken several weeks to reach West Point from Boston and even longer to reach a company in the field. Assuming, as I do, that a skirmish with DS could not have taken place before June–July 1782, at that time Towne would still have been called an ensign because the news of his promotion had not arrived.

18. Benjamin Rush, *Directions for the Health of Soldiers* . . . (Philadelphia, 1777).

19. Calvin Munn to *New York Evening Post,* June 30, 1827; David Willard, *History of Greenfield* (Greenfield, MA, 1838), 160, summarizes the career of Munn who lived in Greenfield after 1792 as a tavern keeper. Willard paraphrases the short letter and adds the comment about Mann's book not in the letter, "She was not wounded as is therein related," which he could only have gotten in conversation with Munn. In 1833, Munn filed Pension Application Massachusetts 29,994, NA.

20. For this and the following paragraphs, Mann, *FR,* 165–71.

21. Keiter, "Deborah Sampson," part 2, *Westchester Historian* 76 (Spring 2000): 52–60, gives background on Crompond (variously spelled at the time), identifies Von Hoite, and locates the site of a possible cave.

22. For the French encampment: Heath, *Memoirs,* Sept. 18 to Oct. 22, 353–57; Elizabeth Ellet, *The Women of the American Revolution,* 3 vols. (New York, 1848–50), 2:130, was told by her informant, who allegedly heard it from Gannett, that "about four months after her first wound she received another severe one, being shot through the shoulder." Ellet is not generally reliable, but four months after the first skirmish (which most likely took place in June–July 1782) would also place it in the fall of 1782, within the time frame of the temporary French encampment at Crompond. Keiter, "Deborah Sampson," part 2, asserts that Sampson was treated by a French surgeon in an American army hospital in Crompond, but in the *FR,* 170, Mann refers to "the French surgeon" in "the old hospital" in "the French encampment." In his revised MS, he referred to "the French surgeon" in "the French hospital" (Mann, "Heroine," 306–07), offering dialogue in comic pidgin French by the French surgeon.

23. Mann, *FR,* 167; Mann, "Heroine," 305–09.

24. Granville Temple Sproat, "Old Folks Traditions of Deborah Sampson," unpublished paper, reported in a column-length letter by M. M. Copeland entitled "Deborah Sampson," to *Boston Evening Traveller,* Jan. 19, 1889, p. 6, col. 9 (AAS). A handwritten copy of this is in Pauline Moody's Papers, SPL; Ellet, *Women of the Revolution,* 2:130; for the Freneau documents, see chapter 6 below; Gannett, *Address,* 17; for family memories, Zilpah Tolman to Eugene Tappan, Jan. 29, 1902, in Tappan, "Deborah Sampson Gannett Dinner . . . Sharon, April 3, 1902," MS, 74–75, SPL.

25. For the officer's report: *New York Independent Gazette,* Jan. 10, 1784; DG, petition to the Senate and House, Dec. 25, 1809, MS Photostat, MHS; for Patience Payson's testimony on behalf of Benjamin Gannett's petition, see chapter 9.

26. For Hannah Snell, [Robert Walker], *The Female Soldier* (1750), 16–17.

27. For pension requirements, see chapter 6; for testimony on behalf of Benjamin Gannett's pension application, see chapter 9.

28. For documentation, see chapter 6 and esp. chapter 8; Henry Dearborn [Secretary of War] to Benjamin Austin [pension agent], March 11, 1805, in Vinton, intro. to Mann, *FR,* xix.

29. Holly A. Mayer, *Belonging to the Army: Camp Followers and Community During the American Revolution* (Columbia, SC, 1996), 222–23; Richard L. Blanco, "American Army Hospitals in Pennsylvania During the Revolutionary War," *Pennsylvania History* 48 (1981): 347–68.

30. It is possible Sampson was in only one skirmish, not two. Some of the later accounts passed on in oral tradition give the impression there was one, but this could be a normal telescoping of events. In Mann's 1797 memoir, as we shall see, her sex was discovered after she was near death in a Philadelphia hospital. A summary of her life in the [Dedham] *Village Register and Norfolk County Advertiser,* Dec. 29, 1820, the Mann family paper (on the occasion of her application for a general pension), adds a new note. It reports that she was "twice wounded by musket balls," and she concealed her sex "till at length a severe wound which she received in battle and which had well nigh closed her earthly career, occasioned the discovery. On her recovery she quitted the army." This account is puzzling because it reports her "discovery" after being wounded "in battle," not after being sick at a Philadelphia hospital, as in Mann's book and revised MS. It is hard to construct a scenario for this version; it may have been written by Mann, Jr., who was telescoping events.

31. Mann, *FR,* 171–75.

32. Keiter, "Deborah Sampson," part 3, *Westchester Historian* 76 (Summer 2000): 84–93.

33. "Roll of Capt. Webb's Light Infantry, November 17, 1782," Webb Papers, AAS; for Richard Snow, *Mass. S&S,* 14:621.

34. Mann, "Heroine," 313.

35. Mann, *FR,* 175–77.

36. Benjamin Gilbert Diary, MS, Oct. 25, 1782; Keiter, "Deborah Sampson," part 4, *Westchester Historian* 76 (Fall 2000): 119–21.

37. Mann, *FR,* 177–80 (stretched out to several pages to accommodate Vinton's lengthy footnotes from the revised MS); Mann, "Heroine," 322–47.

38. My thanks to Helen Tanner, who convinced me of the presence of white Anglo-Americans living with eastern Indians. See June Namias, *White Captives: Gender and Ethnicity on the American Frontier* (Chapel Hill, NC, 1993).

39. For the state of Indians within New York, see Barbara Graymont, *The Iroquois in the American Revolution* (Syracuse, NY, 1972); Dean Snow, an anthropologist and an authority on the Indians of this area, writes: "I cannot imagine that there was even a Seneca village (or much of one)" in this location—Snow to Alfred Young, Oct. 23, 1995. Don R. Gerlach, *Philip Schuyler and the War for Independence, 1775–1783* (Syracuse, NY, 1987), 486–91, suggests that at this time Schuyler very likely was not at his home.

40. Mann, *FR,* 145 (want of shoes); 155 (destitute of shoes); 156 (lost her toenails); 180 (feet crimsoned the snow).

CHAPTER 5: THE GENERAL'S WAITER

1. *New York Independent Journal,* Jan. 10, 1784; Mann, *FR,* chap. 9; DG, Diary, Nov. 11, 1802.

2. Mann, *FR,* 157, 236.

3. Mann, *FR*, 182; David Zabecki, "Decorations, Military," in Richard Blanco, ed., *The American Revolution: An Encyclopedia*, 2 vols. (New York, 1993), 1:449–50; Edward Boynton, comp., *General Orders of George Washington. Issued at Newburgh on the Hudson, 1782–1783*, ed. Alan Aimone (1883; Harrison, NY, 1973), April 27, 1783; Aug. 7, 1782, 8–9, 34–35; Charles Royster, *A Revolutionary People at War: The Continental Army and American Character, 1775–1783* (Chapel Hill, NC, 1979), 331–32.

4. Mann, *FR*, 181–83; Mann, "Heroine," 181.

5. Thomas Egleston, *The Life of John Paterson, Major General in the Revolutionary Army* (New York, 1898), Appendix, 408, lists his location month-by-month on the basis of the monthly returns. He is at New Windsor in November–December 1782 and January–February 1783, and then at Newburgh in March–June 1783. Therefore, Sampson may also have been with him at Newburgh, a few miles from the encampment, where a number of officers besides Washington were housed in private homes. For the move to West Point, Paterson to Henry Knox, Knox to Paterson, Knox to Washington, June 21, 22, 1783, in Egleston, *Paterson*, 294–95.

6. *OED*, s.v. "waiter": one historical meaning relevant to the army, since lost, is "a man (rarely a woman) whose office or privilege it is to attend upon a superior"; Royall Tyler, *The Contrast: A Comedy in Five Acts* (Philadelphia, 1790), act 2, scene 2; Kenneth Silverman, *A Cultural History of the American Revolution . . . 1763–1789* (New York, 1976), 558–63; Gordon Wood, *Radicalism of the American Revolution* (New York, 1991), 184–85.

7. Mann, *FR*, 247–48; Mann, "Heroine," 351–52 (Reverend Avery); for Phelan: Egleston, *Life of Paterson*, 289; for Haskell: *Mass. S&S* 7:434–35.

8. Charles Neimeyer to Alfred Young, Memorandum, September 1997.

9. Holly A. Mayer, *Belonging to the Army: Camp Followers and Community in the American Revolution* (Columbia, SC, 1996), 169–77; "Considerations and Proposals on the Impropriety of Employing Soldiers as Servants to the Officers," unsigned, Jan. 31, 1782, in United States Revolution MS, Box 4, Folder 1, AAS.

10. John Adams cited in Richard Brown, "Where Have All the Great Men Gone?" in Brown, ed., *Major Problems in the Era of the American Revolution* (Lexington, MA, 1992), 615; for Agrippa Hull: Sidney Kaplan, *The Black Presence in the American Revolution* (Washington, DC, 1975), 36–39, and plate 3 (portrait).

11. Egleston, *Life of Paterson*, passim, the source of most of our knowledge of Paterson; Edward E. Curtis, "John Paterson," *DAB*, 7:292–93 ("commanding presence"); Baron von Steuben, *Regulations for the Order and Discipline of the Troops of the United States* (Boston, 1794), 135. In his "Instructions for the Captain," Steuben writes, "His first object should be to gain the love of his men, by treating them with every possible kindness and humanity. . . ."

12. Chastellux and Paterson cited in Janet Dempsey, *Washington's Last Cantonment: "High Time for Peace"* (Monroe, NY, 1987), 71–72 and chaps. 4, 5.

13. Dempsey, *Last Cantonment*, chaps 4, 5 (conditions); GW, *Writings*, 26: Orders of the Day, Jan. 25, Feb. 10, 1783, 68, 111–12 (necessaries); John Shy to Alfred Young, comment on MS, 1995. Shy edited *Winding Down: The Revolutionary War Letters of Lieutenant Benjamin Gilbert of Massachusetts, 1780–1783* (Ann Arbor, MI, 1989).

14. Mann, *FR*, 181; Dempsey, *Last Cantonment*, chap. 6.

15. William Tarbell, "An Original View of the Encampment of the Massachusetts Soldiers During the Last Year of the Revolutionary War," a line drawing, n.d., WH.1971.400.R, New York State Office of Parks, Washington Headquarters State Historic Site, depicts three lines of huts for each regiment with separate houses for the regimental commander in front of them. In the drawing, Paterson, commander of a wing of the encampment, is not given a house; presumably it is set off still further from the enlisted men. This is a schematic rendering of the encampment copied from an original done at the time by a soldier in the Seventh Massachusetts.

16. Holly A. Mayer, "Soldierly Subordination: The Issue of Deference in the Continental Army," in Peter Karsten, ed., *The Military and Society,* vol. 2: *The Training and Socializing of Military Personnel* (New York, 1988), 293–307; for Edward Phelan as aide, Egleston, *Life of Paterson,* 289–90; *Mass. S&S* 12:279–80, 285, 289–90 lists him as in the cantonment from December 1782, and as an aide to Paterson May–August 1783; Mann, "Heroine," 355 (lame horse).

17. For the tone of life for officers in 1783: Heath, *Memoirs,* passim; Gilbert, "Diary," January 1783ff.; Shy, ed., *Winding Down,* 86–87, 98 (seraglio); Dempsey, *Last Cantonment,* chaps. 6, 7, 8.

18. Paul J. Sanborn, "Newburgh Conspiracy," in Blanco, ed., *Encyclopedia of the Revolution,* 1191–95; Richard H. Kohn, "The Inside History of the Newburgh Conspiracy: America and the Coup d'Etat," *WMQ* 27 (1970): 187–220; Skeen, "The Newburgh Conspiracy Reconsidered," *WMQ* 31 (1974): 273–90; Royster, *A Revolutionary People at War,* 333–41. No one has claimed that Paterson was a member of the cabal, but his name invariably is near the top of the signers of petitions.

19. Gilbert, "Diary," March 26–29, 1783; Joseph Plumb Martin, *Private Yankee Doodle: Being a Narrative of Some of the Adventures, Dangers and Sufferings of a Revolutionary War Soldier,* ed. George F. Scheer (Hallowell, ME, 1830; Boston, 1962), 278–79.

20. For the dispersal of the army, Dempsey, *Last Cantonment,* chaps. 10, 11; for troop strength, Charles Lesser, *The Sinews of Independence: Monthly Strength Reports of the Continental Army* (Chicago, 1976), 250, 254, 255; Gilbert, June 10, 1783, in Shy, ed., *Winding Down,* 107; Martin, *Private Yankee Doodle,* 279.

21. Mann, *FR,* 185–93.

22. DG, *Address,* 19.

23. For Binney's children, see below, note 34; Charles Brockden Brown, *Arthur Mervyn; or Memoirs of the Year 1793* (Philadelphia and New York, 1799–1800).

24. I am indebted to Konstantin Dierks for indefatigable research tracking the hospital, army medical history, Binney and his family. My thanks to Whitfield Bell of the American Philosophical Society for advice.

25. Andrew A. Zellers-Frederick, "Mutiny in Pennsylvania," in Blanco, ed., *Encyclopedia of the Revolution,* 1147–51; Kenneth R. Bowling, "New Light on the Philadelphia Mutiny of 1783: Federal-State Confrontation at the Close of the War for Independence," *Pennsylvania Magazine of History and Biography* 101 (1977): 419–50; Mary A. Y. Gallagher, "Reinterpreting the 'Very Trifling Mutiny' at Philadelphia in June 1783," *Pennsylvania Magazine of History and Biography* 119 (1995): 3–35; Charles P. Neimeyer, *America Goes to War: A Social History of the Continental Army* (New York, 1996), 155–58.

26. GW to Major General Robert Howe, June 25, July 4, 1783; GW to President of the Congress, June 24; GW to Howe, Aug. 13, 1783; all in GW, *Writings,* 27:32–35, 42–43, 100.

27. Knox to Paterson, June 25; Paterson to Knox, June 26; Knox to Paterson, June 26, 1783, in Egleston, *Life of Paterson,* 296–29; for Paterson's activities and location, June–Sept. 25, 1783, ibid., 298–99, 418; *Pennsylvania Gazette,* July 23, 1783 [CD-ROM edn]; Captain Nathaniel Cushing, Orderly Book, for sentence of the courts-martial by Captain Elinathan Haskell (at that point aide-de-camp to General Howe), Sept. 21, 1783 (Orderly Book No. 32, AAS).

28. Mann, *FR,* 185–87.

29. General Howe's Orders of the Day, July 6, 7, 8, 1783, are in Captain Nathaniel Cushing Orderly Book, June 21–Sept. 25, 1783, AAS. Elizabeth A. Fenn, *Pox Americana: The Great Smallpox Epidemic of 1775–82* (New York, 2001), chaps. 2, 3. Mann, in a previous passage (*FR,* 156–57), claims that Sampson avoided an army order for inoculation to escape detection. He places this at West Point early in 1782 on her return from Yorktown. The army carried out an inoculation of two thousand soldiers in January 1782, before Sampson arrived in May or June 1782. See Heath, *Memoirs,* 340–43, and Fenn, *Pox Americana,* 133.

30. In Philadelphia City Archives Record Group 35: "Guardians of the Poor. Treasurer's Accounts, 1766-1796," 2 vols., vol. 1780–1796, 35.1: Feb. 8, 1783, "By cash rec'd from . . . Robert Morris for Rent for the East end of the House which is occupied as an hospital. . . ." 337.10, and Dec. 23, 1783, a receipt for ten months rent, 375. (Robert Morris was U.S. Superintendent of Finances.) Alms House Managers, Minutes, 1766–1788, 3 vols., vol. 1780–1788 (35.3), also lists "Rent for the Eastern wing of the House . . . occupied as a Continental Hospital" for 1782–84. Richard Blanco, "American Army Hospitals in Pennsylvania During the Revolution," *Pennsylvania History* 48 (1981): 347–68 (for the Bettering House, 1776–77); Mary C. Gillett, *The Army Medical Department, 1775–1818* (Washington, DC, 1990), 127. My thanks to Ms. Gillett for clarifying army medical records.

31. James Thacher, *Military Journal of the American Revolution* (1823; Hartford, CT, 1862), 321, Sept. 10, 1782; Esther Forbes, *Paul Revere and the World He Lived In* (Boston, 1942), 12.

32. Louis C. Duncan, *Medical Men in the American Revolution* (Carlisle Barracks, PA, 1931), Appendix B, lists Binney as Hospital Surgeon from May 1776, and Hospital Physician and Surgeon from Oct. 6, 1780, to the end of the war; his portrait by Charles Willson Peale is in Society of the Cincinnati, Washington, DC; Mayer, *Belonging to the Army,* 195–96, 219–21 (status of physicians); for receipts: Numbered Record Books Concerning Military Operations and Service, as follows: Pay and Settlement of Accounts in the War Dept. Collection of Revolutionary War Records. Record Group 93 (M853), Reel 29, 148:50, 65, 72, 74, 80 has line items for Forage for Binney, 1783–84; Reel 34, 104: 88, 109, 134 has Quartermaster Receipts for Binney 1783–84, as does Reel 36 Military Stores Account Book and Commissary Ledger for these years.

33. *Pennsylvania Gazette,* Feb. 12, 1767 [CD-ROM edn]; Papers of the Continental Congress Microfilm, Reel 92:78:4, p. 61, "Return of the Officers &c in the Gen'l Hospital of the United States," July 23, 1781, lists "Barnabas Binney. Where stationed &c Philda. attended ye Sick in Jail &c" and "Mary Parker, Matron, Where stationed &C: Philadelphia." While this entry is for another hospital two years earlier, it establishes Mary Parker as a matron

associated with Binney. *McPherson's Directory of Philadelphia* (1785) lists five Widow Joneses and three Widow Parkers with no occupations; Edmund Hogan, *The Prospect of Philadelphia* (1795), 51, lists Rosanna Jones, widow, as "nurse for the sick."

34. Charles J. F. Binney, comp., *Genealogy of the Binney Family in the United States* (Albany, 1886), 246–49, 235 (origin of name); William A. Goddard, *Memoir of the Rev. James Manning, D.D., First President of Brown University* (Boston, 1839), 20–21. This memoir by a descendant is among the "Biographical Sketches of Early Graduates of Brown University." In 1785, Binney's sister, Avis, married Nicholas Brown, after whom Brown University was named. My thanks to Martha L. Mitchill, University Archivist, and Joyce M. Botelho of the John Nicholas Brown Center for searching for Binney material at Brown University.

35. Binney, *Genealogy*, 247.

36. Calvin Munn, letter to the editor, *New York Evening Post*, June 30, 1827.

37. Mann, *FR*, chaps. 9–11.

38. Mann, "Heroine," 375ff. Jane Keiter, author of the series of four articles about Deborah Sampson in Westchester County (cited in chapter 4), writes me: "I believe that Miss P existed and that I know her identity. I do not have any hard proof since neither Deborah nor Miss P left any primary source evidence that I know of. I trust Mann more than you do. I took all the clues that he gave in his ms. [the 1830s revised MS in DHS] and matched them to a girl (and I think that there is only one possible match). Mann claims that Deborah met Miss P in Annapolis on the way to Yorktown so you are going to have trouble with this in any case. It makes sense as the army spent four days there and jibes with the rest of the story which is complex. A document that I have is the will of a relative whose gift of money Miss P was to receive 'at the age of twenty one years or at the day of marriage which shall first happen.' Mann says Miss P 'was heiress to an ample fortune, a legacy from a rich relation, which she was to possess on her marriage—.' Since most everything about Miss P checks out, I tend to believe that Mann got this information from Deborah who got it from Miss P"—Jane Keiter to Alfred Young, Aug. 17, 2001. Keiter anticipates my skepticism. In general, I have less confidence in Mann's 1830s MS than in his published text, and I find no convincing evidence that Sampson enlisted in 1781 or was at Yorktown.

39. Samuel Willard Crompton, "Deborah Sampson," *American National Biography*, 24 vols. (New York, 1999), 19:230–31, accepts the claim in Elizabeth Evans, *Weathering the Storm: Women and the American Revolution* (New York, 1975), 312, that in 1783 Sampson "joined a contingent of Eleventh Massachusetts Regiment soldiers on a land surveying expedition towards the Ohio River." The Eleventh with Colonel Benjamin Tupper, however, was disbanded Jan. 1, 1781, at West Point (see Wright, *The Continental Army*, 212). Colonel Tupper, who commanded the Eleventh until Jan. 1, 1781, was transferred to the Sixth Massachusetts until June 12, 1783 (see Heitman, *Historical Register of Officers*, 559; Benjamin Tupper, *Mass. S&S*, 16:144–45; "Benjamin Tupper," *DAB* 10:52–53). None of Tupper's activities in the west can be dated to 1783; see Archer B. Hulbert, ed., *Records of the Original Proceedings of the Ohio Company*, 2 vols. (Marietta, OH, 1917). I think Tupper was another name Mann got from DG, which he threw in for verisimilitude. Neither Crompton nor Evans cite a source for the claim about DG and Tupper.

40. I tried to locate the sites Mann mentioned in one sentence in his 1797 account: "The

travelers] hired one of the tribe to pilot them over the Allegany. Passing the Jumetta Creek and the Fork of the Pennsylvania and Glade Roads, about 40 miles from the Jumetta, they came to the foot of the Dry Ridge. . . . They visited a tribe near a place called Medskar" (202–03). William Skull, "A Map of Pennsylvania . . ." (London, 1775), Newberry Library, the map closest in time to an expedition allegedly in 1783, shows an unnamed east-west road in western Pennsylvania north of a branch of the Potomac River which passes the branches of the Juniata River, Allegheny Ridge, and Laurel Hill Ridge (sometimes known as Dry Ridge), and also passes Long Glade and Great Glade. Thus, while Mann's geography is confusing and his spelling off, he did not invent the places he named. (There is no Medskar on the map.) Where he got the names of these places is a puzzle. Mann, in the 1830s in "Heroine," chap. 26, offers more description and expands his coverage of the journey, but is no clearer as to the geography. My thanks to Robert W. Karrow, Curator of Special Collections, Newberry Library, for helping me to locate and analyze maps of Pennsylvania.

41. June Namias, *White Captives: Gender and Ethnicity on the American Frontier* (Chapel Hill, NC, 1993), 94–95, for the Abraham Panther work, which had twenty-four printings from 1787 to 1812.

42. Elizabeth Ellet, *Women of the American Revolution*, 3 vols. (New York, 1848–50), 2:131; Carroll Smith-Rosenberg, "The Female World of Love and Ritual: Relations Between Women in Nineteenth-Century America," *Signs* 1 (1975): 18; Nancy Cott, *The Bonds of Womanhood: "Woman's Sphere" in New England, 1780–1835* (New Haven, CT, 1977), chap. 5; Lucia Bergamasco, "Friendship, Love and Spirituality in New England in the Eighteenth Century: The Experience of Esther Burr and Sarah Prince," *Annales, ESC* 41, no. 2 (1986): 295–323.

43. Tyler, *The Contrast*, 12 (act 1, scene 2): Julie Wheelwright, *Amazons and Military Maids: Women Who Dressed as Men in Pursuit of Life, Liberty and Happiness* (London, 1989), 53–54.

44. Charles Brockden Brown, *Ormond; or The Secret Witness* (Philadelphia, 1799), chap. 25; for the distinctions being drawn in England, Tim Hitchcock, *English Sexualities, 1700–1800* (New York, 1997), chap. 6; Emma Donoghue, *Passions Between Women: British Lesbian Culture, 1668–1801* (London, 1993), chap. 4; Terry Castle, *The Apparitional Lesbian: Female Homosexuality and Modern Culture* (New York, 1993), intro., chap. 5; Randolph Trumbach, "London's Sapphists: From Three Sexes to Four Genders in the Making of Modern Culture," in Julia Epstein and Kristina Straub, eds., *Body Guards: The Cultural Politics of Gender Ambiguity* (New York, 1991), 112–41.

45. Mann, *FR,* chaps. 9–12; Mann "Heroine," chaps. 25–27. In the 1830s MS, when Robert Shurtliff returns to "the amiable Miss P.," he vows "to throw off the veil of my own sex." In Mann's language, writing as if he were Sampson, "I am a female," he exclaims, and after doing so, "I voluntarily half hid my face in the robe that covered her snowy bosom. Scarcely was the last fairly articulated, when she sallied and would have dropped upon the floor, had she not been partly enclosed in my arms. A paleness like the hue of death was upon her when I rested her upon the sofa." Miss P. is overcome. "A Female. O sir do not cajole, do not play upon me by words." At which point, Mann writes, "I then cast off my coat and vest, and unlacing a silk bandage about my breast, I flung open my bosom, as I did my conscience, to ►er astonished view and contemplation. She thrust her soft hands into my bosom for a con-

firmation of the naked truth and to ascertain whether I had a pulsation there like her own. My God! She exclaimed, at the same time holding me to an embrace that shot a thrill of extasy [*sic*] through every fibre of my body and sense of soul." Miss P. now responds: "My dear and doubly interesting Sister . . . or how shall I address you? I can hardly decide on which costume I would again have you arrayed." The erotic exchange intensifies. Miss P. asks her to stay and, Deborah, in Mann's narration, tells us, "I am not ashamed to acknowledge that I remained two or three days companion to this lady, both in her parlour and bedroom, without the formality of the marriage rites—the first female embrace into which I had naturally fallen for three years. And could my desires have controlled my destiny, I should have spun out the remaining thread of my life in the sweet, inspiring atmosphere of this eden-abode." I read this scene as explicitly sexual.

For changing American tastes in erotic literature, see Helen Lefkowitz Horowitz, *Rereading Sex: Battles over Sexual Knowledge and Suppression in Nineteenth-Century America* (New York, 2003), chap. 2; David S. Reynolds, *Beneath the American Renaissance: The Subversive Imagination in the Age of Emerson and Melville* (New York, 1988), 213–15; and Timothy J. Gilfoyle, *City of Eros: New York City, Prostitution, and the Commercialization of Sex, 1790–1920* (New York, 1992), chaps. 6, 7. For Herman Mann's involvement with "Fanny Hill," the English pornographic classic, Richard J. Wolfe, *Marbled Paper: Its History, Techniques and Patterns* (Philadelphia, 1990), 90–98. My thanks to James Green of the Library Company of Philadelphia for bringing this to my attention.

46. Resolve of the General Court on the Petition of Deborah Gannett, Mass. Laws (1791–92), chap. 23, Jan. 20, 1792, and MS version, MA, which accepted Oct. 23, 1783, as the date of discharge; Henry Jackson, Certificate, Aug. 1, 1786, reprinted in Vinton, intro. to Mann, *FR*, xxv; DG, Petition, Sept. 14, 1818, NA ("served until November 1783").

47. Wright, *The Continental Army*, 206.

48. Ellet, *Women of the American Revolution*, 2:133–34. My thanks to Philander D. Chase, senior associate editor of the Papers of George Washington, and to Robert Haggard, for searching their files in 1997, without finding any sign of Washington having contact with Sampson Gannett at any time. Paul Uek searched the Henry Knox Papers, MHS, finding no evidence of any comment about Sampson by Knox.

49. Mann, *FR*, 217–19.

50. [Juror's Report], Massachusetts Superior Court judicature, Boston, August 1777, reprinted in The History Project, *Improper Bostonians* (Boston, 1998), 30, gives John Paterson as colonel of the regiment in which Ann Bailey practiced her deception. This has to be the same John Paterson, although there is some question as to when his promotion from colonel to general became effective. "Sam Gay" is listed in *Mass. S&S*, 6:340 as having been in Brigadier General Paterson's regiment. In 1777, there is only one John Paterson in *Mass. S&S*, vol. 11, with the rank of colonel who was promoted the same year to be a general; see Egleston, *Life of Paterson*, 416–17. See Patrick J. Leonard, "Ann Bailey: Mystery Woma· Warrior of 1777," *Minerva* 11 (1993): 1–4.

51. GW, *Writings*, 26: General Orders, Feb. 8, March 5, March 13, 1783, pp. 109–10, 191, 200 General Paterson at the courts-martial, Captain Nathaniel Cushing, Orderly Book N AAS; on army punishments: Neimeyer, *America Goes to War*, chap. 7; John Shy, *A*

Numerous and Armed: Reflections on the Military Struggle for American Independence (rev. edn, Ann Arbor, MI, 1990), 25–26.

52. Mayer, *Belonging to the Army,* chap. 7, esp. 246–47; [Walker], *The Female Soldier,* 8–10.
53. Flucker cited in Royster, *A Revolutionary People at War,* 367.
54. Sproat, "Old Folks Traditions," in M. M. Copland, "Deborah Sampson," *Boston Evening Traveller,* Jan. 19, 1889; Julie Wheelwright, *Amazons and Military Maids: Women Who Dressed as Men in the Pursuit of Life, Liberty and Happiness* (London, 1989), 66–67.
55. Sproat, "Old Folks Traditions."
56. Elizabeth D. Leonard, *All the Daring of the Soldier: Women of the Civil War Armies* (New York, 1999), 186–87 (the middle sentence in quotation marks is Leonard's paraphrase of the soldier, Robert Horan).
57. For numbers: John Rees, " 'The Multitude of Women': An Examination of the Numbers of Female Camp Followers with the Continental Army," *Minerva* 14 (1996): 1–47, esp. 27–30.
58. Mayer, *Belonging to the Army,* chap. 3.
59. Washington (1776) and Adams (1777), cited in Mayer, *Belonging to the Army,* 61; Dempsey, *Last Cantonment,* 87–88, 116.
60. Royster, *A Revolutionary People at War,* 248–50; David W. Conroy, *In Public Houses: Drink and the Revolution of Authority in Colonial Massachusetts* (Chapel Hill, NC, 1995); Peter Thompson, *Rum Punch and Revolution: Taverngoing and Public Life in Eighteenth Century Philadelphia* (Philadelphia, 2001); Gregory Knouff, "The Common People's Revolution: Class, Race, Masculinity, and Locale in Pennsylvania, 1775–1783," (Ph.D. diss., Rutgers Univ., 1996), chap. 2.
61. Quotations in Royster, *A Revolutionary People at War,* 76–77.
62. Julie Wheelwright, *Amazons and Military Maids,* 56–57 (Snell); Edward Boynton, comp., *General Orders of George Washington. Issued at Newburgh on the Hudson, 1782–1783,* ed. Alan Aimone (1883; Harrison, NY, 1973), Appendix, 98 (Corbin); Linda Grant De Pauw, *Battle Cries and Lullabies: Women in War from Prehistory to the Present* (Norman, OK, 1998), 128–31 (McCauley).
63. Mayer, *Belonging to the Army,* 110–13 (prostitution); James Neagles, *Summer Soldiers: A Survey and Index of Revolutionary War Courts-Martial* (Salt Lake City, 1986).
64. Martin, *Private Yankee Doodle,* 280.
65. Descriptive List of Deserters, Fourth Massachusetts Regiment, Aug. 29, 1782, M 246, Jacket No. 6 (Call no. 324, Roll 36), NA; Heath, *Memoirs,* May 6, 15, 1782, 345–46; GW to Congress, June 24, 1783, in GW, *Writings,* 28:32–35; Martin, *Private Yankee Doodle,* 280.
66. Mann, *FR,* 156.

PART THREE · "THE CELEBRATED MRS. GANNETT"
CHAPTER 6: A GANNETT IN SHARON

. Dedham *Village Register,* May 3, 1827.
Mann, *FR,* 224–32; Vinton, ibid., 225n.
Zilpah Tolman to Eugene Tappan, Jan. 29, 1902, in Tappan, "Deborah Sampson Din-

ner . . . Sharon, April 3, 1902," MS, SPL, 75. DG lived first with her aunt and uncle in Stoughton, the town bordering Sharon, but she became a resident of Sharon when she married Benjamin Gannett, Jr. Stoughton, incorporated in 1726, originally included what was later Sharon and Canton. In 1740, a separate precinct was created, which in 1765 was incorporated as a district, and in 1775 became a legal town named Stoughtonham. On Feb. 25, 1783, Stoughtonham changed its name to Sharon. See D. Hamilton Hurd, *History of Norfolk County, Massachusetts*, 2 vols. (Philadelphia, 1884), 1:257–64.

4. Mann, *FR,* 160–64, 208.

5. Ibid., 225–32, 216 (chapter outline); Ephraim Sampson, Pension Mass. W 11053, NA.

6. Mann, "Catalogue of the Principal Works . . . of Herman Mann . . . 1827," MS, DHS. Mann writes: "I removed [from Walpole] to Dedham in June 1797 for the purpose of correcting the press to which it was [word unclear] when but little more than a sheet of ms was finished."

7. *OED,* s.v. "friend" and "correspondence"; Mann, *FR,* 225n (Vinton).

8. Mann, *FR,* 253–60.

9. For the original full version, see [Anon.], *History of Constantius and Pulchera, or Constancy Rewarded: The First American Novel* (1789–90, Boston, 1794). Pulchera also cross-dresses as a soldier named Valorus and ends up in France. See Cathy N. Davidson, *Revolution and the Word: The Rise of the Novel in America* (New York, 1986), 182–85.

10. Mann, *FR,* 242–44.

11. Frederick Endicott, ed., *The Records of Births, Marriages and Deaths and Intentions to Marriage in the Town of Stoughton from 1727 to 1800 and in the Town of Canton from 1797 to 1845* (Canton, MA, 1896), 149, 156; Thomas Baldwin, comp., *Vital Records of Sharon, Massachusetts to the Year 1850* (Boston, 1909), 28, lists under births for Gannett, "Mary, Dec. 17, 1788. G.R." without the customary names of a father and mother. "G.R." stands for "gravestone record" and is used elsewhere in the vital records to indicate a child who died as an infant. So this might possibly have been a child born to Deborah and Benjamin Junior after Polly, Dec. 19, 1787, and before Patience, Nov. 25, 1790. More likely, however, judging by the birth intervals, it might have been a child born to Joseph (Benjamin's brother) and Abagail [*sic*] Gannett, between the birth of their son Bradish, Nov. 17, 1785, and their daughter Huldah, May 16, 1790. My thanks to David B. Ingram for calling my attention to this record.

12. Daniel Scott Smith, "Population, Family and Society in Hingham, Massachusetts, 1635–1880" (Ph.D. diss., Univ. of California, Berkeley, 1973), 289–90. In Hingham, between 1761 and 1780, only 23 of 125 couples had an interval of more than six months between notice of intention to marry and marriage. I am indebted to Dan Smith for discussions of this and related demographic issues.

13. [Robert Walker], *The Female Soldier* (London, 1750), 39. Mann, *FR,* 250.

14. Louisa May Alcott, cited in Elaine Showalter, intro. to Alcott, *Little Women* (1868; New York, 1989), xiii, xix, xxvi. For overviews, see Virginia Chambers-Schiller, *Liberty a Bet Husband: Single Women in America: The Generations of 1780–1840* (New Haven, CT, 19 intro. and chap. 1; Susan K. Lanser, "Singular Politics: The Rise of the British Natio the Production of the Old Maid," in Judith M. Bennett and Amy Froide, eds., *Singl in the European Past, 1250–1800* (Philadelphia, 1999), 297–323.

15. Mann, preface to DG, *Address.*

16. Paul Revere to William Eustis, Feb. 20, 1804, Revere MS, MHS. For Benjamin Gannett's later life, see chapter 9 below.

17. For overviews, Richard Godbeer, *Sexual Revolution in Early America* (Baltimore, 2002), 227–33; Daniel S. Smith and Michael Hindus, "Premarital Pregnancy in America, 1640–1971: An Overview and an Interpretation," *Journal of Interdisciplinary History* 5 (1975): 537–70; for an example of a town in a comparable time period, Laurel Thatcher Ulrich, *A Midwife's Tale: The Life of Martha Ballard Based on Her Diary, 1785–1812* (New York, 1990), 155–56. Forty of 106 babies delivered by Martha Ballard were conceived out of wedlock—"The average interval between marriage and delivery was 5.6 months."

18. See "Report No. 172 on Benjamin Gannett to accompany bill H.R. No. 890," Jan. 31, 1837, by The Committee on Revolutionary Pensions, and Report to accompany H.R. 184, Dec. 22, 1837, Twenty-fifth Congress, 2nd sess. The report opened: "That the petitioner represents that he is the surviving husband of Deborah Gannett, to whom he was lawfully married on the 7th day of April, 1784." The family continued to use the 1784 date. In 1905, Eugene Tappan, secretary of the Sharon Historical Society (SHS), who was close to the family, published 1784 as the date and then received a letter from George Wentworth, Town Clerk of Stoughton, April 20, 1905, providing the correct date, followed by a "Certificate of Marriage" he issued April 22, 1905, attesting to April 7, 1785, as the date (copies, Sampson Documents, SPL). Tappan then printed an "erratum" slip correcting the date, which he inserted in SHS *Publications* (1905), vol. 2.

19. Mann added nothing to this interlude in his 1830s version—see Mann, "Heroine," 424. Neither did his son, Herman Mann, Jr., who revised his father's manuscript.

20. *Descendants,* 87 (Earl's children); Ann Gilbert to Alfred Young, Sept. 24, 1994 (line of descent). I saw the dress at Beatrice Bostock's home in Truro, Cape Cod, in the summer of 1994, and commissioned a report by Nancy Rexford of Danvers, Massachusetts, a costume historian. Beatrice Helen Weeks Bostock (1904–1995) was the daughter of Helen Louise Weeks, daughter of Edward Monk, who was the son of Mary Gannett Monk, daughter of Earl Gannett, our Deborah's son. The transmission of the dress is further strengthened by the fact that Mrs. Bostock also inherited a cup plate whose authenticity can be established (see chapter 9), a copy of Mann's 1797 book, and a copy of an almanac for 1776 interlineated with diary entries. Beatrice Bostock died in 1995, Ann Gilbert in 2000. The dress was given to the Society for the Preservation of New England Antiquities, Boston.

21. Nancy E. Rexford, Memorandum, July 11, 1995, and letters to Alfred Young, 1994–95. Rexford, former Curator of Costume at the Northampton Historical Society, is the author of *Women's Clothing in America, 1795–1930,* a work in progress, the first volume of which is *Women's Shoes in America, 1775–1930* (Kent, OH, 2000). She is illustrator for Meredith Wright, *Thy Beautiful Garment: Rural New England Clothing, 1783–1800* (East Montpelier, VT, 1990), republished as *Everyday Dress in Rural America, 1783–1800* (New York, 1992).

 ̄ndicott, *Records of Births, Marriages and Deaths,* 149, 156. Crossman, a physician, was the ̄n clerk for many years. See Daniel T. V. Huntoon, *History of the Town of Canton* (Cam- ̄ɡe, MA, 1893), 566–67.

23. Bettye Hobbs Pruitt, comp., *The Massachusetts Tax Valuation List of 1771* (Boston, 1978), "Stoughtonham," 542.

24. Jeremiah Gould, "Annals of Sharon, Massachusetts, 1830," in SHS *Publications* (1904): 3–21. The essay was "originally delivered" in 1831. Gould was at times a Sharon selectman; *Mass. S&S,* 6: 250–51.

25. *Descendants,* 46–50; Sharon Town Records, Book 1, 1753–1807, Photocopy, SPL, 110–237 passim, for appointments for Benjamin Senior, Benjamin Junior, and Joseph (1780–1797). In 1778, Gannett, Sr., was a member of the Committee of Safety that raised bounties for men drafted from the militia to reinforce the Continental Army (see "We the Subscribers," Stoughtonham, June 30, 1778, MS, SHS Records, SPL). David B. Ingram of Foxborough established the author of the diary as Colonel Richard Gridley, chief engineer of the Continental Army, a partner of Edmund Quincy, Jr., of Sharon who married Hannah Gannett, sister of Benjamin Gannett, Jr. (which accounts for the diary being in the Gannett family). Ingram, "Notes re Benjamin Gannett, c. 1728–1813," Dec. 30, 1975, and March 3, 1996, and letters to Alfred Young, 1996. My thanks to David B. Ingram for sharing this research.

26. Deed, "Benjamin Ganett to my son Benjamin Ganett . . . having arrived at the age of twenty one . . ." The grant within the deed is Sept. 3, 1781; the date of registry, June 8, 1785, Suffolk County Registry of Deeds. For the taxes: "A List of the Valuation or Single Rate, also the Ministerial and Town Rate," 1778–83 [Stoughtonham], 1783–1838 [Sharon], transcriptions Sharon Town Hall. I am indebted to Paul Uek, who tracked down real estate and tax records. Uek photocopied the pages listing the Gannetts for each year and photocopied the entire town tax list at five-year intervals. In the early 1900s, Eugene Tappan copied the Sharon entries for the Federal Tax of 1798, in SHS Scrapbook 1: 73ff., SPL.

27. Tax records cited above for 1785, 1795, and 1805.

28. William R. Mann, "Recollections, 1831 to 1850," SHS Scrapbook 1:46, SPL; Eugene Tappan, intro. to DG, Diary, 7 (copies SHS, DHS), reprints the entry about the labor exchange, writing: "the pages in different parts of the book left unfilled by the diary, were utilized for the record of charges for farm work." Given the date of the entry, June 1802, a month before DG left on her tour, it was the other way around. DG took the account book used by her husband for her tour diary. A receipt to Joseph Gannett from Paul Revere, Sept. 23, 1803, for charcoal, is mentioned in Moody, *DS,* 26, as being "still in Sharon" (1975), possibly SPL.

29. Mann, *FR,* 250; Paul Revere to William Eustis, Feb. 20, 1804, Revere MS, MHS, reprinted in Esther Forbes, *Paul Revere and the World He Lived In* (Boston, 1942), 433.

30. Rodney Monk, "Extract from Talk with Grandmother [Rhoda] Monk, Nov. 3, 1901," MS, kindly provided by Mrs. Roger Myrick, Rodney Monk's daughter, Temple, New Hampshire, with other notes by Monk. Monk (1883–1975), a farmer of Groton, Massachusett occasionally returned to the house and farm on East Street, where he visited with Arguimbaus, the present owners. He wrote several letters to Pauline Moody, author c biography of DG (1975), and to Daniel Arguimbau about Deborah and life in Sharon deposited copies of these "Monk Papers" with SPL. His daughter is writing his bio

31. Monk, "Grandmother Monk"; *Descendants,* 66–69.

32. *Descendants,* 87, 113; for the third Benjamin Gannett, *Biographical Review . . . Norfolk County, Massachusetts* (Boston, 1898).

33. DG, Diary, May 28, Sept. 8, Nov. 11, 1802, facsimile of MS, SPL.

34. The editions of Robert Cushman, *The Sin and Danger of Self Love . . . 1621* (Nathan Coverly, Plymouth, 1785) are discussed in Henry W. Cushman, "Robert Cushman's Sermon, Delivered in 1621," *New England Historic and Genealogical Register* (1861), 169–72. Henry Wyles Cushman, a descendant of Robert and an avid antiquarian, examined eleven editions of the original sermon. He wrote: "the copy of Coverly's edition, now before me, has the autograph of 'Deborah Sampson, her book, 1785,' in two places written on it." I regret that I have not been able to locate this particular copy, either in the extensive Henry Wyles Cushman Collection, New England Historic Genealogical Society, or in any of eight research libraries listed in Evans as holding copies of this 1785 edition.

　　While Cushman thought that it probably belonged to "the famous Deborah Sampson," he was also aware that her sister, Sylvia, had married Jacob Cushman of Plymouth and thought that the copy he held might have been owned by that branch of the family. It is not likely that this copy belonged to our Deborah's mother, who still lived in Plympton; she probably would have signed it "Deborah Bradford Samson." Our Deborah was married April 7, 1785, and thus would have had to acquire the pamphlet before then to sign it with her maiden name. If a copy of this particular copy can be located, it would be possible to compare the signature to autographs we have of Robert Shurtliff on the bounty receipt and Deborah Gannett on her pension receipt. In John Adams Vinton, *Genealogical Memoirs of the Sampson Family in America . . .* (Boston, 1864), I count six women named Deborah Sampson born between 1747 and 1773 (listed on 19, 26, 30, 32, 37).

35. For Patience Payson: *Vital Records of Sharon,* 50 (her birth, adoption, death, burial); for her adoption by Gannett, Sr., Rodney Monk to Pauline Moody, August 1970, Moody MS, SPL; *Descendants,* 87 (names); for the use of terms, Charles Janson, *The Stranger in America* (1807), cited in Faye Dudden, *Serving Women: Household Service in Nineteenth-Century America* (Middletown, CT, 1983), 73, 1–11; see also H. L. Mencken, *The American Language,* one-vol. abridged, ed. Raven I. McDavid, Jr. (New York, 1967), 347.

36. Mann, *FR,* 250 (school), 99n (weaving).

37. John Hayward, *Gazetteer of Norfolk County* (Boston, 1849), 267; "A Map of the Town of Sharon according to an actual survey made in the year 1794 & 1795," MA, Maps and Plans, 1794 series, vol. 7, p. 4, no. 1224, reprinted in *Sharon, Massachusetts: A History* (Sharon, MA, 1976), 340–41, with a list of the families on the map.

38. The 1794–95 map cited above for the sites; Eugene Tappan, "Sharon Landowners in 1798," Aug. 12, 1904, SHS Scrapbook 1:73–84.

39. Gould, "Annals," 3 (mileage), 5 (post office); Hayward, *Gazetteer,* says Sharon was seventeen miles from Boston and nine from Dedham; for Dedham, see Stephen Davis, "From Plowshares to Spindles: Dedham, Massachusetts, 1790–1840" (Ph.D. diss., Univ. of Wisconsin, 73), chap. 1.

　　the trends: Gould, "Annals," passim; David B. Ingram, "Notes Pertaining to Benjamin ett from Sharon Town Records, 1765–1780," Dec. 30, 1995. Paul Uek tracked the Gan-
the Town Records.

41. Mann, preface to DG, *Address,* n.p.
42. See the entries for Susanna Baker and Oliver Shephard in Thomas W. Baldwin, comp., *Vital Records of Sharon, Massachusetts to the Year 1850* (Boston, 1909). The entries for 1796–97 in "The Church Records of Rev. Philip Curtis of Sharon, 1742–1797," ed. John G. Phillips, in *SHS Publications* (1908) 5, show that Curtis neither married the parents nor baptized the child.
43. For patterns in fertility, see Susan E. Klepp, "Revolutionary Bodies: Women and the Fertility Transition in the Mid-Atlantic Region, 1760–1820," *Journal of American History* 85 (1998): 910–45; Maris Vinovskis, *Fertility in Massachusetts from the Revolution to the Civil War* (New York, 1981), esp. 14, 23; for one town, Nancy Osterud and John Fulton, "Family Limitation and Age of Marriage: Fertility Decline in Sturbridge, Massachusetts, 1730–1850," *Population Studies* 30 (1977): 481–94.
44. Certificate, Henry Jackson, Aug. 1, 1786, MS, MA, reprinted in Mann, *FR,* Appendix, 248. In Mann's original 1797 edition, the date on Jackson's certificate was misprinted as 1797; in the Boston Public Library copy, someone has penciled in a correction; Vinton also corrected the date in 1866. Certificate, Eliphalet Thorp, Dec. 10, 1791, MA, attests to the date of enlistment.
45. Memorial of Deborah Gannett, Jan. 11, 1792, MA, reprinted in Vinton, intro. to Mann, *FR,* xxiii–xxiv. Africa Hamlin signed receipts in Colonel William Shepard's Regiment, Shepard Papers, LC, and Africa Hamlin is identified as a paymaster in Pension Application 3648 Maine, NA. *Mass. S&S,* 163–64, spells the name Hamlen. A pension application by America Hamlin, Maine 18242, NA, suggests the Hamlins may have been brothers (and that their father had a sense of the continents).
46. *Resolves Massachusetts Legislature,* 1791, January sess., chap. 23. Resolve on the Petition of Deborah Gannett, House of Representatives, Commonwealth of Massachusetts, Jan. 19, 1792, MS, MA. Sometime between the 1860s, when John Adams Vinton copied DG's petition from the original in MA, and the 1970s, the petition disappeared from the legislative docket for the resolution of 1792. The docket still contains Captain Thorp's 1791 attestation for mustering DG in 1782 and the MS copy of the resolution adopted and published by the legislature.

   Julia Ward Stickley, an archivist at the National Archives who was convinced that DS enlisted in 1781, asserted that the MS resolution with the 1782 date "appears to have been altered." I have examined an enlarged copy of this MS and asked J. Michael Comeau of MA to examine it. "It is difficult," Comeau writes, "even looking at the original, to determine if the date was 'doctored' in any way; at the very least the ink is blotted." In my opinion, one has to want to believe such an action to reach such a conclusion. Moreover, the printed resolution (with the 1782) could only have been taken from the handwritten version of the resolution, which in turn was based on the petition.

   The Gannett family perpetuated the 1781 date. My guess is that a family member friend, sometime around 1900, when DG was being rediscovered, took the original p from MA and may have attempted to alter the MS version of the resolve, but gave u Ward Stickley, "The Records of Deborah Sampson Gannett, Woman Soldier of th tion," *Prologue, the Journal of the National Archives* 4 (1972): 233–42; Stickle

Papers on DG, MS Box, MA; Leo Flaherty to Stickley, Sept 22, 1975, photocopy, Stickley Papers, MA; J. Michael Comeau, letter to Alfred Young, October 10, 2001.

47. "Female Heroism," [Worcester] *Massachusetts Spy,* Jan. 26, 1792.

48. Herman Mann, "Catalogue of the Principal Works, published and unpublished, of Herman Mann," [1827], Preface, Mann Papers, DHS; *Columbian Minerva, Dec.* 6, 1796, May 9, Sept. 26, 1797. The printers were Nathaniel and Benjamin Heaton, both subsequently bought out by Mann.

49. Mann, preface to "Heroine," MS, and Mann, "Catalogue," MS, Mann Papers, DHS. "Prospectus of a New Work to be Published by Subscription, The Heroine: or Memoirs of Miss Deborah Sampson . . . ," broadside, Dedham, August 1, 1829, DHS copy.

50. For perceptive studies of Mann by a scholar of literature, see Judith Hiltner, " 'She Bled in Secret': Deborah Sampson, Herman Mann and *The Female Review,*" *Early American Literature* 34 (1999): 190–220, and Hiltner, " 'Like a Bewildered Star': Deborah Sampson, Herman Mann and *Address Delivered with Applause,*" *Rhetoric Society Quarterly* 29 (1999): 5–24. Hiltner has suggested to me that Mann had an affiliation of some sort with Rhode Island College, a Baptist institution, which could have been referred to then as a seminary. She points out that thirty-five subscribers to *FR* identified themselves not by town but as "R.I. College," which could only mean they were students. However, Hiltner found no record of Mann as a student in Brown University Archives; perhaps he studied with a teacher there; later he lived in Providence. For his career, see Richard J. Wolfe, *The Role of the Mann Family of Dedham, Massachusetts in the Marbling of Paper in Nineteenth-Century America and in the Printing of Music, the Making of Cards, and other Booktrade Activities* (Quincy, MA, 1981).

51. Robert B. Hanson, *Dedham, Massachusetts, 1635–1890* (Dedham, MA, 1976), 172–74 (politics); Hannah Adams, *A Summary History of New England* (Dedham, MA, 1799); AAS computer printout of Dedham imprints in AAS provided by Judith Hiltner; *Columbian Minerva,* Aug. 10, 1802, has "Books for Sale or Circulation by H. Mann."

52. Ann Maria Pickford, "Dedham Branch of the Mann Family," *Dedham Historical Register* 7 (1896): 32–33, 60–63; Herman Mann, Jr., *Historical Annals of Dedham* (Dedham, MA, 1847), 75–77, gives a history of the Mann family newspapers.

53. For Revolutionary War memoirs: Michael Kammen, *A Season of Youth: The American Revolution and the Historical Imagination* (New York, 1978), chaps. 1 and 2, and Sarah J. Purcell, *Sealed with Blood: National Identity and Public Memory of the Revolutionary War, 1775–1825* (Philadelphia, 2002); for early American plebeian autobiographies: Mechal Sobel, *Teach Me Dreams: The Search for Self in the Revolutionary Era* (Princeton, NJ, 2000), and Ann Fabian, *The Unvarnished Truth: Personal Narratives in Nineteenth-Century America* (Berkeley, CA, 2000), intro. and chaps. 1 and 2; for the absence of women's historical narratives: Nina Baym, *American Women Writers and the Work of History, 1790–1860* (New Brunswick, NJ, 1995); for religious narratives: Catherine A. Brekus, *Strangers and Pilgrims: ᵣmale Preaching in America, 1740–1845* (Chapel Hill, NC, 1998); Rebecca Larson, *Daugh- of Light: Quaker Women Preaching and Prophesying in the Colonies and Abroad, ᵣ1775* (Chapel Hill, NC, 1999); and Carla Gerona, "Stairways to Heaven: A Cultural

History of Early American Quaker Dreams" (Ph.D. diss., Johns Hopkins Univ., 1998), chap. 5; for captivity narratives: Christopher Castiglia, *Bound and Determined: Captivity, Culture-Crossing, and White Womanhood from Mary Rowlandson to Patty Hearst* (Chicago, 1996).

54. Joseph Stone, portrait of Deborah Sampson, oil on paper, 14½ by 10½ inches, Rhode Island Historical Society. Linda Eppich, Chief Curator, RIHS, informs me that the painting was acquired in 1900 as a gift from Jesse Metcalf, publisher of the *Providence Journal* and an art collector. Its provenance is otherwise unknown; my guess is that it was passed down in Herman Mann's family and came to light about 1900, a time when DG's reputation was being revived. For Stone: Arthur B. and Sybil B. Kern, "Joseph Stone and Warren Nixon of Framingham, Massachusetts," *Antiques* 124 (September 1983): 514–18. Very little is known about Stone, who is not entered in any of the standard directories of American artists. For the engraving: William Beastall is credited with the portrait on the engraving by George H. Graham. Both names appear faintly on the frontispiece in Mann, *FR*. New-York Historical Society, *Dictionary of Artisans in America, 1564–1860* (New Haven, CT, 1957), identifies Beastall as a painter of miniatures who advertised in Portsmouth, New Hampshire, 1795, and Graham as an engraver in Philadelphia who moved to Boston c. 1796, where he was living in 1798. The copperplate for the engraving is in DHS. I am indebted to Georgia Barnhill, AAS, for examining portrait, engraving, and copperplate; to Linda Eppich of the RIHS for the provenance; and to Paul Uek for tracking the image and the artisans.

55. Nancy Rexford, "1797 Deborah Sampson Portrait Dress," Memorandum, Nov. 12, 1994, prepared for Alfred Young.

56. See Edward Savage, *Liberty as Goddess of Youth*, 1796 engraving, LC, in Joshua C. Taylor, *America as Art* (Washington, DC, 1976), 12, and in a folk artist's version, *Liberty and Washington*, unknown artist (c. 1800–10), New York State Historical Association, Cooperstown, NY, reprinted in Kerber, *Women of the Republic*, 286. The pioneer discussion of this image is by E. McClung Fleming, "From Indian Princess to Greek Goddess: The American Image, 1783–1815," *Winterthur Portfolio* 3 (1967): 37–66.

57. Mann, *FR*, 253–60; at the end of his subscription list he added about thirty names, mostly from western Massachusetts. [Dedham] *Minerva*, Oct. 10, 1797, for a notice dated Sept. 19, "now ready." In this same issue, Mann published a notice dated Sept. 11, 1797, stating that he had deposited a copy of *FR*, identifying himself as the claimant to the copyright. The author listed on the title page is "A Citizen of Massachusetts." The women subscribers and their towns were Susanna Gay (Wrentham), Alice Leavens (Walpole), Hannah Orne (Boston), Lucinda Smith (Norton), Hannah Wright (Foxborough), and Mrs. Sarah Chandler (Boston). I have not made an effort to track the subscribers, but I have looked at numerous copies of the 1797 edition of the book and have found virtually no marginalia. Nor did Cathy N. Davidson, who, in *Revolution and the Word: The Rise of the Novel in America* (New York, 1986), made a study of reader response to novels, including Mann's memoir. Almost all extant copies are pristine.

58. Mann, "Catalogue" (printing "devoured"); *Catalogue of Books &c. now Selling by Ros Douglas* (Petersburg, VA), 12, brought to my attention by Susan Branson.

59. William Ellis to William Jackson, Feb. 4, 1837, William Ellis MS, LC, with thanks to J

Sellers of LC for providing a copy. This, I believe, is a copy made for Peter Force, the antiquarian, originally in Force's file, LC, about Gannett. Typescript in Bricknell, PHS, and SPL.

60. Benjamin Mutschler, "The Province of Affliction: Illness in New England, 1690–1820" (Ph.D. diss., Columbia Univ., 2000), chap. 5 on "decisive disability"; Kenneth R. Bowling et al., eds., *Petition Histories: Revolutionary War-Related Claims*, vol. 7 of *Documentary History of the First Federal Congress of the United States of America* (Baltimore, 1997), 7:332–35. My thanks to William diGiacomantonio, associate editor, for interpreting these laws to me and for providing an advance copy of the text.

61. Lewis Leary, *That Rascal Freneau: A Study in Literary Failure* (New Brunswick, NJ, 1941).

62. Fred Patee, comp., *Poems of Philip Freneau*, 3 vols. (Princeton, NJ, 1902), 3:182, reprints the poem and the note from his daughter; for MS Notes: Hammel Receipt Book, typescript MS, Collection No. 21, Philip Freneau, Monmouth County [New Jersey] Historical Association. This seems to have been transcribed by a researcher in 1936 from MS notes no longer available and includes biographical notes on Helena Freneau. My thanks to Jane Reynolds-Peck of the association for providing a copy.

63. Gales and Seaton, eds., *Annals of Congress* 7, Nov. 28, 1797; *Philadelphia Gazette,* Nov. 29, 1797, under "Congress of the United States: House of Representatives, Tuesday Nov. 28"; *Gazette of the United States,* Nov. 29, 1797. Gerda Lerner, ed., *The Female Experience: An American Documentary* (Indianapolis, 1977), 395–96, reprints the abbreviated petition and committee rejection from MS copies, Huntington Library. The petition was first copied, I have since discovered, by the antiquarian historian Benjamin Lossing, but was never used in his numerous publications on the Revolution (see Benjamin Lossing MS, Huntington Lib.).

64. *Time Piece and Literary Companion,* Dec. 1, 1797, under "New York, December 1, 1797."

65. *Journals of the House of Representatives:* 3:220; "Report on the Petitions of James Brown, Deborah Gannett [et al.], March 9, 1798," MS [location not clear], photocopy in Bricknell, PHS. The report speaks of the applications of the four petitioners as being for pensions, and maintains, "[I]f anything is to be done for the payment of back pensions, it should be a general and not a partial measure," indicating that DG's ambiguous plea was interpreted as a petition for a pension.

66. *Annals of Congress,* 7: Nov. 28, 1797, and *Philadelphia Gazette,* Nov. 29, 1797. A search of the correspondence in Harrison Gray Otis Papers, MHS, by Paul Uek turned up no relevant letters, and there is no sign in the *Annals* of Otis, or any other congressman, speaking on her behalf; Philip Marsh, *Philip Freneau: Poet and Journalist* (Minneapolis, 1967), 241–46 (the attacks on Freneau); James M. Smith, *Freedom's Fetters: The Alien and Sedition Laws and American Civil Liberties* (Ithaca, NY, 1956), 3–93 (political climate); 204–20 (John Daly Burk); and passim for Otis and Ames as ultra-Federalists.

67. Judith Hiltner, ed., *The Newspaper Verse of Philip Freneau: An Edition and Bibliographic Survey* (Troy, NY, 1986), 605–06, reprints the version from *Time Piece,* Dec. 4, 1797; Patee, ed., *Poems of Freneau,* 3:182–83, reprints this version (with slight revisions by the poet) from Freneau, *A Collection of Poems on American Affairs,* 2 vols. (New York, 1815), 1:70–72. I have followed the wording and format in the original newspaper (as reprinted by Hiltner).

contemporary reprints: *Reif's Philadelphia Gazette,* July 19, 1798, brought to my attention by Susan Branson, and [Newark] *Centinel of Freedom,* Dec. 12, 1797, brought to my attention by Rosemarie Zagarri; *South Carolina Gazette,* Aug. 24, 1798, cited by Hiltner.

CHAPTER 7: A GANNETT ON TOUR

1. *Columbian Minerva,* March 23, 1802 (plans); "Diary of Deborah Sampson Gannett in 1802" (cited hereafter as DG, Diary). My citations are taken from a facsimile of the handwritten transcription made from the original by Eugene Tappan, Secretary, SHS, copies in SPL and DHS. Tappan, a lawyer and clerk of the probate court in Boston, seems to have made a fastidious transcription faithful to DG's spelling, capitalization, punctuation, and sentence structure. According to his preface, written in 1901–02, the diary was "in the possession of a descendant" who, he said, "received it from his mother who was born and bred in the Gannett mansion" on East Street, Sharon. This would make the owner either a grandson or great-grandson of Deborah. A descendant read passages from it at the 1902 dinner in Sharon celebrating the 100th anniversary of the delivery of the address in Boston. I have not been able to locate either the original diary by DG or the original of Tappan's handwritten transcription.

2. My own research on the tour, with the assistance of Paul Uek, as well as the independent research of Sandra Gustafson which she generously shared with me, establishes DG's presence in the towns she listed, wherever there is a newspaper for the town. There are several discrepancies in her entries, e.g., she advertised an appearance in Worcester in the *Massachusetts Spy,* July 21, 1802, but made an entry in her diary only for a lecture in nearby Holden. She did not make an entry for a performance in New York City established by other sources. Otherwise, there are only frustrating gaps.

   I have taken the mileages (where they exist) from contemporary almanacs published 1802–04 in Dedham, Boston, Worcester, Cooperstown, Albany, Rome, Catskill, and New York City, in AAS, researched by Paul Uek. My mileage estimates are conservative. None of these almanacs offers mileage for a road west from Catskill, although there was a Catskill Turnpike about half the way to Lisle. Andrew Beers, *The Farmer's Diary; or Catskill Almanack, for . . . 1820* (Catskill, NY, 1820), lists the Susquehanna Turnpike with a mileage of 140 miles from Catskill to a point near Lisle, which is the same in a modern computerized calculation for Catskill to Whitney Point (a town next to Lisle).

3. Mrs. Deborah Ganett [*sic*], *An Adress* [*sic*] *Delivered with Applause, at the Federal-Street Theatre, Boston, Four Successive Nights of the Different Plays, Beginning March 22, 1802; and after at other principal towns, a number of nights successively at each place . . .* (Dedham, Printed and Sold by H. Mann for Mrs Gannett at the Minerva Office, 1802), preface by Herman Mann, 3–4 (cited hereafter as DG, *Address*). SHS reprinted this (Sharon, MA, 1905) with an introduction by Eugene Tappan. I follow the pagination in the original 1802 printing (taken from a copy in Clements Library, Univ. of Michigan, also available in Evans microprint).

4. DG, Diary, May 28, 1802.

5. Sally Mann, "Diary, 1800–1805," entries loosely dated April and May 1802, unpaged, Mann Papers, DHS.

6. Mann, preface to DG, *Address,* 4 ("verbatim"); Eugene Tappan, intro. to DG, Diary, 7.
·7. [Robert Walker], *The Female Soldier; or, the Surprising Life of Hannah Snell . . .* (London, 1750), 40; for Hannah Snell, see Julie Wheelwright, *Amazons and Military Maids: Women Who Dressed as Men in Pursuit of Life, Liberty and Happiness* (London, 1989), 111–12, and David Cordingly, *Women Sailors and Sailors' Women: An Untold Maritime History* (New York, 2001), 68–69; Charles Brockden Brown, *Ormond; or The Secret Witness* (New York, 1799), esp. chap. 21; Sandra Gustafson, "The Genders of Nationalism: Patriotic Violence, Patriotic Sentiment in the Performances of Deborah Sampson Gannett," in Robert Blair St. George, ed., *Possible Pasts: Becoming Colonial in Early America* (Ithaca, NY, 2000), 380–99, quotation at 389.
8. For women in public life: David Waldstreicher, *In the Midst of Perpetual Fetes: The Making of American Nationalism, 1776–1820* (Chapel Hill, NC, 1997), 82–84, 122–23, 166–72, 232–41; Simon Newman, *Parades and the Politics of the Street: Festive Culture in the Early American Republic* (Philadelphia, 1997), passim; for women speakers: Susan Branson, *These Fiery Frenchified Dames: Women and Political Culture in Early National Philadelphia* (Philadelphia, 2001), chap. 2, and Christopher Grasso, *A Speaking Aristocracy: Transforming Public Discourse in Eighteenth-Century Connecticut* (Chapel Hill, NC, 1999), 419–24; for women in the churches: Catherine A. Brekus, *Strangers and Pilgrims: Female Preaching in America, 1740–1845* (Chapel Hill, NC, 1998), chap. 2 (Jefferson quotation at 73), and Susan Juster, " 'Neither Male nor Female': Jemima Wilkinson and the Politics of Gender in Post-Revolutionary America," in St. George, ed., *Possible Pasts,* 357–79.
9. Carolyn Eastman, "A Nation of Speechifiers: Oratory, Print, and the Making of a Gendered American Public" (Ph.D. diss., Johns Hopkins Univ., 2001) chaps. 2, 4. See, e.g., "An Oration upon Female Education Pronounced by a Member of the Public Schools of Boston, September 1791," in Caleb Bingham, comp., *The Columbian Orator* (9th edn, Boston, 1801), 47–51.
10. *Albany Gazette,* Aug. 31, Sept. 3, 1802; [Worcester] *Massachusetts Spy,* July 21, 1802. [Providence] *United States Chronicle,* May 6, 1802, is the only advertisement located, aside from Boston, which promises the manual exercise. DG's most common entry in her diary is "delivered an oration" or "delivered an address" (see DG, Diary, Aug. 13, 18, 21; Sept. 1, 7, 19, 1802). On women lecturing, see Kenneth Cmiel, *Democratic Eloquence: The Fight over Popular Speech in Nineteenth-Century America* (New York, 1990), 69–71; Eastman, "A Nation of Speechifiers," chap. 2, sec. 1 (on school "exhibitions").
11. *Mercury and New England Palladium,* March 23, 26, 1802; *Boston Gazette,* March 22 ("Theatrical Notice"), 25, 29, 1802; *Boston Columbian Cinticel,* March 20, 24, 27, 1802; *Independent Chronicle,* March 22, 25, 29, 1802 [Republican paper]. Broadsides are for the Federal Street Theatre for *The Will* (March 22) and *The Way to Get Married* (March 26), both in Boston Public Library, Rare Books (my thanks to Henry Cooke and David Dearborn, New England Historic Genealogical Society, for helping me track these). William Clapp, *A Record of the Boston Stage* (Boston, 1853), 19, 42, 52, 74–75, 78–79. For d'Eon: Gary Kates, *Monsieur 'Eon Is a Woman: A Tale of Political Intrigue and Sexual Masquerade* (New York, 1995); "emoirs of Mademoiselle D'Eon de Beaumont; Commonly Called the Chevalier D'Eon," *Boston Magazine* 1 (June 1784): 313–16, with an engraving by J. Norman in which d'Eon

is dressed half as a woman, half as a man, reprinted in [Boston] *Omnium Gatherum* 1 (September 1810): 481–86.

12. Gustafson, "Genders of Nationalism," 395. See the works of Judith Hiltner and Michelle Navarre-Cleary cited in note 44 below.

13. *Columbian Minerva,* March 23, 1802.

14. *Regulations for the Order and Discipline of the Troops of the United States Part I* (Philadelphia, 1779), "The Manual Exercise," 1–17. My thanks to Emily G. Pingot, Boston National Historical Park, for a copy of this edition. "To All Brave, Healthy, Able Bodied and Well Disposed Young Men . . . Take Notice," broadside, n.d., n.p., LC and Pennsylvania Historical Society, illustrates thirteen positions in the exercise. Although undated, internal evidence indicates this recruiting poster was issued not during the Revolutionary War, but in 1799, during the quasi-war with France. Lieutenant Colonel Aaron Ogden, listed on the poster as commander of the unit to which recruits were asked to report, held that rank from Jan. 8, 1799, through June 15, 1800.

15. [Providence] *United States Chronicle,* May 6, 1802. Sandra Gustafson examined the following papers for cities where Gannett performed: for Providence, *Providence Gazette,* April 24, May 1, 8, 1802; *Providence Phoenix,* May 11, 1802; *United States Chronicle,* April 29, May 6, 13, 1802; for Worcester, *Massachusetts Spy,* July 7–Sept. 29, 1802; *National Aegis,* July 21, 1802; for Springfield, *Federal Spy,* Aug. 10–31, 1802; for Northampton, *Hampshire Gazette,* Aug. 18–Sept. 8, 1802; for Albany, *Albany Gazette,* Aug. 23–Oct. 11, 1802, Feb. 14–March 14, 1803. Gustafson also looked at the [Cooperstown] *Otsego Herald,* Oct. 7, 1802–Jan. 13, 1803, and *Hudson Balance,* Oct. 12, 1802–Jan. 11, 1803, in search of notices of Gannett's travels in western New York. I am indebted to Gustafson for sharing this material with me.

16. *Albany Gazette,* Aug. 31, Sept. 3, 1802, Feb. 18, 1803.

17. Jack Larkin, *The Reshaping of Everyday Life, 1790–1840* (New York, 1988), 218–24 (Maria Tracy at 223); Patricia Cline Cohen, "Women at Large: Travel in Antebellum America," *History Today* 44 (1994): 44–50; Cohen, "Safety and Danger: Women on American Public Transport, 1750–1850," in Dorothy O. Helly and Susan M. Reverby, eds., *Gendered Domains: Rethinking Public and Private in Women's History* (Ithaca, NY, 1992), chap. 6.

18. DG, Diary, May 3, Oct. 13–16, 1802.

19. Ibid., Aug. 24, Sept. 7, 1802.

20. Ibid., May 8, Sept. 11–Oct. 19, 1802; Jan. 3–6, 1803.

21. Ibid., after Feb. 23, 1803 (for Albany); "Bill of Expense" (for Boston).

22. Vinton, in Mann, *FR,* 228–29.

23. [Northampton] *Hampshire Gazette,* Sept. 1, 1802. My thanks to Thomas Foster, who brought this article to my attention; to Judith Hiltner, who gave me her notes; and to Philip Lampi of AAS, who supplied a copy. I assume from the pseudonym, "Gill Blass," as well as from the tone and content, that the author was a man. *The Adventures of Gil Blas of San* lane by Alaine-René Lesage, a French picaresque novel, was translated into English Tobias Smollett in 1795. My thanks to Laura Green for this reference.

24. DG, Diary, May 3, 5, 1802.

25. Ibid., July 30, Aug. 9, 13, Sept. 7, 1802.

26. Ibid., July 10, 30, August 3, 1802; Samuel Damon, *History of Holden* . . . (Worc

1841), 48–49, 147 (commendation from Lafayette, May 15, 1781); David Estes, *History of Holden, Massachusetts* (Worcester, MA, 1894), 330; DG to George Webb, June 2, 1804, Webb Papers, Miscellaneous Manuscripts "S," AAS.

27. Thomas Egleston, *The Life of John Paterson* (New York, 1898); Edward E. Curtis, "John Paterson," *DAB*, 7: 292–93; Paterson is identified as a Republican in Kenneth C. Martis, *The Historical Atlas of Political Parties in the United States Congress, 1789–1989* (New York, 1989), 77, 273, and by Philip Lampi, director of a project collecting early American voting statistics, AAS. For the political processes on the New York frontier, see Alfred F. Young, *The Democratic Republicans of New York: The Origins, 1763–1797* (Chapel Hill, NC, 1967), chap. 23, and Alan Taylor, *William Cooper's Town: Power and Persuasion on the Frontier of the Early American Republic* (New York, 1996). My thanks, again, to Sandra Gustafson (and to her mother), who searched for papers of Paterson without success in Broome County libraries.

28. DG, Diary, Nov. 11–Dec. 11, 1802.

29. This entry with the parable in DG, Diary, is out of order in Tappan's transcription, following the list of places at which she stayed. It belongs after the entry for Sept. 6, and before Sept. 9, 1802, her entry for the springs at Ballston. Ballston is north of Albany, Bethlehem to the south.

30. DG, Diary, Feb. 23, 1802; March 22, 1803.

31. Ibid., "Bill of Expenses," March 22, 1803.

32. Paul Uek discovered and tracked down this hitherto unknown New York leg of Gannett's tour, for which there are no entries in the Diary: [New York] *Commercial Advertiser,* April 12, 1803 (report), April 13, 1803 (theatre notice); *New York Herald,* April 13, 1803; *New York Evening Post,* April 24, 1803; William Dunlap, *History of the Theater* (New York, 1832), 314 (Smith's recommendation); G. C. D. Odell, *Annals of the New York Stage,* 14 vols. (New York, 1927), 2:175–76 (the play).

33. [New York] *Chronicle Express,* April 18, 1803, under the heading, "Thursday April 4." In Dedham, Mann's *Columbian Minerva,* April 26, 1803, picked up a report from New York "by one of the morning papers of last week" of Mrs. Gannett "in this city on her way to the Southward," but from March through June the paper carried nothing about a performance. The same item ran in the [Cooperstown] *Otsego Herald,* April 25, 1803.

34. Washington Irving, "Jonathan Oldstyle, Letter II," [*New York*] *Morning Chronicle,* 1801, in Montrose J. Moses and John Mason Brown, eds., *The American Theatre as Seen by Its Critics, 1752–1934* (New York, 1934), 40, brought to my attention by Tryna Zeedyk; Dunlap, *History of the Theatre,* 314 (comment on the play).

35. Earlier, Gannett recorded where she was even when deathly ill and marking time. There are no entries, however, indicating where she was between Albany, Feb. 23, 1803, and Newport, June [n.d.] 1803. Systematic in listing her expenses and where she stayed, she omitted New York City altogether, which leads me to conclude she blotted the experience out of her memory. Pages may have been lost from the diary, or perhaps she made entries and tore them out r. For Philadelphia, there is no mention of her in the *Philadelphia Aurora,* a leading blican paper, April–June 1803, or in William Wood, *Old Drury of Philadelphia: A History the Philadelphia Stage, 1800–1835,* ed. James Reese (Philadelphia, 1932), or James

Reese, *Cradle of Culture: 1800–1810, The Philadelphia Stage* (Philadelphia, 1957). For her subsequent illness: Paul Revere to William Eustis, Feb. 20, 1804, MS, MHS.

36. Comment on Wright in Cmiel, *Democratic Eloquence,* 70–71; for the Sharon reactions to the lecture in 1902, see chapter 10 below.

37. For the results of the Revolution for women: Linda Kerber, *Women of the Republic: Intellect and Ideology in Revolutionary America* (Chapel Hill, NC, 1980), chaps. 5–9; Mary Beth Norton, *Liberty's Daughters: The Revolutionary Experience of American Women* (Boston, 1980; Ithaca, NY, 1996, with a new preface), chaps. 6–9 and conclusion, quotation by Priscilla Mason at 296; Joan Hoff Wilson, "The Illusion of Change: Women and the American Revolution," in Alfred F. Young, ed., *The American Revolution: Explorations in the History of American Radicalism* (Dekalb, IL, 1976), 383–446; Ronald Hoffman and Peter J. Albert, eds., *Women in the Age of the American Revolution* (Charlottesville, VA, 1989); *The Female Advocate* (New Haven, CT, 1801), 7.

38. Mary Wollstonecraft, *A Vindication of the Rights of Woman with Strictures on Political and Moral Subjects* (Philadelphia, 1792, 1794; Boston, 1792), esp. chap. 3 ("Revolution in Female Manners") and chap. 9; for the response to Wollstonecraft, see Kerber, *Women of the Republic,* 222–25, 282–83; Rosemarie Zagarri, "The Rights of Man and Woman in Post-Revolutionary America," *WMQ* 60 (1998): 203–30; Branson, *These Fiery Frenchified Dames,* chap. 1; Elaine F. Crane, ed., *The Diary of Elizabeth Drinker,* 3 vols. (Boston, 1991), April 22, 1796; and Elizabeth Hewson to Thomas Hewson, Nov. 6, 1796, Microfilm Reel 103, Hewson Family Papers, American Philosophical Society, brought to my attention by Susan Branson.

39. Judith Sargent Murray, *The Gleaner: A Miscellaneous Production in Three Volumes,* 3 vols. (Boston, 1798); reprinted with an intro. by Nina Baym as *The Gleaner* (Schenectady, NY, 1992), 1:167–68; Sheila L. Skemp, *Judith Sargent Murray: A Brief Biography with Documents* (Boston, 1998).

40. Linda Kerber, *Toward an Intellectual History of Women* (Chapel Hill, NC, 1997), 42–62, 63–99, quotation at 98.

41. Zagarri, "The Rights of Man and Woman," 216ff.; Kerber, *Women of the Republic,* 279–80; Chandos Michael Brown, "Mary Wollstonecraft, or The Female Illuminati: The Campaign Against Women and 'Modern Philosophy' in the Early Republic," *Journal of the Early Republic* 15 (1995): 389–424, 426 (Silliman); "Morpheus" [Timothy Dwight], part 2, no. 1, in [Boston] *Mercury and New England Palladium,* March 2, 5, 1802; *The Female Advocate,* 21, 25.

42. Rosemarie Zagarri, *A Woman's Dilemma: Mercy Otis Warren and the American Revolution* (Wheeling, IL, 1995), chap. 6; Joan Hoff, *Law, Gender, and Injustice: A Legal History of U.S. Women* (New York, 1991), 66–79; Murray, *The Gleaner,* 3:217–24; Wollstonecraft, *Vindication,* chap. 9.

43. For Mann's politics, see chapter 6 above; Charles W. Akers. *Abigail Adams: An America Woman* (Boston 1980), 116.

44. In interpreting the address, I have benefited from scholars who generously shared their w in progress with me: Sandra Gustafson, *Eloquence Is Power: Oratory & Performan Early America* (Chapel Hill, NC, 2000), 246–57; Judith R. Hiltner, " 'Like a Bew' Star': Deborah Sampson, Herman Mann and *Address, Delivered with Applause,*"

Society Quarterly 29 (1999): 5–24; and Michelle Navarre-Cleary, "Women Under Cover: The Role of the Female Character in Early American Texts" (Ph.D. diss., Northwestern Univ., 1995).

45. Hiltner, " 'Like a Bewildered Star,' " 6–8.

46. Carolyn Eastman, "A Nation of Speechifiers," chap. 1; Cmiel, *Democratic Eloquence,* chap. 1 (for the Ciceronian verbal style); "A Correspondent," *Hampshire Gazette,* Sept. 1, 1802.

47. DG, *Address,* 3–7. The address has been reprinted in Judith Anderson, ed., *Outspoken Women: Speeches of American Women Reformers, 1635–1935* (Dubuque, IA, 1984), 135–41, and in Elizabeth Evans, *Weathering the Storm: Women of the American Revolution* (New York, 1975), 317–29. My citations are to the original 1802 Dedham printing, also available in Evans microprint.

48. DG, *Address,* 7–11.

49. Ibid., 11–12.

50. Ibid., 12–13.

51. Ibid., 17–19.

52. Ibid., 20–23.

53. Ibid., 24–26.

54. Ibid., 27.

55. Ibid., 28–29.

56. Bingham, *The Columbian Orator,* 47–51 (Boston schoolgirl).

PART FOUR · "OLD SOLDIER"

CHAPTER 8: PUBLIC WOMAN

1. William Ellis to William Jackson, Feb. 4, 1837, Ellis MS, LC, copies in Bricknell, PHS and SPL; Paul Revere to William Eustis, Feb. 24, 1804, Revere MS, MHS.

2. Claude M. Fuess, "William Eustis," *DAB,* 3:193–95; [Dedham] *Columbian Minerva,* March 30, 1802; Thomas Egleston, *Life of John Paterson* (New York, 1898), 393.

3. DG to George Webb, June 2, 1804, Webb Papers, Misc. MSS "S," AAS.

4. *United States Statutes at Large,* Eighth Congress, sess. 2, chap. 44, March 3, 1805 (emphasis added). This may be compared to Seventh Congress, sess. 2, chap. 37, 242–43. Before I became aware that no action by Congress was required for an invalid petition between 1803 and 1806, I made a search of the records of the House of Representatives, for which I thank Diane L. Dimkoff, Center for Legislative Archives, NA, and Steven L. Pastore. See "List of Private Claims Presented to the House of Representatives from the 1st to the 31st Congress," in *Digested Summary of Alphabetical List of Private Claims* (Washington, DC, 1853), 692, which lists DG petitions only for 1798 and 1810. The claim that the documents were destroyed in the War of 1812 is in numerous documents in later years from the War Department to private citizens in DG's Pension File, S 32722, NA.

Henry Dearborn to Benjamin Austin, March 11, 1805, and Receipt Received of Benjamin Austin, April 10, 1805, $104.53½ signed "Deborah Ganett," both reprinted in Vinton, intro. Mann, *FR,* xviii–xix. Another receipt for $24, May 13, 1806, for Sept. 4, 1805, to March 6,

1806, signed "Deborah Gannet," is pasted on the inside cover of the Vinton edition of Mann, *FR,* New York Public Library, Rare Books Division.

6. See the tax assessment discussed below, chapter 9, sec. 2.

7. DG to Paul Revere, Feb. 22, 1806, Revere MS, MHS.

8. My thanks to Konstantine Dierks for interpreting the character of DG's two letters— conversation with the author, June 2000. See Dierks, "Letter Writing, Gender and Class in America, 1750–1800" (Ph.D. diss., Brown Univ., 1999), and Tamara P. Thornton, *Handwriting in America: A Cultural History* (New Haven, CT, 1966), chap. 1.

9. *Sharon, Massachusetts: A History* (Sharon, MA, 1976) reprints a photograph of the tavern in the late nineteenth century. The late Chandler Jones was my host for a visit to the tavern room in 1994 and Patrick Leonard was my guide.

10. Petition, Deborah Gannett to the Senate and House, Dec. 25, 1809, MS, photostat, MHS, which records on the back: "Petition of Deborah Gannett 12 Feby, 1810. Referred to the Committee on the Petition of Thomas Cambell. 27 March 1810 reported and rejected," copy in Bricknell, PHS. I have not seen the originals, which may be in the Legislative Records of the House of Representatives for the Eleventh Congress, Records Group 233, NA. Julia Ward Stickley, an archivist at NA, listed them as such among her sources (Stickley Papers, MA) but did not reproduce the documents. Emil F. Guba reports this as in *House Proceedings,* Eleventh Congress, 1st and 2nd sess. (May 22 to May 1, 1810), 1405–06. Congressman Wheaton of Massachusetts presented the petition, Feb. 12, 1810. There apparently was no debate. For a short summary, see Emil F. Guba, *Deborah Samson alias Robert Shurtliff, Revolutionary War Soldier* (Kingston, MA, privately printed, 1994), 118–19. I did research in the Legislative Records of the House, NA, with the assistance of archivists, but was frustrated in locating these and other documents.

11. John Resch, *Suffering Soldiers: Revolutionary War Veterans, Moral Sentiment, and Political Culture in the Early Republic* (Amherst, 1999), chaps. 3, 4, quotation at 53. *Dedham Gazette,* March 20, May 8, 1818.

12. DG, Deposition, Sept. 19, 1818, DG Pension Records, S 32722, NA. The name of the judge, as best I can make out, is Davis. Elsewhere I have seen him identified as John Davis. This document was exhibited on the "Freedom Train" in 1948 and is in Frank Monaghan, *Heritage of Freedom: The History and Significance of the Basic Documents of American Liberty* (Princeton, NJ, 1947), 99–100.

This 1818 petition is the only one we know of in which Mrs. Gannett claimed she enlisted in 1781 and was at the Battle of Yorktown. In the only prior petition whose details we know— her 1792 petition for back pay to Massachusetts—she said she enlisted May 23, 1782, and was discharged Oct. 23, 1783, and made no claim for Yorktown. Her mustering officer testified to May 20, 1782, as the date of enlistment, and the receipt she signed for a bounty is dated May 23, 1782 (see chapter 2). Herman Mann in his book (1797) had her enlisting in 1781 and at th Battle of Yorktown, and she in her address (1802), written by Mann, said of Yorktown, "I w there."

Most likely, in 1818, when she was very anxious to transfer to the better-paying g pension roll, she did not want to repudiate these claims which might undermine he

ity as having served at all. She was very aware of the cachet of a claim to Yorktown. Intent aside, there are internal signs of a lack of exactness in the petition ("enlisted in April, 1781" and served "until November, 1783" and "served in Massachusetts and New York," omitting Virginia).

The two twentieth-century historians who accept the claim for an enlistment in 1781, Julia Ward Stickley and Jane Keiter, are both impressed that she swore under oath for the 1818 petition. Stickley insisted that a federal document took precedence over a state document and was convinced that the state documents were altered. Keiter, whose work I cited in chapter 4, has great confidence in both Herman Mann's book and the revised MS.

13. Resch, *Suffering Soldiers,* chap. 5.

14. In Pension Files 32722, NA: Deposition, March 16, 1819; Judge J. M. Davis to John C. Calhoun, March 20, 1819.

15. [Dedham] *Village Register and Norfolk County Advertiser,* July 21, 1820, and July 7, 14, for opinion, and Oct. 27, Nov. 10, 1820, for lists of men who had received "notifications . . . relative to the continuance of their Pensions"—Resch, *Suffering Soldiers,* 134 (pension statistics).

16. [Dedham] *Village Register,* Dec. 29, 1820. The original certificate is not in the pension file, but DG's affidavit, Dec. 19, 1820, states, "my former certificate was 13434," and the file contains a form from Dept. of Interior, Bureau of Pensions, Oct. 9, 1916, stating she was pensioned by certificate No. 13434, issued July 31, 1819.

17. The "Schedule of Property" is not dated, but the printed statement she signed Dec. 19, 1820, refers to a schedule. Julia Stickley, "The Records of Deborah Sampson Gannett, Woman Soldier of the Revolution," *Prologue, the Journal of the National Archives* 4 (1972): 233–41, reprints some of the documents, 1792–1820, with captions obsessively correcting documents that offer 1782, and not 1781, as Gannett's date of enlistment. Stickley Papers, MA, has copies of some of the documents. For a brief account of Gannett's petitioning, see Guba, *Deborah Samson,* chap. 11.

18. DG, Petition to the House, Jan. 20, 1820, reprinted in Vinton, intro. to Mann, *FR,* xvi–xvii; Vinton reports the petition was forwarded to Congressman Marcus Morton and "was referred, March 28, 1820, to the Committee on Pensions and Revolutionary Claims. March 31 [where] it was considered, but not allowed. The original petition is now before me." I have not tracked this in House records but am willing to take the word of the meticulous Vinton, who visited the National Archives in Washington.

19. Resch, *Suffering Soldiers,* chap. 7, quotation at 194, 179.

20. Ruth Bogin, "Petitioning and the New Moral Economy of Post-Revolutionary America," *WMQ* 45 (1988): 391–425; Linda G. Kerber, *Women of the Republic: Intellect and Ideology in Revolutionary America* (Chapel Hill, NC, 1980), 93–99.

21. Laurel Thatcher Ulrich, *Good Wives: Image and Reality in the Lives of Women in Northern New England, 1650–1750* (New York, 1980), chap. 2 (deputy husbands).

. Paul Revere to William Eustis, Feb. 20, 1804, Revere MS, MHS, reprinted in Esther Forbes, *Paul Revere and the World He Lived In* (Boston, 1943), 433.

"Correspondent," *Hampshire Gazette,* Sept. 1, 1802.

erman Mann, Jr., "Journal," May 1834, 26–29 ("frequent and welcome visitor"); Dec. 18, , 97–100, MS, DHS, reprinting the article "Female Pensioner" from *Village Register,*

Nov. 20, 1820, but dating it Dec. 20, 1820. I assume this article is by Mann, Jr., not by his father. Mann, Jr.'s "Journal" is full of articles that appeared in the Dedham paper, edited either by his father or by himself.

25. William Ellis to William Jackson, Feb. 4, 1837, Ellis MS, LC, copies in Bricknell, PHS, and SPL. Death Notice, *Norfolk Democrat,* Dec. 10, 1852, lists Ellis as seventy-two and "one of our most useful citizens." The title, "Notes of William Ellis, of Dedham, Pension Comm[ission?]," on a MS notebook, DHS, suggests he was either a pension agent or commissioner of some sort. Ellis, incorrectly identified in some reports as a U.S. senator, was elected to the Massachusetts House and Senate and served as a member of the state's Executive Council. My thanks to Paul Uek for tracking Ellis.

26. Charles Brockden Brown, *Alcuin; A Dialogue* (New York, 1798). For postwar salons, see Susan Branson, *These Fiery Frenchified Dames: Women and Political Culture in Early National Philadelphia* (Philadelphia, 2001), chap. 4. For the colonial era, David S. Shields, *Civil Tongues and Polite Letters in British America* (Chapel Hill, NC, 1997), chap. 4.

27. James M. Banner, Jr., *To the Hartford Convention: The Federalists and the Origins of Party Politics in Massachusetts, 1789–1815* (New York, 1970), chap. 8; Earl Gannett is identified as a captain by the tax assessor in the 1820s, and in a review of his life, as a militia captain in the War of 1812.

28. Philip Lampi to Alfred Young, Dec. 23, 1996. My thanks to Lampi, director of the monumental vote-collecting project, AAS, who provided me with local returns for congressional, presidential, and gubernatorial elections, 1788–1820. The interpretation of the statistics is mine.

29. Letter to [Boston] *Daily Advertiser,* March 8, 1816, by Enoch Hewin et al., in SHS Scrapbook 2:71, SPL.

30. Ronald P. Formisano, *The Transformation of Political Culture: Massachusetts Parties, 1790s–1840s* (New York, 1983), part 1, esp. chap. 7 and pp. 79–81 ("The Last of the Old Patriots: William Eustis").

31. Rosemarie Zagarri, "Gender and the First Party System," in Barbara Oberg and Doron Ben-Atar, eds., *Federalists Reconsidered* (Charlottesville, VA, 1999), 118–34 (quotation about Mrs. Murray at 128); Brown, *Alcuin,* 51–52.

32. Jeremiah Gould, "Annals of Sharon, Massachusetts, 1830," in *Publications SHS* (Boston, 1904), 1:17–18, 21; George Willis Cooke, *Origin and Early History of the First Parish Church, Sharon, Massachusetts* (Boston, 1903), 23. Sidney Ahlstrom and Jonathan S. Cary, *An American Reformation: A Documentary History of Unitarian Christianity* (Middletown, CT, 1985), intro., 3–41.

33. Gould, "Annals of Sharon," 18–19; Cooke, *First Parish Church,* 18–19.

34. I am indebted to Paul Uek for pursuing the church records of Sharon. Unfortunately, a fire destroyed the early records of the First Congregational Parish, Unitarian, but Uek was able to run down some records in the home of Elizabeth McGregor, who calls her trunk the "Unitarian Church of Sharon Archives." Almost all of these records, carefully inventorie are for a period after 1822, with the exception of a few cited below. My thanks to M McGregor for making these records available and to Shirley Schofield for assisting Uek the records of the Congregational Church.

35. Mann, *FR*, 100–06.
36. Minutes and List of Members of the Baptist Church, dated Oct. 10, 26, 1814, MS, First Baptist Church of Sharon. My thanks to Marion Cunningham, clerk of the church, for copies of these, and for hunting for church records. Ms. Cunningham in a letter to me, June 10, 1999, writes: "a little over a year ago two very old record books, in fact the originals, appeared on the doorstep of one of our members. Apparently the member was not at home at the time as we do not know who left them. These books are the missing link, the proof who the founders were and Benjamin Gannett was one of them." Lyman Partridge, *History of the Baptist Church in Sharon, Mass.* (Mansfield, MA, 1882), 8–9, provides a sketch of the members, including Gannett. A certificate attesting to Benjamin Gannett as a member of the Baptist Society, Feb. 25, 1818, is in the McGregor Unitarian Archives cited above. His name is also on a list, "The Ministerial Tax for 1821," in SHS Scrapbook, 2:86ff., SPL. Partridge, *Baptist Church*, 5, 7 (comments on Baptists); Records of the Clerk of the Parish [Unitarian], 1822–31, 12, 17, 34, and 39, in McGregor's Unitarian Archives, show Earl Gannett as an active member.
37. In the absence of records, it is difficult to reconstruct Deborah Gannett's relationship to the Congregational Church of Sharon. Under Reverend Philip Curtis, she may have been alienated from the church; Curtis neither married Deborah and Benjamin nor baptized their three children. Under Reverend Jonathan Whitaker, there are signs she was part of the church early in the century before he became controversial. She and Benjamin are among fifty-nine individuals who made a gift of a newly printed Bible to Whitaker (before 1806), and her daughter Polly (Mary in the will) was married by Whitaker in 1808. For marriages and baptisms, see "Church Records of Rev. Philip Curtis of Sharon, 1742–1797," in *Publications SHS* (Boston, 1908), vol. 5; "List of contributors for the purchase of a Bible" is within *Old Parish Bible* (Philadelphia, 1798), in McGregor Unitarian Archives cited above. This list, made, it seems, before 1806, appears to be copied from the original.
38. Susan Juster, *Disorderly Women: Sexual Politics and Evangelicalism in Revolutionary New England* (Ithaca, NY, 1994), 164–65.
39. See David D. Hall, *Cultures of Print: Essays in the History of the Book* (Amherst, MA, 1996), 36–78, 151–68; Hall, "Books and Reading in Eighteenth-Century America," in Cary Carson, Ronald Hoffman, and Peter J. Albert, eds., *Of Consuming Interests: The Style of Life in the Eighteenth Century* (Charlottesville, VA, 1994), 354–72; William J. Gilmore, *Reading Becomes a Necessity of Life: Material and Cultural Life in Rural New England, 1780–1835* (Knoxville, TN, 1988); and Cathy N. Davidson, *Revolution and the Word: The Rise of the Novel in America* (New York, 1986), chap. 2.
40. For Mann's library: "Books for Sale or Circulation by H. Mann," [Dedham] *Columbian Minerva*, Aug. 10, 1802, which also has a notice, "Circulating Library," with rules; [Dedham] *Norfolk Repository*, March 25, 1806, advertisement for books and *Catalogue of the Norfolk Circulating Library* (H. and W. H. Mann, Dedham, 1823).

For works published by Mann, I have used Shaw-Shoemaker, *American Bibliography*, 1801–19, and a printout of Dedham imprints at AAS. For Mann as a printer: Richard J. Wolfe, *The Role of the Mann Family of Dedham, Massachusetts in the Marbling of Paper in*

Nineteenth-Century America and in the Printing of Music, the Making of Cards, and other Booktrade Activities (Quincy, MA, 1981), and Wolfe, " 'Elegant Work by a Country Bookbinder': Two Gilt-Era Bindings Attributed to Herman Mann, Dedham, Massachusetts, c. 1812," *Proceedings AAS* 99 (1989): 89–111.

For Mann's sensational literature: Daniel A. Cohen, "Social Injustice, Sexual Violence, Spiritual Transcendence: Constructions of Interracial Rape in Early American Crime Literature, 1767–1817," *WMQ* 51 (1999): 508–12. For analysis of Mann's reading tastes: Judith Hiltner, " 'She Bled in Secret': Deborah Sampson, Herman Mann and *The Female Review*," *Early American Literature* 34 (1999): 190–220. I am very much indebted to Judith Hiltner for materials she made available to me and for conversations on Mann. DG subscribed to one book published by Mann, William De Britaine, *Human Prudence* (H. Mann, Dedham, 1806), discussed below, chapter 9, sec. 4.

41. *Benjamin Franklin's Autobiography*, ed. J. A. Leo Lemay and P. M. Zall (New York, 1986), 13–14.

CHAPTER 9: PRIVATE WOMAN

1. References below to members of the family are drawn from Michael R. Gannett, *Gannett Descendants of Matthew and Hannah Gannett of Scituate, Massachusetts* (Chevy Chase, MD, 1976, cited hereafter as *Descendants*). I am indebted to Michael R. Gannett of Cornwall, Connecticut, for sharing his knowledge of the family. My thanks, too, to Janet and Robert Gay of Springfield, Virginia, who made available their geneaology of the Gannett descendants (typescript, 1992). New England Historic Genealogical Society has a printed genealogical chart of the descendants of Deborah Sampson and Benjamin Gannett (1916); Charles Bricknell compiled "A Chart of Deborah's Descendants" (typescript, 1974), in Bricknell, PHS.

2. Deed, Benjamin Gannett [Sr.], tanner, to Joseph Gannett, labourer, Aug. 25, 1805, Norfolk County Registry of Deeds (NCRD), 24:155, brought to my attention by David B. Ingram; for Joseph: Deeds, Benjamin Gannett [Sr.], tanner, to Joseph Gannett, Nov. 23, 1805, 23:192 (12 acres); Joseph Gannett, yeoman, to Javen Morse [Jr.], Nov. 23, 1805, 23:192 (18 acres); and Joseph Gannett to Javen Morse, Nov. 23, 1805, 23:193 (46 acres), all in NCRD. Occupations are given in the deeds.

3. Deeds: Benjamin Gannett [Sr.], tanner, to Earl Gannett, labourer, May 30, 1811, book 39, p. 127; Benjamin Gannet Jun., yeoman, to Benjamin Gannet [Sr.], yeoman, Oct. 24, 1811, 40:142; Benjamin Gannett [Sr.], gentleman, to Earl Gannett and Seth Gay, yeoman, April 21, 1812, 41:163, all NCRD. It is possible the grandfather loaned the money to the two for which he accepted a note and that he canceled the debt in his will. It may have been the custom to list a price on the sale of land even when no money passed hands to establish its value. No will has surfaced for Benjamin Gannett, Sr.

4. Jack Larkin, *The Reshaping of Everyday Life, 1790–1840* (New York, 1988), 105–09; Asl Benjamin, *American Builder's Companion* (1806; rev. 6th edn, Charlestown, MA, 1811), widely used.

5. Rodney Monk, "Extract from Talk with Grandmother [Rhoda] Monk, Nov. 3, 1901,

nal with Mrs. Roger M. Myrick, Temple, New Hampshire, kindly made available by Mrs. Myrick, Rodney Monk's daughter, copy in SPL; *Descendants,* 87. Rhoda Monk (1820–1904) was interviewed by her grandson, Rodney Monk (1883–1975), when he was a young man.

6. Paul Uek tracked the Gannett land transactions in the Norfolk County Registry of Deeds, Dedham, in Grantor Index, 1793–1849, and Grantee Index, 1793–1889; and for the period before Norfolk was a separate county, he tracked them in Suffolk County Registry of Deeds, Grantor and Grantee lists from 1750 to 1793. Most of the deeds noted are in NCRD; some are in the possession of Muriel Nelson of Sharon. One is in the SPL, donated by Claire Cowell, a descendant. For tax assessments, the "List of the Valuation or Single Rate, also the Ministerial or Town Rate" (copy in Sharon Town Hall), was consulted for 1778 to 1839. My thanks to Uek, David B. Ingram of Foxborough, and Daniel Arguimbau for help in interpreting the deeds.

7. The extant documents after 1813 are: Bond, Earl Gannett to Benjamin Gannett, May 21, 1816, for $1,000, and Seth Gay to Earl Gannett, May 6, 1817, for four acres of land (in possession of Muriel Nelson); Deeds at NCRD: Seth Gay to Benjamin Gannett and Earl Gannett, Feb. 19, 1822, 66:53, for six acres [indicating Benjamin and Earl were joint owners]; Benjamin Gannett, yeoman, to Earl Gannett, yeoman, Feb. 19, 1822, 66:53, for one half of "five several pieces of land" and "for the other half of said house & barn after said Benjamin Gannett and his wife decease" (signed by Benjamin in a very shaky hand, suggesting illness). These deeds indicate the joint ownership of the farm and buildings by Benjamin and Earl some time prior to 1822, and that Benjamin provided for the sale of his half after his death and Deborah's.

8. "A List of the Valuation or Single Rate . . . for the Town of Sharon for 1824," Sharon Town Hall. This list of valuations up to 1824 lists Earl and Benjamin on separate lines (separated by a few other names), with only a total sum in the columns for real and personal property. The 1824 valuation is the first to change the format and to itemize kinds of land and personal property, which the assessors continued to do until 1833. I interpret this listing as evidence of co-ownership. Benjamin died in 1837, and in 1838, Earl became the sole Gannett on the assessor's list. I have not attempted to compare the Gannett total valuation to others in a systematic way; my impression is there were many other farms of similar size and value. Paul Uek helped in this analysis.

9. For what is common in family arrangements in New England, I am indebted to conversations with Daniel S. Smith. Three families under the same roof was unusual, but Seth Gay and Patience moved out within a few years, probably back to Roxbury, Gay's hometown, although precisely when is not clear.

10. Benjamin Gannett, Will, June 3, 1828, with Certificate Declaring Earl Gannett Executor of the Estate, Feb. 1, 1837, Norfolk County Court of Probate. The notice states that Benjamin "at the time of his decease [had] goods and estate about the value of $300." For his petition to Congress, see below, sec. 5. I have not attempted to track the daughters, Mary Gilbert (1787–1854) [Mary in the will, Polly in the birth records] and Patience Gay (1790–1865). Probate Papers of Earl Gannett of Sharon, Record No. 7683, Probate Division, Dedham, JCRD. This extensive file includes a very full inventory of the land and property (discussed ʼow), an itemized list of claims against the estate, various papers of the court-appointed

executors, and a poster, "Administrator's Sale of Real Estate," for an auction of the outlying lands, May 11, 1846.

12. Rodney Monk, "Grandmother Monk, Nov. 3, 1901." For Benjamin Gannett (1825–1901), see *Descendants,* 113–14, and *Biographical Review Containing the Sketches of Leading Citizens of Norfolk County, Massachusetts* (Boston, 1898). Conversation with Muriel Nelson, 1995, about her grandfather.

13. Monk, "Grandmother Monk, Nov. 3, 1901." "Mansion" was also used as a legal term for a dwelling house; it appeared occasionally in Benjamin Gannett, Sr.'s, deeds, but this was not the intent of the usage I am referring to; *Descendants,* 87 (for Barzillai Monk, who by occupation was a house mover).

14. Edward A. Chapell, "Housing a Nation: The Transformation of Living Standards in Early America," in Cary Carson, Ronald Hoffman, and Peter Albert, eds., *Of Consuming Interests: The Style of Life in the Eighteenth Century* (Charlottesville, VA, 1994), 167–232, 207–09 (1798 federal inventory).

15. The two pieces I saw in Muriel Nelson's home in Sharon in 1995–96 were donated to SHS. She told me the furniture had never been examined by a curator or appraised. For similar hutch-table pieces: Wallace Nutting, *Furniture of the Pilgrim Century (of American Origin) 1620–1720* (New York; 1924, 1965), figs. 655–71; also Jane C. Nylander, *Our Own Snug Fireside: Images of the New England Home 1760–1860* (New York, 1993), for a picture of a triple-purpose kitchen "settee table" of a later period with a fold-down top for ironing and a storage chest beneath the seat.

16. Larkin, *Reshaping of Everyday Life,* 109–21, quotation at 118; Virginia and Lee McCalester, *A Field Guide to American Houses* (New York, 1994), 152–68. The tax assessments on the house are something of a puzzle. In the 1824 list cited in note 8, which breaks down types of property, "house and barn" are assessed for $200 each to Earl and Benjamin for a combined total of $400. However, earlier assessments on the two men were much higher: 1816: $900 and $400, total $1,300; 1817: $675 and $375, total $1,050; 1818: $450 and $600, total $1,050. These larger totals seem more consistent with the house's size. Scanning the Sharon tax assessments for this period, my rough impression is that, assuming joint Gannett assessments in the range of $1,050–$1,300, the house was assessed somewhere in the middle.

17. Laurel Thatcher Ulrich, "Martha Ballard and Her Girls: Women's Work in Eighteenth-Century Maine," in Stephen Innes, ed., *Work and Labor in Early America* (Chapel Hill, NC, 1988), 70–105, concludes, 99, that "the most reliable servants were relatives." Patience Payson had been adopted by Benjamin Gannett, Sr., and passed on to Deborah and Benjamin Junior.

18. Richard L. Bushman, *The Refinement of America: Persons, Houses, Cities* (New York, 1992), 251–55, quotation at 251; DG, Diary, Aug. 24, 1802, SPL; Pauline Moody, *Massachusetts' Deborah Sampson* (Attleborough, MA, 1975, cited hereafter as *DS*), 32, wrote that Ernest H Gilbert, Mary Clark Gannett's grandson, "bequeathed Deborah's parlor table to his neig' bors on Bay Road [Sharon/Stoughton], Mr. and Mrs. John E. Forrest," clearly imply there was a parlor. I don't know where this piece ended up.

19. Alexander Corbett, "America's Jean d'Arc . . . ," newspaper article after Jan. 2, 1901.

paper unnamed, typescript, SPL; Nylander, *Our Snug Fireside,* chap. 5 (housework), chap. 8 (kitchens).

20. Bushman, *Refinement of America,* 256–62, quotation at 260; Mann, *FR,* 230–31 (Pratt). Pratt of Middleborough described the house after a visit about 1850.

21. Mrs. F. G. Moody, "Deborah Sampson's Willow" (Jan. 6, 1904), and Edward G. Smith, "Sharon Memories" (Jan. 30, 1904), SHS Scrapbook 1:58, 65, SPL; Corbett, "America's Jean D'Arc" (Jan. 2, 1901); for the revival of the Liberty Tree, see Alfred F. Young, *The Shoemaker and the Tea Party: Memory and the American Revolution* (Boston, 1999), 98, 107, 118, 139–40.

22. Earl B. Gannett, Probate Inventory, Sept. 2, 1845, No. 7683, NCRD. There are two separate lists: one, "Articles taken by Mary Gannett, widow of the deceased," i.e., to which she as widow was entitled, consisting of household furnishings and farm equipment; the other, a printed legal form headed "Personal Estate," on which the assessors filled in farm capital (real estate, animals, tools, etc.) but left blank almost all the categories for household goods. I interpret this to mean there were none other than the articles set aside for Earl's wife. It is possible, judging by the information cited above about a parlor table that ended up with a descendant of Mary Gilbert, that Earl's two sisters received some household goods after the death of their father in 1837.

For standards and procedures in probate inventories: Gloria L. Main, "Probate Records as a Source for Early American History," *WMQ* 32 (1975): 89–99; Peter Benes, ed., *Early American Probate Inventories* (Dublin Seminar for New England Folklore, 1987), intro. and 6–16; and Alice Hanson Jones, *American Colonial Wealth Documents and Methods,* 3 vols. (New York, 1977), 1:1–36, intro.

23. Pauline Moody, *DS,* chap. 4, written by a family member then living in Sharon, rounds up the information she had in 1975 about these artifacts.

24. Rodney Monk to Pauline Moody, May 26, 1966, Monk Papers, SPL; Rodney Monk of Groton (1883–1975) wrote letters to Pauline Moody, the family biographer of DG, and to Daniel Arguimbau in the 1960s and 1970s. I am indebted to his daughter, Mrs. Roger Myrick, and Daniel Arguimbau for sharing these documents, and have deposited copies with SPL as Monk Papers. See Amy H. B. Crehore Falcon, *Crehore and Kin, 1629–1961* (Evanston, IL, 1961), 212–13.

25. Gilbert Thompson to Eugene Tappan, May 1, 1905, in SHS Scrapbook 1:103, SPL. As of 1995–2000, the following artifacts claimed to be descended from Deborah Gannett were in the possession of the following descendants: with Muriel Nelson, a hutch table and a pine cupboard (since donated to SHS); with Beatrice Bostock and her daughters Ann Gilbert (both deceased) and Susan Goldstone, a cup plate (in addition to the wedding dress donated to the Society for the Preservation of New England Antiquities); with Christine Penn, Madison, North Carolina (since deceased), two porringers; with her brother Peter Seibert, Vail, Colorado (since deceased), a mirror; and with Carolyn Myrick, Temple, New Hampshire, a porringer. I have authenticated the cup plate, but I have no reason, on the basis of lines of descent, to doubt the authenticity of the other items.

Other alleged possessions have "disappeared." *Sharon Advocate,* Sept. 26, 1902, reports a wooden army canteen passed down via descendants of Hannah Sampson, Deborah's sister, donated to the Town of Sharon. The canteen and a tin foot-warmer, donated I believe by the Gannetts of the East Street house around 1900, were supposedly in SPL but disappeared some decades ago. Pauline Moody, *DS,* also mentions a wooden pie-crimper allegedly whittled by Deborah in her youth in possession of Wilda Keevy Brown of Hanson, Massachusetts, and a parlor table with Mr. and Mrs. John E. Forrest of Sharon/Stoughton. Charles Bricknell drew up a list, "Location of Deborah Sampson's Possessions," c. 1972 (Bricknell, PHS), which, in addition to many of the above items, mentioned a small three-legged table given to PHS by a Sampson descendant, c. 1970. Mrs. Muriel Nelson also showed me a cast-metal eagle allegedly worn on Deborah's hat or uniform in the war. This could be the "silver eagle" which a note in SHS Scrapbooks says Seth R. Boyden, Dec. 8, 1894, presented, to whom is not clear.

26. The cup plate was identified on the basis of photographs by Susan Meyers, Curator of Ceramics, Smithsonian Institution, conversation with author, February 1995; my thanks also to Katherine Zugmun, Assistant Curator of Decorative Arts, Chicago Historical Society, who compared the plate to those in the society's collection. Richard Nylander, Curator, SPNEA, who examined the plate for Ann Gilbert, identified it as "transferware Staffordshire called Pearlware," on the basis of "the blueish glaze applied over the common clay [which] produces the more refined white look"—Ann Gilbert to Alfred Young, Aug. 14, 1997. For the genre: Richard H. and Virginia A. Wood, "A Check List of Historical China Cup Plates," *The Antiques Journal* (1958): 15–16, and Jane S. Spillman, "Cup Plates in Early America," *Magazine Antiques* 104 (1973): 2, 216–19; *Benjamin Franklin's Autobiography,* ed. J. A. Leo Lemay and P. M. Zall (New York, 1986), 65 (comment on chinaware).

27. Nylander, *Our Own Snug Fireside,* 243–44 (Caroline King), 236 (Susan Blunt); Rodris Roth, "Tea-Drinking in Eighteenth Century America: Its Etiquette and Equipage," *Contributions from the Museum of History and Technology: U.S. National Museum Bulletin 225* (Washington, DC, 1961), 61–91, reprinted in Robert B. St. George, ed., *Material Life in America, 1600–1800* (Boston, 1988), 439–62.

28. Bushman, *Refinement of America,* 184–85.

29. William Ellis to William Jackson, Feb. 4, 1837, Ellis MS, LC.

30. Reverend Lyman Partridge to Eugene Tappan, Jan. 27, 28, 1902, SHS Scrapbook 1:70–71, SPL. While Partridge, the Baptist minister, is suspect as a biased source, he said he passed on the report from Mrs. Holmes, a granddaughter; Moody, *DS,* 36 (for George Washington Gay).

31. Moody, *DS;* Corbett, "Sharon's Jean D'Arc," cited above; Rodney Monk, "Grandmother Monk," cited above.

32. Monk, "Grandmother Monk"; Daniel Johnson cited in Eugene Tappan, intro., DG, *Address, SHS Publications* (Boston, 1908), vol. 5; Elisha Horton, "Recollections of Past Events, Jan. 1, 1858," MS, SPL, filed under "Industry, Cotton Beaumont."

33. Reverend Lyman Partridge to Eugene Tappan, Nov. 27, 1902, SHS Scrapbooks.

34. Mann, preface, DG, *Address* (1802); Mann, "Prospectus of a New Work to be Published Subscription, The Heroine . . . ," broadside, Dedham, Aug. 1, 1829, MHS.

35. William De Britaine, *Human Prudence: or, The Art by Which a Man & a Woman*

Advanced to a Fortune, to Permanent Honour, and to Real Grandeur (London, 8th edn, reprinted, Herman Mann, Dedham, 1806). Herman Mann adapted this for American readers. Priced first at $2, it was lowered to 85 cents. The aphorisms cited are from 53, 54, and 55; DG to George Webb, June 2, 1804, Webb MS, AAS. Mann dedicated the book "To the American Citizen and Youth of Both Sexes."

36. Herman Mann, Jr., "Journal," May 4, 1850, 28–29, MS, DHS; Ellis to Jackson, Feb. 4, 1837, Ellis MS, LC.

37. Herman Mann [Sr.], "The Heroine," MS, and Herman Mann, Jr., "The American Heroine," MS, both DHS. A typed version of the latter is in Bricknell, PHS, which Bricknell was also unable to publish in the 1970s. For the Mann family correspondence about payment for the later Vinton edition of the 1797 book with Wiggin & Lunt, the Boston publishers of the edition, see an exchange of letters, Mann Papers, DHS. After Mann, Sr., died, a broadside advertising a subscription to "The Heroine" dated 1829 was reissued by his son, with the date of proposed publication changed in handwriting to 1835 or 1836 and the terms of sale altered.

38. Mary Beth Norton, *Founding Mothers and Fathers: Gendered Power and the Forming of American Society* (New York, 1996), 256–77, quotations at 256, 277.

39. DG to George Webb, June 2, 1804, miscellaneous MS "S," AAS.

40. Linda Kerber, " 'History Can Do It No Justice': Women and the Reinterpretation of the American Revolution," in Kerber, *Toward an Intellectual History of Women* (Chapel Hill, NC, 1997), 63–99.

41. George Adams to Lewis Bradford, March 3, 1850, Bricknell, PHS; "The Temperance Movement in Sharon," SHS Scrapbook 3:42, SPL.

42. Barbara Lambert Merrick, "The Secret Life of Jonathan Sampson," *The Mayflower Quarterly* 48 (1982): 172–77, reprints excerpts from the Plympton and Fayette Town Records. Charles Bricknell, "Deborah Bradford Samson Gannett, Alias Timothy Thayer, Alias Robert Shurtliff," unpublished article, 11-page typescript, PHS. My thanks to Patrick Leonard, who provided me with typed excerpts from the Plympton Selectmen's Records and other documents based on his research in Maine. Jonathan Sampson returned briefly to Plympton in 1794 for a land transaction with his sisters. See also Guba, *Deborah Samson*, chap. 4, "The Mystery of Deborah's Parents."

43. George Quintal tracked Nehemiah Sampson in Maine and New Hampshire local history without finding additional information. For his family genealogy, see Ezra S. Stearns, comp., *Genealogical and Family History of the State of New Hampshire*, 4 vols. (New York 1908), 2:961. See chapter 11 below for a discussion of the claim that he was a mulatto. For Ephraim, see Ephraim Sampson Pension File W 11052, NA, M 804, Roll 2113. Bricknell, PHS, has a few notes on the brothers and sisters.

44. Mrs. Cyrus Tolman (Zilpah Tolman) to Eugene Tappan, Dec. 4, 1903, SHS Scrapbook 1:109–10, SPL. Tolman to Tappan, Jan. 29, 1902, typescript, Bricknell, PHS, says the same thing. A letter of Irene Soule is in Ephraim Sampson Pension File, NA. In 1797, Captain John Soule of Middleborough bought six copies of Mann's book.

e chapter 4 for a discussion of the evidence concerning DG's wound. The testimony submitted with the petition is summarized in *Journal of the House of Representatives* (Washington, DC, 1837): Twenty-fifth Congress, 2nd sess., Report No. 172 (Jan. 31, 1837), to accompany H.R. 890, 1–2, and in Report No. 159 (Dec. 22, 1837) to accompany H.R. 184, 1–2. The latter is also in typescript in DG Pension File S 32722, NA.

46. DG, Pension File, for a summary of the medical costs with no details; "Fees Charged by Boston Medical Association, Feb., 1806," in *Medicine in Colonial Massachusetts, 1620–1820, Publications Colonial Society of Massachusetts* 57 (1980), after p. 150; for 1817 Boston fees, George Rosen, "Fees and Fee Bills: Some Economic Aspects of Medical Practice in Nineteenth Century America," *Bulletin of the History of Medicine,* Suppl. 6 (Baltimore, 1946): 5–6. My thanks to Steven L. Pastore for tracking medical fees. Pension: March 1827, receipt for payment by The Bank of the United States at Boston, Fogg Collection, Maine Historical Society, copy in Bricknell, PHS.

47. [Dedham] *Village Register,* May 3, 1827, probably by Herman Mann, Jr.; "A Female Veteran," *Niles Register,* May 26, 1827, 217; in Boston, 1827: "Another Revolution Soldier No More," *Columbian Centinel,* May 5; *Daily Advertiser,* May 2; *American Traveller,* May 18; "Another Revolutionary Character Gone," *Commercial Gazette,* May 7. The AAS index to *Early American Periodicals* lists only a notice in *Ariel* [Philadelphia], May 25, 1827. *Army and Navy Chronicle* IV, Feb. 16, 1837, reports the death of Benjamin Gannett, husband of "The Celebrated Deborah Sampson."

48. For this larger process of erasure and the sanitizing of heroes of the Revolution, see Young, *The Shoemaker and the Tea Party,* part 2.

49. Will of Benjamin Gannett, n.d.; Bond of Earl Gannett as executor of the estate, Feb. 7, 1837, Probate Court, NCRD 7680; Mann, *FR,* 232 (drawing of gravestones).

50. Mann, *FR,* 250–51.

51. See DG, Diary, entries for June 28 and Nov. 11, 1802. She sent money home "to her family," not to her husband.

52. Mrs. F. [Florence G.] Moody, "Deborah Sampson's Willow," SHS Scrapbook 1:58, SPL.

53. Twenty-fifth Congress, 2nd sess., Report No. 159, Dec. 22, 1837, by Mr. Morgan from the Committee on Revolutionary Pensions, typescript, DG, Pension File S 32722, NA.

54. A letter from "Commissioner," Pension Office, to Peter Force, Sept. 18, 1838, summing up Benjamin Gannett's pension history, reports that Congress passed a special act (*Statutes at Large,* vol. 6, p. 735) on July 7, 1838, awarding the heirs the money. This and other letters of 1837–38 are in DG's Pension File.

55. Vinton, *The Sampson Family* (Boston, 1864); for names, I rely on the index to Michael Gannett, *Descendants,* and on the genealogy by Janet and Robert Day (typescript, 1992); see an interview with Rodney Monk in *Worcester Telegram,* March 15, 1936. Among present-day Gannetts, Deborah Gannett Brooks (1947–) of Brookline, Massachusetts, seems to be one of the few women named Deborah. Among Sampson descendants, I have encountered Deborah Sampson Shinn, at the time Curator of Applied Arts, Cooper-Hewitt National Design Museum, New York, who informs me that her mother named her after the famous Debo-

56. Michael Gannett's file on Deborah Sampson has an undated Ripley's "Believe It or N cartoon featuring Benjamin Gannett, possibly from the 1970s.

1. For the changing ways Americans have viewed the Revolution, see Michael Kammen, *A Season of Youth: The American Revolution and the Historical Imagination* (New York, 1978; Ithaca, NY, 1988).

2. For Paine's reputation, see my "*Common Sense* and *The Rights of Man* in America: The Celebration and Damnation of Thomas Paine," in Kostas Gavroglu et al., eds., *Science, Mind and Art . . . Essays in Honor of Robert S. Cohen* (Dordrecht, Netherlands, 1995), 411–39; John Adams to Joseph Ward, June 6, 1809, and Aug. 31, 1809, Joseph Ward Papers, Chicago Historical Society, the former letter reprinted in Alfred F. Young, Terry J. Fife, and Mary E. Janzen, *We the People: Voices and Images of the New Nation* (Philadelphia, 1993), 191.

3. For the erasure of radicalism, see my *The Shoemaker and the Tea Party: Memory and the American Revolution* (Boston, 1999), part 2, and Harlow E. Shiedley, *Sectional Nationalism: The Culture and Politics of the Massachusetts Conservative Elite, 1815–1836* (Boston, 1998).

4. Michael Kammen, *Mystic Chords of Memory, The Transformation of Tradition in American Culture* (New York, 1991), 3–39, quotations at 9–10.

5. Gloria Steinem, *Outrageous Acts and Everyday Rebellions* (New York, 1983; 2nd edn, 1995), xix. Steinem attributes this phrasing, as well as the idea, to Gerda Lerner, but Lerner says that while she expressed the idea many times, "nothing sounds like this" in her writings— Lerner to the author, July 9, 14, 2001. See Lerner, *The Creation of Feminist Consciousness: From the Middle Ages to Eighteen-Seventy* (New York, 1993), esp. 166, 281.

6. Quotations cited in Rosemarie Zagarri, *A Woman's Dilemma: Mercy Otis Warren and the American Revolution* (Wheeling, IL, 1995), 140–47; Mercy Otis Warren, *History of the Rise, Progress and Termination of the American Revolution,* ed. Lester Cohen, 3 vols. (Boston, 1805; Indianapolis, 1988), 1:211, 236–38. Interestingly, this elaborately indexed modern edition has only three citations to women in the index; Joan Hoff, *Law, Gender and Injustice: A Legal History of U.S. Women* (New York, 1991), 66–79.

7. Judith Sargent Murray, *The Gleaner: A Miscellaneous Production in Three Volumes,* 3 vols. (Boston, 1798), 1-vol. reprint, ed. Nina Baym (Schenectady, NY, 1992), chap. 91; Sheila L. Skemp, *Judith Sargent Murray: A Brief Biography with Documents* (Boston, 1998).

8. Surprisingly, Adams's encomium to DSG in this speech has gone unnoticed by celebrants of either Deborah or Adams. I came across it in Linda Kerber, *Women of the Republic: Intellect and Ideology in Revolutionary America* (Chapel Hill, NC, 1980), 112–13, who discusses the speech as it bears on women's citizenship.

9. See chapter 9 above. William Jackson, representing Norfolk County, introduced and seems to have shepherded Benjamin Gannett's petition through Congress. There is no record of involvement by Adams. J. Q. Adams in Charles Francis Adams, ed., *Memoirs of John Quincy Adams, Comprising Portions of His Diary from 1789 to 1848,* 12 vols. (Philadelphia, 1876), 10:26–27, lists Deborah Gannett as a topic he took up in his speech but has no other entries for her or for Benjamin Gannett. Richard Alan Ryerson, editor-in-chief of the Adams ▪pers, MHS, informed me that there is no evidence of a correspondence between Mrs. ▪nnett and Adams, and no reference in the published *Memoirs.* "I should add, however,

that we cannot say whether Gannett is mentioned in John Quincy Adams's manuscript Diary, which is nearly three times as long as the 12-volume *Memoirs*, because the Diary has never been indexed"—Ryerson to the author, Dec. 16, 1996.

10. For the debate and context, see William Lee Miller, *Arguing About Slavery: John Quincy Adams and the Great Battle in the United States Congress* (New York, 1995); for Adams's role, Samuel Flagg Bemis, *John Quincy Adams and the Union* (New York, 1965), chaps. 17, 18.

11. Bemis, *John Quincy Adams*, 368.

12. *Speech of John Quincy Adams of Massachusetts, Upon the Rights of the People, Men and Women, to Petition; on the Freedom of Speech and of Debate in the House of Representatives of the United States . . .* (Gales & Seaton, Washington, DC, 1838), 22–23. This reprints Adams's speech in the House verbatim.

13. Adams, *Speech*, 66–67 (June 26); Miller, *Arguing About Slavery,* 314–17. For his possible sources, see Angelina Grimké, *An Appeal to the Christian Women of the South* (1836); Angelina Grimké, *Appeal to the Women of the Nominally Free States* (1837); and Sarah Grimké, *Letters on the Equality of the Sexes and the Condition of Women* (1838), summarized in Nina Baym, *American Women Writers and the Work of History, 1790–1860* (New Brunswick, NJ, 1995), 223–24.

14. Adams, *Speech,* 67–70.

15. Ibid., 72–73 (June 28).

16. Ibid., 76–77. My thanks to Judith Hiltner for identifying Aspasia.

17. Bemis, *John Quincy Adams,* 372.

18. For nineteenth-century trends in cross-dressing: Vern L. Bullough and Bonnie Bullough, *Cross Dressing, Sex, and Gender* (Philadelphia, 1993), 157–68; D. Michael Quinn, *Same-Sex Dynamics Among Nineteenth-Century Americans: A Mormon Example* (Urbana, IL, 1996), 134–36; for summaries of the social changes: Jack Larkin, *The Reshaping of Everyday Life, 1790–1840* (New York, 1988) chap. 5, quotation at 204, and Edward Countryman, *Americans: A Collision of Histories* (New York, 1996), chaps. 6, 7.

19. I am indebted to Shane White, who was doing research for his book with Graham White, *Stylin': African American Expressive Culture from Its Beginnings to the Zoot Suit* (Ithaca, NY, 1998)—White to Young, June 11, 1996. The sources are: [New York] *National Advocate,* Aug. 25, 1817, Oct. 19, 1820; [New York] *American,* Sept. 21, 1821; [New York] *Commercial Advertiser,* June 12, 1832; and [Philadelphia] *Public Ledger,* Aug. 15, 25, 1836, March 4, 10, 1837.

20. For other examples of women cross-dressing: "The Life and Writings of Minerva Mayo, 1820–1822," MS, Old Sturbridge Village Research Library, transcribed and edited by Jack Larkin; Larry Gara, "Ellen Craft," *NAW* 1:396–98, brought to my attention by Mary O'Keefe Young; see also *A Narrative of the Life, Occurrences, Vicissitudes and Present Situation of K. White* ["A Tale of Woe"], *Compiled and Narrated by Herself* (Schenectady, NY, for the authoress, 1809), 63, 67, 104–05, brought to my attention by Christopher Castiglia, who believes the narrative is "embellished if not entirely fabricated."

21. For examples of the genre: "Mademoiselle de Beaumont or the Chevalier d'Eon," engravi͏ in [Boston] *Omnium Gatherum* (September 1810); *The Widow in Masquerade; or the Fen Warrior . . . The Life and Adventures of Hannah Snell* (Northampton, MA, 1809);

Adams Vinton in Mann *FR*, xxx (women at Waterloo); on the decline of the genre, see Dianne Dugaw, *Warrior Women and Popular Balladry, 1650–1850* (Cambridge, UK, 1989), chap. 3.

22. For bibliography and analysis, see Estelle C. Jelinek, *The Traditions of Women's Autobiography: From Antiquity to the Present* (Boston, 1988), chap. 6, and Jelinek, "Disguise Autobiographies: Women Masquerading as Men," *Women's Studies International Forum* 10 (1987): 53–62. AAS recently added to its collection *A Sketch of the Life of Elizabeth Emmons, or The Female Sailor Who Was Brutally Murdered While at Sea . . .* (Boston, 1841).

23. *The Female Marine and Related Works: Narratives of Cross-Dressing and Urban Vice in the America's Early Republic,* ed. Daniel A. Cohen (Amherst, MA, 1997). Dianne Dugaw provided the information from her workbooks that Nathaniel Coverly & Son was also the printer of *The Female Drummer* and *The Bristol Bridegroom*—letter to the author, May 2, 1995. For Ann Street, New York City, as the center of erotic publishing, see Helen Lefkowitz Horowitz, *Rereading Sex: Battles over Sexual Knowledge and Suppression in Nineteenth-Century America* (New York, 2002), 132–33, 244–45.

24. *The Female Marine, or the Adventures of Lucy Brewer* (Boston, 1816), quotations at 71, 75, and 82 in the Cohen edition.

25. *The Cabin-Boy's Life; or, Singular and Surprising Adventures of Mrs. Ellen Stephens . . .* (New York, 1840), 12.

26. *The Friendless Orphan, An Affecting Narrative of the Trials and Afflictions of Sophia Johnson* (New York, 1841), 23.

27. William Dunlap, *The Glory of Columbia, Her Yeomanry! A Play in Five Acts* (New York, 1817), 12–19; Michael Schuldiner, "The Historical Drama of Mordecai Noah's *She Would Be a Soldier,*" in Schuldiner and Daniel Kleinfield, eds., *The Selected Writings of Mordecai Noah* (Westport, CT, 1999), 13–16. My thanks to Loretta Mannucci, who called my attention to these plays.

28. Mary Livermore, *My Story of the War* (Hartford, CT, 1889), 111–16; Linda Grant De Pauw, *Battle Cries and Lullabies: Women in War from Prehistory to the Present* (Norman, OK, 1998), 147–56; Elizabeth Young, *Disarming the Nation: Women's Writing and the Civil War* (Chicago, 1999), chap. 4.

29. Michael Denning, *Mechanic Accents: Dime Novels and Working-Class Culture in America* (New York, 1987), 11 (circulation figures); *Traditions and Romances of Border and Revolutionary Times,* ed. Edward S. Ellis, in *Complete Beadle's Dime Tales,* no. 2 (New York, n.d., c. 1862), 18–22. My thanks to Timothy Malone and Samuel Huang for locating this copy in the Northern Illinois University Library, Special Collections.

30. Mann, *FR* (Vinton ed., 1866), xxx. The Vinton edition was also reprinted during World War I in *Magazine of History with Notes and Queries,* extra no. 47 (Tarrytown, NY, 1916), but not again until 1972 in a series of first-person sources of the Revolutionary War.

31. Charles F. Adams, ed., *Letters of Mrs. Adams,* 2 vols. (Boston 1840), 1:xxi–ii; Alma Lutz, "Elizabeth Ellet," *NAW* 1:569–70.

32. For women historians: Baym, *American Women Writers,* chap. 10; for male historians: Peter Force Papers, LC, which has letters to Force from pension clerks and a draft of an article, unpublished, it seems; Benjamin Lossing, "The Female Review," n.d., 23-page MS, Huntington Library, which appears to be a summary of Gannett's life based on Mann's 1797 book.

Lossing published Gannett's letter of 1804 to Captain Webb in his magazine, *American Historical Record* 2 (1873): 562–63, and a letter from C. Harold Vinton, ibid., 3 (1874): 79–80.

33. Elizabeth Ellet, *The Women of the American Revolution,* 3 vols. (New York, 1848–50), quotations at 1:18. In 1856, Baker & Scribner published the 6th edition of the work. There were other printings in 1900, 1951, 1969, 1980; Ellet, *Domestic History of the American Revolution* (New York, 1850); Linda Kerber, "History Can Do It No Justice: Women and the Reinterpretation of the American Revolution," in Kerber, *Intellectual History of Women* (Chapel Hill, NC, 1997), 63–99, quotation at 65. For the women's movement: Eleanor Flexner, *Century of Struggle: The Woman's Rights Movement in the United States* (New York, 1959, 1968), chaps. 4–6; Ellen C. DuBois, *Feminism and Suffrage: The Emergence of an Independent Woman's Movement in America, 1848–1869* (Ithaca, NY, 1978).

34. Ellet, *Women of the Revolution,* 2:123.

35. See the discussion in chapter 2 of Sampson's first enlistment as "Timothy Thayer." Ellet identifies the source as "a niece of Captain Tisdale," the officer with whom DSG stayed for a few days in 1802. See DG, Diary, July 3, 20, 1802. The story is that in 1778 she stayed at the home of Nathaniel Thayer, where she had the flirtation.

36. Ellet, *Women of the Revolution,* 2:124–26. Binney had a niece who lived in another city; the nineteenth-century Binney family rejected the notion of an affair with her.

37. Ibid., 2:133–35.

38. Sarah Josepha Hale, *Woman's Record; or Sketches of all Distinguished Women from "the Beginning" Till A.D. 1850* . . . (New York, 1853), 497; Paul Boyer, "Sarah Hale," *NAW* 2:110–14; see also Jesse Clement, ed., *Noble Deeds of American Women* (Boston, 1869), 450–58; for an account blending Mann with Ellet, see Thomas Wyatt, "Deborah Sampson, The Heroine of '76," in *Graham's American Monthly Magazine* 39 (September 1851): 147–53; *Appleton's Cyclopedia of American Biography* (1888), 5:382; *The National Cyclopedia of American Biography* (New York, 1909), "Deborah Sampson"; and Oliver Wendell Holmes, *The Guardian Angel* (Boston, 1867), 74–75.

39. For an overview of trends, see Kammen, *Mystic Chords of Memory,* chaps. 7–9; for the Revolution in this era, Kammen, *Season of Youth,* 59–65; for late-nineteenth-century patriotism, Cecilia Elizabeth O'Leary, *To Die For: The Paradox of American Patriotism* (Princeton, NJ, 1999).

40. Robert E. Riegel, "Mary Livermore," *NAW* 2:410–13; for the women's movement of this era, see Flexner, *Century of Struggle,* chaps. 10–13; Ellen DuBois, *Woman's Suffrage and Women's Rights* (New York, 1998), 30–42, 68–80, 160–75.

41. Jane Austin, *Dr. LeBaron and His Daughters: A Story of the Old Colony* (Boston, 1891); for Austin, see *DAB,* 1:431–35; Mary P. Haskell, "The Girl Who Fought in the Revolution," *Ladies' Home Journal* 17 (July 1900): 12; Kate Gannett Wells, "Deborah Sampson, Heroine of the American Revolution," *New England Magazine* 19 (October 1895): 156–58; SHS Scrapbooks, SPL, has the following clippings for these years: "A Yankee Jeanne D'Arc," Boston *Evening Transcript,* 1895; Greenough White, "A Sharon Celebrity," 2-col. article, n.d., very likely from a Boston paper c. 1901; and Alexander Corbett, Jr., "An American Joan of Arc," from an unnamed Boston paper, clearly 1901.

42. Benjamin Gannett, obituary of Jan. 4, 1901, from an unidentified paper, SHS Scrapbook

43. Kammen, *Mystic Chords of Memory,* 218–20; I have consulted the ancestry files, DAR Library, Washington, DC; *Canton Journal,* Nov. 28, 1890 (about Gilbert Thompson); Alexander Corbett, Jr., "An American Jean D'Arc," SPL; for Helen Weeks—author's conversation with Beatrice Weeks Bostock, her daughter, and Ann Gilbert, her granddaughter, Truro, Massachusetts, summer 1995.

44. John Goddard Phillips, ed., *A Memorial to Eugene Tappan, Esq.* (Sharon, MA, 1910), *SHS Publications* (Boston, 1904), 6:34–49. In 1901, Tappan transcribed Mrs. Gannett's Diary.

45. My account in this and the following paragraphs is based on Eugene Tappan, "Deborah Sampson Gannett Dinner in the Town Hall, Sharon, Massachusetts, April 3, 1802," MS, SPL, filed as "Banquet, 1902." The attendees are listed 23–33. For the Baptists, see Rev. L. Partridge to Eugene Tappan, Jan. 27, 28, 1902, SHS Scrapbook 1: 70–71.

46. Tappan, "Dinner," 22–23, 49–50.

47. Ibid., 34–39 (Livermore talk); Rodney Monk, "About Deborah Sampson Gannett, August, 1970," 2-page MS, personal papers of Mrs. Roger Myrick, copy in Monk Papers, SPL; see also Mary Livermore to Eugene Tappan, Feb. 10, 1902, SHS Scrapbook 1:57, SPL.

48. Tappan, "Dinner," 38.

49. Ibid., 53–69.

50. Picture postcards: for the Sharon house, in possession of Muriel Nelson; for the Thomas house on Sachem Street, Middleborough, cards in possession of Kenneth Crest, reproduced in chapter 1. My thanks to Walter Thompson of Middleborough for showing me his extensive collection of local postcards and to the Curt Teich Postcard Archives, Lake County Museum, Wauconda, Illinois, for searching their collections. This archive houses 386,000 image records of postcards.

51. Pauline Moody, *Massachusetts' Deborah Sampson* (Attleborough, MA, 1975), chap. 5 for a brief summary; a clipping likely from a Boston paper, May 21, 1908, SPL, filed under "Monument in Sharon."

52. Conversations of the author with Muriel Nelson, Sharon, 1994, 1995.

53. Muriel Nelson to the author, June 12, 1994.

CHAPTER 11: LOST AND FOUND

1. I base this on conversations with Daniel Arguimbau, the present owner of the Gannett house and farm, Sharon, December 1996; on the family scrapbook of clippings in possession of Muriel Nelson, Sharon; and on articles listed in the *Reader's Guide to Periodical Literature.*

2. *Worcester Sunday Telegram,* Oct. 12, 1919, Automobile, Amusement and Women's News section, 1; for Potter, see *Mass. S&S,* 12:622–23; Federal Writers Project of the Works Progress Administration for Massachusetts, *Massachusetts: A Guide to Its Places and People* (Boston, 1937), 535; for the HABS error, see my discussion of Middleborough houses in chapter 1.

3. Robert Ripley, "Believe It or Not!" cartoon panel, n.d., in Michael Gannett Personal Papers (Ripley recycled his oddities; this may also have appeared earlier); "Middleboro Soldier Girl Is Theme of Sparkling Comedy," a review of *Damn Deborah* by Walter Charles Robert the Cape Cod Playhouse, Dennis, Massachusetts, after Aug. 15, 1937, clipping possibly

from *Boston Herald,* provided by Dr. and Mrs. David Browne, Plympton; New York Public Library for the Performing Arts (Lincoln Center, NY) has a file on the play, indicating that it was performed elsewhere in the 1930s and 1940s; Morris Bishop, "Private Deborah Sampson, U.S.A.," *The New Yorker,* July 3, 1937; Richardson Wright, *Forgotten Ladies: Nine Portraits from the American Family Album* (Philadelphia, 1928); Stewart Holbrooke, *Lost Men of American History* (New York, 1946); "A Forgotten Woman in History: Deborah Sampson," *True Comics* (August 1941), 3:9–11; for the continuing genre: "Hoaxes of the Ages," *U.S. News & World Report,* July 24–31, 2000, and James Chenoweth, *Oddity Odyssey: A Journey Through New England's Colorful Past* (New York, 1997).

4. Pauline Moody, *Massachusetts' Deborah Sampson* (Attleborough, MA, 1975), 42; for Frank E. Gannett, see *Current Biography* (1945), 215–19, and Martin Fausold, "Frank. E. Gannett," *DAB Supplement* 6 (1956–60), 226–27. For the ship: *The Ganneteer* (May 1944, a publication of the Gannett Newspaper Group), 4; John Gorley Bunke, *Liberty Ships: Ugly Ducklings of World War II* (Annapolis, MD, 1972), 227. My thanks to Tarra Connell and Jackie Jolly of the Gannett Foundation for searching their files for links to Deborah Gannett.

5. Frank Monaghan, *Heritage of Freedom: The History and Significance of the Basic Documents of American Liberty* (New York, 1947), 99–100 (document); 145–46 (the committee).

6. Conversation of the author with Daniel Arguimbau, 1995; with Michael Gannett, 1995; family scrapbook in possession of Muriel Nelson, Sharon; copies of Rodney Monk's letters are deposited in the Monk Collection, SPL; "Profile Charles Bricknell and the Other Woman," in [Kingston, MA] *Silver Lake News,* Feb. 10, 1977; Charles Bricknell to Michael Gannett, Oct. 29, 1975 (about Middleborough), in Michael Gannett Personal Papers.

7. For the military statistics: Linda K. Kerber, *No Constitutional Rights to Be Ladies: Women and the Obligations of Citizenship* (New York, 1998), 265; for historiography: Peter Novick, *That Noble Dream: The "Objectivity Question" and the American Historical Profession* (New York, 1988), chap. 10, and Esther Forbes, *Paul Revere and the World He Lived In* (Boston, 1942), 432–34.

8. Cynthia Costello, Shan Miles, and Anna Stone, eds., *The American Woman, 1999–2000* (Women's Research and Education Institute, New York, 1998), 348–51; for the number of women veterans by state, The Women's Memorial, "Statistics on Women in the Military" (typescript, Washington, DC, 2000).

9. Sara M. Evans, *Born for Liberty: A History of Women in America* (New York, 1989), 243–314.

10. For a brief survey of historical scholarship as of 1990: Linda Kerber, "The Revolutionary Generation: Ideology, Politics, and Culture in the Early Republic," and Linda Gordon, "U.S. Women's History," both in Eric Foner, ed., *The New American History* (Philadelphia, 1990), 25–49, 185–210, also available as pamphlets from the American Historical Association; for contexts, Joan Wallach Scott, *Gender and the Politics of History* (New York, 1988), "Women's History," 15–27, and "American Women Historians, 1884–1984," 178–98; for seminal essays, Gerda Lerner, *The Majority Finds Its Past: Placing Women in History* (New York, 1979).

11. Kerber, "The Revolutionary Generation," 26; on the overall changes in history, see No[ ] *That Noble Dream,* chap. 14; on changes in the history of the Revolution, see my "American Historians Confront 'The Transforming Hand of Revolution,' " in Rona[ ]

man and Peter J. Albert, eds., *The Transforming Hand of Revolution: Reconsidering the American Revolution as a Social Movement* (Charlottesville, VA, 1996), 422–54; on the women's movement and history, Ruth Rosen, *The World Split Open: How the Modern Women's Movement Changed America* (New York, 2000), 225, 266–67; on gay history, Martin Duberman, Martha Vicinus, and George Chauncey, Jr., eds., *Hidden from History: Reclaiming the Gay and Lesbian Past* (New York, 1989), intro., 1–13.

12. Emil F. Guba, *Deborah Samson alias Robert Shurtliff, Revolutionary War Soldier* (Kingston, MA, privately printed, 1994), 150–89, sums up the achievements of the group; foreword by Patrick Leonard, viii–xii; Leonard, "Deborah Samson: Official Heroine of the State of Massachusetts" (Canton Historical Society <Samson@Canton.org>); Bricknell to Michael Gannett, Oct. 11, 1975, Michael Gannett Personal Papers; Pauline Moody, *Massachusetts' Deborah Sampson;* Michael R. Gannett, *Gannett Descendants of Matthew and Hannah Gannett of Scituate, Massachusetts* (Chevy Chase, MD, 1976). My knowledge of the efforts of the group is based on conversations with Leonard, Jan Lewis Nelson, and Michael R. Gannett, and on their correspondence in Bricknell, PHS, and the private collections of Leonard and Gannett. The group also succeeded in having the National Woman's Hall of Fame at Seneca Falls, New York, declare DG a member and in having the Capitol Historical Society in Washington, DC, issue a medallion with her image.

13. See Julia Ward Howe Stickley, "The Records of Deborah Sampson Gannett, Woman Soldier of the Revolution," *Prologue, the Journal of the National Archives* 4 (1972): 233–41, and in Julia Ward Stickley Papers, MA; Stickley to Pauline Moody (a mean-spirited put-down); Stickley to Michael Gannett, Nov. 4, 5, 16 ("commies" at Harvard), Nov. 24, 1975; Gannett to Stickley, Nov. 8, 23, 1975, all in Michael Gannett Personal Papers. For the claim of Deborah as black, see the next section of this chapter; for the lost battle to put Sampson on a postage stamp, Guba, *Deborah Samson,* chap. 16.

14. In response to my article, "Searching for Deborah Sampson," *Middleboro Gazette,* Sept. 5, 1995, and Grechen Fehrenbacher, "Desperately Seeking Deborah," [New Bedford] *Standard Times,* Oct. 6, 1995, a dozen people offered help. Edwina Wood to author, Nov. 24, 1995.

15. Sampson is in Elizabeth Evans, *Weathering the Storm: Women of the American Revolution* (New York, 1975); Lonnelle Aikman, "Patriots in Petticoats," *National Geographic* (October 1975), 475–93; Linda Grant De Pauw and Conover Hunt, *"Remember the Ladies": Women in America, 1750–1815* (New York, 1975), a pathbreaking book based on the exhibit.

16. The sourcebook: Eleanor Wachs, comp., *Deborah Sampson Gannett (1760–1827), America's First Woman Soldier, A Source Booklet* (Commonwealth Museum, Secretary of the Commonwealth of Massachusetts, 1980, 1990); the lesson plan for fifth-grade level: Lora Barney, "Deborah Sampson," <http:/teacherlink.ed.usu.edu/res>. Library of Congress catalogues books about Sampson as follows: for children, by Ann McGovern (1975), Harold Felton (1976), Bryna Stevens (1984), and Rick Blake (2003); as juvenile fiction, Cora Cheyney (1967) and Patrica Clapp (1977). Cheyney, *The Incredible Deborah: A Story Based on the Life of Deborah Sampson* (New York, 1967), now out of print, struck me as an imaginative juvenile biography. Other authors, beside Herman Mann (1797), are Vera Laska (1976) and Lucy Freeman and Alma Bond (1992). The catalogue omits Florence Moody (1975) and Emil Guba (1994), two self-published works.

17. For the significance of the *American National Biography,* see Edmund S. Morgan and Marie Morgan, "Who's Really Who," *New York Review of Books* 47 (March 9, 2001): 38–43. The entry in *ANB* is by Samuel Willard Crompton. Gerda Lerner, ed., *The Female Experience: An American Documentary* in "The American Heritage Series," ed. Leonard W. Levy and Alfred F. Young (Indianapolis, 1977), 295–96. The first modern scholarly article, well researched, is by Vera O. Laska, "Deborah Sampson Gannett," in Laska, *"Remember the Ladies": Outstanding Women of the American Revolution* (Commonwealth of Massachusetts Bicentennial Publication, May 1976), 61–100. For scholarship on Herman Mann, see the works by Cathy N. Davidson and Judith Hiltner cited in the Prologue; on her military service, see the articles by Jane Keiter cited in chapter 4 on the war in Westchester; on her performance, see the works cited in chapter 7 on DG as a lecturer by Sandra Gustafson and Michelle Navarre-Cleary; for representations, Thomas A. Foster, " 'In Defense of All That Is Dear and Lovely': Revolutionary War Soldier Deborah Sampson and the Permeability of War-Time Gender Norms" (M.A. thesis, North Carolina State Univ., 1995).

18. See works cited earlier by Linda Grant De Pauw, Holly A. Mayer, Julie Wheelwright, Dianne Dugaw; for a philosophic discussion, see Jean Bethke Elshtain, *Women and War* (Chicago, 1987, 1995), 174–75; for encyclopedia entries: "Deborah Sampson Gannett," in Jack P. Greene and J. R. Pole, eds., *The Blackwell Encyclopedia of the American Revolution* (Oxford, 1991, with four errors in fourteen lines); Holly Mayer, "Deborah Sampson," in Richard L. Blanco, ed., *The American Revolution, 1775–1783: An Encyclopedia,* 2 vols. (New York, 1993); "Deborah Sampson" in Marc Boatner, *Encyclopedia of the American Revolution* (New York, 1974).

19. For Corbin, see Linda Grant De Pauw, *Battle Cries and Lullabies: Women in War from Prehistory to the Present* (Norman, OK, 1996), 130; for the illustration by Herbert Knotel at West Point, see the Epilogue below. My thanks to Allan Aimone, Librarian at the West Point Academy, for discussing their holdings on DSG. Part of the cantonment at New Windsor is managed by the National Temple Hill Association, which maintains the huts, and part by the New York State Office of Parks, which maintains a museum. For information about the Pentagon exhibit, my thanks to Linda Grant De Pauw and her friends.

20. For the museum dedication: Linda Witt, ed., *The Day the Nation Said Thanks* (Washington, DC, 1999); conversation with Brigadier General Wilma Vaught, April 11, 2000. My thanks to Judith A. Bellafaire and Linda Witt for information about the plan of The Women's Memorial to include Sampson in an exhibit, "Early Patriots." See also First Lieutenant Henry Singer, USA, Ret., "UnCommon Soldier," *The Retired Officer Magazine* (July 1992): 35–38, brought to my attention by Adelaide Atwood, retired navy nurse.

21. *New York Times,* July 21, 1999; *Chicago Tribune,* May 26, 1997; "Woman's History Month, 1991, by the President of the United States of America, A Proclamation" (White House press release, March 1, 1999).

22. The coloring book: Jill Canon, *Heroines of the American Revolution: A Bellerophon Coloring Book* (Santa Barbara, CA, 1996); "Trivial Pursuits" in a unit "U.S.A. Trivia"; for the folk song written by Sarah Lifton in the 1970s, see Dianne Dugaw, *Warrior Women: Women and Popular Balladry, 1690–1850* (Cambridge, UK, 1989), 89, note 42; *National Enquirer,* F 1992, also May 9, 1971. I know of the following research centers (outside Massac...

which provide information about DSG: Minerva Center, Pasadena, MD; National Women's History Project, Windsor, CA; American Association of University Women Women's History Project, Camarillo, CA; Lesbian Herstory Archives, New York, NY; and the Lesbian History Project, Los Angeles.

23. On the Web search engine Google, the keywords Deborah Sampson, without enclosing them in quotation marks, produced some 20,000 entries, most of which are not relevant. For the results of searching with more specific entries, see the next section of this chapter. I am drawing a distinction between Google and the specialized search engines designed for scholars, such as J-Stor for journals or OCLC for manuscripts, which an Internet user has to access through a research or university library. I am indebted to Paul Uek, John Aubrey, and Marilyn M. Young, who made Internet searches for me, and to Linda Grant De Pauw, H. Giles Carter, and Ian McGiver, who sent me Internet materials.

24. Michael Frisch, "American History and the Structures of Collective Memory: A Modest Exercise in Empirical Iconography," *Journal of American History* 75 (1989): 1130–55, reporting polls he took of his university students over many years up to 2000—conversation with Michael Frisch, April 10, 2000.

25. Roy Rosenzweig, "The Road to Xanadu: Public and Private Pathways on the History Web," *Journal of American History* 88 (2001): 548–79. For annotated lists of history Web sites, see Center for History and New Media and American Social History Project, *History Matters: The U.S. Survey Course on the Web*, <http://historymatters.gmu.edu>, and Dennis A. Trinkle and Scott A. Merriman, eds., *The U.S. History Highway: A Guide to Internet Resources* (Armonk, NY, 2002).

26. Merrill Peterson, *The Jefferson Image in the American Mind* (New York, 1960), a classic.

27. Entries found in a Google search, Sept. 3, 2002. Not all these entries refer to Deborah Sampson as a black person; in some the word "black" appears, as in "a black dress" or "black and white illustration." I estimate the number of specific linkages. For the encyclopedias, see note 37 below.

28. William C. Nell, *The Colored Patriots of the American Revolution with Sketches of Several Distinguished Colored Persons* (Boston, 1855; New York, 1968); Harold Villard, "William C. Nell," *DAB,* 7:413.

29. Nell, *Colored Patriots,* 21–23. For Seymour Burr, Pension Application W 23726, NA, M 804, Roll 425, Frames 285, 317, which establishes him in the Fourth Massachusetts Regiment under the command of Colonel Henry Jackson, discharged Dec. 21, 1783, at West Point; and death notice, *Columbian Centinel,* Feb. 25, 1837 (death in Canton). For Jeremiah Jones or Jonas, U.S. Pension Application S 32924, NA, M 804, Roll 1440, Frame 7504, establishes him in the army 1781–83, "to the end of the war," and discharged at West Point. My thanks to George Quintal for conducting this research.

30. See Larry Gara, "Ellen Craft," *NAW* 1:396–98; for a recently discovered novel of the 1850s by an African-American woman which has this theme, see Hannah Crafts, *The Bondwoman's Narrative,* ed. Henry Louis Gates, Jr. (New York, 2002).
    In 1866, Vinton wrote in a footnote to Mann, *FR,* x: "Some years ago as the editor has been informed, a volume made its appearance, professing to give memoirs of eminent colored men, and Deborah Sampson was included as one of the number!" This may be a garbled

reference to Nell or to another work of the pre-Civil War period. Langston Hughes and Milton Meltzer, *The Pictorial History of the Negro in America* (New York, 1956; 4th edn, 1983), 56–57. For earlier assertions that Sampson was a Negro: Rev. W. Spencer Carpenter, *African Methodist Episcopal Church Review* 29 (1913): 217–18, and works by Herbert Aptheker (1940) (who later said he was wrong), Saunders Redding (1950), and W. Schulte Nordhoff (1960). For Benjamin Quarles, see his preface to the 1968 reprint of Nell's book, and Quarles, *The Negro in the American Revolution* (Chapel Hill, NC, 1961), xi; Bricknell refers to a letter he received from John Hope Franklin, c. 1970, in Bricknell, "Deborah Sampson Gannett," Memorandum, 6-page TS, n.d., PHS; for second thoughts by editors: for *Minneapolis Tribune,* see Wallace Allen, managing editor, to Lewis Gannett, Aug. 7, 1968, and for *Look,* Ernest Dunbar, senior editor, to Clara Gannett Barker, April 5, 1962, both in Michael Gannett Personal Papers.

32. *The Crisis* (December 1976): 36; "Soul Corner," cartoon feature syndicated in black newspapers (January 1976); Guba, *Deborah Samson,* chap. 3, reviews this debate; Charles Bricknell, "Deborah Samson Gannett," Memorandum, Bricknell, PHS, sums up the case against the claim. Marianna Davis, ed., *Contributions of Black Women to America, 1776–1976,* 10 vols. (Newton, MA, c. 1981). I have not seen the entry for Sampson in this work. See Charles Bricknell to Dr. Marianna W. Davis, Benedict College, Jan. 19, 29, 1981; Davis to Bricknell, Jan. 14, 1981, in Bricknell, PHS; and Michael Gannett to Davis, March 31, 1981, Michael Gannett Personal Papers.

33. For army racial identifications: *Minority Service, Massachusetts, 1775–1783* (National Society of the Daughters of the American Revolution, Washington, DC, 1989), and George Quintal, *"Patriots of Color, 'A Peculiar Beauty and Merit'": African Americans and Native Americans at Battle Road and Bunker Hill* (National Park Service, Boston, 2002); the Plympton Town Records, Book 2, and its index were combed by Charles Bricknell for references to members of the Sampson family and to others (see Bricknell MS, PHS, cited above).

34. Mann, *FR,* 134; Mann, "Heroine," 179–80; "A Correspondent," [Northampton] *Hampshire Gazette,* Sept. 1, 1802.

35. Gordon Greenwood Sampson, *Our New England Sampsons and Some Related Families* (privately published, 1953), 38 (for Nehemiah's vital statistics and children) and 46 (for "A Personality Sketch"), sent to Michael Gannett by Deveda McClintock Boseker of Columbia, Ohio, descendent of Nehemiah. Boseker enclosed a letter to Marianna Davis, March 1981, protesting her identifying Sampson as black.

   Mass. S&S, 13:762, has the identification of Nehemiah taken from the original, a "Descriptive List of Mass. 24th Division, July 22, 1780, under command of Capt. William Scott," MA, Muster Rolls, Roll 24 for vols. 34 and 35, p. 206. In NA, Nehemiah Sampson is on index card #371733015 with no further information (M 881, Roll 415, Frames 436–37).

   In local histories of Readfield, Maine, and Rochester, New Hampshire, which mentio⟨ Nehemiah, there is no indication of color for him or his six children. The genealogy lis⟨ above lists his birth in Sharon as July 17, 1764, which would fit the muster roll designatic⟨ age sixteen. However, Ezra S. Stearns, comp., *Genealogical and Family History of the⟨ of New Hampshire,* 4 vols. (New York, 1908), 2:961, offers as his date of birth July 16,⟨ accurate, this would have made him only fourteen at the time of his enlistment; he cc⟨

passed himself off as sixteen (or this might have been another Nehemiah Sampson). My thanks to George Quintal for this research.

36. Hughes and Meltzer, *Pictorial History,* 56–57.

37. "Deborah Sampson (Robert Shurtleff)," in Jesse Carnie Smith, ed., *Notable Black American Women* (Detroit, 1992), 973–75; Larry Martin, "Deborah Sampson Gannett," in Darlene Clark Hine, ed., *Black Women in America: An Historical Encyclopedia,* 2 vols. (Brooklyn, NY, 1993), 1:477–78; see also Jim Haskins, *African American Military Heroes* (Black Star Series, New York, 1998).

Darlene Clark Hine, editor of *Black Women in America,* after reading these pages in manuscript, said: "I am completely persuaded by your argument. The article in the *Encyclopedia* is just wrong. Too often people grasp for symbols and models when there is no need to. There are so many real African Americans who made contributions to American history. If I were putting out a revised edition of the *Encyclopedia,* I would ask the question, why is there such a compulsion to claim?"—telephone conversation with the author, May 5, 2002.

38. For discussion of the issue of Sampson's alleged color on the Internet with postings by about ten users, see H-Women list, <http://www2.h-net.msu.edu/> (Feb. 8–12, 2000). In this exchange, Kimberly Gannett wrote: "Yes, in fact Deborah Sampson Gannett was black. I am related to her . . . I am certainly proud to be related to her." I enumerate descendants with whom I have had contact in my acknowledgments. Ann Hurlbert talked to me about her mother, Ann Cole Gannett (1916–1997), a Republican member of the Massachusetts legislature in the 1970s who, she said, was at odds with a caucus of black legislators over their claiming Deborah as black.

39. The History Project, *Improper Bostonians: Lesbian and Gay History from the Puritans to Playland* (Boston, 1998), 30–31; Steve Hogan and Lee Hudson, eds., *Completely Queer: The Gay and Lesbian Encyclopedia* (New York, 1999), xi–xii, 435, 612 (entries for Deborah Sampson). For an example of an Internet listing, see The Lesbian History Project, *Notable Lesbians of All Colors (List),* <http://www.lib.usc.edu/~retter/database.html> (June 2001). For a novel, Paul Lussier, *Last Refuge of Scoundrels: A Revolutionary Novel* (New York, 1999). In an author's note, Lussier says that his character Deborah Simpson is "a composite of several characters who actually lived, primarily Deborah Sampson"; David Bahr, "Say You Want a Revolution," *The Advocate* (March 13, 2001), identifiies Lussier as a gay producer for TV and quotes him as identifying his character as "a cross-dressing whore."

40. Richard Godbeer, *Sexual Revolution in Early America* (Baltimore, 2002), chap. 7, and Godbeer, "The Cry of Sodom: Discourse, Intercourse, and Desire in Colonial New England," *WMQ* 52 (1995): 259–86.

41. The classic works on female friendships are: Carroll Smith-Rosenberg, "The Female World of Love and Ritual: Relations Between Women in Nineteenth-Century America," *Signs* 1 (1975): 1–29, and Nancy F. Cott, *The Bonds of Womanhood "Woman's Sphere" in New England, 1780–1835* (New Haven, CT, 1977).

For the emergence of historical scholarship, see intro. to Duberman, Vicinus, and Chauncey, ds., *Hidden from History,* 1–13. For the history of the modern gay and lesbian movements, Rosen, *The World Split Open,* 164–77, and John D'Emilio and Estelle Freedman,

Intimate Matters: A History of Sexuality in America (New York, 1988; Chicago, 1997), 318–25.

43. Jonathan Ned Katz, *Gay American History: Lesbians and Gay Men in the U.S.A.: A Documentary History* (New York, 1976; rev. edn, 1992), quotation at 209–11, document at 212–14; Katz, *Gay/Lesbian Almanac: A New Documentary* (New York, 1983), 634n. Katz informed me that the wording in the 1992 revised edition from which I am quoting is the same as in the 1976 edition.

Lillian Faderman, *Surpassing the Love of Men: Romantic Friendships Between Women from the Renaissance to the Present* (New York, 1981), 58–60, refers to Sampson's "apparent transvestite Lesbianism." Faderman, using the Vinton edition of "Herbert [*sic*] Mann," mixes quotations from the original book with quotations from Mann's unpublished MS in Vinton's footnotes.

44. Martha Vicinus, "Lesbian History: All Theory and No Facts or All Facts and No Theory," *Radical History Review* 60 (1994): 55–75, quotations at 60, 61.

45. Martin Duberman, "A Matter of Difference," *The Nation* 257 (July 5, 1993): 22–24 (I have reversed the order of the sentences); Duberman, *Left Out: The Politics of Exclusion: Essays 1964–2002* (New York, 2002), reprints this piece amalgamated with another essay from *Gay Advocate*, Dec. 24, 1996.

46. Lucy Freeman and Alma Bond, *America's First Woman Warrior: The Courage of Deborah Sampson* (New York, 1992), 208–09.

47. Gerda Lerner, *The Creation of Feminist Consciousness: From the Middle Ages to Eighteen-Seventy* (New York, 1993), 274; see also Lerner, *The Creation of Patriarchy* (New York, 1986), 231–43, "Definitions."

48. Kerber, *No Constitutional Rights to Be Ladies,* 299–302.

49. See comments by Captain Alison Weir and Linda Grant De Pauw, H-net Humanities and Social Sciences OnLine, "Feminists and the American Revolution," <http://h-net2.msu.edu/~women> (May 20–22, 1996, with additions, May 24–25, June 12, 1996).

50. Rev. Cora Cheyney Partridge to Patrick Leonard, n.d., c. 1983, Leonard Private Papers; Jan Nelson, conversation with the author, 2000.

51. Theresa Ramppen Gaydos to author, n.d., 1995; Salima Kahn's essay, "Deborah Sampson" (1997), *The Bronx Mall "Kids Connection,"* <http:/www.bronxmall.com/kids/district10/num10/html>.

52. On American monuments: Kirk Savage, *Standing Soldiers, Kneeling Slaves: Race, War, and Monument in Nineteenth-Century America* (Princeton, NJ, 1997); Sanford Levinson, *Written in Stone: Public Monuments in Changing Societies* (Durham, NC, 1998); for the women's Vietnam War monument: *Celebration of Patriotism and Courage* (Washington, DC: Vietnam Women's Memorial Project, 1993), a booklet prepared for the dedication of the statue. The description is from Lynn Sherr and Jurate Kazickas, *Susan B. Anthony Slept Here: A Guide to American Women's Landmarks* (New York, 1976, 1995), 88.

53. Sherr and Kazickas, *Susan B. Anthony Slept Here,* 207 and 276 (Hannah Duston); 28 (Molly Pitcher); 303–04 (Sybil Luddington); 335–36 (Margaret Corbin); 383 (Mc Pitcher); see also Marion Tinling, *Women Remembered: A Guide to the Landmark*

Women's History in the United States (New York, 1986), 422–23 (Margaret Corbin); 430ff. (Molly Pitcher). For Molly Pitcher, see Elizabeth Cometti, "Mary Ludwig Hays McCauley," NAW, 2:448–49; De Pauw, *Battle Cries and Lullabies: Women in War from Prehistory to the Present* (Norman, OK, 1998), 126–31; Carol Klaver, "An Introduction to the Legend of Molly Pitcher," *Minerva: Quarterly Report on Women in the Military* 7 (1994): 35–61.

54. Sharon Cooper, "Sculptor Chisels Away Conventions," *Patriot Ledger,* Nov. 15, 1989; for Stubbs's public sculpture: Marty Carlock, *A Guide to Public Art in Greater Boston* (Boston, 1993), 8, 64, 65, 82, 169, 223. I also draw on brochures by Stubbs.

55. Lu Stubbs, "The Look on Deborah Sampson's Face," *The Sharon Advocate,* from which the quotations that follow are taken. Liz Kowalczyk, "This Woman's Place Was in the Revolution," *Patriot Ledger,* Oct. 24, 1988; Lu Stubbs to Charles Bricknell, Nov. 29, 1988, and Bricknell to Stubbs, Dec. 1, 1988, Bricknell, PHS; Guba, *Deborah Samson,* 144–47, was also critical. Newspaper clippings, Deborah Sampson Statue, SPL. Interview by the author with Lu Stubbs, 1995. Stubbs moved to Northampton in 2001.

56. Stubbs to author, Mar. 19, 1995 ("her spirit").

EPILOGUE: THE SEAGULL

1. Louisa May Alcott, *Little Women,* ed. Elaine Showalter (Boston, 1868; New York, 1989), quotations from chaps. 1 and 36. Jane Austin, *Dr. LeBaron and His Daughters: A Story of the Old Colony* (Boston, 1891), 399, used a similar figure of speech to describe Deborah. For the civil war as a "defining presence" in Alcott's writings, see Elizabeth Young, *Disarming the Nation: Women's Writing and the American Civil War* (Chicago, 1999), chap. 2.

2. David Ramsay, *The History of the American Revolution,* 2 vols. (Philadelphia, 1789; Indianapolis, 1990), 2:629–31.

3. Valerie Traub, *The Renaissance of Lesbianism in Early Modern Europe* (Cambridge, UK, 2002), intro.; [Robert Walker], *The Female Soldier; or the Surprising Life and Adventures of Hannah Snell* (London, 1750; reprint, Los Angeles, 1989), intro. by Dianne Dugaw, 28.

4. Joseph Plumb Martin, *Private Yankee Doodle: Being a Narrative of Some of the Adventures, Dangers and Sufferings of a Revolutionary Soldier,* ed. George F. Scheer (Hallowell, ME, 1830; Boston, 1962), 283.

5. Alcott, *Journals* (April 1861), 105, cited in Young, *Disarming the Nation,* 78.

Acknowledgments

My acknowledgments may demonstrate one reason more scholars do not undertake biographies of unsung heroes who make a mark on history but leave so little evidence. Such biographies are labor-intensive, requiring a great deal of detective work in the field tracking small clues. They also demand acquiring mastery of a wide range of fields to understand the world the subject moves in. You can't do this only by sitting in a library or an archive reading a person's papers, especially when there are no papers. And you can't do it without the help of a lot of other people.

In 1975, Vera Laska, the first scholar to do a documented article about Deborah Sampson Gannett, mused that a full-scale biography would require "a graduate seminar with a dozen doctoral candidates working on various aspects of her life." Or, maybe, a very prosperous artisan who could command the services of a band of skilled journeymen and apprentice artisans. I had neither seminar nor craft shop. I was able to (under)pay a few researchers for specific projects, but I got by essentially with a little help from my friends and the many kindnesses of strangers. It gives me great pleasure to acknowledge them. And I hope the amount of support given me encourages others who seek to do likewise.

This book began as a paper at a conference in Williamsburg, Virginia, in November 1993, sponsored by the Omohundro Institute of Early American History, the theme of which was the search for personal identity in early America. Unable to fit Deborah Sampson to the theme, I could not condense my paper to fit the time limits for my session or squeeze her life into an essay for the insightful volume that emerged from the conference. About that time, Peter Dimock, then an editor at Knopf/Random House, asked me if I would be interested in writing a book about how one goes about doing life histories of ordinary people in early American history. I had tried my hand at this in an article about George Robert Twelves Hewes, a Boston shoemaker in the American Revolution, which appeared in the *William and Mary Quarterly* and has since become book. I replied that I thought the process might best be explained while working out the life of o ordinary person, especially one for whom the historical record is sparse. And that's how this b was born. I am indebted to Ronald Hoffman, Director of the Omohundro Institute, for inv me to do the paper, and to Peter Dimock for inviting me to do the book. Both are enablers, risk-taking and patient.

One set of individuals helped me in searching for evidence, another gave me the benefit of their research on either aspects of Sampson or historical contexts of her life, and still others favored me with their expertise by reading versions of the manuscript.

In the early stages of research I would have been lost without scholars who steered me over unfamiliar terrain, sometimes by a conversation, sometimes by demonstrating their mastery of a field. My thanks go to: Linda Grant De Pauw, editor of *Minerva: Quarterly Report on Women and the Military,* who knows as much as any scholar about women in wars; Mary Beth Norton for her command of the status of women in early America; John Shy for his sense of the social history of the Revolutionary War; Daniel Scott Smith for his mastery of family history; Martha Vicinus for her knowledge of "passing" women; and Richard Godbeer and Valerie Traub for their pioneering syntheses in the history of sexuality. By uncovering little-known fields of knowledge, some scholars inspired me to pursue lines of inquiry I had no idea were possible: Holly A. Mayer, the army as a community; Elizabeth Carroll Reilly, popular reading; Nancy E. Rexford, historical clothing; Mechal Sobel, the dreams of ordinary people; and Elizabeth Young, women in the Civil War who crossed boundaries. As a guide, Elizabeth Young was indispensable.

In pursuit of Sampson, I was fortunate to be walking over paths already blazed by the Massachusetts enthusiasts who labored for years to have her declared the official state heroine. Patrick Leonard of Braintree, my first guide, took me to the sites of her life, introduced me to descendants, and generously shared the sources he had unearthed. Pat, in turn, led me to the work of his fellow musketeers, Charles Bricknell of Plympton and Emil Guba of Kingston. I poured over Bricknell's bulging scrapbooks of sources, correspondence, and memoranda at the Plympton Historical Society, and read Guba's book debunking the myths about Deborah, completed while he was in his late nineties and legally blind and deaf. I met Bricknell and briefly corresponded with Guba. Both men have since passed on. Jan Lewis Nelson of Gloucester, originally from Middleborough, also gave me the benefit of her discoveries, since incorporated into a novel, and walked me around young Deborah's haunts.

Gannett descendants proved invaluable. Muriel Nelson of Sharon, Deborah's great-great-granddaughter, who was a child in the Gannett home in Sharon before World War I, shared her memories of the family as well as scrapbooks with a century of public notices of Sampson; she also showed me real estate deeds and two pieces of furniture passed down. Beatrice Bostock of Truro, another great-great-granddaughter, and her daughter Ann Gilbert, both since deceased, allowed me to examine the dress, cup plate, and almanac they inherited. Caroline Monk Myrick of Temple, New Hampshire, gave me copies of the notes and letters left by her father, Rodney Monk, Deborah's great-grandson, a link to the family of 1900, and assembled snapshots of her sister Polly Monk Wise, said by her father to resemble Deborah. Michael R. Gannett (descended from a collateral line of Gannetts), author of the essential Gannett genealogy, shared his collections and correspondence. Janet and Robert Gay sent me a copy of the family genealogy they compiled. ̣escendants who sent me documents or photographs are: Lois Cowell Anderson, Claire Cowell, ̣k Fawkes, Keri Scofield Lawson, the late Christine Penn, and Alice K. Shepard. Descendants whom I had conversations, in addition to many of those listed above, are Richard Buckman,

Acknowledgments

Deborah Gannett Brooks, Kimberly Gannett, Peter Cole Gannett, Thomas Brattle Gannett, Ann Hurlburt, Deborah Sampson Shinn, and Rachel Sampson Wilcox.

I was welcomed by owners of the three surviving houses in which Sampson lived. My thanks to Dr. and Mrs. David Browne, owners of the house where she was born in Plympton; to Mr. and Mrs. Kenneth Crest, owners of the Jeremiah Thomas house in Middleborough where she was a servant; and to Daniel and Peggy Arguimbau, owners of the house and farm where the Gannetts lived after 1813. My debt to Daniel, a teacher of agronomy, is large: he helped me imagine what house, farm, and town might have been like in Gannett's day. In my field trips: for Sharon, Daniel was my guide. For Middleborough, my indefatigable guide was Janet Thomas Griffith, past secretary of the town's Historical Commission, who took me to sites and sources and helped me to puzzle out one mystery after another. My thanks also go to Reverend Brian M. Cooke, George Decas, Ted Eayrs, Mary J. Fuller, Loraine Skidmore, Lee Smith, Stetson Thomas, Walter Thompson, and Janet and Warren Whipple.

I have a heavy debt to researchers who undertook projects for me: first and foremost, Paul Uek, the historian and librarian who pursued Mrs. Gannett's later life from 1784 to 1827 in Sharon and on her tour. He patiently ran down real estate and tax records, newspapers, town and church records, manuscripts and ephemera. I could not have told this part of her story without his painstaking research. He also hunted for illustrations. For Sampson at war: Jon Parmenter ran down the pension applications of members of her light infantry company; Constantine Diercks sleuthed the Philadelphia story and Dr. Barnabas Binney; and George Quintal, military detective par excellence, tracked her brother Nehemiah and a host of soldiers supposedly connected to her. Nancy E. Rexford, who authenticated the 1780s dress, lived up to her reputation as one of the country's foremost costume historians. My thanks, too, to Steven L. Pastore for a task in the National Archives and to Ralph Pugh for transcribing Deborah's diary.

I was fortunate in having scholars working on phases of Sampson's life who could not have been more generous in sharing research in progress and in talking to me. I am indebted to Judith Hiltner, a scholar of literature, for her insightful work about Herman Mann; to Jane Oxford Keiter for her meticulous research on Sampson's military exploits in Westchester County; to Mechal Sobel for her passage on Deborah in her pathbreaking book about dreams; to Sandra Gustafson for her innovative scholarship on Gannett's oration and tour; to Michelle Navarre-Cleary for a chapter in her dissertation on this subject; and to Thomas A. Foster for first charting Sampson's reputation.

Other scholars allowed me to read their work in progress on subjects that established contexts for Sampson's life: on sexuality, Valerie Traub, Richard Godbeer, Kirsten Fischer, Susan S. Lanser, Thomas A. Foster, and Rebecca Bach; on religion and society in New England, Douglas Winiarski and Leigh Johnsen; on women in eighteenth-century public life, Susan Branson, Sheila L. Skemp, and Rosemarie Zagarri. Others who shared their scholarship include Robert E. Cray and Sarah J. Purcell (on the historical memory of the Revolution), Dianne Dugaw (on women warriors), Carolyn Eastman (on women's oratory), Alan Kulikoff (on yeoman farmers), Marcus Rediker (on women pirates), and John Resch (on veterans).

In a project where small clues turned out to be so important, I am grateful to the many individuals who sent me documents, or called my attention to sources I otherwise would not [

found, or answered my inquiries: Nina Baym, J. L. Bell, Michael Bellesiles, Lucia Bergamasco, Wayne Bodle, Patricia U. Bonomi, Kenneth Bowling, Catherine A. Brekus, Kathleen M. Brown, H. Gilles Carter, Christopher Castiglia, Daniel A. Cohen, Patricia Cline Cohen, Samuel Willard Crompton, Cathy N. Davidson, Cornelia Hughes Dayton, Martin B. Duberman, Terry J. Fife, Nona C. Flores, Wayne Franklin, Michael Frisch, Timothy J. Gilfoyle, Eliot Gorn, Anne L. Guba, Tobias Higbie, the late Bridget Hill, Thomas Humphrey, Jonathan Ned Katz, Alan Kulikoff, Lt. Col. M. Landahl-Smidt, USAF (Ret.), Jean Lee, Gerda Lerner, Kenneth Lockridge, John Long, Lisa Lubow, Tim Malone, Loretta Mannucci, Brendon McConville, Ian McGiver, Simon Newman, Gregory Nobles, Mary Beth Norton, Grey Osterud, Cora Cheney Partridge, Dennis Pessis, M.D., Jonathan Prude, Elizabeth Reis, Donna Rilling, Mary Beth Rose, Lois Rudnick, Mary Sheldon, Barbara Sicherman, Susan Sleeper-Smith, Barbara Clark Smith, Dean R. Snow, Richard Steckel, Lu Stubbs, Helen Tanner, Alan J. Taylor, Roger Thompson, Len Travers, Randolph Trumbach, the late Alex Tulsky, M.D., Laurel Thatcher Ulrich, Charles C. Wells, Julie Wheelwright, Shane White, and Mary O'Keefe Young. I thank you all very much!

Military reenactors of the Revolution, east and midwest, enlightened me: Andrea and Paul Ackerman, Susan Cifaldi, Paul Dickfoss, Theresa Ramppen Gaydos, Don H. Hagist, David C. Jahntz, and the members of the Northwest Alliance who challenged my presentation to them about how Sampson got away with her disguise. I profited especially from conversations with Henry Cooke IV, historical costumer; with Cathy Stanton, historian of reenactors; and with Joan Gatturna, who reenacts Sampson in Massachusetts.

The unsung keepers of the past are librarians, archivists, curators in historical societies, museums, and historic sites, and editors of publication projects. A small regiment of them, paraded here by state, gave me assistance for which I am grateful.

California. Los Angeles Lesbian History Project: Yolanda Retter.

Massachusetts. The Adams Papers: Richard Ryerson and Celeste Walker. American Antiquarian Society: Georgia Barnhill, Nancy Burkett, Joanne D. Chaisin, John Hench, Thomas Knoles, and Philip Lampi. Andover Newton Theological School: Diana Yount. Bellingham Historical Commission: Ernest Taft. Boston National Historical Park: Martin Blatt, Matt Greif, and Emily Pingot. Boston Public Library: Roberta Zonghi and R. Eugene Zepp. Dedham Historical Society: Ronald F. Frazier. Harvard Medical School Library: Richard Wolfe. Massachusetts Archives: J. Michael Comeau. Massachusetts Historical Society: William Fowler, Peter Drummey, Chris Steele, and Virginia Smith. Massachusetts Supreme Judicial Court Archives: Elizabeth C. Bouvier. Middleborough Historical Association: the late Robert Beals and Dorothy Thayer. Middleborough Public Library: Betty Brown, Marjorie Judd, and George Barden. New England Historic Genealogical Society: David Dearborn. Old Sturbridge Village: Jack Larkin. Pilgrim Hall Museum: Peggy M. Baker. Paul Revere Memorial Association: Patrick Leehey. Plympton Historical Association: Carolyn McGuire, Lois Wheelock, Les Waterman, and Edwina Wood. Sharon Baptist Church: Marion Cunningham. Sharon Historical Association: Shirley Schofield and Nancy Glynn. Sharon Public Library: Barbara Katz, Rebecca Case, Bonnie Strong, and David ˜ssman. Sharon Unitarian Church: Beth McGregor. Society for the Preservation of New England Antiquities: Richard Nylander.

Michigan. Clements Library, University of Michigan: John Dann and Arlene Shy.

New Hampshire. American Independence Museum: Bill Widell.

Acknowledgments

New Jersey. Monmouth County Historical Association: Jane Reynolds-Peck.

New York. Hancock Shaker Village: Sharon Duane Koomler. Lesbian Herstory Archives: Deborah Edel. National Temple Hill Association: Mrs. William Fulton. New Windsor Encampment Historic Site: E. Jane Townshend. Papers of Robert Morris, Queens College: Elizabeth Nuxoll. Thomas Paine Historical Association, New Rochelle: Catherine T. Goulding. U.S. Military Academy Library: Alan C. Aimone, David M. Reel, and David Meschutt.

Pennsylvania: American Philosophical Society: Edward C. Carter II and Whitfield Bell. David Library of the American Revolution: David J. Fowler and Gregory Knouff. The Library Company of Philadelphia: James Green.

Rhode Island. Brown University: Martha Mitchell and Joyce Botelho. Rhode Island Historical Society: Linda Eppich and Dana Signe Munroe.

Virginia. Gannett Foundation: Tarra Connell and Jackie Jolly. The Papers of George Washington, University of Virginia: William Abbott, Philander D. Chase, and Robert Haggard.

Washington, DC. Daughters of the American Revolution Library: Eric Grundset. Documentary History of the First Federal Congress: William C. diGiacomantonio. Library of Congress, Manuscripts Division: John Sellers. National Archives: De Anne Blanton and Diane L. Dimkoff. National Museum of American History, The Smithsonian Institution: Barbara Clark Smith and Susan H. Myers. National Park Service: Dwight Pitcaithley. Society of the Cincinnati: Kory W. Rogers and Rachel Bradshaw. U.S. Army Center for Military History: Mary Gillett. Women In Military Service For America Memorial: Brig. Gen. Wilma L. Vaught, USAF (Ret.), Linda Witt, and Judith A. Bellafaire.

My major debt is to the Newberry Library, Chicago, my home base, a scholar's paradise, where I have been a Senior Research Fellow since my retirement from Northern Illinois University in 1990. I am grateful to its presidents, Charles Cullen and the late Lawrence W. Towner, and to its directors of research, past and present, Richard H. Brown, Fred Hoxie, and James Grossman, all of whom have been so successful in making the Newberry a center for intellectual inquiry. I deeply appreciate the services of its dedicated librarians, John Aubrey (who made my project his own), John Brady, Christine Colburn, JoEllen Dickie, Susan Fagan, Rhonda Frevert, Hjordis Halvorson, Robert Karrow, Paul Saenger, and the late David Thackery.

I have been blessed by a large number of people who read all of parts of the manuscript at various stages. Three scholars with an enviable command of women's history in early America who read the entire manuscript are Linda Kerber, who read an early version and gave me the confidence to go on; Mary Beth Norton, who read the penultimate version and guided me in telling Deborah's tale more concisely; and Kirsten Fischer, who after reading earlier chapters and becoming an enthusiast of Deborah, read the final version with acumen. Linda Grant De Pauw and Judith Hiltner read an array of chapters perceptively. The military chapters were read expertly by De Pauw, John Shy, Charles Neimeyer, Jane Keiter, Holly A. Mayer, and George Quintal. Jan Lewis Nelson and Elizabeth C. Reilly read about young Deborah in Middleborough; Susan Juster, Leigh Johnsen, and Douglas Winiarski about religion in Middleborough; Mechal Sobel Carla Gerona, and Sharon Block challenged me on the dream; Daniel Arguimbau, David E Ingram, and Paul Uek kept me on my toes in the chapters on Sharon. A long chapter on sexual since distributed in the book, was read to my great advantage by Valerie Traub, Kirsten Fisc

Acknowledgments

Richard Godbeer, Thomas A. Foster, Amy Froide, Ann Little, and Rebecca Bach, as well as by members of the Fellows Seminar of the Newberry Library. Part 5, Passing into History, was improved by De Pauw, Foster, and Hiltner. At the outset, I profited from the formal comments on my paper at the Omohundro Institute conference by Gordon Wood and Robert Gross, as well as from comment by John Demos, Jesse Lemisch, and Kenneth Lockridge.

Jane N. Garrett has been a wise, perceptive, and patient editor and Ann Adelman an incisive copyeditor.

Needless to say, while these readers sharpened my understanding and saved me from error, none are responsible for errors of fact that remain or for my vagaries of interpretation.

In my travels, I have enjoyed the generous hospitality of friends. In Boston: from Robin and Robert Cohen; in Worcester: from Elizabeth and Jerry Reilly; in Sharon: from Lois Palken Rudnick and Steven Rudnick; in Washington, DC: from Ira and Martha Berlin and Greg LeRoy. In Westchester County, over the years, I was taken to historic sites by the late Ora Young, my sister-in-law. My niece, Amy Young Geiger, along with Larry and Pamela Geiger, were wonderful companions on a tour of Hudson Valley sites.

My wife, Marilyn Mills Young, in addition to being a guide to the Internet, has been an insightful reader and a demanding editor. Her labor has made it possible to bring this project to completion. Her love has made it all worthwhile. The book is dedicated to my three daughters, Sarah Young, Emily Young, and Elizabeth Young, a source of wisdom, encouragement, and love.

Index

Index

Index

Index

Index

Index

Printed in the United States
by Baker & Taylor Publisher Services